T0338223

PROJECT RECOVERY

PROJECT RECOVERY
Case Studies and Techniques for Overcoming Project Failure

Harold Kerzner, PH.D.

Library of Congress Cataloging-in-Publication Data

Kerzner, Harold.
    Project recovery : case studies and techniques for overcoming project failure / Harold Kerzner.
       pages   cm
     Includes index.
     ISBN 978-1-118-80919-8 (cloth); ISBN 978-1-118-80917-4 (ebk);
     ISBN 978-1-118-80919-8 (ebk); ISBN 978-1-118-84161-7 (ebk)
       1. Project management.   I. Title.
    HD69.P75K4955   2013
    658.4'04—dc23   2013035013

Printed in the United States of America
10 9 8 7 6 5 4 3 2 1

To our children Jackie, Andrea, Jason, Lindsey, Jason Berk, and our first grandchild, Stella Harper Berk. The title of this book was in no way created with our children in mind.

CONTENTS

10 TECHNIQUES FOR RECOVERING FAILING PROJECTS **289**

PREFACE

Having spent nearly five decades involved in project management, my greatest frustration has been how little we have learned over the years from project failures. Newspaper and journal articles thrive on project disasters. The greater the disaster and the larger the financial investment or loss, the greater the number of articles that appear.

We also have a poor definition of what constitutes a failure. When something fails, you generally assume that it cannot be corrected. Articles have been written that describe the opening day of terminal 5 at London Heathrow as a failure. Rather, it should be called a disaster because the opening day problems were corrected. Had it been a failure, terminal 5 would never have opened.

The same holds true for the problems with Boeing's 787 Dreamliner and the Airbus A380. These two projects are not failures. History will show that they will be regarded as successes. The problems that they have had may be regarded as glitches or partial disasters but not failures as they are sometimes called in the literature.

The book discusses several large project case studies where there are multiple causes for the problems that happened. There are also shorter or condensed cases and smaller situations. The smaller situations generally focus on just one cause. Even though some of the cases and situations are more than a decade old, what is important are the lessons that were learned.

After reading through these cases and situations, you probably recall having lived through many of these situations. Project management has existed for more than half a century. During that time, we have documented mistakes that led to more than a trillion dollars wasted just in IT alone. Every year, many of us read the latest Chaos Report prepared by the Standish Group which lists the causes of IT failures. Then we must ask ourselves: If we know what the causes are, then why do the same causes repeat themselves every year? Why aren't we doing anything about it? Why are we afraid of admitting that we made a mistake? Why don't we try to prevent these problems from happening again?

Some industries are more prone to these mistakes than others. But we are learning. We have university degrees in project management where these case studies are prime learning tools. The people coming through these courses will be the project management leaders of tomorrow. Wishful thinking says that we would like books like this not to be necessary in the future.

What is important about many of the case studies identified in this book is that effective recovery techniques may have been able to reduce the impact of or even eliminate many of these disasters. Usually there are early warning signs of disaster that signal us to begin the recovery process. In each of the case studies and situations are lessons learned that provide us with insight in techniques we should use to recover failing projects. There are tools that can be used as well to support the techniques.[1] The first nine chapters of this book are designed as feeders for Chapter 10, which focuses directly on techniques for the recovery process.

HAROLD KERZNER
The International Institute for Learning

---

1. An excellent reference for some tools that can support the techniques discussed in this book can be found in Cynthia Stackpole Snyder, *A Project Manager's Book of Forms: A Companion to the PMBOK® Guide*, Second Edition, Wiley, Hoboken, NJ, 2013.

1 UNDERSTANDING SUCCESS AND FAILURE

1.0 INTRODUCTION

Most people have a relatively poor understanding of what is meant by project success and project failure. As an example, let's assume you purchase a new car that contains a lot of electronic gadgetry. After a few days, some of the electronics fail to work correctly. Was the purchase of the new car a success or a failure? Most people would refer to this as a glitch or small problem that can be corrected. If the problem is corrected, then you would consider the purchase of the new car as a success.

But now let's assume you purchase a $10 million software package for your company. The software fails to work correctly and your company loses $50 million in sales before the software bugs are removed and the system operates as expected. In this example, the literature would abound with stories about the failure of your software package and how much money your company lost in the process. But if the software package is now bug free and your company is generating revenue from use of the package, then why should the literature refer to this as a failure? Was the purchase and eventual use of the software package a success or a failure? Some people might consider this as a success with glitches along the way that had to be overcome. And we all know that software development rarely occurs without glitches.

Defining success and failure is not clear cut. We all seem to understand what is meant by total success or total failure. But the majority of projects fall into the grey area between success and failure where there may not be any clear definition of the meaning of partial success or partial failure.

Project success has traditionally been defined as completing the requirements within the triple constraints of time, cost and scope (or performance). This is the answer that had been expected of students on most exams. In the same breath, project failure had been defined as the inability to meet the requirements within time, cost and scope. Unfortunately, these definitions do not provide a clear picture or understanding of the health of the project and whether or not success has been achieved. And to make matters worse, the definition of success or failure is treated like

1

the definition of beauty; it is in the eyes of the beholder. Today, we are finally beginning to scrutinize the definitions of project success and project failure.

1.1 SUCCESS: HISTORICAL PERSPECTIVE

The complexities with defining project success and failure can be traced back to the early days of project management. The birth and initial growth of project management began with the Department of Defense (DOD) in the United States. With thousands of contractors, the DOD wanted some form of standardization with regard to project performance reporting. The earned value measurement system (EVMS) was created primarily for this purpose.

For the EVMS to be effective, metrics were needed to track performance and measure or predict project success. Everybody knew that measuring success was complicated and that predicting project success correctly required several metrics. Unfortunately, our understanding of metrics and metric measurement techniques was relatively poor at that time. The result was the implementation of the rule of inversion. The rule of inversion states that the metrics with the highest informational value, especially for decision making and measuring success, should be avoided or never measured because of the difficulty in data collection. Metrics like time and cost are the easiest to measure and should therefore be used. The result was that we then spent too much time on these variables that may have had the least impact on decision making and measuring and predicting project success or project failure. The EVMS, for all practical purposes, had two and only two metrics: time and cost. Several formulas were developed as part of the EVMS, and they were all manipulations of time and cost.

The definition of success was now predicated heavily upon the information that came out of the EVMS, namely time and cost. The triple constraints of time, cost and scope were established as the norm for measuring and predicting project success.

Unfortunately, good intentions often go astray. DOD contracts with the aerospace and defense industry were heavily based upon the performance of the engineering community. In the eyes of the typical engineer, each of the triple constraints did not carry equal importance. For many engineers, scope and especially technical achievement were significantly more important than time or cost. The DOD tried to reinforce the importance of time and cost, but as long as the DOD was willing to pay for the cost overruns and allow schedule slippages, project success was measured by how well performance was achieved regardless of the cost overruns, which could exceed several hundred percent. To make matters worse, many of the engineers viewed project success as the ability to exceed rather than just meet specifications, and to do it using DOD funding. Even though the triple constraints were being promoted as the definition of success, performance actually became the single success criterion.

1.2 EARLY MODIFICATIONS TO TRIPLE CONSTRAINTS

The DOD's willingness to tolerate schedule slippages and cost overruns for the sake of performance gave the project management community the opportunity to consider another constraint, namely customer acceptance. Projects, by definition, are most often unique opportunities that you may never have attempted before and may never attempt again. As such, having accurate estimating databases that can be used to predict the time and cost to achieve success was wishful thinking. Projects that required a great deal of innovation were certainly susceptible to these issues as well as significant cost overruns. To make matters worse, the time and cost estimates were being established by people that knew very little about the complexities of project management and had never been involved in innovation activities.

People began to realize that meeting the time and cost constraints precisely would involve some degree of luck. Would the customer still be willing to accept the deliverables if the project was late by one week, two weeks or three weeks? Would the customer still be willing to accept the deliverables if the cost overrun was $10,000, $20,000, or $100,000?

Now it became apparent that success may not appear as just a single point as shown in Figure 1-1. The small circle within the cube in Figure 1-1 represents the budget, schedule and scope requirements defined by the customer. However, given the risks of the project, success may be identified as all points within the cube. In other words, if the schedule were to slip by

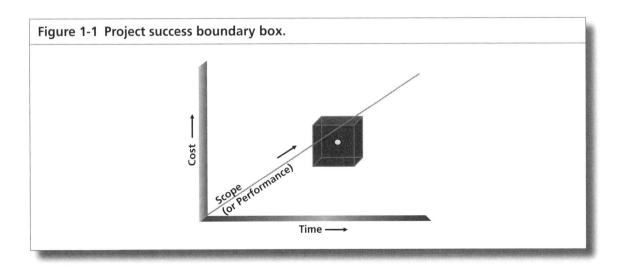

Figure 1-1 Project success boundary box.

Figure 1-2 Project success defined as customer satisfaction.

up to two weeks, and the budget was exceeded by up to $50,000, and the client was able to receive up to 92% of the initial requirements, then the project might still be regarded as a success. Therefore, success is not just a single point. The hard part is identifying the size and boundaries of the success cube.

Using Figure 1-1, the only definition of success was now customer satisfaction or customer acceptance. For some customers and contractors, time and cost were insignificant compared to customer satisfaction. Having the deliverables late or over budget was certainly better than having no deliverables at all. But customers were not willing to say that success was merely customer acceptance. Time and cost were still important to the customers. As such, the triple constraints were still used but surrounded by a circle of customer satisfaction, as shown in Figure 1-2.

Figure 1-2 made it clear that there may be several definitions of project success because not all constraints carry equal importance. On some projects, customer acceptance may be heavily biased toward cost containment whereas on other projects the scheduled delivery date may be critical.

1.3 PRIMARY AND SECONDARY CONSTRAINTS

As projects became more complex, organizations soon found that the triple constraints were insufficient to clearly define project success even if the constraints were prioritized. There were other constraints that were often more important than time, cost and scope. These "other" constraints were referred to as secondary constraints with time, cost and scope being regarded as the primary constraints. Typical secondary constraints included:

- Using the customer's name as reference at the completion of the project
- Probability of obtaining follow-on work
- Financial success (i.e., profit maximization)
- Achieving technical superiority (i.e., competitive advantage)
- Aesthetic value and usability
- Alignment with strategic planning objectives
- Maintaining regulatory agency requirements
- Abiding by health and safety laws
- Maintaining environmental protection standards
- Enhancing the corporate reputation and image
- Meeting the personal needs of the employees (opportunities for advancement)
- Supporting and maintaining ethical conduct (Sarbannes-Oxley law)

The secondary constraints created challenges for many companies. The EVMS was created to track and report only the primary constraints. To solve the tracking problem, companies created enterprise project management methodologies (EPMs) that incorporated the EVMS and also tracked and reported many of the secondary constraints. This was of critical importance for some companies because the secondary constraints could be more important than the primary constraints. As an example, consider the following situation:

Situation: A vendor was awarded a contract from a new client. The vendor had won the contract because they underbid the job by approximately 40%. When asked why they had grossly underbid the contract, the vendor stated that their definition of success on this contract was the ability to use the client's name as a reference when bidding on other contracts for other clients. Completing the contract at a loss was not as important as using the client's name as a reference in the future.

LESSON LEARNED It is important to have a clear definition of success (and failure) at the beginning of the project.

Even though we now had both primary and secondary constraints, companies still felt compelled to use the traditional triple constraints of time, cost and scope as the primary means for defining success. As shown in Figure 1-3, all of the secondary constraints were inserted within the triangle representing the triple constraints. In this example, shown in Figure 1-3, image/reputation, quality, risk and value were treated as secondary constraints. Discussions over the secondary constraints were made by analyzing the impact they had on the primary constraints, namely whether the secondary constraints elongated or compressed any of the primary constraints.

Figure 1-3 Competing constraints.

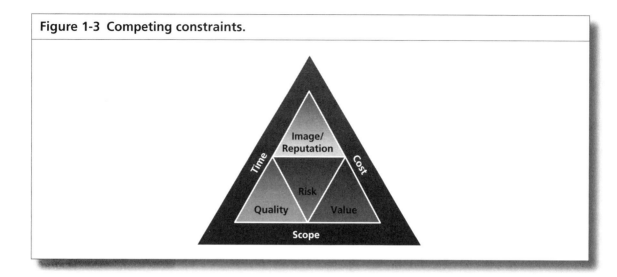

1.4 PRIORITIZATION OF CONSTRAINTS

As the number of constraints on a project began to grow, it became important to prioritize the constraints. Not all constraints carry the same weight. As an example, many years ago I had the opportunity to work with some of Disney's project managers at Disneyland and Disneyworld. These were the project managers responsible for creating new attractions. At Disney, there were six constraints on most projects:

- Time
- Cost
- Scope
- Safety
- Quality
- Aesthetic value

At Disney, safety was considered as the single most important constraint, followed by quality and aesthetic value. These three were considered as the high-priority constraints never to undergo any tradeoffs. If tradeoffs were to be made, then the tradeoffs must be made on time, cost or scope. The need for prioritization of the success criteria was now quite clear.

1.5 FROM TRIPLE CONSTRAINTS TO COMPETING CONSTRAINTS

When the Project Management Institute (PMI) released the fourth edition of the *PMBOK® Guide*, the use of the term triple constraints was replaced with the term "competing constraints." Defining project success was now becoming significantly more complicated because of the increasing number of constraints and their importance in defining project success. Everybody knows and understands that "what gets measured, gets done." Therefore, there were three challenges that soon appeared:

- Each new constraint has to be tracked the same way that we traditionally tracked time and cost.
- In order to track the new constraints, we need to establish metrics for each of the constraints. You cannot have a constraint without having a metric to confirm that the constraint is being met.
- Metrics are measurements. We must understand the various measurement techniques available for tracking the new metrics that will be used to predict and report success.

Project success, metrics and measurement techniques were now inter-related. Historically, success was measured using only two knowledge areas of the *PMBOK® Guide*, namely time management and cost management. Today, success metrics can come from any of the 10 knowledge areas in the fifth edition of the *PMBOK® Guide*. It is entirely possibly that, in the future, we will modify the inputs, tools and outputs discussed in the *PMBOK® Guide* to include a metric library as shown in Figure 1-4. In future editions of the *PMBOK® Guide* we may even have supplemental handouts for each knowledge area describing the metrics that are available and how they can be used to track and predict project success. This is shown in Figure 1-5.

Figure 1-4 Future *PMBOK® Guide* and metrics.

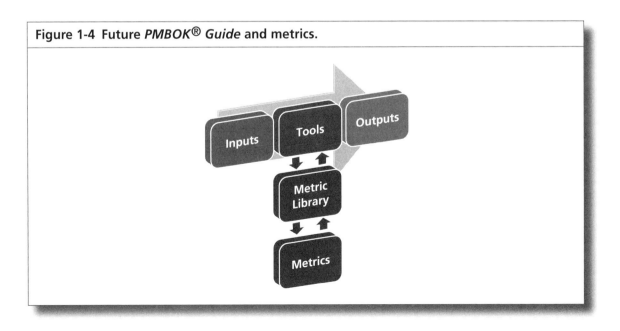

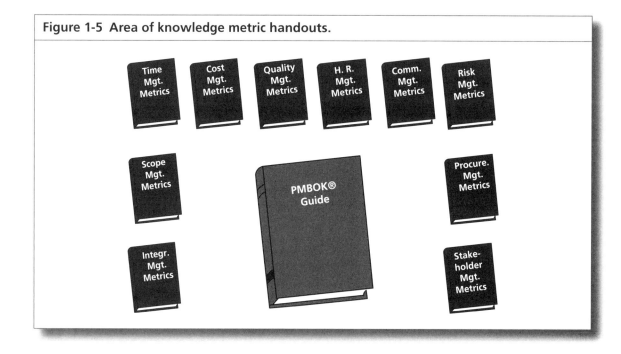

Figure 1-5 Area of knowledge metric handouts.

1.6 FUTURE DEFINITIONS OF PROJECT SUCCESS

Advances in metrics and measurement techniques have allowed us to change our definition of project success and failure. Previously, we stated the importance of customer acceptance as a success criterion. But today, even the term "customer acceptance" is being challenged. According to a study ("Customer Value Management: Gaining Strategic Advantage," The American Productivity and Quality Center [APQC], © 1998, p. 8):

> Although customer satisfaction is still measured and used in decision-making, the majority of partner organizations [used in this study] have shifted their focus from customer satisfaction to customer value.

Advances in measurement techniques have now allowed us to measure such items as value, image reputation and goodwill. Therefore, we can now establish a rather sophisticated and pin-pointed approach to defining project success. Value may become the most important term in defining project success. Having a significant cost overrun and/or schedule slippage may be acceptable as long as business value was created. During the selection of the projects that go into the portfolio of projects, value may become the driver for project selection. After all, why work on a project if the intent is not to create some form of business value? Value may also change the way we define a project. As an example, consider the following:

- *PMBOK® Guide—*Fifth Edition, definition of a project: A temporary endeavor undertaken to create a unique product, service or result.
- **Future definition of a project:** A collection of sustainable business value scheduled for realization.

Value can also be used to define project success. As an example:

- **Traditional definition of project success:** Completion of the project within the triple constraints of time, cost and scope.
- **Future definition of project success:** Achieving the desired business value within the competing constraints.

The above definitions make it clear that there is now a business and/or value component added to our definition of project success. Value may very well become the driver for how we measure success or failure in the future. Success or failure is no longer being measured solely by time and cost.

Measuring value by itself is extremely difficult. To overcome the potential problems, it may be easier to define the value success constraint as a composition of other constraints or attributes as shown in Figure 1-6. In other words, constraints from all or part of the six interrelated components in Figure 1-6 will make up the value success constraint.

To illustrate how this might work in the future, let's consider the following scenario. The project manager will meet with the client and possibly the stakeholders at project initiation to come to an agreement as to what is meant by value since value will be perhaps the primary measurement of project success. You show the client the six success constraint categories as listed in Figure 1-6. You and the client must then agree on which constraints will make up the success or value constraint. Let's assume that the client defines project value according to a mixture of the four constraints listed in Table 1-1.

Once the client's value factors are known, you and the client jointly determine which constraints can be used for measurement purposes, the metrics that will be used and how points will be assigned for staying within each constraint. You and the client must then agree on the weighting factor importance of each of the constraints.

Using this method, success is being measured by the ability to meet the value constraint even though the value constraint is composed of four other constraints. It is entirely possible that you are not maintaining performance within one of the constraints, such as the time constraint, but your performance within the other three constraints more than makes up for it to the point where the client perceives that value is still being accomplished and the project is a success.

Figure 1-6 Components of value success constraint.

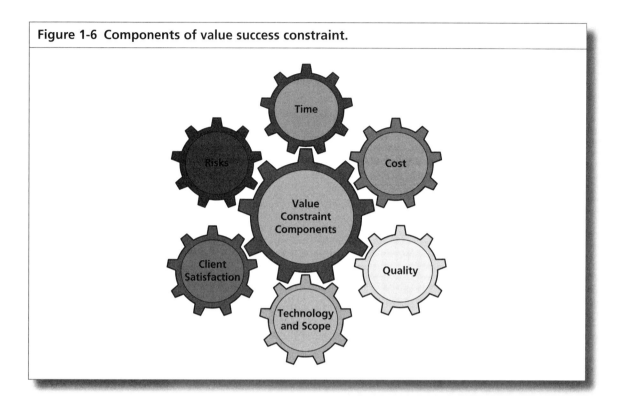

TABLE 1-1   Components of Client's Value/Success Constraint

CLIENT'S VALUE FACTORS	SUCCESS CONSTRAINT	WEIGHTING FACTOR, %
Quality	Quality	20
Delivery date	Time	30
Usability	Performance	35
Risk minimization	Risk	15

You will also notice in this example that cost was not selected as a component of the success criteria or the value constraint. This does not mean that cost is not important. Cost is still being tracked and reported as part of the project management activities but the client does not consider cost as that critical and as part of the success criteria.

As our projects become larger and more complex, the number of constraints used to define success can grow. And to make matters worse, our definition of success can change over the life of the project. Therefore, our definition of success may be organic. Companies will need to establish metrics for tracking the number of success constraints.

The importance of a project success criterion that includes a value component is critical. All too often, projects are completed just to find out that no business value was created. You can end up creating products that nobody will buy. As an example, consider the following example:

Situation: The Iridium Project[1] was designed to create a worldwide wireless handheld mobile phone system with the ability to communicate anywhere in the world at any time. Executives at both Motorola and Iridium LLP regarded the project as the eighth wonder of the world. But more than a decade later and after investors put up billions of dollars, Iridium had solved a problem that very few customers needed solved.

The Iridium Project was both a success and a failure at the same time. As a success, the 11-year project was completed just 1 month late and more than 1000 patents were created. As a failure, investors lost more than $4 billion because the marketplace for the product had changed significantly over the life of the project. In retrospect, it appears that project success was measured solely by technical performance and the schedule. Had there been a more complete definition of success, including value constraints based upon a valid business case, the project would have been cancelled due to eroding business value well before billions of dollars were wasted.

LESSON LEARNED Revalidation of the business case is a necessity especially on long-term projects.

1.7 DIFFERENT DEFINITIONS OF PROJECT SUCCESS

The use of a value constraint to define success can work well as long as everyone agrees on the definition of success. But on large complex projects involving a governance committee made up of several stakeholders, there can be many definitions of success. There can also be more than one definition of success being used for team members working on the same project. As an example:

Situation: During a project management training program for the R&D group of a paint manufacturer, the question was asked: "How does the R&D group define project success?" The answer was simple and concise: "The commercialization of the product." When asked what happens if nobody purchases the product, the R&D personnel responded, "That's not our problem. That headache belongs to marketing and sales. We did our job and were highly successful."

LESSON LEARNED The business case for a project must have a clearly understood definition of success and hopefully be agreed to by all participants.

---

1. For information on the Iridium Project, see Harold Kerzner, "The Rise, Fall and Resurrection of Iridium: A Project Management Perspective," *Project Management Case Studies*, Wiley, Hoboken, NJ, 2013, pp. 327–366. A modified version of the case study appears in Section 3.6.

1.8 UNDERSTANDING PROJECT FAILURE

Most companies seem to have a relatively poor understanding of what is meant by project failure. Project failure is not necessarily the opposite of project success. Simply because we could not meet the project's success criteria is not an indication that the project was a total failure. Consider the following example:

Situation: During an internal meeting to discuss the health of various projects undertaken to create new products, a vice president complained that less than 20% of the R&D projects were successful and reached the product commercialization stage. He then blamed poor project management for the failures of the other 80% of the projects. The director of the Project Management Office then spoke up asserting that most of the other 80% of the projects were not failures. They had in fact created intellectual property that was later used on other R&D projects (i.e., spinoffs) to create commercially successful products.

> **LESSON LEARNED** Projects that create intellectual property, perhaps for future use, should not always be regarded as a total failure.

The above example should make it clear that the definition of project failure is more of a grey area than pure black and white. If knowledge and/or intellectual property is gained on the project, then perhaps the project should not be considered as a complete failure. All project managers know that things may not always go according to plan. Replanning is a necessity in project management. We can begin a project with the best of intentions and prepare a plan based upon the least risk. Unfortunately, the least risk plan usually requires more time and more money. If the project must be replanned using least time as the primary success criterion, then we must be willing to incur more risk and perhaps additional costs.

There is no universally accepted diagnosis as to why projects fail because each project has its own set of requirements, its own unique project team and its own success criteria and can succumb to changes in the enterprise environmental factors. Failures can and will happen on some projects regardless of the company's maturity level in project management. As seen in Figure 1-7, it often takes companies two years or longer to become reasonably good at project management and perhaps another five years to reach some degree of excellence. Excellence in project management is defined as a continuous stream of projects that meet the company's project success criteria.

But as seen in Figure 1-7, even with a high degree of project management excellence, some projects can and will fail. There are three reasons for this:

Figure 1-7 Some projects will fail.

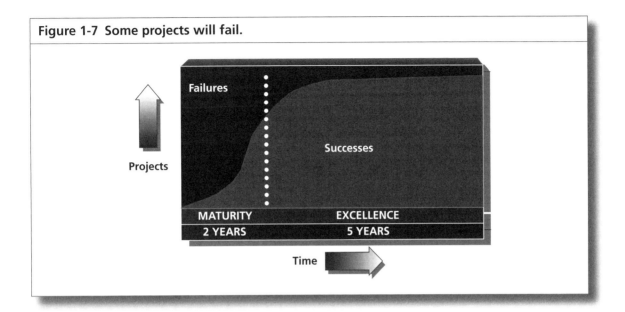

- Any executive that always makes the right decision certainly isn't making enough decisions.
- Effective project management practices can increase your chances of project success but cannot guarantee that success will be achieved.
- Business survival is often based upon how well the company is able to accept and manage business risks. Knowing which risks are worth accepting is a difficult process.

1.9 DEGREES OF PROJECT FAILURE

One of the most commonly read reports on why IT projects fail is the Chaos Report prepared by the Standish Group. The Chaos Report identifies three types of IT project outcomes:

- **Success:** A project that gets accolades and corporatewide recognition for having been completed on time, within budget and meeting all specification requirements.
- **Challenged:** A project that finally reaches conclusion, but there were cost overruns and schedule slippages, and perhaps not all of the specifications were met.
- **Failure:** A project that was abandoned or cancelled due to some form of project management failure.

It is interesting to note how quickly IT personnel blame project management as the primary reason for an IT failure. Although these categories may be acceptable for IT projects, it may be better to use the following breakdown for all projects in general:

- **Complete success:** The project met the success criteria, value was created and all constraints were adhered to.
- **Partial success:** The project met the success criteria, the client accepted the deliverables and value was created although one or more of the success constraints were not met.
- **Partial failure:** The project was not completed as expected and may have been cancelled early on in the life cycle. However, knowledge and/or intellectual property was created that may be used on future projects.
- **Complete failure:** The project was abandoned and nothing was learned from the project.

The following situations provide examples of each of these categories.

Situation: A company undertook a 1-year R&D project designed to create a new product. Assuming the product could be developed, the company had hoped to sell 500,000 units over a 2-year period. During the R&D effort, the R&D project team informed management that they could add significant value to the product if they were given more money and if the schedule were allowed to slip by about 6 months. Management agreed to the schedule slippage and the cost overrun despite resistance from sales and marketing. More than 700,000 units were sold over the first 12 months after product release. The increase in sales more than made up for the cost overrun.

LESSON LEARNED   In this situation, the project was considered as a complete success even though there was a schedule slippage and a cost overrun. Significant value was added to the business.

Situation: A company won a contract through competitive bidding. The contract stipulated that the final product had to perform within a certain range dictated by the product's specifications. Although there were no cost overruns or schedule slippages, the final product could meet only 90% of the specification's performance requirements. The client reluctantly accepted the product and later gave the contractor a follow-on contract to see if they could reach 100% of the specification's performance requirements.

LESSON LEARNED   This situation was considered as a partial success. Had the client not accepted the deliverable, the project may have been classified as a failure.

Situation: A company had a desperate need for software for part of its business. A project was established to determine whether to create the software from scratch or to purchase an off-the-shelf package.

The decision was made to purchase an expensive software package shortly after one of the senior managers in a software company made an excellent presentation on the benefits the company would see after purchasing and using the software as stated. After purchasing the software, the company realized that it could not get the expected benefits unless the software was custom designed to its business model. The software company refused to do any customization and reiterated that the benefits would be there if the software was used as stated. Unfortunately, it could not be used as stated, and the package was shelved.

Situation: A hospital had a policy where physicians and administrators would act as sponsors on large projects even though they had virtually no knowledge about project management. Most of the sponsors also served on the committee that established the portfolio of projects. When time came to purchase software for project management applications, a project team was established to select the package to be procured. The project team was composed entirely of project sponsors that had limited knowledge of project management. Thinking that they were doing a good thing, the committee purchased a $130,000 software package with the expectation that it would be used by all of the project managers. The committee quickly discovered that the organization was reasonably immature in project management and that the software was beyond the capabilities of most project team members. The software was never used.

LESSON LEARNED In the above situation, the company considered the project as a total failure. No value was received for the money spent. Eventually the company committed funds to create its own software package customized for its business applications.

LESSON LEARNED The above situation, just like the previous situation, was considered as a complete failure.

Situation: A company was having difficulty with its projects and hired a consulting company for project management assistance. The decision to hire the company was largely due to a presentation made by one of the partners that had more than 20 years of project management experience.

After the consulting contract was signed, the consulting company assigned a small team of people, most of which were recent college graduates with virtually no project management experience. The consulting team was given offices in the client's company and use of client's computers.

The consulting team acted merely as note-takers in meetings. The quarterly reports they provide to the client were simply a consolidation of the notes they would take during project team meetings. The consulting team was fired since they were providing no value. The client was able to recover from the company's computers several of the e-mails

LESSON LEARNED   In the above example, the client eventually sued the consulting company for failure to perform and collected some damages. The client considered the consulting project as a complete failure.

LESSON LEARNED   Although this project was a partial failure, it did create intellectual property that could be used later.

sent from the consultants to their superiors. One of the e-mails that came from the headquarters of the consulting company stated, "We know we didn't give you a qualified team, but do the best you can with what you have." The client never paid the consulting company the balance of the money due on the contract.

Situation: A company worked on an R&D project for more than a year just to discover that what it wanted to do simply would not happen. However, during the research, the company found some interesting results that later could be used in creating other products.

1.10 OTHER CATEGORIES OF PROJECT FAILURE

Rather than defining failure as either partial or total failure, some articles define failure as preimplementation failure and postimplementation failure. With preimplementation failure, the project is never completed. This could be the result of a poor business case, inability of the team to deliver, a change in the enterprise environmental factors, changing business needs, higher priority projects or any other factors which mandate that senior management pull the plug. The result could be a partial or total failure.

With postimplementation failure, the project is completed and everyone may have high expectations that the deliverables will perform as expected. However, as is the case in IT, postimplementation is when the software bugs appear sometimes causing major systems to be shut down until repairs can be made. The larger and more complex the software package, the less likely it is that sufficient test cases have been made for every possible scenario that could happen in implementation. If daily business operations are predicated upon a system that must be shut down, the failure and resulting losses can run into the hundreds of millions of dollars. Consider the following examples:

- In 2008, the London Stock Exchange's clients were trading more than $17 billion each day. On what was expected to be one of the busiest trading days in months largely due to the U.S. government's takeover of Fannie Mae and Freddie Mac, 352 million shares worth $2.5 billion were traded in the first hour of trading right before the system shut down. For more than 7 hours, investors were unable to buy or sell shares.
- In October 2005, British food retailer Sainsbury scrapped a $528 million investment in an automated supply chain management system that was unable to get merchandise from its warehouses to its retail stores.

Eventually, the company was forced to hire 3000 additional employees to stock the shelves manually.

- In May 2005 Toyota recalled 160,000 Prius hybrid vehicles because warning lights were illuminating unexpectedly and the cars' gasoline engines began stalling. The culprit was a software bug that was in the car's embedded code.
- On April 16, 2013, a glitch in the reservation system at American Airlines grounded all flights leaving thousands stranded for hours. American Airlines has 3500 flights daily on a worldwide basis and an estimated 100,000 passengers were affected by the delays. Approximately 720 flights were cancelled. Although American Airlines rebooked passengers on other flights, American Airlines also warned that delays could continue for several days, thus affecting future flights. A similar situation occurred at Comair Airlines a few years earlier where more than 1000 flights were cancelled. The glitch was also in the reservation system.

Postimplementation failures can become so costly that a company may find itself on the brink of bankruptcy.

1.11 SUMMARY OF LESSONS LEARNED

It is much more difficult than people believe to have a clear understanding of success and failure. Project complexity will force us to better understand those constraints that have a direct bearing upon the project's success criteria. Advances must be made in the use of metrics and metric measurement techniques to assist us with a better understanding of success and failure.

A checklist of techniques that might be used for a better understanding of success and failure includes:

- ☐ Work with the client and the stakeholders to see if an agreement can be reached on the definition of success and failure.
- ☐ Work with the client and the stakeholders to identify the critical success factors.
- ☐ Establish the necessary metrics for each of the critical success factors.
- ☐ Prioritize the critical success factors and the metrics.
- ☐ Throughout the project, revalidate the business case and the accompanying critical success factors.
- ☐ Project failures will happen and it may not be the result of poor project management practices.
- ☐ Project complexity will force us to better understand those constraints that have a direct bearing upon the project's success criteria.
- ☐ Advances must be made in the use of metrics and metric measurement techniques.

TABLE 1-2 *PMBOK® Guide* Alignment to Lessons Learned

LESSONS LEARNED	PMBOK® GUIDE SECTIONS
Defining success and failure is not easy.	1.3, 1.4, 2.2.3
Definitions can change from project to project.	2.2.3
Defining success and failure requires a combination of metrics that can be unique for each project and program.	1.3, 1.4, 2.2.3, 8.1.3.3, 8.2.1.3, 8.3.1.2
Not all success and failure constraints carry the same level of importance.	1.4, 2.2.3, 8.3.3.3
There must be a clear definition of success at the beginning of a project and all parties must agree to it.	1.3, 1.4, 2.2.3, 3.3
A project value success factor, which is a combination of several constraints, may be used rather than reporting on all of the constraints.	1.6, 8.1.3.3, 8.2.1.3, 8.3.1.2
Every project should have a business and/or value constraint.	1.6
Revalidation of the business case must be done periodically to make sure that we are still creating business value.	1.4.3, 1.6
There are degrees of project success and failure.	1.3, 1.4, 2.2.3
Project replanning can change the definitions of project success and failure.	2.2.3
The expectation that all projects will be successful is unrealistic.	2.2.3

Table 1-2 provides a summary of the lessons learned and alignment to various sections of the *PMBOK® Guide* where additional or supporting information can be found. In some cases, these sections of the *PMBOK® Guide* simply provide supporting information related to the lesson learned. There are numerous sections of the *PMBOK® Guide* that could be aligned for each lesson learned. For simplicity sake, only a few are listed.

2 CAUSES OF PROJECT FAILURE

2.0 INTRODUCTION

Projects can fail in any life-cycle phase. When analyzing where failures can occur, we most frequently look at three phases: the project formulation phase, the project implementation phase and the postimplementation phase. Not very many projects fail in the formulation stage. More often than not, the failure occurs during the execution or postimplementation phase. This is particularly true for IT implementation when companies do not spend sufficient time understanding how implementation actually works. During project formulation we assume that the business case is correct. The mistake we make is that we lack an understanding of what questions to ask and to whom the questions should be asked during project formulation. This relates to users not being involved early enough or even throughout the project.

2.1 FACTS ABOUT PROJECT FAILURE

Over the years, we have recognized several facts related to project failures. They include:

- Very few projects fail by themselves; rather, it's the people that fail and the decisions that people make are the wrong decisions.
- Even the most reliable systems will fail during implementation—It's just a matter of when the bugs will appear.
- Project failures are more common than most people believe.
- There's no clear definition of project failure.
- The line between success and failure is not clear; it is a grey area.
- There's no clear magic bullet to guarantee success or prevent failure.
- Failure can occur after successful execution of a project plan because of changing market conditions or the inability to fill an auditorium for a concert.
- Factors we use to define success or failure include time, cost, safety, revenue, profits, promotions, loss of employment, customer satisfaction, product deployment and business value.
- We can have R&D success and marketing launch failure, i.e., different definitions of success and failure on the same project.

2.2 CAUSES OF PROJECT FAILURE

There are numerous causes that lead to project failure. The causes are not necessarily restricted to specific industries. However, IT projects that fail seem to include many of the causes on the list. For almost 17 years, the Chaos Report has blamed project management for the failure of IT projects. Even though many of these causes are the result of poor project management practices, the real question should be: "Why have these same causes of failure appeared year after year, and we persist in doing nothing to correct the situation?"

Knowing the causes of project failure does not help a company unless the company plans on taking action. Most companies simply do not know what to do to recover a failing project. Other companies do not have sufficient metrics on many of their projects that can be used as early warning indicators and then failure occurs too late for any corrective action to take place.

When a project is completed successfully, we go through excruciating pain to capture best practices and lessons learned. Everyone wants to broadcast to the world what they did well on the project to achieve success. But the same is not true for project failures. For personal reasons, people are reluctant to discuss failures even though more best practices can be learned from failures than from successes. People fear that failures may be used against them during performance reviews.

The list of reasons why projects fail is quite large. Yet most companies either do not recognize the symptoms of failure or disregard the symptoms when they do appear. Even if they see the symptoms, they do not know what actions to take. Typical reasons for failure include:

- End-user stakeholders not involved throughout the project
- Minimal or no stakeholder backing; lack of ownership
- Weak initial business case
- Business case deterioration
- Business case requirements that changed significantly over the life of the project
- Technical obsolescence
- Technologically unrealistic requirements
- Lack of a clear vision
- New executive team in place with different visions and goals
- Corporate goals and/or vision not understood at the lower organizational levels
- Plan that asks for too much in too little time
- Poor estimates, especially financial
- Unclear stakeholder requirements
- Passive user stakeholder involvement after handoff
- Unclear or unrealistic expectations
- Unrealistic assumptions, if they exist at all

- Plans based upon insufficient data
- No systemization of the planning process
- Planning performed by a planning group
- Inadequate or incomplete requirements
- Lack of resources
- Assigned resources that lack experience or the necessary skills
- Resources that lack focus or motivation
- Staffing requirements that are not fully known
- Constantly changing resources
- Poor overall project planning
- Established milestones not measurable
- Established milestones too far apart
- Environmental factors that have changes causing outdated scope
- Missed deadlines and no recovery plan
- Budgets exceeded and out of control
- Lack of replanning on a regular basis
- Lack of attention provided to human and organizational aspects of project
- Project estimates that are best guesses and not based upon history or standards
- Not enough time provided for estimating
- Exact major milestone dates or due dates for reporting not known
- Team members working with conflicting requirements
- People shuffled in and out of project with little regard for schedule
- Poor or fragmented cost control
- Each stakeholder uses different organizational process assets, which may be incompatible with each other
- Weak project and stakeholder communications
- Poor assessment of risks, if done at all
- Wrong type of contract
- Poor project management; team members possess a poor understanding of project management, especially virtual team members
- Technical objectives that are more important than business objectives
- Assigning critically skilled workers, including the project manager, on a part-time basis

Not all of the causes of failure are the result of actions taken by the project manager. As an example, procurement often selects the lowest bidder without verifying that the bidders know what the work entails and whether their bid is realistic. After go-ahead, we end up with scope changes that result in cost overruns and schedule delays.

Although any single cause can induce failure, it is more likely that the actual failure is caused by a combination of these causes. Several of the important causes of failure are discussed in the remainder of this chapter. Some of the critical causes of failure are discussed separately in some of the chapters that follow.

2.3 SCHEDULE FAILURE

The literature abounds with causes of project failure and authors are very quick to blame project management. Unfortunately, not all of the causes are or should be attributed to project management. Setting the schedule falls into this category.

Project managers would like nothing better than to be able to establish the schedule for their project after coordination with the key project team members. Unfortunately, more often than not, the schedule, and possibly the budget as well, is dictated to them at the onset of the project by decision makers that may have very little understanding about the complexity of the project and even less of an understanding about project management. These same decision makers persist in establishing end dates that may be unrealistic and refuse to hear the bad news when the project manager states that the schedule is unrealistic. The decision makers also refuse to understand the importance of "schedule slack" and expect the project manager to effectively manage all scheduling risks, often with very little support from senior management.

If project managers are forced to accept an unrealistic schedule, then the real fault should rest with the decision makers at the origination of the project. The two most common mistakes made by decision makers is not understanding the technology or the complexity of the project and making decisions for personal or political reasons.

Decision makers are rarely technical experts. They must rely upon the recommendations of others. When NASA's Space Shuttle Program was on the drawing board, a study was conducted to determine the cost of delivering a payload into space. The study showed that the cost would be approximately $100 per pound and NASA could launch five Space Shuttles each month. Later, it was determined that the actual cost would be closer to $2000 per pound, a 20-fold increase in cost, and the paperwork nightmare at NASA allowed for one Space Shuttle launch each month at best. The people conducting the original study sought the advice of the contractors that would most likely be bidding on the job and, as expected, they lowballed their estimates in hopes of winning a lucrative contract. Because cost containment was an issue, and the payload costs had increased by 2000%, NASA committed insufficient funds to other areas of the project such as safety and risk management. This decision was part of the problem that later resulted in the deaths of seven astronauts on the Space Shuttle *Challenger* launch. While hindsight is always 20–20, it is often a better philosophy to obtain expert advice from people that have no financial interests in the outcome of the project.

A similar example would be the baggage-handling system at Denver International Airport (DIA). The stakeholders were more excited over the idea than the feasibility. Forecasting was impossible because of no precedent. Granting tenants changes to drawings is an acceptable practice as long as the technology is reasonably well known and the complexity of the project is understood. When the decision was made to install an automated baggage-handling system for the entire airport, a launch date two years down the road was established. The contractor was pressured into accepting this date. Unfortunately, the only airline with such a system was Lufthansa in Munich and that system wasn't anywhere near the complexity of the DIA system. Furthermore, the Lufthansa system took approximately eight years to complete and the system was tested 24 hours a day, seven days a week, for six months to extract all of the bugs. Expecting a more complex system to be installed in two years at DIA was more wishful thinking than reality.

Whether or not decision makers understand the complexity of the project, decisions are often made for political purposes or for the personal interest of the decision makers. As an example, the decision makers correctly decided that DIA should remain closed for the two-year period when the baggage-handling system was to be installed. Ripping up concrete, installing unproven technology and having planes moving about would be serious safety risks that DIA officials were not willing to accept. But by keeping the airport closed for two additional years and without any income from landing fees, DIA would be hemorrhaging cash at the rate of $1.1 million each day to service its debt. Therefore, there was significant pressure placed upon the project teams to have the baggage-handling system up and running within two years.

In another example, the CIO of a company told the project team that a software package had to be installed and running by the first week in December. The pressure placed upon the project team was based entirely upon the CIO's desire for the largest possible year-end bonus for himself and this would surely happen if the software launch date could be met. The project team however knew that perhaps less than 10% of the software would be up and running by the beginning of December and it would probably be June of the following year before the entire software package would be operational. Yet the CIO kept pressuring the team to meet an unrealistic and impossible deadline. The team was forced to work significant overtime and the morale of the team was extremely poor. The CIO never realized that he was making the situation worse rather than better.

2.4 FAILURES DUE TO UNKNOWN TECHNOLOGY

Many people believe that large, long-term projects are the easiest to manage because there is sufficient time available for contingency planning and/or recovery planning if necessary. While this may be true in some industries, the critical factor is whether or not we are dealing with known or new technology. The greater the unknowns in the technology or software, the greater the likelihood that bugs will be there and scope changes will be necessary.

When technology is reasonably well known, design freezes are possible, which, in turn, allows for fewer scope changes. When dealing with IT, business needs can change rapidly, making design freezes perhaps impossible and opening the door for the addition of possibly unnecessary bells and whistles.

Most schedules are finish-to-start schedules regardless of whether the technology is known or unknown. However, when dealing with new technology, untested technology or replacing old technology with newer technology as in IT, we know that the risks have increased and we tend to perform some of the work in parallel rather than in series hoping to mitigate these risks. If rework is necessary, then significantly more activities can require rework than with pure finish-to-start schedules, and the critical path may change significantly. In IT, generally no more than 20% of the activities should be done in parallel.

2.5 PROJECT SIZE AND SUCCESS/FAILURE RISK

We very rarely hear about the failure of a $100 million construction project because the planning is usually meticulous even though we may have some large cost overruns. Effective planning is a necessity when the failure of the project could result in the loss of human life. The construction of Denver International Airport, the "Big Dig" in Boston and the tunnel in the channel between England and France are good examples of project successes accompanied by significant cost overruns. However, in other industries such as IT, we frequently hear about failures even though the IT package is eventually operational.

In general, larger and more complex projects have a greater chance of failure than smaller projects. This is shown in Figure 2-1. The slope of the curve is very sensitive to the industry at hand. Figure 2-1 might be representative of industries such as IT. When dealing with large IT projects that include new or untested software, the project should be broken down into smaller projects where the bugs are more easily identified and corrections can be made in small increments. Identifying bugs and then making corrections after $5 million has been spent on a $100 million IT project is less costly than making corrections after $75 million has been spent.

There are many projects where the risk or complexity makes it difficult for the project manager to accept all of the responsibility for the successful delivery of a project. Even the existence of a project sponsor may not be enough. Therefore, as shown in Figure 2-1, there may exist a point in a project where the cost, complexity, risk or length cannot be effectively governed by a single individual or project sponsor. In such cases, committee governance may be necessary and the decision to save or cancel the project

Figure 2-1 Typical success rate curve versus project costs.

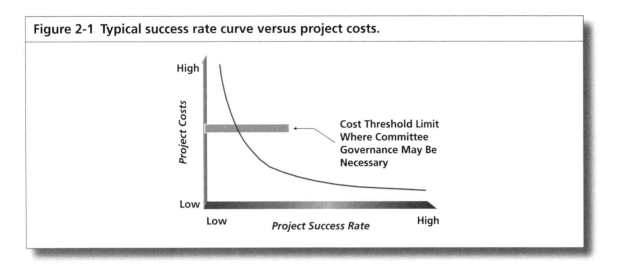

becomes more difficult. In addition, the larger the project, the greater the impact of politics in the decision-making processes.

On the plus side, today's executives are more knowledgeable about project management than their predecessors. As such, we can expect the governance teams to get a better understanding of what information they need for decision making such that more projects can be recovered rather than terminated. This can also change the slope of the curve in Figure 2-1.

2.6 FAILURE DUE TO IMPROPER CRITICAL FAILURE FACTORS

Researchers prepare lists that identify critical success factors and critical failure factures. While these lists have merit, there is no guarantee that the inverse of a critical success factor will be a critical failure factor. For example, in IT user involvement is usually one of the top 10 critical success factors. However, based upon the complexity of the project, the lack of user involvement may not appear as one of the critical failure factors. These lists have merit but they are industry and perhaps even company specific.

In most industries, project managers focus heavily on critical success factors only. This is the result of project management education which emphasizes information captured from best practices and lessons learned. This approach may be beneficial for those industries where there are significantly more successes than failures. But in industries such as IT where the reverse is the norm, project managers should identify and track both critical success factors and critical failure factors.

2.7 FAILURE TO ESTABLISH TRACKING METRICS

If you know the reasons why projects fail, then common sense says that we should establish metrics to track these potential causes of failure on future projects. It is a lot easier to correct an out-of-tolerance condition when the problem is small than when the problem grows. Capers Jones published a book in 1994 in which he concluded that the two primary causes of IT failure seem to be: (1) inaccurate selection of metrics and (2) inadequate measurement.[1] These conclusions appeared the year before the Chaos Reports appeared and yet not much has been done concerning his conclusions.

If project failure is to be reduced, then we must develop constraints and accompanying metrics around the causes of failure. These constraints and metrics could very easily become part of the success criteria and will force project teams to better understand the causes of project failure and techniques for eliminating them. If the metrics indicate that we should pull the plug on the project early, then this might be considered as partial success because we will no longer be squandering money on a bad project.

2.8 FAILING TO RECOGNIZE EARLY WARNING SIGNS

Project success usually occurs only at the end of a project even though we may have success tracking metrics. Failure, however, can occur anywhere in the project's life cycle. There are both quantitative and behavioral early warning signs that failure may be imminent. Some of these include:

- Believing that project success is driven by methodologies and processes rather than people
- Lack of project governance
- Lack of agreement or understanding between the project manager and the governance group over authority and decision-making relationships
- Key stakeholders using words such as "you're in charge," "It's your decision to make," "You're the project manager" and "I'm too busy to help you right now"
- Lack of project team focus on the constraints, especially the constraints related to project success
- Failing to recognize that project replanning is a necessity

There is no guarantee that the existence of these tell-tale signs will definitely lead to failure, but the chances may be good that failure is a possibility.

---

1. Capers Jones, *Assessment and Control of Software Risks*, Prentice Hall, Upper Saddle River, NJ, 1994.

2.9 IMPROPER SELECTION OF CRITICAL TEAM MEMBERS

Large, complex projects are managed by a team of people called the project office rather than just the project manager. The people that reside in the project office are referred to as assistant project managers (APMs). This is shown in Figure 2-2.

Because the complexity of today's projects appears to be increasing, executives must become concerned about who should be assigned as an assistant project manager. Historically, executive attention was given only to the selection of the project manager rather than the selection of the entire project office. On large technical projects, there may be a need for an APM for engineering, manufacturing, cost control, scheduling, quality and several other functional disciplines.

To understand the problem, we must begin first with understanding the job description of the APM. Historically, on large projects, the project manager would find it almost impossible to single-handedly manage the coordination of all of the personnel assigned to the project. The simplest solution seemed to be the designation of an APM. As an example, let's assume that there are 20 engineers assigned to the project. Rather than asking the project manager to perform the integration of activities among the 20 engineers, one of the engineers is designated as the APM for engineering and the APM handles the coordination. Sometimes this person would be referred to as the lead engineer. Now the project manager needs to interface with just one person, the APM for engineering, when discussing the engineering activities.

Figure 2-2 Project organization.

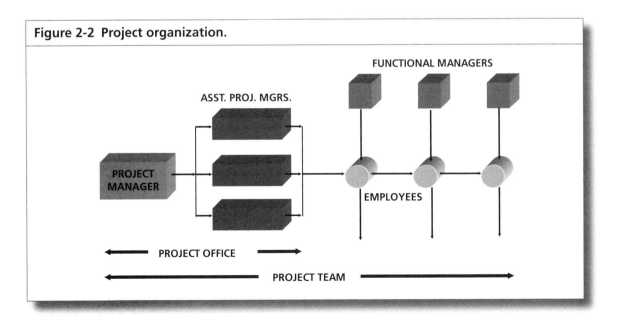

While this approach looks good on paper, problems can occur that lead to project failure:

- The people assigned as APMs considered themselves as lead experts in their disciplines and, as such, believed that knowledge of project management was unnecessary for them to perform their jobs.
- The APMs viewed their chances for promotion to be based upon their technical knowledge rather than project management capability or project success.
- Project management work was an add-on to their normal job and their functional managers that evaluated them for promotion had limited project management knowledge and therefore did not consider APM performance during the promotion cycles.
- Highly technical APMs began changing the direction of the project for their own personal satisfaction.
- APMs were making decisions that were in the best interest of their own functional area rather than the best interest of the project or the company.
- The project manager had to manage the interfacing between APMs since many of the APMs did not communicate with one another.

It soon became apparent that the project manager's job was becoming more difficult rather than easier because the APMs had just a cursory understanding of project management. This led to work integration failures and elongated the schedule. The next step was to assign people as APMs that had previous experience as project managers. It was then entirely possible that someone could be a project manager part time on one project and an APM part time on another project. While this technique had merit, there were still issues that the APMs understood project management but had difficulty coordinating functional activities because of a lack of knowledge of the functional area.

Today, we are training functional employees in project management so that they can perform properly as APMs. Functional managers are also being trained in project management. The result is that those functional employees that are asked to perform as APMs are being evaluated on their technical ability by their functional managers and their project management performance by both the project manager (on an informal basis) and their functional managers. This now gives us the best of both worlds and provides functional employees with long-term career path opportunities in either the functional arena or the project management arena.

If you believe the Chaos Report, which argues that most failures are attributed to project management, then you see the importance of having people properly trained in project management. And, as expected, the training should go well beyond just the project manager.

Situation: A hospital undertook a project designed to create a "cafeteria" benefits package that could be customized for more than 8000 employees. Each employee would walk through the cafeteria and select what benefits they wanted from the shelves. At the end of the cafeteria line would be a cashier that would tell them the cost of their package and how much they must pay out of pocket.

A consultant was brought in by the vice president of Human Resources to help with the initiation of the project. The first decision was the selection of project manager. The Human Resources Department wanted the project manager to come from their group because they thought up the idea for the project. The Accounting Department wanted the project manager to come from their group because they were responsible for standing at the payroll window and telling everyone how the deductions would be made from their paychecks and how much. The IT Department wanted control of the project because they were responsible for creating the software. The consultant wanted a professional project manager to be hired because none of the three departments had any project management experience.

The vice president of Human Resources was displeased with the consultant's recommendation believing that Human Resources should manage the project even though nobody in Human Resources had even been trained in project management. The consultant was fired and Human Resources took control of the project. The project nearly failed but eventually most of the project was completed, late by more than one year, over budget and with conflicts galore just about everywhere. Parts of the project were delayed but scheduled to be completed the following year.

LESSON LEARNED The Human Resources Department was under the impression that anyone can be a project manager. Their belief changed significantly after this project. Today, they have professionally trained and certified project managers throughout the hospital.

2.10 UNCERTAIN REWARDS

When people are assigned to a project team, they immediately wonder what's in it for them if the project is a success. This includes the project manager as well. Likewise, people may worry about what will happen to them if the project fails.

In some environments, such as pharmaceutical R&D, a typical project is 3000 days to reach the commercialization stage and at a cost of $850 million to $1.5 billion. Given the fact that probably less than 2% of the projects are considered as total successes whereby they generate $500 million a year in revenue, you could retire from a pharmaceutical company having worked on just three or four projects and having all failures. Not all projects will be successful regardless of the industry.

Project managers are expected to take risks when managing a project. There must be criteria established for how project managers will be evaluated. If project managers are downgraded during performance reviews for managing a project that failed, the chances are good that very few people will want to become project managers and even fewer people will volunteer to manage high-risk projects.

Situation: In the early 1980s, a health care provider ambitiously undertook the development of an IT package to come up with a better way to reimburse physicians. Having very little knowledge about project management, the company was unsure as to who should be appointed as the project manager. Rather than training people to perform as project managers, the organization decided to simply appoint various IT personnel as "temporary" project managers just for components of this large project. These individuals still had other functional duties to perform in addition to their work on this project. The temporary project managers knew that they still had a home in the functional area if the project failed and that their rewards would be based more upon their traditional functional duties than their performance on the project.

Integrating all of the work became a migraine headache. People were working massive overtime and morale was quite low. After having spent almost $1 billion over a two-year period, the project was cancelled because it was obvious that the organization had bitten off more than it could chew. The people assigned as full-time project managers received poor performance reviews whereas the part-time project managers received average to above-average performance reviews.

People developed a hatred for project management believing that it would never work in their organization and a project management assignment would be detrimental to their career. But senior management had a different idea. Senior management believed that project management would be an essential component for the organization's future. The organization created a position called the vice president of projects. Project managers could come from anywhere in the organization and be assigned administratively full time to the vice president until the project ended. Based upon the size of the project, it was believed that all project managers must be full time, but at completion of the project they may still return to their functional areas if they wished.

The organization realized many of the mistakes that had been made on the $1 billion disaster. A week-long training program was established for 50 people in the organization. The participants attending the program were never told that they would probably be in the resource pool to be assigned as future project managers. The instructor was the only person told which people in the class would be assigned as project managers shortly after the class was finished. Furthermore, the instructor was asked to provide feedback to the vice president as to which employees would best be able to function as a project manager based upon classroom observation.

One woman in the class appeared to have a really good grasp as to what project management was all about. The week following the class, the vice president told the woman that she would be assigned as the project manager on the next large project. Her response was very clear: "I would rather resign from the company than become a project manager!"

2.11 ESTIMATING FAILURES

It is not uncommon on large projects to ask an estimating group to establish the cost and schedule. This is particularly true if the company has an estimating database. The problem is that many companies do not ask the project managers to validate the estimates. And even if the project manager is asked to state whether the estimates are realistic, it happens after contract award.

Estimating groups can work well on low-risk projects where technical complexity is at a minimum. But on large projects with high degrees of complexity, the people that will be doing the work should be allowed to participate in establishing or revalidating the estimates. If this does not happen, then the team may not be committed to the estimates and some degree of failure can be expected.

Situation: Barbara just received the good news; she was assigned as the project manager for a very large project that her company won through competitive bidding. Whenever a request for proposal (RFP) comes into Barbara's company, a committee composed mainly of senior managers reviews the RFP. If the decision is made to bid on the job, the RFP is turned over to the Proposal Department. Part of the Proposal Department is an estimating group that is responsible for estimating all work. If the estimating group has no previous history concerning some of the deliverables or work packages and is unsure about the time and cost for the work, the estimating team will then ask the functional managers for assistance with estimating.

Project managers like Barbara do not often participate in the bidding process. Usually, their first knowledge about the project comes after the contract is awarded to their company and they are assigned as the project manager. Some project managers are highly optimistic and trust the estimates that were submitted in the bid implicitly unless, of course, a significant time span has elapsed between the date of submittal of the proposal and the final contract award date. Barbara, however, was somewhat pessimistic because the estimating group required almost six months to prepare the estimates and then submit the proposal. Barbara believed that accepting the estimates as they were submitted in the proposal was like playing Russian roulette. As such, Barbara preferred to review the estimates.

Barbara concluded that the estimates were way off of the mark. The only way that this project could ever be completed in the allotted time would be to reduce the scope significantly. Barbara believed that the estimating group had not considered any complexity factors with their estimates.

Barbara's estimate was that the project would take closer to four years rather than three years to complete. During the first quarterly report after the project began, Barbara was honest in her belief on what the estimated time would be to complete the project. The customer reacted swiftly and cancelled the project.

LESSONS LEARNED Expecting a project manager to accept an unrealistic estimate is an invitation for failure. The larger and more complex the project, the greater the need to have the participation of the project manager and key team members during proposal preparation.

2.12 STAFFING FAILURES

Very few companies have the ability to manage large, complex projects by themselves without support from vendors. The problem is how much time both the parent company and the vendors need to ramp up to full manpower on the project.

Clients usually perform their own internal analysis on the time and cost to perform the work. However, the so-called true cost will not appear until after the vendors submit their bids and the bids are reviewed. The client may need to arrange for funding for the project prior to making the announcement of contract awards. The vendors may need months to fully ramp up for the project and hire experienced personnel or train their own personnel. In any case, there can be a gap of one to six months, or even longer, between the contract award date and the official go-ahead date.

Situation: After go-ahead, Sarah reviewed the information she had on the project and believed it was more complex than any other project she had managed. Sarah's company had a philosophy that the project manager would be assigned during proposal preparation, assist in the preparation of the proposal, validate the estimates as best he or she could and take on the role of the project manager after contract award, assuming the company would be awarded the contract.

Usually, contract go-ahead would take place within a week or two after contract award. That made project staffing relatively easy for most of the project managers. It also allowed the company to include in the proposal a detailed schedule based upon resources that would be assigned upon contract award and go-ahead. During proposal preparation, the functional managers would anticipate who would be available for assignment to this project over the next few weeks. The functional managers could then estimate with reasonable accuracy the duration and effort required based upon the grade level of the resources to be assigned. Since the go-ahead date was usually within two weeks of contract award, and the fact that the contract award was usually within a week or so after proposal submittal, the schedule that appeared in the proposal was usually the same schedule for the actual project with very few changes. This entire process was based upon the actual availability of resources rather than the functional managers assuming unlimited resources and using various estimating techniques.

While this approach worked well on most projects, Sarah's new project had a go-ahead date of six months after contract award. For the functional managers, this created a problem estimating the effort and duration. Estimating now had to be made based upon the assumption of unlimited availability rather than the availability of limited resources. Functional managers were unsure as to who would be available six months from now, yet some type of schedule had to appear in the proposal.

Sarah knew the risks. When estimates were being prepared for Sarah's proposal, the functional managers assumed that the higher skilled workers in the department would be available and assigned to the project after go-ahead. The effort and duration estimates were then made based upon the higher skilled employees.

Sarah's company was awarded the contract. Sarah had silently hoped that the company would not get the contract, but it did. As expected, the go-ahead date was six months later. This created a problem for Sarah because she was unsure as to when to begin the preparation of the detailed schedule. The functional managers told her that they could not commit to an effort and duration based upon actual limited resource availability until somewhere around two to three weeks prior to the actual go-ahead date. The resources were already spread thin across several projects and many of the projects were having trouble. In addition, a reprioritization of projects had occurred and Sarah's project now had other higher priority efforts ahead of her. This meant that the higher skilled resources may be committed elsewhere, and there was not enough time available to hire additional workers and train them. Sarah was afraid that the worst case scenario would come true and that the actual completion date would be longer than what was in the proposal. Sarah was certainly not happy about explaining this to the client should it be necessary to do so.

As the go-ahead date neared, Sarah negotiated with the functional managers for resources. Unfortunately, her worst fears came true when, for the most part, she would be provided with only average or above-average resources. The best resources were in demand elsewhere and it was obvious that they would not be available for her project.

Using the efforts and durations provided by the functional managers, Sarah prepared the new schedule. Much to her chagrin, she would be several months late. The client would have to be told about this. But before telling the client, Sarah decided to look at ways to compress the schedule. Working overtime was a possibility, but Sarah knew that overtime could lead to burned-out workers and the possibility of mistakes being made would increase. Also, Sarah knew that the workers really did not want to work overtime. Crashing the project by adding more resources was impossible because there were no other resources available. Outsourcing some of the work was likewise not possible because the statement of work identified that proprietary information would be provided by the client and that the contractor would not be allowed any outsourcing of the work to a third party. Because of the nature of the work, doing some of the work in parallel rather than series was not possible. There was always a chance that the assigned resources could get the job done ahead of schedule but Sarah believed that a schedule delay was inevitable.

Sarah had to make a decision about when and how to inform the client of the impending schedule delay. If she told the truth to the client right now, the client might understand but also might believe that her company lied in the proposal. That would be an embarrassment for her company. If she delayed informing the client, there is a chance that the original schedule in the proposal might be adhered to, however slim. If the client was informed at the last minute about the delay, it could be costly for the client and equally embarrassing for her company.

LESSONS LEARNED Honesty with the client is always the best policy. The client should be treated as an ally rather than as a combatant.

Sarah decided that this was a decision that senior management should make. The decision was made to tell the client about the possible staffing issues and the possibility for a late completion date. The client understood the problem and agreed to let the project continue on.

2.13 PLANNING FAILURES

We all strive to develop the perfect project plan. However, what usually happens is that we develop an optimistic plan or a pessimistic plan. With an optimistic plan, we assume the best and hope nothing can go wrong. When things do go wrong, as happened with the automated baggage-handling system at Denver International Airport and with the opening of terminal 5 at London Heathrow Airport, we write off the mistakes as optimistic planning failure. If we prepare a pessimistic plan, then we may end up providing the client with less performance than what was possible. This is referred to as pessimistic planning failure.

Figures 2-3 and 2-4 illustrate optimistic and pessimistic failures.[2] For simplicity sake, let's define failure as unmet expectations. Furthermore, let's assume that there are two components of failure; planning failure and perceived failure. Planning failure is the difference between what was achievable and what was planned. Perceived failure is the difference between what was planned and what was actually accomplished. Perceived failure could be the result of poor performance. The actual failure is the difference between what was achievable and what was actually accomplished.

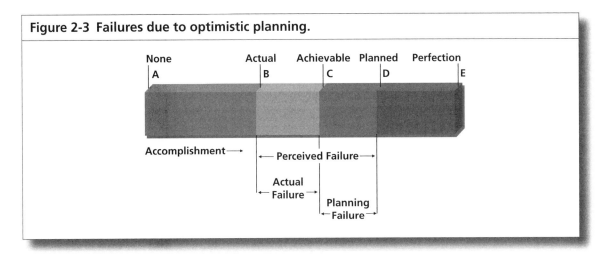

Figure 2-3 Failures due to optimistic planning.

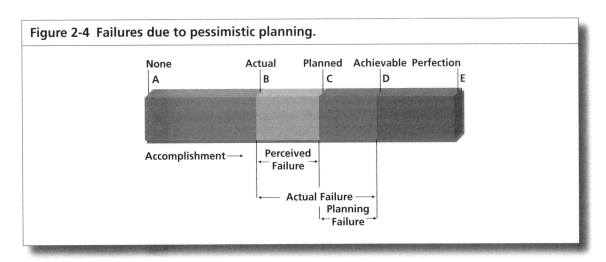

Figure 2-4 Failures due to pessimistic planning.

2. Figures 2-3 and 2-4 adapted from Robert D. Galbreath, *Winning at Project Management,* Wiley, Hoboken, NJ, 1986, pp. 2–6.

In Figure 2-3, the project manager knew what was achievable (C) but laid out a plan telling the client that D would be accomplished. If the project's performance reached C, then the perceived failure would have been just the planning failure. If the actual performance was at B, where we accomplished less than what was achievable, then the perceived failure is the sum of the actual and planning failures.

In Figure 2-4, the project team lays out a plan (C) for less than what was achievable (D). The difference is the planning failure due to pessimism. If the actual accomplishment is less than what was planned (B), then the actual failure would be the sum of the perceived and planning failures. If the actual performance was greater than what was planned (C) but less than what was achievable (D), then there would be no perceived failure and the actual failure would be less than the planning failure.

2.14 RISK MANAGEMENT FAILURES

In Figures 2-3 and 2-4 we defined perceived failure as the difference between what was planned and what was achieved. Let's assume that the plan was to meet the customer's expectations. We tend to explain the perceived failure in terms of a lack of technical accomplishment. But, as can be seen in Figure 2-5, the difference is often due partially to the inability to effectively manage the project's risks. Until companies become reasonably mature with effective risk management practices, project failure must have a risk failure component.

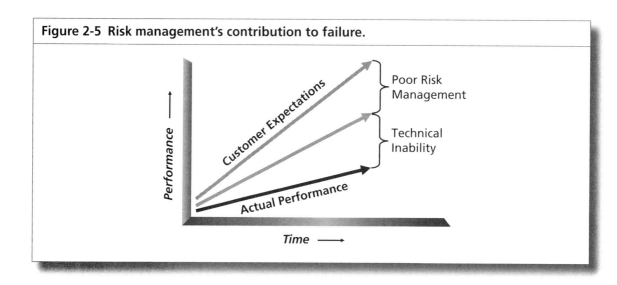

Figure 2-5 Risk management's contribution to failure.

2.15 MANAGEMENT MISTAKES

Project managers are not infallible. They make mistakes like anyone else. Sometimes project managers make decisions or take actions that they believe are in the best interest of the project but instead create problems that may not directly cause failure immediately but may plant the seeds for a possible failure downstream. As an example, consider the following situation:

Situation: A company received a contract to produce a large quantity of units for a client. Each unit required approximately 3 hours of uninterrupted assembly work. Once assembly of a unit began, because of the chemicals that were used, work had to continue until the assembly of the unit was completed. The schedule called for the assembly of two full units per day: one in the morning and one in the afternoon.

Optimistically, the project manager assumed that 10 units would be produced each week for the duration of the project. The team members understood the importance of the meeting scheduled milestones and agreed not to take any vacation days until the manufacturing and assembly schedule was fulfilled.

The project manager scheduled two team meetings a week: one meeting on Monday morning and the second team meeting on Thursday morning. The team meetings began at 10:00 a.m. and lasted between 1.5 and 2 hours. The assembly workers complained that the team meetings were robbing them of valuable assembly time. The project manager did not heed their warnings and simply recommended that they start work early the day of the team meeting or work overtime. Unfortunately, not all of the assembly workers could start work early or work overtime as a group. The schedule began to slip to the point where the client became irate and considered cancelling the remaining work.

LESSON LEARNED Project managers must make decisions according to work ethics and culture of the team members rather than solely the project manager's work ethic and desires.

In the above situation, the project was not cancelled. The project manager eventually went to one team meeting a week and it was a lunchtime meeting where the project paid for pizza and/or sandwiches. The schedule of two assembled units per day was then fulfilled.

While the project manager believed that two team meetings a week was a necessity, he failed to realize that he was robbing the assembly team of time they needed to do their work. In project management courses, we generally discuss the time-robbers that directly affect the performance of the project manager. We seem to neglect discussing the actions of the project manager that can rob team members of their precious time.

Here's another situation where the project manager believed that he was doing the right thing but a disaster soon occurred.

Situation: A project that was strategically important to a company was in serious trouble. Rather than risk failure, management assigned a new project manager that had some expertise in ways to recover a failing project. The new project manager decided to stop work on the project and scrap the existing schedule while telling the team (that prepared the schedule and estimates) that the existing schedule was irreversibly flawed and based upon unrealistic estimates. Furthermore, the project manager stated that he would personally create a new schedule and see how much business value could be salvaged from this point forth. This could take up to a week.

When the new schedule was completed, the project manager tried to reconvene the project team. Unfortunately, many of the previous team members had asked to be reassigned to other projects because they were led to believe that they were the reasons for the problems. Even though the new schedule had merit, the dismantling of the project team would make it impossible to meet the new schedule. It would be like starting from scratch at the bottom of the learning curve. The project was then cancelled and written off as a failure.

> **LESSONS LEARNED** The words that the project manager used made the team feel that they had failed personally. The project manager destroyed the morale of the team and made the situation worse. There are better ways to handle this type of situation.

Albert Einstein once stated, "We cannot solve our problems with the same thinking we used when we created them." While this statement has merit, it certainly should not mean replacing all or most of the team members. Recovery of a failing project cannot take place in a vacuum. Stopping the project and replanning are the right ideas, but the process should be done with the team because they know what will work and what probably will not work. Stopping the project and making the team feel personally responsible for failure were an invitation for "rats to desert a sinking ship."

These are just some examples of mistakes we make inadvertently believing we are doing the right thing. Later, we may find that we have made things worse rather than better.

2.16 LACKING SUFFICIENT TOOLS

Most companies today have tools for managing projects. Enterprise project management methodologies fall into this category. Some companies have more than 50 tools they use whereas other companies have at best just a handful. Working on projects without the correct tools is an invitation for failure.

Situation: A home appliance company had eight different IT systems development project management methodologies that could be used for IT projects. At the beginning of each project, the project team would convene and decide which methodology would be best for a particular project. With eight methodologies to select from, it became an impossible task to get total agreement. Many team members were quite familiar with perhaps just two or three methodologies and were quite unhappy having to work with unfamiliar methodologies. Management learned quickly after several IT failures that it would be best to have just one systems development methodology that everyone could follow.

We should make it clear that we are not discussing a singular methodology for an entire company. While this may be an altruistic goal for some companies, large firms may have different methodologies for various parts of the business. For example, at General Motors, there was a methodology for new car development and a second methodology for just IT projects. Having more than one methodology can work. The problem occurs when the project bridges several functional areas that have their own methodology.

> **LESSONS LEARNED** Having tools to support project management activities is the correct approach. But what is better is having the right tools.

2.17 FAILURE OF SUCCESS

Any single project can be driven to success with a sledge hammer, brute force, the use of formal authority and overzealous and unnecessary executive interference. But what if the success of this project had a detrimental effect on other projects that sacrificed their resources to make this project a success? What happens if the people on this project refuse to work again for this project manager? What happens if the executive is successful doing this on one project and then believes he o she can continue doing it on other projects? This is called the failure of success. Care must be taken in how we define success. Perhaps project management success should be defined as a stream of successfully managed projects where the organizational process assets were used correctly. There is a difference between overall project management success and success on an individual project.

The greater the number of individual successes, the greater the tendency that a company can become complacent and miss opportunities for improvements. As an example, consider a project manager that has had two or three projects in a row that were considered to be successful. For the moment, let's forget about whether the successes were blind luck or exceptional project management performance.

As the project manager begins to close out his or her current project, the team is debriefed to capture lessons learned and best practices. My experience has shown that the greater the number of prior successes, or the stronger the project manager's reputation, the greater the tendency that lessons learned and best practices will be examined only from the things that went well on the project. Best practices can be learned from what went wrong or even failures as well as what went right. Yet the more successes we have, the more we are led to believe the mistakes we made may have been a fluke and there was nothing to be learned from them. When the truth finally appears, the results can be devastating.

Sometimes, we can learn more from failures than successes, but the greater the number of successes, the greater the chance that critical mistakes that lead to failure will be hidden. Too much success can lead to failure if we become complacent and refuse to examine both good and bad performance as part of continuous improvement efforts. Companies that have colossal failures or enter bankruptcy seem to improve their project management performance at a faster rate than those that believe that they are already successful. When survival of the firm is at stake, improvements occur rapidly.

Success can be a form of blindness that permeates all levels of management and nobody realizes that they may be infected with a blinding disease until they see the competition making inroads into their market share. Executives are blinded by the number of successes and the size of their Christmas bonuses. This could lead management to misbelieve that the current portfolio of projects is sufficient to prepare the firm for the future or that they have a superior project management methodology that will endure for the next several years. They could also falsely believe that the competition cannot catch them. Project managers see their successes as opportunities for career advancement and workers see this as job security.

There are tell-tale early warning signs indicating the failure of success:

- Continuous improvements in project management have slowed down significantly.
- People refuse to discuss mistakes made and what can be learned from them.
- Mistakes are often hidden from all levels of management.
- Bad news, if it does exist and is reported, is filtered as it proceeds up the chain of command.
- There is a high degree of complacency in the way projects are managed.
- Project management methodologies have become more rigid than flexible.
- The project manager is provided with very little freedom in how to apply the methodology to a particular client's needs.
- Everyone uses exactly the same metrics for managing projects.
- Budgets for training and education in project management are diminishing.

If a company is fortunate to have a great many successes, then why doesn't the company ask itself, "How do we maintain our leadership position and prevent the competition from catching up to us?" Only on rare occasions have executives and project managers asked me this question.

Perhaps the real issue is, "Who is looking out for the future of project management in the firm?" An organization must have a central group responsible for the management of project management intellectual property. This group is often the project management office, project management community of practice or the project management center of excellence. If this group is doing their job effectively, then they should have metrics in place to show that their actions improve the overall effectiveness of the firm. There should be expertise in the group on how to differentiate project success from project failure. The group should also possess facilitation capability in how to effectively debrief project teams and capture those critical best practices needed for continuous improvements. The group can and must correct the blindness before it becomes critical.

2.18 MOTIVATION TO FAIL

It is a mistake to believe that all people that work on projects want the project to succeed. For projects internal to the company, people may want the project to fail if they believe that they personally will be adversely affected by the outcome of the project. This is particularly true for projects designed to improve efficiency, eliminate certain waste and downsize the organization. The outcome from the project may force employees to work differently or could result in a downsizing of the organization. Executives may want the project to fail if they believe that the size of their empire will diminish resulting in a loss of power, authority, prestige or even salary. Workers may want the project to fail if they believe that they must learn new tools, work differently, change their work habits, be reassigned to other positions in the company or even lose their job. Even active user involvement cannot overcome many of these fears.

Planned failure can be classified as follows:

- Preimplementation failure
- Postimplementation failure

With preimplementation failure, workers may try to sabotage the project as the project develops. This assumes that they fully understand the impact if the project were implemented successfully. This type of project failure can occur as the result of the actions of one person or perhaps a small group of people. Once the project is implemented, it is more difficult to commit sabotage. Postimplementation failure generally requires the efforts of several people who team up and find numerous reasons why the project's deliverables do not perform as need.

Situation: The FoxMeyer ERP Program[3] In 1993, FoxMeyer Drugs was the fourth largest distributor of pharmaceuticals in the United States, worth $5 billion. In an attempt to increase efficiency, FoxMeyer purchased an SAP system and a warehouse automation system and hired Andersen Consulting to integrate and implement the two in what was supposed to be a $35 million project. By 1996, the company was bankrupt; it was eventually sold to a competitor for a mere $80 million.

The reasons for the failure are familiar. First, FoxMeyer set up an unrealistically aggressive time line—the entire system was supposed to be implemented in 18 months. Second, the warehouse employees whose jobs were affected—more accurately, threatened—by the automated system were not supportive of the project, to say the least. After three existing warehouses were closed, the first warehouse to be automated was plagued by sabotage, with inventory damaged by workers and orders going unfilled.

Finally, the new system turned out to be less capable than the one it replaced: By 1994, the SAP system was processing only 10,000 orders a night, compared with 420,000 orders under the old mainframe. FoxMeyer also alleged that both Andersen and SAP used the automation project as a training tool for junior employees, rather than assigning their best workers to it.

In 1998, two years after filing for bankruptcy, FoxMeyer sued Andersen and SAP for $500 million each, claiming it had paid twice the estimate to get the system in a quarter of the intended sites. The suits were settled and/or dismissed in 2004.

> **LESSON LEARNED** No one plans to fail, but even so, make sure your operation can survive the failure of a project.

2.19 TRADEOFF FAILURES

Given the likelihood that projects will get into trouble, project managers must be prepared to perform tradeoffs for each of the variables identified as critical success or failure factors. As identified in Figure 2-6, for each variable there are tradeoff risks. For some of the risks, whether they are high risks or low risks, there exists a threshold limit when executive involvement may be necessary. Executives may have a better understanding of how the tradeoffs and accompanying risks will impact the business.

---

3. Jake Widman, "Lessons Learned: IT's Biggest Project Failures," *Computerworld*, October 9, 2008.

Figure 2-6 Tradeoff risks.

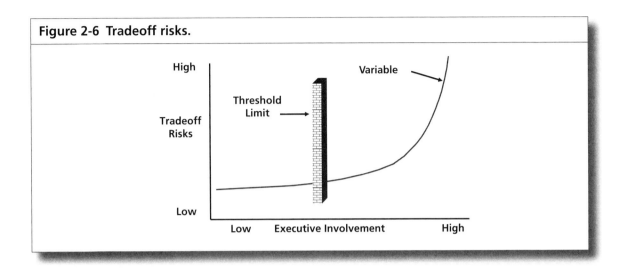

2.20 SUMMARY OF LESSONS LEARNED

There are numerous causes of project failure. Not all causes can be predicted, but there are usually some early warning signs that provide us with sufficient time to take corrective action. Effective risk management is probably the most effective tool for understanding the causes of failure.

A checklist of techniques that might be used to understand causes of failure might include:

☐ Work with the client and the stakeholders to identify what the major causes of project failure might be.
☐ The larger the project, the greater the risk of failure and the greater the need for effective governance. Strive for effective governance.
☐ Carefully review all risk triggers and early warning signs of trouble.
☐ Understand the capabilities of your organizational process assets.
☐ You must understand that most mistakes may be able to be repaired quickly. However, dishonesty with the client, stakeholders and the team may never be repaired.

Table 2-1 provides a summary of the lessons learned and alignment to various sections of the *PMBOK® Guide* where additional or supporting information can be found. In some cases, these sections of the *PMBOK® Guide* simply provide supporting information related to the lesson learned. There are numerous sections of the *PMBOK® Guide* that could be aligned for each lesson learned. For simplicity sake, only a few are listed.

TABLE 2-1   *PMBOK® Guide* **Alignment to Lessons Learned**

LESSONS LEARNED	PMBOK® GUIDE SECTIONS
Get user and stakeholder involvement as early as possible during project initiation and be prepared to ask the right questions.	3.3
The hardest failure to predict is a schedule failure because of all of the interconnected factors.	6.7
Not all projects are initiated with known technology. Even if technology is unknown, technical documentation must be prepared to the best of the team's ability.	4.1.1.1, 4.1.1.2, 4.4.3.2, 12.3.1.5
Effective monitoring and controlling of a project require a good project management information system (PMIS). However, the PMIS may not be able to prevent failure if the wrong critical success factors (CSFs) are selected.	3.6, 4.3.2.2, 4.4.2.3
Not everyone is qualified to perform as a project manager regardless of their educational background.	1.7.1, 1.7.2
If project managers have split loyalties in the workplace and are not dedicated to the success of the project, the foundation for possible failure exists.	1.7.1, 1.7.2
During project staffing activities, project managers must validate that the assigned resources have the necessary skills and the proper attitude.	2.3.1, 9.2
Project managers must be actively involved in planning activities, not having others do the work for them.	3.4
Project managers must maintain honesty with the client and stakeholders.	1.7.1, 1.7.2, 2.2, 2.2.1
The project manager must know and respect the work ethic of the members of the project team.	1.7.2, 2.1.1, 9.3.2.1
Project managers that use poor communication skills when dealing with the project team can induce failure. This includes making promises that cannot be fulfilled, especially with regard to awards.	9.3.2.6, 10.2
Risk triggers cannot be monitored without effective organizational process assets.	2.1.4
Tradeoffs are a necessity on every project.	4.5

3 BUSINESS CASE FAILURE

3.0 INTRODUCTION

Perhaps the worst possible cause of failure is when the business case for the project either is faulty from the onset of the project or changes unfavorably during the execution of the project and nobody realizes it or wants to admit it. Usually the governance personnel have a better insight into the validity of the business case than does the project manager. When a business case is flawed at the beginning of a project, it is usually because not enough time was provided for an investigation to validate the objectives. Project managers generally assume that the business case is valid when starting out on the project.

3.1 CHANGING STAKEHOLDERS

That a project has a valid business case based upon a justifiable need and can be completed within the existing technology does not mean that it will be a success. Ineffective stakeholder relations management is usually the ultimate culprit. When stakeholders change over the life of a project, the likelihood that the business case will change increases significantly.

In the early years of project management, we learned a great deal about the issues with changing stakeholders and the impact on the business case. On long-term government projects, especially those involving military personnel functioning as stakeholders for the DOD, changes in stakeholders can take place several times over the life of the project. Some stakeholders will make decisions based upon what's in it for them personally, such as a promotion or reassignment to another promotable position, rather than for the best interest of the project. If the project is going well, some stakeholders may try to accelerate the schedule regardless of the cost or associated risks if a successful project can get them promoted while they are in command of the project. If the project is in trouble, other DOD stakeholders may be unwilling to admit failure if it means being passed over for promotion. In this case, they will stick with the bad decisions they have made but add in additional scope changes to elongate the project so that it does not interfere with their reassignment to another position. Therefore, the person replacing them will have to deal with all of the headaches.

3.2 REVALIDATION OF ASSUMPTIONS

Project management has been in existence for more than 50 years. Yet in all that time there is still one critical mistake that we repeat over and over again: a failure to revalidate the project's assumptions identified in the business case. Project managers are often brought on board a project after the project has been approved and the assumptions and constraints have been documented in the project charter. The charter is then handed to the project manager and the project manager may mistakenly believe that the assumptions are correct and still valid.

The problem is that the project could have been approved months before rather than just left waiting on the back burner for funding to be approved. While sitting on the back burner, the assumptions for the project may have changed significantly to the point where the business case is no longer valid and the project should no longer be considered or should be considered but redirected toward different objectives. In either case, completing a project based upon faulty assumptions may result in completing a project that provides no business value.

We provide project managers with software to assist them in tracking time, cost, scope, risk and many other project functions. But we do not provide them with the necessary tools to track the ongoing validity of the assumptions and the business case. For most project managers, assuming that they do this at all, it is a manual process. Input from the project sponsor is essential and there is a valid argument that this should be part of the sponsor's job description.

In any case, assumptions and business cases can and do change. Examples of assumptions that are likely to change over the duration of a project, especially on a long-term project, might include:

- The cost of borrowing money and financing the project will remain fixed.
- The procurement costs will not increase.
- The breakthrough in technology will take place as scheduled.
- The resources with the necessary skills will be available when needed.
- The marketplace will readily accept the product.
- Our competitors will not catch up to us.
- The risks are low and can be easily mitigated.
- The political environment in the host country will not change.

The problem with having faulty assumptions is that they can lead to faulty conclusions, bad results and unhappy customers. The best defense against poor assumptions is good preparation at project initiation, including the development of risk mitigation strategies. One possible way to do this is with a validation checklist as shown in Table 3-1.

It may seem futile to track the assumptions as closely as we track time, cost and scope. But at a minimum, assumptions should be revalidated

TABLE 3-1 Assumption Validation Checklist

CHECKLIST FOR VALIDATING ASSUMPTIONS	YES	NO
Assumption is outside of the control of the project.		
Assumption is outside of the control of the stakeholder(s).		
The assumption can be validated as correct.		
Changes in the assumption can be controlled.		
The assumed condition is not fatal.		
The probability of the assumption holding true is clear.		
The consequences of this assumption pose a serious risk to the project.		
Unfavorable changes in the assumption can be fatal to the project.		

prior to each gate review meeting. This may help eliminate unfavorable downstream surprises.

3.3 MANAGING INNOVATION[1]

Innovation is generally regarded as a new way of doing something. For innovation to take place, the new way of doing something should be substantially different from the way it was done before rather than a small incremental change such as with continuous improvement activities. The ultimate goal of innovation is to create hopefully long-lasting additional value for the company, the users and the deliverable itself. Innovation can be viewed as the conversion of an idea into cash or a cash equivalent.

While the goal of successful innovation is to add value, the outcome can be negative or even destructive if it results in poor team morale, an unfavorable cultural change or a radical departure from existing ways of doing work. The failure of an innovation project can lead to demoralizing the organization and causing talented people to be risk avoiders in the future rather than risk takers.

Not all project managers are capable of managing projects involving innovation. The characteristics of innovation projects include an understanding that:

- Specific innovation tools and decision-making techniques may be necessary.
- It may be impossible to prepare a detailed schedule showing when an innovation breakthrough will actually occur.

---

1. Adapted from Harold Kerzner, *Project Management: A Systems Approach to Planning, Scheduling and Controlling*, 11th edition, Wiley, Hoboken, NJ, 2013, pp. 427–430.

- It may be impossible to determine a realistic budget for innovation.
- Innovation simply may not be possible and there comes a time when one must simply "give up."
- The deliverable from the innovation project may need extra "bells and whistles," which would make it too costly to users.

Failure is an inevitable part of many innovation projects. The greater the degree of innovation desired, the greater the need for effective risk management practices to be in place. Without effective risk management, it may be impossible within a reasonable time period to "pull the plug" on a project that is a cash drain and with no likelihood of achieving success.

Standard project management methodologies do not necessarily lend themselves to projects requiring innovation. It is impossible to prepare a schedule that pinpoints the exact time when a technical breakthrough will occur. Frameworks may be more appropriate than methodologies. Methodologies work well when there exists a well-defined statement of work and reasonable estimates. Schedules and work breakdown structure (WBS) development for innovation projects are normally based upon rolling wave or progressive planning since it is unlikely that we can develop a detailed plan and schedule for the entire project.

Decision makers responsible for business case formulation frequently have much less information available to evaluate candidate innovation projects. Uncertainties often surround the success likelihood of a project and market response, the ultimate market value of the project, its total cost to completion and the probability of commercial success and/or a technical breakthrough.

Project selection and evaluation decisions are often confounded by several behavioral and organizational factors. Departmental loyalties, conflicts in desires, differences in perspectives and an unwillingness to openly share information can stymie the project selection and evaluation process. Adding to these, the uncertainties of innovation and possibly a lack of understanding of the complexities of the innovation project can make decision making riskier than for projects where innovation may be unnecessary. Much project evaluation data and information used to formulate the business case are necessarily subjective in nature.

3.4 EXAMPLES OF CHANGING BUSINESS CASES

Companies today seem to do a reasonable job identifying the business case. But for long-term projects, the opportunities for changes to the business case are endless. Changes can result from new technologies, new customers, new competitors, changes in the marketplace, changes in economic conditions and changes resulting from political intervention. Most project managers have limited knowledge of how the competitive forces impact their project and therefore may need continuous feedback from sponsors and governance committees. The following examples show what happens when business cases can change, often quickly.

Situation: The Iridium Project[2] When the Iridium Project was first developed, the need for a global wireless cell phone was quite apparent. All Iridium needed was about 1% of the market to be highly successful. But the Iridium Project was an 11-year project. As expected, new competitors entered into the marketplace and gave the consumers the option for less expensive cell phones and cheaper long-distance rates. Over the 11 years of development of the Iridium phone system, technology changed to the point where Iridium could no longer guarantee the customer base it desperately needed to cover its debt load. The business case that started out with valid objectives suddenly became flawed.

> **LESSONS LEARNED** When systems are highly complex, take a decade to complete and are designed to create unique products or services, the risk is great because it may be impossible to know if the end user will appreciate what was created. The need that existed at the beginning of the decade may not be the same need at the end of the decade.

Situation: Denver International Airport[3] Denver International Airport (DIA) started out with a valid case: the need for a new airport to service Denver and handle the expected load of more than 66 million passengers per year. But when it became time to sign a lease agreement with United Airlines for the new airport, DIA's decision makers did not fully understand the complexity of the scope changes that United Airlines was demanding before signing the lease. To make matters worse, DIA's decision makers increased the complexity of the project with added requirements without fully understanding the impact. A consultant was hired to evaluate one of the scope changes, namely the feasibility of an automated baggage-handling system to be used just for the United Airlines concourse. The consultant stated that the request by United Airlines for an automated baggage-handling system was not feasible. Rather than believe the consultant's opinion, the DIA decision makers decided to expand the automated baggage-handling system to cover the entire airport. Now, part of the business case was definitely flawed. After spending close to $5 billion over 14 years to get the automated baggage-handling system to work, DIA officials finally pulled the plug on the project in August 2005. The business case became flawed when they tried to develop an entire system from scratch based upon unproven technology and refusing to heed the warnings of the

---

2. The full Iridium Project Case Study appears in Section 3.6.

3. The case studies on Denver International Airport and the Automated Baggage Handling System appear in Sections 4.11 and 4.12.

LESSON LEARNED   Even as little as one scope change can significantly alter the business case. Continuous revalidation is a necessity.

technical experts. When complexity is not fully understood, a project can be overwhelmed with uncertainty and risk. The chance of project failure increases significantly. The effect on the morale of the team and the organization's culture can be devastating.

Sometimes, even when technology is known with reasonable certainty, changes in the enterprise environment factors, such as changing economic conditions due to a declining housing market accompanied by lower disposal income, can have a significant impact on a project's business case. When the bubble burst in the housing market, leisure entertainment took a big hit because of the expected lower consumer spending. This affected leisure entertainment construction projects such as the Fontainebleau Las Vegas.

Situation: Fontainebleau Las Vegas[4] Fontainebleau Las Vegas is a $2.9 billion, 3889-room, 68-story unfinished hotel/condo-hotel/casino development near the north end of the Las Vegas Strip on the 24.5-acre site previously occupied by the El Rancho and Algiers hotels in Paradise, Nevada. It was intended to be a sister property to the well-known 1950s-era Fontainebleau Miami Beach. The building is currently the tallest in the Las Vegas Valley.

The project, upon completion was expected to include: a 95,000-ft^2 casino, a 60,000-ft^2 spa, a 3300-seat performing arts theater, 1018 condo-hotel units, 180,000 ft^2 of retail space, 400,000 ft^2 of indoor and outdoor conference space, nightclubs and 24 restaurants and lounges.

Groundbreaking was officially announced to have begun on April 30, 2007. Gaming revenue on the Las Vegas Strip peaked at the end of October 2007. The tower was topped out on November 2008.

Fontainebleau Resorts CEO Glenn Schaeffer, the former chief financial officer of Mandalay Resort Group, which generated record profits before it was sold to MGM Mirage in 2005, left Fontainebleau Resorts without comment in May 2009. Schaeffer was primarily responsible for securing more than $3 billion in loans for the project. Also, Bank of America, the resort's largest lender, refused to provide financing on its committed line of credit for the project around this time; as a result, the resort's operator, Fontainebleau Las Vegas LLC, filed for Chapter 11 bankruptcy protection in June 2009. Construction work stopped on the project, which was about 70% complete; the grand opening had been scheduled for October 2009.

---

4. Adapted from Fontainebleau Las Vegas, *Wikipedia, the Free Encyclopedia.*

In October 2009, Penn National Gaming was considering purchasing the partially completed resort and the 24.5 acres of land for $300 million. At that rate the land was being sold for $12.25 million per acre. Two years earlier land was going for over $30 million per acre on the Strip. Over $2 billion has already been invested in the topped-out building on the site. Penn National has been looking for an opportunity to enter the Las Vegas gaming market.

However, in bankruptcy court in Miami, Florida, on November 23, 2009, corporate raider and financier Carl Icahn, who until 2008 controlled major casino/resort operator American Casino & Entertainment Properties, offered $156 million in cash and financing, outbidding Penn National Gaming for control of the Fontainebleau. Icahn's bid included a $51 million debtor-in-possession loan, which, until the resort would be auctioned, would provide funding to stabilize the building, cover employees' salaries, cover previous costs and eliminate the need for the resort to ask the bankruptcy court each week to borrow and spend money. Penn National dropped out of the bidding after going as high as $145 million; Penn had offered $101.5 million in cash and loans.

As of November 2009, the cost to complete the resort was an estimated $1 to 1.5 billion.

On February 18, 2010, Carl Icahn assumed part ownership of the project without an auction by being the only qualified bidder, paying $150 million.

In October 2010, Icahn auctioned off the furnishings previously intended for the building. For example, the Plaza Hotel & Casino in Downtown Las Vegas bought rugs, furniture and mattresses from the sale and used them in a refurbishment that was completed in late 2011. Future plans for the hotel project have not yet been disclosed to the public.

LESSON LEARNED When business cases are highly dependent upon market conditions, it is extremely important to understand the present and be able to predict the future.

What is important in the three examples provided here is how we define project success and project failure. The Iridium Project ended up as a phenomenal technical success as well as a financial failure for investors. The business case appeared to have both a technical component and a financial component. From a technical perspective, the Iridium Project ended up as a technical success creating a worldwide satellite phone system. It was also seen as a project management success where the launch date of the 11-year project was missed by about 1 month. But from a financial viewpoint, the project failed miserably having only 11,000 subscribers rather than the 400,000 subscribers that were projected. Good money was thrown away after bad money.

The business case for Denver International Airport called for the construction of a world class airport capable of satisfying Denver's needs for the next century. The fiasco with the automated baggage-handling system was a technical failure but did not prevent the airport from being considered as a business case success. Wanting to satisfy its tenants is the right thing to do, but within reason. Even though some bad technical decisions may have been made, the airport is still regarded as a very successful project despite the cost overruns.

The Fontainebleau Las Vegas Project can be considered as a total failure. While the project was on schedule, within budget and meeting all requirements, the fact remains that there was already overcapacity in Las Vegas. Unlike the Iridium Project where market capacity for the project was probably correct at project initiation but diminished over the 11 years it took for the project to be completed, the Fontainebleau Las Vegas Project was probably a mistake from the start. Even without considering the impending recession, the city's overcapacity should have been a warning sign that the business case was flawed and without any reasonable definition of project success from a business perspective.

3.5 PROLOGUE TO THE IRIDIUM CASE STUDY

The case study on the Iridium Project is rich with information. It shows how a business case changed over the 11 years it took to complete the Iridium Project.

When reading over the case study, focus on the following:

- Does there appear to be a business case for the Iridium Project?
- If so, what was the business case?
- What caused the business case to change?
- How did management react to the changes in the business case?
- When should the decision have been made to pull the plug?
- Were there any behavioral factors that influenced how management reacted to the changes in the environment?
- Was the Iridium Project a success, a failure or both?

3.6 RISE, FALL AND RESURRECTION OF IRIDIUM[5]

The Iridium Project was designed to create a worldwide wireless handheld mobile phone system with the ability to communicate anywhere in the world at any time. Executives at Motorola regarded the project as the eighth

---

5. Copyright © 2013 by Harold Kerzner.

wonder of the world. But more than a decade later and after investing billions of dollars, Iridium had solved a problem that very few customers needed solved. What went wrong? How did the Iridium Project transform from a leading-edge technical marvel to a multibillion-dollar blunder? Could the potential catastrophe have been prevented?

> What it looks like now is a multibillion-dollar science project. There are fundamental problems: The handset is big, the service is expensive, and the customers haven't really been identified.
> —Chris Chaney, Analyst, A.G. Edwards, 1999

> There was never a business case for Iridium. There was never market demand. The decision to build Iridium wasn't a rational business decision. It was more of a religious decision. The remarkable thing is that this happened at a big corporation, and that there was not a rational decision-making process in place to pull the plug. Technology for technology's sake may not be a good business case.[6]
> —Herschel Shosteck, Telecommunication Consultant

> Iridium is likely to be some of the most expensive space debris ever.
> —William Kidd, Analyst, C.E. Unterberg, Towbin

In 1985, Bary Bertiger, chief engineer in Motorola's strategic electronics division, and his wife Karen were on a vacation in the Bahamas. Karen tried unsuccessfully to make a cellular telephone call back to her home near the Motorola facility in Chandler, Arizona, to close a real estate transaction. Unsuccessful, she asked her husband why it would not be possible to create a telephone system that would work anywhere in the world, even in remote locations.

At this time, cell technology was in the infancy stage but was expected to grow at an astounding rate. AT&T projected as many as 40 million subscribers by 2000.[7] Cell technology was based upon tower-to-tower transmission, as shown in Figure 3-1.[8] Each tower or "gateway" ground station reached a limited geographic area or cell and had to be within the satellite's field of view. Cell phone users likewise had to be near a gateway that would uplink the transmission to a satellite. The satellite would then downlink the signal to another gateway that would connect the transmission to a ground telephone system. This type of communication is often

---

6. Stephanie Paterik, "Iridium Alive and Well," *The Arizona Republic*, April 27, 2005, p. D5.

7. Judith Bird, "Cellular Technology in Telephones," *Data Processing*, Vol. 27, No. 8, October 1985, p. 37.

8. Source for Figure 3-1 has been adapted from Part 3 of Section 1 (Satellite Communications—A Short Course) of *Satellite Communications*, prepared by Dr. Regis Leonard for NASA Lewis Research Center.

Figure 3-1 Typical satellite communication architecture.

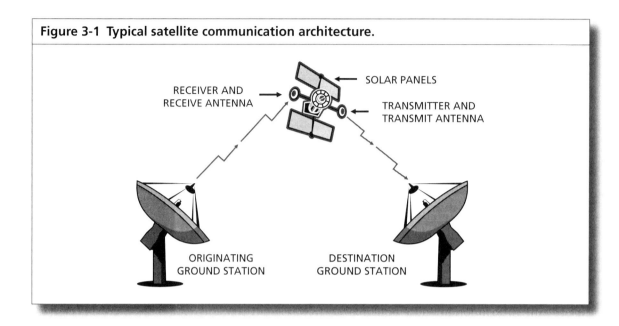

referred to as bent-pipe architecture. Physical barriers between the senders/ receivers and the gateways, such as mountains, tunnels and oceans, created interference problems and therefore limited service to high-density communities. Simply stated, cell phones couldn't leave home. And, if they did, there would be additional "roaming" charges. To make matters worse, every country had their own standards and some cell phones were inoperable when traveling in other countries.

Communications satellites, in use since the 1960s, were typically geostationary satellites that orbited at altitudes of more than 22,300 miles. At this altitude, three geosynchronous satellites and just a few gateways could cover most of Earth. But satellites at this altitude meant large phones and annoying quarter-second voice delays. Comsat's Planet 1 phone, for example, weighed in at a computer-case-sized 4.5 pounds. Geosynchronous satellites require signals with a great deal of power. Small mobile phones, with a 1-watt signal, could not work with satellites positioned at this altitude. Increasing the power output of the mobile phones would damage human tissue. The alternative was therefore to move the satellites closer to Earth such that less power would be needed. This would require significantly more satellites the closer we get to Earth and additional gateways. Geosynchronous satellites, which are 100 times further away from Earth than low Earth-orbiting (LEO) satellites, could require almost 10,000 times as much power as LEO satellites, if everything else were the same.[9]

---

9. Ibid.

When Bary Bertiger returned to Motorola, he teamed up with Dr. Raymond Leopold and Kenneth Peterson to see if such a worldwide system could be developed while overcoming all of the limitations of existing cell technology. There was also the problem that LEO satellites would be orbiting Earth rapidly and going through damaging temperature variations—from the heat of the sun to the cold shadow of Earth.[10] The LEO satellites would most likely need to be replaced every five years. Numerous alternative terrestrial designs were discussed and abandoned. In 1987 research began on a constellation of LEO satellites moving in polar orbits that could communicate directly with telephone systems on the ground and with one another.

Iridium's innovation was to use a large constellation of low-orbiting satellites approximately 400-450 miles in altitude. Because Iridium's satellites were closer to Earth, the phones could be much smaller and the voice delay imperceptible. But there were still major technical design problems. With the existing design, a large number of gateways would be required, thus substantially increasing the cost of the system. As they left work one day in 1988, Dr. Leopold proposed a critical design element. The entire system would be inverted whereby the transmission would go from satellite to satellite until the transmission reached the satellite directly above the person who would be receiving the message. With this approach, only one gateway Earth station would be required to connect mobile-to-landline calls to existing land-based telephone systems. This was considered to be the sought-after solution and was immediately written in outline format on a whiteboard in a security guard's office. Thus came forth the idea behind a worldwide wireless handheld mobile phone with the ability to communicate anywhere and anytime.

Naming the Project "Iridium"

Motorola cellular telephone system engineer Jim Williams, from the Motorola facility near Chicago, suggested the name Iridium. The proposed 77-satellite constellation reminded him of the electrons that encircle the nucleus in the classical Bohr model of the atom. When he consulted the periodic table of the elements to discover which atom had 77 electrons, he found Iridium—a creative name that had a nice ring. Fortunately, the system had not yet been scaled back to 66 satellites, or else he might have suggested the name Dysprosium.

Obtaining Executive Support

Initially Bertiger's colleagues and superiors at Motorola had rejected the Iridium concept because of its cost. Originally, the Iridium concept was

---

10. Bruce Gerding, "Personal Communications via Satellite: An Overview,"
Telecommunications, Vol. 30, No. 2, February 1996, pp. 35, 77.

considered perfect for the U.S. government. Unfortunately, the era of lucrative government-funded projects was coming to an end and it was unlikely that the government would fund a project of this magnitude. However, the idea behind the Iridium concept intrigued Durrell Hillis, the senior vice president and general manager of Motorola's Space and Technology Group. Hillis believed that Iridium was workable if it could be developed as a commercial system. Hillis instructed Bertiger and his team to continue working on the Iridium concept but to keep it quiet.

> "I created a bootleg project with secrecy so no one in the company would know about it," Hillis recalls. He was worried that if word leaked out, the ferociously competitive business units at Motorola, all of which had to fight for R&D funds, would smother the project with nay-saying.[11]

After 14 months of rewrites on the commercialized business plan, Hillis and the Iridium team leaders presented the idea to Robert Galvin, Motorola's chairman at the time, who gave approval to go ahead with the project. Robert Galvin, and later his successor and son Christopher Galvin, viewed Iridium as a potential symbol of Motorola's technological prowess and believed that this would become the eighth wonder in the world. In one of the initial meetings, Robert Galvin turned to John Mitchell, Motorola's President and Chief Operating Officer, and said, "If you don't write out a check for this John, I will, out of my own pocket."[12] To the engineers at Motorola, the challenge of launching Iridium's constellation provided considerable motivation. They continued developing the project that resulted in initial service in November 1998 at a total cost of over $5 billion.

Launching the Venture

On June 26, 1990, Hillis and his team formally announced the launch of the Iridium Project to the general public. The response was not very pleasing to Motorola with skepticism over the fact that this would be a new technology, the target markets were too small, the revenue model was questionable, obtaining licenses to operate in 170 countries could be a problem and the cost of a phone call might be overpriced. Local phone companies that Motorola assumed would buy into the project viewed Iridium as a potential competitor since the Iridium system bypassed traditional landlines. In many countries, Postal Telephone and Telegraph (PTT) operators are state owned and a major source of revenue because of the high profit margins. Another issue was that the Iridium Project was announced before

---

11. David S. Bennahum, "The United Nations of Iridium," *Wired*, Issue 6.10, October 1998, p. 194.

12. Quentin Hardy, "How a Wife's Question Led Motorola to Chase a Global Cell-Phone Plan," *Wall Street Journal* (Eastern edition), New York, December 16, 1996. p. A1.

permission was granted by the Federal Communications Commission (FCC) to operate at the desired frequencies.

Both Mitchell and Galvin made it clear that Motorola would not go it alone and absorb the initial financial risk for a hefty price tag of about $3.5 billion. Funds would need to be obtained from public markets and private investors. In order to minimize Motorola's exposure to financial risk, Iridium would need to be set up as a project-financed company. Project financing involves the establishment of a legally independent project company where the providers of funds are repaid out of cash flow and earnings and where the assets of the unit (and only the unit) are used as collateral for the loans. Debt repayment would come from the project company only rather than from any other entity. A risk with project financing is that the capital assets may have a limited life. The potential limited life constraint often makes it difficult to get lenders to agree to long-term financial arrangements.

Another critical issue with project financing especially for high-technology projects is that the projects are generally long term. It would be nearly eight years before service would begin, and in terms of technology, eight years is an eternity. The Iridium Project was certainly a "bet on the future." And if the project were to fail, the company could be worth nothing after liquidation.

In 1991, Motorola established Iridium Limited Liability Corporation (Iridium LLC) as a separate company. In December of 1991, Iridium promoted Leo Mondale to vice president of Iridium International. Financing the project was still a critical issue. Mondale decided that, instead of having just 1 gateway, there should be as many as 12 regional gateways that plugged into local, ground-based telephone lines. This would make Iridium a truly global project rather than appear as an American-based project designed to seize market share from state-run telephone companies. This would also make it easier to get regulatory approval to operate in 170 countries. Investors would pay $40 million for the right to own their own regional gateway. As stated by Flower:

> The motive of the investors is clear: They are taking a chance on owning a slice of a de-facto world monopoly. Each of them will not only have a piece of the company, they will own the Iridium gateways and act as the local distributors in their respective home markets. For them it's a game worth playing.[13]

There were political ramifications with selling regional gateways. What if in the future the U.S. government forbids shipment of replacement parts to certain gateways? What if sanctions are imposed? What if Iridium were to become a political tool during international diplomacy because of the number of jobs it creates?

---

13. Joe Flower, "Iridium," *Wired*, Issue 1.05, November 1993.

In addition to financial incentives, gateway owners were granted seats on the board of directors. As described by David Bennahum, reporter for *Wired*:

> Four times a year, 28 Iridium board members from 17 countries gather to coordinate overall business decisions. They met around the world, shuttling between Moscow, London, Kyoto, Rio de Janeiro, and Rome, surrounded by an entourage of assistants and translators. Resembling a United Nations in miniature, board meetings were conducted with simultaneous translation in Russian, Japanese, Chinese, and English.[14]

The partner with the largest equity share was Motorola. For its contribution of $400 million, Motorola originally received an equity stake of 25% and 6 of 28 seats on Iridium's board. Additionally, Motorola made loan guarantees to Iridium of $750 million, with Iridium holding an option for an additional $350 million loan.

For its part, Iridium agreed to $6.6 billion in long-term contracts with Motorola that included a $3.4 billion firm-fixed-price contract for satellite design and launch and $2.9 billion for operations and maintenance. Iridium also exposed Motorola to developing satellite technology that would provide the latter with significant expertise in building satellite communications systems as well as vast intellectual property.

Iridium System[15]

The Iridium system is a satellite-based, wireless personal communications network providing a robust suite of voice features to virtually any destination anywhere on Earth.

The Iridium system comprises three principal components: the satellite network, the ground network and the Iridium subscriber products, including phones and pagers. The design of the Iridium network allows voice and data to be routed virtually anywhere in the world. Voice and data calls are relayed from one satellite to another until they reach the satellite above the Iridium subscriber unit (handset) and the signal is relayed back to Earth.

Terrestial and Space-Based Network[16]

The Iridium constellation consists of 66 operational satellites and 11 spares orbiting in a constellation of six polar planes. Each plane has 11 mission satellites performing as nodes in the telephony network. The remaining 11 satellites orbit as spares ready to replace any unserviceable satellite. This

---

14. Bennahum, 1998, p. 136.

15. This is the operational version of the Iridium system today taken from the Iridium website, www.Iridium.com.

16. Ibid.

constellation ensures that every region on the globe is covered by at least one satellite at all times.

The satellites are in a near-polar orbit at an altitude of 485 miles (780 km). They circle Earth once every 100 minutes traveling at a rate of 16,832 miles per hour. The satellite weight is 1500 pounds. Each satellite is approximately 40 feet in length and 12 feet in width. In addition, each satellite has 48 spot beams, 30 miles in diameter per beam.

Each satellite is cross-linked to four other satellites: two satellites in the same orbital plane and two in an adjacent plane. The ground network is comprised of the system control segment and telephony gateways used to connect into the terrestrial telephone system. The system control segment is the central management component for the Iridium system. It provides global operational support and control services for the satellite constellation, delivers satellite-tracking data to the gateways and performs the termination control function of messaging services. The system control segment consists of three main components: four telemetry tracking and control sites, the operational support network and the satellite network operation center. The primary linkage between the system control segment, the satellites and the gateways is via K-band feeder links and cross-links throughout the satellite constellation.

Gateways are the terrestrial infrastructure that provides telephony services, messaging and support to the network operations. The key features of gateways are their support and management of mobile subscribers and the interconnection of the Iridium network to the terrestrial phone system. Gateways also provide network management functions for their own network elements and links.

Project Initiation: Developing Business Case

For the Iridium Project to be a business success rather than just a technical success there had to exist an established customer base. Independent studies conducted by A.T. Kearney, Booz, Allen & Hamilton and Gallup indicated that 34 million people had a demonstrated need for mobile satellite services, with that number expected to grow to 42 million by 2002. Of these 42 million, Iridium anticipated 4.2 million to be satellite-only subscribers, 15.5 million satellite and world terrestrial roaming subscribers and 22.3 million terrestrial roaming-only subscribers.

A universal necessity in conducting business is ensuring that you are never out of touch. Iridium would provide this unique solution to business with the essential communications tool. This proposition of one phone, one number with the capability to be accessed anywhere, anytime was a message that target markets—the global traveler, the mining, rural, maritime industries, government, disaster relief and community aid groups—would readily embrace.

Also at the same time of Iridium's conception, there appeared to be another potentially lucrative opportunity in the telecommunications marketplace. When users of mobile or cellular phones crossed international borders, they soon discovered that there existed a lack of common standards, thus making some phones inoperable. Motorola viewed this as an opportunity to create a worldwide standard allowing phones to be used anywhere in the world.

The expected breakeven market for Iridium was estimated between 400,000 and 600,000 customers globally assuming a reasonable usage rate per customer per month. With a launch date for Iridium service established for 1998, Iridium hoped to recover all of its investment within one year. By 2002, Iridium anticipated a customer base of 5 million users. The initial Iridium target market had been the vertical market, those of the industry, government and world agencies that have defended needs and far-reaching communication requirements. Also important would be both industrial and public sector customers. Often isolated in remote locations outside of cellular coverage, industrial users were expected to use handheld Iridium satellite services to complement or replace their existing radio or satellite communications terminals. The vertical markets for Iridium would include:

- Aviation
- Construction
- Disaster relief/emergency
- Forestry
- Government
- Leisure travel
- Maritime
- Media and entertainment
- Military
- Mining
- Oil and gas
- Utilities

Using their own marketing resources, Iridium appeared to have identified an attractive market segment after having screened over 200,000 people, interviewed 23,000 people from 42 countries and surveyed over 3000 corporations.

Iridium would also need regional strategic partners, not only for investment purposes and to share the risks but also to provide services throughout its territories. The strategic regional partners or gateway operating companies would have exclusive rights to its territories and were obligated to market and sell Iridium services. The gateways would also be responsible for end-user sales, activation and deactivation of Iridium services, account maintenance and billing.

Iridium would need each country to grant full licenses for access to the Iridium system. Iridium would need to identify the "priority" countries that account for the majority of the business plan.

Because of the number of countries involved in the Iridium network, Iridium would need to establish global customer care centers for support services in all languages. No matter where an Iridium user was located, he or she would have access to a customer service representative in their native language. The customer care centers would be strategically located to offer 24-hours-a-day, 7-days-a-week, and 365-days-a-year support.

"Hidden" Business Case

The decision by Motorola to invest heavily into the Iridium Project may have been driven by a secondary or hidden business case. Over the years, Motorola achieved a reputation of being a first mover. With the Iridium Project, Motorola was poised to capture first-mover advantage in providing global telephone service via LEO satellites. In addition, even if the Iridium Project never resulted in providing service, Motorola would still have amassed valuable intellectual property that would make Motorola possibly the major player for years to come in satellite communications. There may have also been the desire of Robert and Christopher Galvin to have their names etched in history as the pioneers in satellite communication.

Risk Management

Good business cases identify the risks that the project must consider. For simplicity sake, the initial risks associated with the Iridium Project could be classified as:

Technology Risks: Although Motorola had some technology available for the Iridium Project, there was still the need to develop additional technology, specifically satellite communications technology. The development process was expected to take years and would eventually result in numerous patents.

Mark Gercenstein, Iridium's vice president of operations, explains the system's technological complexity:

> More than 26 completely impossible things had to happen first, and in the right sequence (before we could begin operations)—like getting capital, access to the marketplace, global spectrum, the same frequency band in every country of operations.[17]

While there was still some risk in the development of new technology, Motorola had the reputation of being a high-tech, can-do company. The engineers at Motorola believed that they could bring forth miracles in technology. Motorola also had a reputation for being a first mover (i.e., first to market) with new ideas and products, and there was no reason to believe that this would not happen on the Iridium Project. There was no competition for Iridium at its inception.

---

17. Peter Grams and Patrick Zerbib, "Caring for Customers in a Global Marketplace," *Satellite Communications*, October 1998, p. 24.

Because the project schedule was more than a decade in duration, there was the risk of technology obsolescence. This required that certain assumptions be made concerning technology a decade downstream. Developing a new product is relatively easy if the environment is stable. But in a high technology environment that is both turbulent and dynamic, it is extremely difficult to determine how customers will perceive and evaluate the product 10 years later.

Development Risks: The satellite communication technology, once developed, had to be manufactured, tested and installed in the satellites and ground equipment. Even though the technology existed or would exist, there was still the transitional or development risks from engineering to manufacturing to implementation which would bring with it additional problems that were not contemplated or foreseen.

Financial Risks: The cost of the Iridium Project would most certainly be measured in the billions of dollars. This would include the costs for technology development and implementation, the manufacture and launch of satellites, the construction of ground support facilities, marketing and supervision. Raising money from Wall Street's credit and equity markets was years away. Investors were unlikely to put up the necessary hundreds of millions of dollars on merely an idea or a vision. The technology needed to be developed and possibly accompanied by the launch of a few satellites before the credit and equity markets would come on board.

Private investors were a possibility, but the greatest source of initial funding would have to come from the members of the Iridium consortium. While sharing the financial risks among the membership seemed appropriate, there was no question that bank loans and lines of credit would be necessary. Since the Iridium Project was basically an idea, the banks would require some form of collateral or guarantee for the loans. Motorola, being the largest stakeholder (and also with the "deepest pockets") would need to guarantee the initial loans.

Marketing Risks: The marketing risks were certainly the greatest risks facing the Iridium membership. Once again, the risks were shared among its membership where each member was expected to sign up customers in their geographic area.

Each consortium member has to aggressively sign up customers for a product that didn't exist yet, no prototypes existed to be shown to the customers, limitations on the equipment were unknown as yet and significant changes in technology could occur between the time the customer signed up and the time the system was ready for use. Companies that see the need for Iridium today may not see the same need 10 years later.

Motivating the consortium partners to begin marketing immediately would be extremely difficult since marketing material was nonexistent. There was also the very real fear that the consortium membership would be motivated more so by the technology rather than the necessary size of the customer base required.

The risks were interrelated. The financial risks were highly dependent upon the marketing risks. If a sufficient customer base could not be signed up, there could be significant difficulty in raising capital.

Collective Belief

Although the literature doesn't clearly identify it, there was most likely a collective belief among the workers assigned to the Iridium Project. The collective belief is a fervent, and perhaps blind, desire to achieve that can permeate the entire team, the project sponsor and even the most senior levels of management. The collective belief can make a rational organization act in an irrational manner.

When a collective belief exists, people are selected based upon their support for the collective belief. Nonbelievers are pressured into supporting the collective belief and team members are not allowed to challenge the results. As the collective belief grows, both advocates and nonbelievers are trampled. The pressure of the collective belief can outweigh the reality of the results.

The larger the project and the greater the financial risk to the firm, the higher up the collective belief resides. On the Iridium Project, the collective belief originated with Galvin, Motorola's CEO. Therefore, who could possibly function as the person willing to cancel the Iridium Project? Since it most likely should be someone higher up than Galvin, oversight should have been done by someone on the board of directors or even the entire Iridium board of directors. Unfortunately, the entire Iridium board of directors was also part of the collective belief and shirked their responsibility for oversight on the Iridium Project. In the end, Iridium had nobody willing to pull the plug.

Large projects incur large cost overruns and schedule slippages. Making the decision to cancel such a project, once it has started, is very difficult, according to David Davis[18]:

> The difficulty of abandoning a project after several million dollars have been committed to it tends to prevent objective review and recosting. For this reason, ideally an independent management team – one not involved in the projects development – should do the recosting and, if possible, the entire review. . . . If the numbers do not holdup in the review and recosting, the company should abandon the project. The number of bad projects that make it to the operational stage serves as proof that their supporters often balk at this decision. . . . Senior managers need to create an environment that rewards honesty and courage and provides for more decision making on the part of project managers. Companies must have an atmosphere that encourages projects to succeed, but executives must allow them to fail.

---

18. David Davis, "New Projects: Beware of False Economics," *Harvard Business Review*, March-April 1985, pp. 100–01. Copyright © 1985 by the President and Fellows of Harvard College. All rights reserved.

The longer the project, the greater the necessity for the exit champions and project sponsors to make sure that the business plan has "exit ramps" such that the project can be terminated before massive resources are committed and consumed. Unfortunately, when a collective belief exists, exit ramps are purposefully omitted from the project and business plans.

Iridium's Infancy Years

By 1992, the Iridium Project attracted such stalwart companies as General Electric, Lockheed and Raytheon. Some companies wanted to be involved to be part of the satellite technology revolution while others were afraid of falling behind the technology curve. In any event, Iridium was lining up strategic partners, but slowly.

The Iridium plan, submitted to the FCC in August 1992, called for a constellation of 66 satellites expected to be in operation by 1998 and more powerful than originally proposed, thus keeping the project's cost at the previously estimated $3.37 billion. But the Iridium Project, while based upon lofty forecasts of available customers, was now attracting other companies competing for FCC approval on similar satellite systems, including Loral Corp., TRW Inc. and Hughes Aircraft Co., a unit of General Motors Corp. There were at least nine companies competing for the potential billions of dollars in untapped revenue possible from satellite communications.

Even with the increased competition, Motorola was signing up partners. Motorola had set an internal deadline of December 15, 1992, to find the necessary funding for Iridium. Signed letters of intent were received from the Brazilian government and United Communications Co., of Bangkok, Thailand, to buy 5% stakes in the project, each now valued at about $80 million. The terms of the agreement implied that the Iridium consortium would finance the project with roughly 50% equity and 50% debt.

When the December 15 deadline arrived, Motorola was relatively silent on the signing of funding partners, fueling speculation that it was having trouble. Motorola did admit that the process was time-consuming because some investors required government approval before proceeding. Motorola was expected to announce at some point, perhaps in the first half of 1993, whether it was ready to proceed with the next step, namely receiving enough cash from its investors, securing loans and ordering satellite and group equipment.

As the competition increased, so did the optimism about the potential size of the customer base.

"We're talking about a business generating billions of dollars in revenue," says John F. Mitchell, Vice Chairman at Motorola. "Do a simple income extrapolation," adds Edward J. Nowacki, a general manager at TRW's Space & Electronics Group, Redondo Beach, Calif., which plans a $1.3 billion, 12-satellite system called Odyssey. "You conclude that even a tiny fraction of the people around the world who can afford our services will make them successful." Mr. Mitchell says that if just 1% to 1.5% of the expected 100 million cellular users in the year 2000 become regular users at $3 a minute, Iridium will breakeven. How does he know this? "Marketing studies," which he won't share. TRW's Mr. Nowacki says Odyssey will blanket the Earth with two-way voice communication service priced at "only a slight premium" to cellular. "With two million subscribers we can get a substantial return on our investment," he says. "Loral Qualcomm Satellite Services, Inc. aims to be the 'friendly' satellite by letting phone-company partners use and run its system's ground stations", says Executive Vice President Anthony Navarra. "By the year 2000 there will be 15 million unserved cellular customers in the world," he says.[19]

But while Motorola and other competitors were trying to justify their investment with "inflated market projections" and a desire from the public for faster and clearer reception, financial market analysts were not so benevolent. First, market analysts questioned the size of the customer base that would be willing to pay $3000 or more for a satellite phone in addition to $3–$7 per minute for a call. Second, the system required a line-of-sight transmission, which meant that the system would not work in buildings or in cars. If a businessman were attending a meeting in Bangkok and needed to call his company, he must exit the building, raise the antenna on his $3000 handset, point the antenna toward the heavens and then make the call. Third, the low-flying satellites would eventually crash into Earth's atmosphere every five to seven years because of atmospheric drag and would need to be replaced. That would most likely result in high capital costs. And fourth, some industry analysts believed that the start-up costs would be closer to $6 billion to $10 billion rather than the $3.37 billion estimated by Iridium. In addition, the land-based cellular phone business was expanding in more countries, thus creating another competitive threat for Iridium.

The original business case needed to be reevaluated periodically. But with strong collective beliefs and no exit champions, the fear of a missed opportunity, irrespective of the cost, took center stage.

Reasonably sure that 18 out of 21 investors were on board, Motorola hoped to start launching test satellites in 1996 and begin commercial service by 1998. But critics argued that Iridium might be obsolete by the time it actually starts working.

Eventually, Iridium was able to attract financial support from 19 strategic partners:

- AIG Affiliated Companies
- China Great Wall Industry Corporation (CGWIC)

---

19. John J. Keller, "Telecommunications: Phone Space Race has Fortune at Stake," *Wall Street Journal* (Eastern edition), New York, January 18, 1993, p. B1.

- Iridium Africa Corporation (based in Cape Town)
- Iridium Canada, Inc.
- Iridium India Telecom Private Ltd. (ITIL)
- Iridium Italia S.p.A.
- Iridium Middle East Corporation
- Iridium SudAmerica Corporation
- Khrunichev State Research and Production Space Center
- Korea Mobile TELECOM
- Lockheed Martin
- Motorola
- Nippon Iridium Corporation
- Pacific Electric Wire & Cable Co. Ltd. (PEWC)
- Raytheon
- STET
- Sprint
- Thai Satellite Telecommunications Co., Ltd.
- Verbacom

Seventeen of the strategic partners also participated in gateway operations with the creation of operating companies.

The Iridium board of directors consisted of 28 telecommunications executives. All but one board member was a member of the consortium as well. This made it very difficult for the board to fulfill its oversight obligation effectively given the members' vested/financial interest in the Iridium Project.

In August 1993, Lockheed announced that it would receive $700 million in revenue for satellite construction. Lockheed would build the satellite structure, solar panels, attitude and propulsion systems, along with other parts and engineering support. Motorola and Raytheon Corp. would build the satellite's communications gear and antenna.

In April 1994, McDonnell Douglas Corp. received from Iridium a $400 million contract to launch 40 satellites for Iridium. Other contracts for launch services would be awarded to Russia's Khrunichev Space Center and China's Great Wall Industry Corporation, both members of the consortium. The lower cost contracts with Russia and China were putting extraordinary pressure on U.S. providers to lower their costs.

Also at the same time, one of Iridium's competitors, the Globalstar system, which was a 48-satellite mobile telephone system led by Loral Corporation, announced that it intended to charge 65 cents per minute in the areas it served. Iridium's critics were arguing that Iridium would be too pricey to attract a high volume of callers.[20]

---

20. Jeff Cole, "McDonnell Douglas Said to Get Contract to Launch 40 Satellites for Iridium Plan," *Wall Street Journal* (Eastern edition), New York, April 12, 1994, p. A4.

Debt Financing

In September 1994, Iridium said that it had completed its equity financing by raising an additional $733.5 million. This brought the total capital committed to Iridium through equity financing to $1.57 billion. The completion of equity financing permitted Iridium to enter into debt financing to build the global wireless satellite network.

In September 1995, Iridium announced that it would be issuing $300 million 10-year senior subordinated discounted notes rated Caa by Moody's and CCC+ by Standard & Poor's, via the investment banker Goldman Sachs, Inc. The bonds were considered to be high-risk, high-yield "junk" bonds after investors concluded that the rewards weren't worth the risk.

The rating agencies cited the reasons for the low rating to be yet-unproven sophisticated technology and the fact that a significant portion of the system's hardware would be located in space. But there were other serious concerns:

- The ultimate cost of the Iridium Project would be more like $6 billion or higher rather than $3.5 billion, and it was unlikely that Iridium would recover that cost.
- Iridium would be hemorrhaging cash for several more years before service would begin.
- The optimistic number of potential customers for satellite phones may not choose the Iridium system.
- The number of competitors had increased since the Iridium concept was first developed.
- If Iridium defaulted on its debt, the investors could lay claim to Iridium's assets. But what would investors do with more than 66 satellites in space waiting to disintegrate upon reentering the atmosphere?

Iridium was set up as "project financing" in which case, if a default occurred, only the assets of Iridium could be attached. With project financing, the consortium's investors would be held harmless for any debt incurred from the stock and bond markets and could simply walk away from Iridium. These risks associated with project financing were well understood by those that invested in the equity and credit markets.

Goldman Sachs & Co., the lead underwriter for the securities offering, determined that for the bond issue to be completed successfully, there would need to exist a completion guarantee from investors with deep pockets, such as Motorola. Goldman Sachs cited a recent $400 million offering by one of Iridium's competitors, Globalstar, which had a guarantee from the managing general partner, Loral Corp.[21]

---

21. Quentin Hardy, "Iridium Pulls $300 Million Bond Offer; Analysts Cite Concerns about Projects," *Wall Street Journal* (Eastern edition), New York, September 22, 1995, p. A5.

Because of the concern by investors, Iridium withdrew its planned $300 million debt offering. Also, Globalstar, even with its loan guarantee, eventually withdrew its $400 million offering. Investors wanted both an equity position in Iridium and a 20% return. Additionally Iridium would need to go back to its original 17-member consortium and arrange for internal financing.

In February 1996, Iridium had raised an additional $315 million from the 17-member consortium and private investors. In August 1996, Iridium had secured a $750 million credit line with 62 banks co-arranged by Chase Securities Inc., a unit of Chase Manhattan Corp. and the investment banking division of Barclays Bank PLC. The credit line was oversubscribed by more than double its original goal because the line of credit was backed by a financial guarantee by Motorola and its AAA credit rating. Because of the guarantee by Motorola, the lending rate was slightly more than the 5.5% baseline international commercial lending rate and significantly lower than the rate in the $300 million bond offering that was eventually recalled.

Despite this initial success, Iridium still faced financial hurdles. By the end of 1996, Iridium planned on raising more than $2.65 billion from investors. It was estimated that more than 300 banks around the globe would be involved and that this would be the largest private debt placement ever. Iridium believed that this debt placement campaign might not be that difficult since the launch date for Iridium services was getting closer.

M-Star Project

In October 1996, Motorola announced that it was working on a new project dubbed M-Star, which would be a $6.1 billion network of 72 low-orbit satellites capable of worldwide voice, video and high-speed data links targeted at the international community. The project was separate from the Iridium venture and was expected to take four years to complete after FCC approval. According to Bary Bertiger, now corporate vice president and general manager of Motorola's satellite communications group, "Unlike Iridium, Motorola has no plans to detach M-Star as a separate entity. We won't fund it ourselves, but we will have fewer partners than in Iridium."[22]

The M-Star Project raised some eyebrows in the investment community. Iridium employed 2000 people but M-Star had only 80. The Iridium Project generated almost 1100 patents for Motorola, and that intellectual property would most likely be transferred to M-Star. Also, Motorola had three contracts with Iridium for construction and operation of the global communication system providing for approximately $6.5 billion in payments to Motorola over a 10-year period that began in 1993. Was M-Star

---

22. Quentin Hardy, "Motorola Is Plotting New Satellite Project—M-Star Would be Faster Than the Iridium System, Pitched to Global Firms," *Wall Street Journal* (Eastern edition), New York, October 14, 1996, p. B4.

being developed at the expense of Iridium? Could M-Star replace Iridium? What would happen to the existing 17-member consortium at Iridium if Motorola were to withdraw its support in lieu of its own internal competitive system?

A New CEO

In 1996, Iridium began forming a very strong top management team with the hiring of Dr. Edward Staiano as CEO and vice chairman. Prior to joining Iridium in 1996, Staiano had worked for Motorola for 23 years, during which time he developed a reputation for being hard-nosed and unforgiving. During his final 11 years with Motorola, Staiano led the company's General Systems Sector to record growth levels. In 1995, the division accounted for approximately 40% of Motorola's total sales of $27 billion. In leaving Motorola's payroll for Iridium's, Staiano gave up a $1.3 million per year contract with Motorola for a $500,000 base salary plus 750,000 Iridium stock options that vested over a 5-year period. Staiano commented:

> I was spending 40 percent to 50 percent of my time (at Motorola) on Iridium anyway . . . If I can make Iridium's dream come true, I'll make a significant amount of money.[23]

Project Management at Motorola (Iridium)

Motorola fully understood the necessity of good project management on an effort of this magnitude. Just building, launching and positioning the satellites would require cooperative efforts of some 6000 engineers located in the United States, Ireland, Italy, Canada, China, India and Germany. The following were part of Motorola's project management practices on the Iridium Project:

- **Selection of partners:** Motorola had to find highly qualified partners that would be willing to be upfront with all problems and willing to work with teams to find resolutions to these problems as soon as they surfaced. Teamwork and open communications would be essential.
- **Existing versus new technology:** Motorola wanted to use as much existing technology as possible rather than completely "reinvent the wheel." This was critical when considering that the Iridium Project would require upwards of 15 million lines of code. Motorola estimated that only about 2 million lines of code would need to be prepared from scratch. The rest would come from existing time-tested legacy software from existing projects.

---

23. Quentin Hardy, "Staiano Is Leaving Motorola to Lead Firm's Iridium Global Satellite Project," *Wall Street Journal* (Eastern edition), New York, December 10, 1996, p. B8.

- **Use of the capability maturity model (CMM):** Each strategic partner was selected and evaluated against their knowledge of the CMM developed by the Software Engineering Institute (SEI) at Carnegie-Mellon University. In many cases, Motorola would offer a crash course in CMM for some strategic partners. In 1995, Motorola had reached level 3 of the five levels in CMM and had planned to reach level 4 by 1996.
- **The WBS:** The WBS was decomposed into major systems, then subsystems and then products.
- **Scheduling systems:** Primavera Project Planner was the prime tool used for planning, tracking progress and quickly spotting scheduling bottlenecks. The level 1 schedule on Primavera was a summary schedule for executive-level briefings. Level 2 was a more detailed schedule. Level 3 schedules were for line managers. Level 4 schedules were for the product teams.
- **Tradeoffs:** Scope change control processes were established for tradeoffs on scope, cost, schedule and risks. Considerable flexibility in product development was provided to the partners and contractors. There was a decentralization of decision making and contractors were empowered to make decisions. These meant that all other product teams that could be affected by a contractor's decision would be notified and provide feedback.

By 1996, 23 out of 47 major milestones were completed on or ahead of schedule and under budget. This was in contradiction to the 1994 Standish Group report that cited that less than 9% of large software projects come in on time and within budget.

Satellite Launches

At 11:28 A.M. on a Friday morning the second week of January 1997, a Delta 2 rocket carrying a global positioning system (GPS) exploded upon launch scattering debris above its Cape Canaveral launch pad. The launch, which was originally scheduled for the third quarter of 1996, would certainly have an impact on Iridium's schedule while an industry board composed of representatives from McDonnell-Douglas and the Air Force determined the cause of the explosion. Other launches had already been delayed for a variety of technical reasons.

In May of 1997, after six failed tries, the first five Iridium satellites were launched. Iridium still believed that the target date for launch of service, September 1998, was still achievable but that all slack in the schedule had been eliminated due to the earlier failures.

By this time, Motorola had amassed tremendous knowledge on how to mass-produce satellites. As described by Bennahum:

> The Iridium constellation was built on an assembly line, with all the attendant reduction in risk and cost that comes from doing something over and over

until it is no longer an art but a process. At the peak of this undertaking, instead of taking 18 to 36 months to build one satellite, the production lines disgorged a finished bird every four and a half days, sealed it in a container, and placed it on the flatbed of an idling truck that drove it to California or Arizona, where a waiting Boeing 747 carried it to a launchpad in the mountains of Taiyuan, China, or on the steppes of Baikonur in Kazakhstan.[24]

Initial Public Offering (IPO)

Iridium was burning cash at the rate of $100 million per month. Iridium filed a preliminary document with the Security and Exchange Commission (SEC) for an initial public offering of 10 million shares to be offered at $19–$21 a share. Because of the launch delays, the IPO was delayed.

In June of 1997, after the first five satellites were placed in orbit, Iridium filed for an IPO of 12 million shares priced at $20 per share. This would cover about three months of operating expenses including satellite purchases and launch costs. The majority of the money would go to Motorola.

Signing Up Customers

The reality of the Iridium concept was now at hand. All that was left to do was to sign up 500,000–600,000 customers, as predicted, to use the service. Iridium set aside $180 million for a marketing campaign including advertising, public relations and a worldwide, direct mail effort. Part of the advertising campaign included direct mail translated into 13 languages, ads on television and on airlines, airport booths and Internet web pages.

How to market Iridium was a challenge. People would certainly hate the phone. According to John Windolph, executive director of marketing communications at Iridium, "It's huge! It will scare people. It is like a brick-size device with an antenna like a stout bread stick. If we had a campaign that featured our product, we'd lose." The decision was to focus on the fears of being out of touch. Thus the marketing campaign began. But Iridium still did not have a clear picture of who would subscribe to the system. An executive earning $700,000 would probably purchase the bulky phone, have his or her assistant carry the phone in their briefcase, be reimbursed by their company for the use of the phone and pay $3–$7 per minute for calls, also a business expense. But are there 600,000 executives worldwide that need the service?

There were several other critical questions that needed to be addressed. How do we hide or downplay the $3400 purchase price of the handset and the usage cost of $7 per minute? How do we avoid discussions about

---

24. Bennahum, 1998, p. 194.

competitors that are offering similar services at a lower cost? With operating licenses in about 180 countries, do we advertise in all of them? Do we take out ads in *Oil and Gas Daily*? Do we advertise in girlie magazines? Do we use full-page or double-page spreads?

Iridium had to rely heavily upon its "gateway" partners for marketing and sales support. Iridium itself would not be able to reach the entire potential audience. Would the gateway partners provide the required marketing and sales support? Do the gateway partners know how to sell the Iridium system and the associated products?

The answer to these questions appeared quickly.

> Over a matter of weeks, more than one million sales inquiries poured into Iridium's sales offices. They were forwarded to Iridium's partners—and many of them promptly disappeared, say several Iridium insiders. With no marketing channels and precious few sales people in place, most global partners were unable to follow up on the inquiries. A mountain of hot sales tips soon went cold.[25]

Iridium's Rapid Ascent

On November 1, 1998, the Iridium system was officially launched. It was truly a remarkable feat that the 11-year project was finally launched, just a little more than a month late.

> After 11 years of hard work, we are proud to announce that we are open for business. Iridium will open up the world of business, commerce, disaster relief and humanitarian assistance with our first-of-its-kind global communications service. . . . The potential use of Iridium products is boundless. Business people who travel the globe and want to stay in touch with home and office, industries that operate in remote areas—all will find Iridium to be the answer to their communications needs.[26]

On November 2, 1998, Iridium began providing service. With the Iridium system finally up and running, most financial analysts issued "buy" recommendations for Iridium stock with expected yearly revenues of $6–$7 billion within five years. On January 25, 1999, Iridium held a news conference call to discuss its earnings for the fourth-quarter of 1998.

> In the fourth quarter of 1998, Iridium made history as we became the first truly global mobile telephone company. Today, a single wireless network, the Iridium Network, covers the planet. And we have moved into 1999

---

25. Leslie Cauley, "Losses in Space—Iridium's Downfall: The Marketing Took a Back Seat to Science—Motorola and Partners Spent Billions on Satellite Links for a Phone Few Wanted," *Wall Street Journal* (Eastern edition), New York, August 18, 1999, p. A1.

26. Excerpts from the Iridium press release, November 1, 1998.

with an aggressive strategy to put a large number of customers on our system, and quickly transform Iridium from a technological event to a revenue generator. We think the prospects for doing this are excellent. Our system is performing at a level beyond expectations.

Financing is now in place through projected cash flow positives. Customer interest remains very high and a number of potentially large customers have now evaluated our service and have given it very high ratings. With all of this going for us, we are in position to sell the service and that is precisely where we are focusing the bulk of our efforts.[27]

—Ed Staiano, CEO, Iridium

Last week Iridium raised approximately $250 million through a very successful 7.5 million-share public offering. This offering had three major benefits. It provided $250 million of cash to our balance sheet. It increased our public float to approximately 20 million shares. And it freed up restrictions placed on $300 million of the $350 million of Motorola guarantees. These restrictions were placed on that particular level of guarantees by our bankers in our $800 million secured credit facility.

With this $250 million, combined with the $350 million of additional guarantees from Motorola, this means we have approximately $600 million of funds in excess of what we need to break cash flow breakeven. This provides a significant contingency for the company.[28]

—Roy Grant, Chief Financial Officer, Iridium

December 1998

In order to make its products and services known to travelers, Iridium agreed to acquire Claircom Corporation from AT&T and Rogers Cantel Mobile Communications for about $65 million. Claircom provided in-flight telephone systems for U.S. planes as well as equipment for international carriers. The purchase of Claircom would be a marketing boost for Iridium.

The problems with large, long-term technology projects were now appearing in the literature. As described by Bennahum:

"This system does not let you do what a lot of wired people want to do," cautions Professor Heather Hudson, who runs the telecommunications program at the University of San Francisco and studies the business of wireless communications. "Nineteen-nineties technologies are changing so fast that it is hard to keep up. Iridium is designed from a 1908s perspective of a global cellular system. Since then, the Internet has grown and cellular telephony is much more pervasive. There are many more opportunities for roaming than were assumed in 1989. So there are fewer businesspeople who need to look for an alternative to a cell phone while they are on the road."[29]

---

27. Excerpts from the Iridium conference call, January 25, 1999.
28. Ibid.
29. Bennahum, 1998, p. 194.

Additionally, toward the late 1990s, some industry observers felt that Motorola had additional incentive to ensure that Iridium succeeded, irrespective of the costs—namely, protecting its reputation. Between 1994 and 1997, Motorola had suffered slowing sales growth, a decline in net income and declining margins. Moreover, the company had experienced several previous business mishaps, including a failure to anticipate the cellular industry's switch to digital cell phones, which played a major role in Motorola's more than 50% share price decline in 1998.

Iridium's Rapid Descent

It took more than a decade for the Iridium Project to ascend and only a few months for descent. In the first week of March, almost 5 weeks after the January teleconference, Iridium's financial woes began to surface. Iridium had expected 200,000 subscribers by the end of 1998 and additional subscribers at a rate of 40,000 per month. Iridium's bond covenants stated a target of 27,000 subscribers by the end of March. Failure to meet such a small target could send investor confidence spiraling downward. Iridium had only 10,000 subscribers. The market that was out there 10 years before was not the market that was there today. Also, 10 years before there was little competition for Iridium.

Iridium cited the main cause of the shortfall in subscriptions as being shortages of phones, glitches in some of the technology, software problems and, most important, a lack of trained sales channels. Iridium found out that it had to train a sales staff and it would have to sell the product, not its distributors. The investor community did not appear pleased with the sales problem that should have been addressed years before, not four months into commercial service.

Iridium's advertising campaign was dubbed "Calling Planet Earth" and promised that you had the freedom to communicate anytime and anywhere. This was not exactly true because the system could not work within buildings or even cars. Furthermore, Iridium underestimated the amount of time subscribers would require to examine and test the system before signing on. In some cases, this would be six months.

Many people blamed marketing and sales for Iridium's rapid descent:

> True, Iridium committed so many marketing and sales mistakes that its experiences could form the basis of a textbook on how not to sell a product. Its phones started out costing $3,000, were the size of a brick, and didn't work as promised. They weren't available in stores when iridium ran a $180 million advertising campaign. And Iridium's prices, which ranged from $3.00 to $7.50 a call, were out of this world.[30]

---

30. James Surowieckipp, "The Latest Satellite Startup Lifts Off. Will It Too Explode?" *Fortune*, October 25, 1999, pp. 237–254.

Iridium's business plan was flawed. With service beginning on November 2, 1998, it was unlikely that 27,000 subscribers would be on board by March of 1999 given the time required to test the product. The original business plan required that the consortium market and sell the product prior to the onset of service. But selling the service from just a brochure was almost impossible. Subscribers want to touch the phone, use it and test it prior to committing to a subscription.

Iridium announced that it was entering into negotiations with its lenders to alter the terms of an $800 million secured credit agreement due to the weaker-than-expected subscriber and revenue numbers. Covenants on the credit agreement included the following[31]:

DATE	CUMULATIVE CASH REVENUE ($ MILLIONS)	CUMULATIVE ACCRUED REVENUE ($ MILLIONS)	NUMBER OF SATELLITE PHONE SUBSCRIBERS	NUMBER OF SYSTEM SUBSCRIBERS[32]
March 31, 1999	$4	$ 30	27,000	52,000
June 30, 1999	50	150	88,000	213,000
Sept. 30, 1999	220	470	173,000	454,000

The stock, which had traded as high as almost $73 per share, was now at approximately $20 per share. And, in yet another setback, Chief Financial Officer Roy T. Grant resigned.

April 1999

Iridium's CEO, Ed Staiano, resigned at the April 22 board meeting. Sources believed that Staiano resigned when the board nixed his plan requesting additional funds to develop Iridium's own marketing and distribution team rather than relying on its strategic partners. Sources also stated another issue in that Staiano had cut costs to the barebones at Iridium but could not get Motorola to reduce its lucrative $500 million service contract with Iridium. Some people believed that Staiano wanted to reduce the Motorola service contract by up to 50%. John Richardson, the CEO of Iridium Africa Corp., was assigned as interim CEO. Richardson's expertise was in corporate restructuring. For the quarter ending March, Iridium said it had a net loss of $505.4 million, or $3.45 a share. The stock fell to $15.62 per share. Iridium managed to attract just 10,294 subscribers five months after commercial rollout.

---

31. Iridium World Communications Ltd., 1998 Annual Report.

32. Total system subscribers include users of Iridium's phone, fax and paging services.

One of Richardson's first tasks was to revamp Iridium's marketing strategy. Iridium was unsure as to what business they were in. According to Richardson:

> The message about what this product was and where it was supposed to go changed from meeting to meeting . . . One day, we'd talk about cellular applications, the next day it was a satellite product. When we launch in November, I'm not sure we had a clear idea of what we wanted to be.[33]

May 1999

Iridium officially announced that it did not expect to meet its targets specified under the $800 million loan agreement. Lenders granted Iridium a two-month extension. The stock dropped to $10.44 per share, partly due to a comment by Motorola that it might withdraw from the ailing venture.

Wall Street began talking about the possibility of bankruptcy. But Iridium stated that it was revamping its business plan and by month's end hoped to have chartered a new course for its financing. Iridium also stated in a regulatory filing that it was uncertain whether it would have enough cash to complete the agreement to purchase Claircom Communications Group Inc., an in-flight telephone service provider, for the promised $65 million in cash and debt.

Iridium had received extensions on debt payments because the lending community knew that it was no small feat transforming from a project plan to an operating business. Another reason why the banks and creditors were willing to grant extensions was because bankruptcy was not a viable alternative. The equity partners owned all Earth stations, all distribution and all regulatory licenses. If the banks and creditors forced Iridium into bankruptcy, they could end up owning a satellite constellation that could not talk to the ground or gateways.

June 1999

Iridium received an additional 30-day extension beyond the 2-month extension it had already received. Iridium was given until June 30 to make a $90 million bond payment. Iridium began laying off 15% of its 550-employee workforce, including two senior officers. The stock had now sunk to $6 per share and the bonds were selling at 19 cents on the dollar.

> We did all of the difficult stuff well, like building the network, and did all of the no-brainer stuff at the end poorly.[34]
>
> —John Richardson, CEO, Iridium

---

33. Carleen Hawn, "High Wireless Act," *Forbes*, June 14, 1999, pp. 60–62.
34. Ibid.

Iridium's major mistake was a premature launch for a product that wasn't ready. People became so obsessed with the technical grandeur of the project that they missed fatal marketing traps . . . Iridium's international structure has proven almost impossible to manage: the 28 members of the board speak multiple languages, turning meetings into mini-U.N. conferences complete with headsets translating the proceedings into five languages.[35]

—John Richardson, CEO, Iridium

We're a classic MBA case study in how not to introduce a product. First we created a marvelous technological achievement. Then we asked how to make money on it.

—John Richardson, CEO, Iridium

Iridium was doing everything possible to avoid bankruptcy. Time was what Iridium needed. Some industrial customers would take six to nine months to try out a new product but would be reluctant to subscribe if it appeared that Iridium would be out of business in six months. In addition, Iridium's competitors were lowering their prices significantly putting further pressure on Iridium. Richardson then began providing price reductions of up to 65% off of the original price for some of Iridium's products and services.

July 1999

The banks and investors agreed to give Iridium yet a third extension to August 11 to meet its financial covenants. Everyone seemed to understand that the restructuring effort was much broader than originally contemplated.

Motorola, Iridium's largest investor and general contractor, admitted that the project may have to be shut down and liquidated as part of bankruptcy proceedings unless a restructuring agreement could be reached. Motorola also stated that if bankruptcy occurred, Motorola would continue to maintain the satellite network, but for a designated time period only.

Iridium had asked its consortium investors and contractors to come up with more money. But to many consortium members, it looked like they would be throwing good money after bad. Several partners made it clear that they would simply walk away from Iridium rather than provide additional funding. That could have a far-reaching effect on the service at some locations. Therefore all partners had to be involved in the restructuring. Wall Street analysts expected Iridium to be allowed to repay its cash payments on its debt over several years or offer debt holders an equity position in Iridium. It was highly unlikely that Iridium's satellites orbiting Earth would be auctioned off in bankruptcy court.

---

35. Leslie Cauley, "Losses in Space—Iridium's Downfall: The Marketing Took a Back Seat to Science," *Wall Street Journal* (Eastern edition), New York, August 18, 1999, p. A1.

August 1999

On August 12, Iridium filed for bankruptcy protection. This was like having "a dagger stuck in their heart" for a company that a few years earlier had predicted financial breakeven in just the first year of operations. This was one of the 20 largest bankruptcy filings up to this time. The stock, which had been trading as little as $3 per share, was suspended from the NASDAQ on August 13, 1999. Iridium's phone calls had been reduced to around $1.40 to $3 per minute and the handsets were reduced to $1500 per unit.

There was little hope for Iridium. Both the business plan and the technical plan were flawed. The business plan for Iridium seemed like it came out of the film "Field of Dreams," where an Iowa corn farmer was compelled to build a baseball field in the middle of a corn crop. A mysterious voice in his head said, "Build it and they will come." In the film, he did, and they came. While this made for a good plot for a Hollywood movie, it made a horrible business plan.

> If you build Iridium, people may come. But what is more likely is, if you build something cheaper, people will come to that first.
> —Herschel Shosteck, Telecommunication Consultant, 1992

The technical plan was designed to build the holy grail of telecommunications. Unfortunately, after spending billions, the need for the technology changed over time. The engineers that designed the system, many of whom had worked previously on military projects, lacked an understanding of the word "affordability" and the need for marketing a system to more than just one customer, namely the DOD.

> Satellite systems are always far behind the technology curve. Iridium was completely lacking the ability to keep up with Internet time.[36]
> —Bruce Egan, Senior Fellow at Columbia University Institute for Tele-Information

September 1999

Leo Mondale resigned as Iridium's chief financial officer. Analysts believed that Mondale's resignation was the result of a successful restructuring no longer being possible. According to one analyst, "If they (Iridium) were close (to a restructuring plan), they wouldn't be bringing in a whole new team."

Iridium "Flu"

The bankruptcy of Iridium was having a flulike effect on the entire industry. ICO Global Communications, one of Iridium's major competitors,

---

36. Stephanie Paterik, "Iridium Alive and Well," *The Arizona Republic*, April 27, 2005, p. D5.

also filed for bankruptcy protection just two weeks after the Iridium filing. ICO failed to raise the $500 million it sought from public-rights offerings that had already been extended twice. Another competitor, the Globalstar Satellite Communications System, was still financially sound.

> They (Iridium) set everybody's expectations way too high.[37]
> —Anthony Navarro, Globalstar Chief Operating Officer

Searching for a White Knight

Iridium desperately needed a qualified bidder who would function as a white knight. It was up to the federal bankruptcy court to determine whether someone was a qualified bidder. A qualified bidder was required to submit a refundable cash deposit or letter of credit issued by a respected bank that would equal the greater of $10 million or 10% of the value of the amount bid to take control of Iridium.

According to bankruptcy court filing, Iridium was generating revenue of $1.5 million per month. On December 9, 1999, Motorola agreed to a $20 million cash infusion for Iridium. Iridium desperately needed a white knight quickly or it could run out of cash by February 15, 2000. With a monthly operating cost of $10 million and a staggering cost of $300 million every few years for satellite replenishment, it was questionable if anyone could make a successful business from Iridium's assets because of asset specificity.

The cellular phone entrepreneur Craig McCaw planned on a short-term cash infusion while he considered a much larger investment to rescue Iridium. He was also leading a group of investors who pledged $1.2 billion to rescue the ICO satellite system that filed for bankruptcy protection shortly after the Iridium filing.[38]

Several supposedly white knights came forth, but Craig McCaw's group was regarded as the only credible candidate. Although McCaw's proposed restructuring plan was not fully disclosed, it was expected that Motorola's involvement would be that of a minority stakeholder. Also, under the restructuring plan, Motorola would reduce its monthly fee for operating and maintaining the Iridium system from $45 million to $8.8 million.[39]

Definition of Failure (October 1999)

The Iridium network was an engineering marvel. Motorola's never-say-die attitude created technical miracles and overcame NASA-level technical

---

37. Quentin Hardy, "Surviving Iridium," *Forbes*, September 6, 1999, pp. 216–217.

38. "Craig McCaw Plans Cash Infusion to Support Cash-Hungry Iridium," *Wall Street Journal* (Eastern edition), New York, February 7, 2000, p. 1.

39. "Iridium Set to Get $75 Million from Investors Led by McCaw," *Wall Street Journal* (Eastern edition), New York, February 10, 2000, p. 1.

problems. Iridium overcame global political issues, international regulatory snafus and a range of other geopolitical issues on seven continents. The Iridium system was, in fact, what Motorola's Galvin called the eighth wonder of the world.

But did the bankruptcy indicate a failure for Motorola? Absolutely not! Motorola collected $3.65 billion in Iridium contracts. Assuming $750 million in profit from these contracts, Motorola's net loss on Iridium was about $1.25 billion. Simply stated, Motorola spent $1.25 billion for a project that would have cost them perhaps as much as $5 billion out of their own pocket had they wished to develop the technology themselves. Iridium provided Motorola with more than 1000 patents in building satellite communication systems. Iridium allowed Motorola to amass a leadership position in the global satellite industry. Motorola was also signed up as the prime contractor to build the 288-satellite "Internet in the Sky," dubbed the Teledesic Project. Backers of the Teledesic Project, which had a price tag of $15 billion to transmit data, video and voice, included Boeing, Microsoft's Chairman Bill Gates and cellular magnate Craig McCaw. Iridium had enhanced Motorola's reputation for decades to come.

Motorola stated that it had no intention of providing additional funding to ailing Iridium, unless of course other consortium members followed suit. Several members of the consortium stated that they would not provide any additional investment and were considering liquidating their involvement in Iridium.[40]

In March 2000 McCaw withdrew his offer to bail out Iridium even at a deep discount asserting that his efforts would be spent on salvaging the ICO satellite system instead. This, in effect, signed Iridium's death warrant. One of the reasons for McCaw's reluctance to rescue Iridium may have been the discontent by some of the investors who would have been completely left out as part of the restructuring effort, thus losing perhaps their entire investment.

Satellite Deorbiting Plan

With the withdrawal of McCaw's financing, Iridium notified the U.S. Bankruptcy Court that Iridium had not been able to attract a qualified buyer by the deadline assigned by the court. Iridium would terminate its commercial service after 11:59 p.m. on March 17, 2000, and it would begin the process of liquidating its assets.

Immediately following the Iridium announcement, Motorola issued the following press release:

> Motorola will maintain the Iridium satellite system for a limited
> period of time while the deorbiting plan is being finalized. During this

---

40. Scott Thurm, "Motorola Inc., McCaw Shift Iridium Tactics," *Wall Street Journal* (Eastern edition), New York, February 18, 2000, p. 1.

period, we also will continue to work with the subscribers in remote locations to obtain alternative communications. However, the continuation of limited Iridium service during this time will depend on whether the individual gateway companies, which are separate operating companies, remain open.

In order to support those customers who purchased Iridium service directly from Motorola, Customer Support Call Centers and a website that are available 24 hours a day, seven days a week have been established by Motorola. Included in the information for customers is a list of alternative satellite communications services.

The deorbiting plan would likely take two years to complete at a cost of $50 to $70 million. This would include all 66 satellites and the other 22 satellites in space serving as spare or decommissioned failures. Iridium would most likely deorbit the satellites four at a time by firing their thrusters to drop them into the atmosphere where they would burn up.

Iridium Is Rescued for $25 Million

In November 2000 a group of investors led by an airline executive won bankruptcy court approval to form Iridium Satellite Corporation and purchase all remaining assets of failed Iridium Corporation. The purchase was at a fire-sale price of $25 million, which was less than a penny on the dollar. As part of the proposed sale, Motorola would turn over responsibility for operating the system to Boeing. Although Motorola would retain a 2% stake in the new system, Motorola would have no further obligations to operate, maintain or decommission the constellation.

Almost immediately after the announcement, Iridium Satellite was awarded a $72 million contract from the Defense Information Systems Agency, which is part of the DOD.

Iridium will not only add to our existing capability, it will provide a commercial alternative to our purely military systems. This may enable real civil/military dual use, keep us closer to leading edge technologically, and provide a real alternative for the future.[41]

—Dave Oliver, Principal Deputy Undersecretary
of Defense for Acquisition

Iridium had been rescued from the brink of extinction. As part of the agreement, the newly formed company acquired all of the assets of the original Iridium and its subsidiaries. This included the satellite constellation, the terrestrial network, Iridium real estate and the intellectual property

---

41. "DoD Awards $72 Million to Revamp Iridium," *Satellite Today*, Vol. 2, No. 227, Potomac, December 7, 2000, p. 1.

originally developed by Iridium. Because of the new company's significantly reduced cost structure, it was able to develop a workable business model based upon a targeted market for Iridium's products and services.

> Everyone thinks the Iridium satellites crashed and burned, but they're all still up there.[42]
> —Weldon Knape, WCC Chief Executive Officer, April 27, 2005

A new Iridium phone costs $1495 and is the size of a cordless home phone. Older, larger models start at $699, or you can rent one for about $75 per week. Service costs $1 to $1.60 a minute.[43]

Epilogue

February 6, 2006, Iridium satellite declared that 2005 was the best year ever. The company had 142,000 subscribers, which was a 24% increase from 2004 and the 2005 revenue was 55% greater than in 2004. According to Carmen Lloyd, Iridium's CEO, "Iridium is on an exceptionally strong financial foundation with a business model that is self-funding."[44]

For the year ending 2006, Iridium had $212 million in sales and $54 million in profit. Iridium had 180,000 subscribers and a forecasted growth rate of 14% to 20% per year. Iridium had changed its business model, focusing on sales and marketing first and hype second. This allowed them to reach out to new customers and new markets.[45]

Shareholder Lawsuits

The benefit to Motorola, potentially at the expense of Iridium and its investors, did not go unnoticed. At least 20 investor groups filed suit against Motorola and Iridium, citing:

- Motorola milked Iridium and used the partners' money to finance its own foray into satellite communication technology.
- By using Iridium, Motorola ensured that its reputation would not be tarnished if the project failed.
- Most of the money raised through the IPOs went to Motorola for designing most of the satellite and ground station hardware and software.
- Iridium used the proceeds of its $1.45 billion in bonds, with interest rates from 10.875% to 14%, mainly to pay Motorola for satellites.

---

42. Stephanie Paterik, Iridium Alive and Well," *The Arizona Republic*, April 27, 2005.

43. Ibid.

44. Iridium Press Release, February 6, 2006.

45. Adapted from Reena Jana, "Companies Known for Inventive Tech Were Dubbed the Next Big Thing and Then Disappeared. Now They're Back and Growing." *Business Week, Innovation*, April 10, 2007.

- Defendants falsely reported achievable subscriber numbers and revenue figures.
- Defendants failed to disclose the seriousness of technical issues.
- Defendants failed to disclose delays in handset deliveries.
- Defendants violated covenants between themselves and their lenders.
- Defendants delayed disclosure of information, provided misleading information, and artificially inflated Iridium's stock price.
- Defendants took advantage of the artificially inflated price to sell significant amounts of their own holdings for millions of dollars in personal profit.

Bankruptcy Court Ruling

On September 4, 2007, after almost 10 months, the Bankruptcy Court in Manhattan ruled in favor or Motorola and irritated the burned creditors that had hoped to get a $3.7 billion judgment against Motorola. The judge ruled that even though the capital markets were "terribly wrong" about Iridium's hopes for huge profits, Iridium was "solvent" during the critical period when it successfully raised rather impressive amounts of debt and equity in the capital markets.

The court said that even though financial experts now know that Iridium was a hopeless one-way cash flow, flawed technology project and doomed business model, Iridium was solvent at the critical period of fundraising. Even when the bad news began to appear, Iridium's investors and underwriters still believed that Iridium had the potential to become a viable enterprise.

The day after the court ruling, newspapers reported that Iridium LLC, the now privately held company, was preparing to raise about $500 million in a private equity offering to be followed by an IPO within the next year or two.

Epilogue (2011)

When Iridium went into bankruptcy, it was considered a technical masterpiece but a business failure. While many people were willing to write off Iridium, it is alive and doing reasonably well. Following the court ruling in 2007, Iridium announced plans for the second-generation Iridium satellites called Iridium NEXT. Satellite launches for Iridium NEXT would begin in 2015 and be completed by 2017. The original Iridium satellites that were expected to have a life expectancy of five to seven years after their launch in 1997–1998 were now expected to be fully operational until 2014–2020.

Iridium was able to receive new contracts from the U.S. government and also attract new users. Iridium also created a consortium of investors that would provide financial support. On June 2, 2010, Iridium announced the award of a $2.9 billion contract to Thales Alenia Space for satellite procurement. At the same time, a $492 million contract was awarded to

Space X for the launch of these satellites from Vandenberg Air Force Base in California.

In 2010, Iridium stock had a high of $11.13 and a low of $6.27. The market capitalization was $656 million and the earnings per share were $0.09. But while Iridium was maintaining its growth, there were new risks that had to be considered:

- There are too many satellites in space and there is a risk that an Iridium satellite will collide with another satellite. (An Iridium satellite did collide with a Russian satellite.) Some people say that this is a defined and acceptable risk.
- There is also the risk of swarms of whirling debris hitting the Iridium satellites.
- Additional spare satellites may be needed and perhaps not every plane will have a spare. Typically, moving satellites can take up to two weeks and consume a great deal of fuel, thus shortening the satellite's life expectancy.
- The original Iridium satellites were manufactured on an assembly line. In its peak during 1997–1998, Iridium produced a satellite every 4.3 days whereas single satellite development was typically 21 days. Iridium was also able to keep construction costs at about $5 million per satellite. This process would have to be duplicated again or even improved upon.
- Some people argue that Iridium's survival is based upon the large number of contracts it receives from the U.S. government. If the government reduces its support or even pulls out of Iridium, the financial risks may significantly increase.

The need for Iridium still exists.

3.7 SUMMARY OF LESSONS LEARNED

The greatest possible cause of failure could very well be a poor business case or a business case that changed and nobody recognized that it had in fact changed. This requires an understanding of the enterprise environmental factors and the assumptions.

A checklist of techniques for managing the business case might include:

- ☐ Work with the client and the stakeholders to identify the business case.
- ☐ Set up a timetable for periodic review of the business case.
- ☐ Make sure you fully understand the enterprise environmental factors and how they can impact the business case.
- ☐ Establish metrics for tracking assumptions in the business case.
- ☐ Determine the impact that all approved scope changes will have on the business case and accompanying assumptions.

TABLE 3-2 *PMBOK® Guide* Alignment to Lessons Learned

LESSONS LEARNED	PMBOK® GUIDE SECTIONS
The longer the project, the more likely it is that the business case will undergo changes.	5.5, 5.5.3.4
Project managers must not rely solely upon the sponsor or governance committee for the creation of the project's business case.	4.1.1.1, 4.1.1.2, 5.2, 5.2.3.1
The assumptions in the business case are always subject to change and therefore must be revalidated. This mandates that the project manager understand enterprise environmental factors.	11.2.2.4, 11.3.3.1, 11.5.3.2, 2.1.5, 5.4.1.4, 6.1.1.3
As little as one scope change can alter the business case.	5.2, 5.2.3.1, 5.3.3.1, 5.3.3.2, 5.4.3.2, 5.5
When the business case depends upon market conditions, it may be impossible to predict the future.	4.1.1.1, 4.1.1.2

Table 3-2 provides a summary of the lessons learned and alignment to various sections of the *PMBOK® Guide* where additional or supporting information can be found. In some cases, these sections of the *PMBOK® Guide* simply provide supporting information related to the lesson learned. There are numerous sections of the *PMBOK® Guide* that could be aligned for each lesson learned. For simplicity sake, only a few are listed.

4 SPONSORSHIP/GOVERNANCE FAILURES

4.0 INTRODUCTION

All projects have the potential of getting into trouble. But in general, project management can work well and reduce the chance of project failure as long as the project's requirements do not impose severe pressure upon the project manager, and a project sponsor or governance committee exists as an ally to assist the project manager when trouble does appear. In today's chaotic environment, the pressure imposed upon projects appears to be increasing because:

- Companies are accepting greater risks and highly complex projects as a necessity for survival.
- Customers are demanding low-volume, high-quality products with some degree of customization.
- Project life cycles and the time for new product development are being compressed.
- Enterprise environmental factors are having a greater impact on project execution, especially on long-term projects.
- Customers and stakeholders want to be more actively involved in the execution of projects.
- Companies are developing strategic partnerships with suppliers, and each supplier can be at a different level of project management maturity.
- Global competition has forced companies to accept projects from customers that are all at a different level of project management maturity and with different reporting requirements.

These pressures tend to slow down the decision-making processes at a time when stakeholders want the projects and processes to be accelerated. One person, while acting as the project sponsor, may have neither the time nor capability to address all of these additional issues. Unless proper governance exists on the project, the result will be a project slowdown. The slowdown occurs because:

- The project manager may be expected to make decisions in areas where he or she has limited knowledge.
- The project manager may hesitate to accept full accountability and ownership for the project.

- Excessive layers of management for reporting and decision making are being superimposed on top of the project's organizational structure.
- Risk management is being pushed up to higher levels in the organizational hierarchy to people with limited knowledge of risk management, resulting in delayed decisions and possibly faulty mitigation strategies.
- The project manager may demonstrate questionable leadership ability on some of the nontraditional or complex projects.

The problems resulting from these pressures may not be resolved easily and in a timely manner with just one person functioning as a project sponsor. These problems are more likely to be resolved using effective project governance.

4.1 DEFINING PROJECT GOVERNANCE

Project governance is actually a framework by which project decisions are made. Governance relates to decisions that define expectations, accountability, responsibility, the granting of power or verifying performance. Governance relates to consistent management and cohesive policies, processes and decision-making rights for a given area of responsibility. Governance enables efficient and effective decision making to take place while maintaining the value expected with the project's outcome. Therefore, the governance groups must understand the benefits of the project, the expected business value, the strategic fit and the probability of success.

Project management textbooks assert that project managers have single-person accountability to produce the assets or deliverables of the project. Accountability is usually defined as responsibility and commensurate authority. However, there are degrees of both authority and responsibility. Project managers almost always have to share some degree of both authority and responsibility with those responsible for governance, and the degree of sharing must be clearly defined at the onset of the project even though it may be subject to change throughout the project.

Every project can have different governance even if each project uses the same enterprise project management methodology. The governance function can operate as a separate process or as part of project management leadership. Governance is designed not necessarily to replace project decision making but to prevent undesirable decisions from being made.

4.2 PROJECT VERSUS CORPORATE GOVERNANCE

Project governance is not the same as corporate governance. Corporate governance consists of the set of processes, customs, policies, laws and institutions affecting the way people direct, administer or control a *corporation*. Corporate governance also includes the relationships among the many players involved (i.e., the *stakeholders*) and the alignment of the results to corporate *goals*. The principal players include the *shareholders*, *management* and *board of directors*. Other stakeholders include employees, suppliers, customers, banks and other lenders, regulators, the environment and the community at large.[1] The people participating in corporate governance can be completely different from the people participating in project governance, and the roles, responsibilities and decision-making rights can be different as well.

Governance on projects and programs sometimes fails because people confuse project governance with corporate governance. The result is that members of the committees are not sure what their role should be and can end up making decisions that lead to project failure. Some of the major differences include:

- **Alignment:** Corporate governance focuses on how well the portfolio of projects is aligned with and satisfies overall business objectives. Project governance focuses on ways to keep a project on track and to verify that value will be created at the project's completion.
- **Direction:** Corporate governance provides strategic direction with a focus on how project success will satisfy corporate objectives. Project governance is more operational direction with decisions based upon predefined parameters with regard to project scope, time, cost and functionality.
- **Dashboards:** Corporate governance dashboards are based upon financial, marketing and sales metrics. Project governance dashboards have operation metrics on time, cost, scope, quality, action items, risks and deliverables.
- **Membership:** Corporate governance committees are composed of the seniormost levels of management. Project governance membership may include some individuals from middle management.

Another factor which could lead to the failure of projects and programs occurs when members of the project or program governance group do not understand project or program management and the differences between them. This can lead to unwanted micromanagement by the governance committee. It can also lead to decisions that are detrimental to effective project management practices. Some people believe that projects deliver value, whereas programs create assets. Another difference more applicable to projects is that project governance may be short-lived.

---

1. Adapted from "Project Governance," *Wikipedia, the Free Encyclopedia.*

4.3 ROLES, RESPONSIBILITIES AND DECISION-MAKING AUTHORITY

Project governance is the management framework within which project decisions are made. Project governance is a critical element of any project, while the accountabilities and responsibilities associated with an organization's business-as-usual activities are laid down in their organizational/corporate governance arrangements. Seldom does an equivalent framework exist to govern the development of its capital investments (i.e., projects). For instance, the organizational chart provides a good indication of who in the organization is responsible for any particular operational activity the organization conducts. But unless an organization has specifically developed a project governance policy, no such chart is likely to exist for a project development activity. Therefore, the role of project governance is to provide a decision-making framework that is logical, robust and repeatable to govern an organization's capital investments. In this way, an organization will have a structured approach to conducting both its business-as-usual activities and its business change, or project, activities.[2]

There is always the question of what decisions must be made by the governance committee and what decisions the project manager can make. Ambiguous or overlapping roles and responsibilities lead to chaos. In general, the project manager should have the authority to make decisions related to actions necessary to maintain the baselines. Governance committees must have the authority to approve scope changes above a certain monetary value and to make decisions necessary to align the project to corporate objectives and strategy. They also have the authority to redirect or cancel the project. Figures 4-1 and 4-2 illustrate some of the possible differences in activities performed by the project manager and the governance groups.

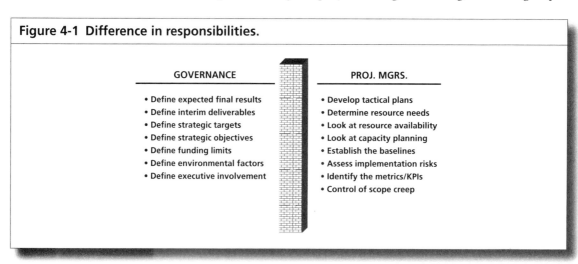

Figure 4-1 Difference in responsibilities.

GOVERNANCE	PROJ. MGRS.
• Define expected final results	• Develop tactical plans
• Define interim deliverables	• Determine resource needs
• Define strategic targets	• Look at resource availability
• Define strategic objectives	• Look at capacity planning
• Define funding limits	• Establish the baselines
• Define environmental factors	• Assess implementation risks
• Define executive involvement	• Identify the metrics/KPIs
	• Control of scope creep

---

2. Adapted from "Project Governance," *Wikipedia, the Free Encyclopedia.*

Figure 4-2 Differences in decision-making authority.

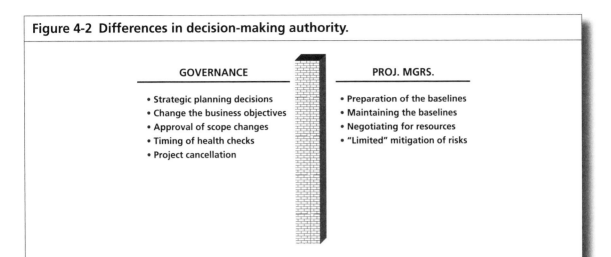

GOVERNANCE	PROJ. MGRS.
• Strategic planning decisions	• Preparation of the baselines
• Change the business objectives	• Maintaining the baselines
• Approval of scope changes	• Negotiating for resources
• Timing of health checks	• "Limited" mitigation of risks
• Project cancellation	

4.4 GOVERNANCE FRAMEWORKS

Historically, governance was provided by a single project sponsor. This was particularly true for internal projects, especially those that were not too complex. Today, governance is provided by a committee that can include representatives from each stakeholder's organization, regardless of whether the project is for a client internal or external to the company.

Table 4-1 shows various governance approaches based upon the type of organizational structure for the project. The membership of each governance committee can change from project to project and from industry to industry. The membership may also vary based upon the number of stakeholders and whether the project is for an internal or external client. On long-term projects, membership can change throughout the project.

For projects external to the company, the number of governance committees can be significant. This is shown in Figure 4-3. The hierarchy of committees can be different for each project. On large complex projects that require significant funding, there may be members on the committee from each funding organization. There can also be significant conflicts and political issues between the members of various governance groups over the amount of money each funding source will put up, the value of the project, scope changes, costs and other such arguments. Getting agreement between members of the committees is difficult to achieve, since each member may have a hidden agenda. Not all members may want to see the project succeed.

Not all information presented to these committees is in the form of paperwork. To eliminate the heavy cost of paperwork, companies are designing dashboard reporting systems, and there can be a different dashboard for each member of each committee based upon their informational requirements.

TABLE 4-1 Project Governance Approaches

PROJECT ORGANIZATIONAL STRUCTURE	DESCRIPTION	GOVERNANCE APPROACH
Dispersed locally	Team members can be full time or part time. They are still attached administratively to their functional area even though a matrix structure exists.	Usually a single person is acting as the sponsor but there may be an internal committee depending upon the project's complexity.
Dispersed geographically	This is a virtual team. The project manager may never see some of the team members. Team members can be full time or part time.	Usually governance by committee and can include stakeholder membership.
Colocated	All of the team members are physically located in close proximity to the project manager. The project manager does not have any responsibility for wage and salary administration.	Usually a single person acting as the sponsor.
Projectized	This is similar to a colocated team, but the project manager generally functions as a line manager and may have wage and salary administration responsibilities.	May be governance by committee based upon the size of the project and the number of strategic partners.

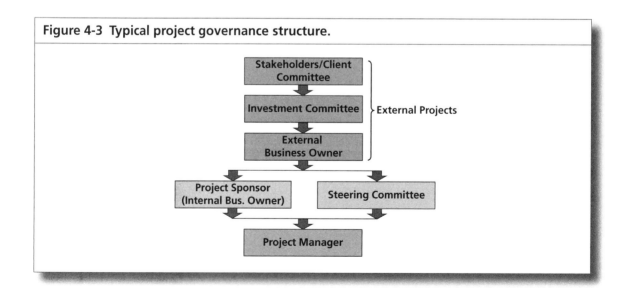

Figure 4-3 Typical project governance structure.

4.5 GOVERNANCE FAILURES

Projects can fail even with excellent governance. However, there are situations where poor governance can lead to project failures. Some common causes of governance failure include:

- There is no clearly defined ownership for the project.
- The governance team cannot agree on the objectives of the project.
- The business case for the project is either nonexistent or poorly defined.
- The governance team is either too large or too small for the project.
- There is no clear accountability for project success, thus slowing down the decision-making process.
- The roles and responsibilities of the board members are not clearly defined.
- The governance boards limit the decision-making authority of the project team, thus elongating the project life cycle.
- Membership in the governance team continuously changes.
- New members bring with them hidden agendas.
- The governance team adds in wasteful scope inclusions, thus elongating the project's life cycle.
- Members of the governance team lack knowledge in risk management.
- The governance team is not provided with the right information on which to base their decision(s).
- The governance team is provided with the correct information, but they lack a process for effective decision making.
- Governance team members allow politics to influence their decisions, such as the timetable for announcements or how the project will impact their community.
- Nobody tries to validate that the project team can accomplish what the governance board requires.
- Members of the governance team do not understand the differences between project and organizational governance, thus focusing on hierarchical decision making rather than serial decision making.
- There is a failure to realize that governance team effectiveness is directly related to stakeholder relations management effectiveness.
- Board members are unable to work together.

Governance on projects is a necessity in today's business environment. Effective governance provides the organization performing the project with a mechanism by which the rights and interests of the stakeholders will be met. Governance is necessary for the successful delivery of business value in projects.

4.6 WHY PROJECTS ARE HARD TO KILL

In general, with new product development it may take 60 or more ideas to come up with one commercially successful product. Each idea is usually constructed in the form of a project for idea evaluation purposes. Therefore, based upon the company's success rate and how the company defines success and failure, the company could have an abundance of failures before discovering a commercially successful product.

Although this example may be oversimplified, it does bring across three important points:

- Not all projects will be successful.
- Not knowing when to pull the plug on a failing project can be costly.
- Not demonstrating a willingness to pull the plug on a failing project can be even more costly.

We rarely hear about the number of small R&D projects that were cancelled because they could not produce any viable results. But we do hear about the alarming number of large projects, especially IT projects, that either failed or were in trouble because these projects were publicized in the media. It is not uncommon to read about IT projects that failed and hundreds of millions of dollars were expended without having any viable results. Once troubled projects get into the media, companies may continue funding the project in hopes of a miracle rather than having to publicly admit defeat. The bad news is that most bailout processes fail unless there is a reasonable chance that some value can be found at completion of the project.

Projects begin with an idea as to what the end result looks like. The end result must be very well understood in order for the project to be a success. Unfortunately, too many projects get funded with just a cursory understanding of the end result. Then, when we get into the depths of the project and discover that certain steps were omitted or problems exist, we try to save face by throwing good money after bad money. However, large high-technology projects such as the Airbus 380 or the Boeing 787 that had well-understood end results can still require additional funding because of technology issues and a high concern for passenger safety. This is a necessity when working in a high-technology environment using state-of-the-art technology.

Projects generally do not fail because the idea was bad. Rather, they fail because the project was not executed correctly. If there are indications that the project should be cancelled and you pull the plug in a timely manner such that the bleeding stops, then this could be viewed as a success because you are no longer squandering resources. The resources can quickly be reassigned to other projects that offer more fruitful opportunities. But if the signs of failure exist and funding continues, then we have a true failure, but more so a failure in project management and project governance.

If the idea for the project has merit and is directly related to strategic business objectives, executives may be reluctant to let the project die. They may be blind-sided by the desire to:

- Eliminate or surpass the competition
- Strengthen the firm's reputation and image
- Reach the ultimate "pot of gold"
- Strengthen the corporate culture

These desires can drastically outweigh the fact that the original idea was unsound and that the business case was unrealistic. However, there are projects that at one time may have had a valid business case but then lose their business value as the project progresses. The Iridium Project is a classic example of a project that started out with a valid business case and lost its glamour in the marketplace over time. Cancelling a project may be difficult because:

- Significant funds have already been spent.
- Plant closing costs are significant and will result in losses.
- There are exit barriers related to customers still using the products.
- Payments must be made to terminated workers.
- There may be penalty clauses for breach of contract with vendors.
- Moving people around may violate seniority and hiring practices.

If executives are to pull the plug in a timely manner, then they need the right information such that they can make informed decisions. Good information systems that provide honesty in reporting allow for decisions to be made in a timely manner. But we must still deal with the critical question, "How bad must the results become before we are willing to pull the plug?" Hoping for the miracle is never a good idea. But sometimes decisions must be made based upon partial information. Consider the following situation:

Situation: On a large, complex project, the lead time for the purchasing of capital equipment was at least a year before any meaningful results would be available. The capital equipment was needed to meet the strategic launch date for a new product. The company purchased the expensive equipment and then discovered that the project was doomed. Rather than admit defeat, the company continued funding the project rather than admit that it had thrown away a sizable sum of money on capital equipment that would not be used.

LESSON LEARNED Throwing good money after bad money is never a good idea.

Information systems for projects performed internally in a company are generally more reliable than information system reports that come from a vendor. It is extremely more difficult to cancel a project where the vendor is responsible for the speed of innovation. The vendor's reports may make it appear that all is well when, in fact, things are progressing poorly. The timeliness of information is critical if projects are to be terminated in a timely manner.

4.7 COLLECTIVE BELIEF

Some projects, especially very long-term projects with full-time workers, often mandate that everyone swear allegiance to the project. This is called a collective belief. The collective belief is a fervent, and perhaps blind, desire to achieve that can permeate the entire team, the project sponsor and even the most senior levels of management.

The collective belief can make a rational organization act in an irrational manner, especially when it comes to cancelling a distressed project Regardless of what the project's metrics indicate and the fact that the business case may no longer be valid. This is particularly true if the project sponsor or the governance committee spearheads the collective belief. When a collective belief exists, people are selected based upon their support for the collective belief. Nonbelievers are pressured into supporting the collective belief and team members are not allowed to challenge the results. As the collective belief grows, both advocates and nonbelievers are trampled. The pressure of the collective belief can outweigh the reality of the results.

The Iridium Project was a classic example where the collective belief permeated not only everyone on the team but also everyone on the board of directors of Iridium. Had the Iridium board been effective in their duties, the project would have been cancelled or redirected several years earlier.

There are several characteristics of the collective belief, which is why some large, high-technology projects are often difficult to kill. These characteristics are directly applicable to people that sit on governance committees:

- Inability or refusal to recognize or admit failure
- Refusing to see the warning signs
- Seeing only what you want to see
- Fearful of exposing mistakes
- Viewing bad news as a personal failure
- Viewing failure as a sign of weakness
- Viewing failure as damage to one's career
- Viewing failure as damage to one's reputation

Because of these characteristics, members of the governance committee often find it very difficult to terminate a project. This is especially true if they have a vested interested in the outcome of the project. It may be beneficial for large and/or complex projects to have some members that are not affected by the outcome of the project and are not financial supporters of the project.

4.8 EXIT CHAMPION

Project sponsors and project champions do everything possible to make their project successful. But what if the project champions, as well as the project team, have blind faith in the success of the project? What happens if the strongly held convictions and the collective belief disregard the early warning signs of imminent danger? What happens if the collective belief drowns out dissent?

In such cases, an exit champion must be assigned. The larger the project and the greater the financial risk to the firm, the higher up the exit champion should reside. If the project champion just happens to be the CEO, then someone on the board of directors or even the entire board of directors should assume the role of the exit champion. Unfortunately, there are situations where the collective belief permeates the entire board of directors. In this case, the collective belief can force the board of directors to shirk their responsibility for oversight.

The exit champion sometimes needs to have some direct involvement in the project in order to have credibility, but direct involvement is not always a necessity. Exit champions must be willing to put their reputation on the line and possibly face the likelihood of being cast out from the project team. According to Isabelle Royer[3]:

> Sometimes it takes an individual, rather than growing evidence, to shake the collective belief of a project team. If the problem with unbridled enthusiasm starts as an unintended consequence of the legitimate work of a project champion, then what may be needed is a countervailing force—an exit champion. These people are more than devil's advocates. Instead of simply raising questions about a project, they seek objective evidence showing that problems in fact exist. This allows them to challenge—or, given the ambiguity of existing data, conceivably even to confirm—the viability of a project. They then take action based on the data.

Large projects incur large cost overruns and schedule slippages. Making the decision to cancel such a project, once it has started, is very difficult, according to David Davis[4]:

> The difficulty of abandoning a project after several million dollars have been committed to it tends to prevent objective review and recosting. For this reason, ideally an independent management team—one not involved

---

3. Isabelle Royer, "Why Bad Projects Are So Hard to Kill," *Harvard Business Review*, February 2003, p.11. Copyright © 2003 by the Harvard Business School Publishing Corporation. All rights reserved.

4. David Davis, "New Projects: Beware of False Economics," *Harvard Business Review*, March–April 1985, pp. 100–101. Copyright © 1985 by the President and Fellows of Harvard College. All rights reserved.

in the projects development—should do the recosting and, if possible, the entire review. . . . If the numbers do not holdup in the review and recosting, the company should abandon the project. The number of bad projects that make it to the operational stage serves as proof that their supporters often balk at this decision. . . . Senior managers need to create an environment that rewards honesty and courage and provides for more decision making on the part of project managers. Companies must have an atmosphere that encourages projects to succeed, but executives must allow them to fail.

The longer the project, the greater the necessity for the exit champions and project sponsors to make sure that the business plan has "exit ramps" such that the project can be terminated before massive resources are committed and consumed. Unfortunately, when a collective belief exists, exit ramps are purposefully omitted from the project and business plans. Another reason for having exit champions is so that the project closure process can occur as quickly as possible. As projects approach their completion, team members often have apprehension about their next assignment and try to stretch out the existing project until they are ready to leave. In this case, the role of the exit champion is to accelerate the closure process without impacting the integrity of the project.

Some organizations use members of a portfolio review board to function as exit champions. Portfolio review boards have the final say in project selection. They also have the final say as to whether or not a project should be terminated. Usually, one member of the board functions as the exit champion and makes the final presentation to the remainder of the board.

4.9 WHEN TO GIVE UP

Not all projects will be completed successfully. Some projects may be partial successes but others may be complete failures. If all of the projects you work on are completed successfully, primarily projects internal to your company, then you either are probably not working on enough projects or are working in a company that is not considered a risk taker.

First and foremost, we must understand that the only real failures are those projects from which nothing is learned. Second, what appears to be more important to the project manager is knowing when to say, "I give up!" The earlier the decision is made to cancel a project, the quicker the resources can be assigned to other projects that may have a greater opportunity for value creation and commercial success. Simply stating that we should wait until the next gate review meeting to make a decision is not a viable way to provide governance to projects. Senior management must create templates or checklists that seek out those critical parameters that indicate that project cancellation should be considered. The decision to cancel a project is not easy, especially if the project's objectives can no longer be met but the project is creating intellectual property that can be used in the future. This could lead to successful spin-offs from the original project.

Establishing criteria for cancelling a project may include factors such as:

- The project's objectives cannot be met and continuation of the project will not necessarily create intellectual property.
- The project's assumptions have changed and we may not be working on the right project.
- The project can be completed but it will not create any sustainable value for the company.
- Market conditions have changed such that the return on investment (ROI) will not be met, or the sales expectations will not be met, or the competition is expected to introduce a more advanced product.
- The final product may become obsolete earlier than expected or the company may not be able to provide customer support for the product to meet customer expectations.
- Costs have risen on the project and the schedule has slipped significantly.
- There are technical difficulties beyond the capabilities of our personnel.
- The problem is just too complex for our company to manage.
- Key resources have left the project or resigned from our company.
- The company is experiencing a significant cash flow problem.
- There has been a significant change in the company's interest and strategy.

It is the responsibility of senior management to be able to make sure that project audits are conducted in a timely manner. Project managers must be willing to bring forth quickly any bad news that may lead to project termination. Likewise, senior management must create a culture where people are not punished for bringing forth bad news.

Even if all of the indications are there for the project to be terminated, there are always situations when the executives will refuse to cancel the project for personal reasons.

Situation: The Irresponsible Sponsors[5] Two vice presidents came up with ideas for pet projects and funded the projects internally using money from their functional areas. Both projects had budgets close to $2 million and schedules of approximately one year. These were somewhat high-risk projects because they both required that a similar technical breakthrough be made. There was no guarantee that the technical breakthrough could be made at all. And even if the technical breakthrough could be made, both executives estimated that the shelf life of both products would be about one year before becoming obsolete but that they could easily recover their R&D costs.

---

5. Copyright © 2010 by Harold Kerzner. Reproduced by permission. All rights reserved.

These two projects were considered as pet projects because they were established at the personal request of two senior managers and without any real business case. Had these two projects been required to go through the formal portfolio selection of projects process neither project would have been approved. The budgets for these projects were way out of line for the value that the company would receive and the ROI would be below minimum levels even if the technical breakthrough could be made. The project management office (PMO), which is actively involved in the portfolio selection of projects process, also stated that it would never recommend approval of a project where the end result would have a shelf life of one year or less. Simply stated, these projects existed for the self-satisfaction of the two executives and to get them prestige from their colleagues.

Nevertheless, both executives found money for their projects and were willing to let the projects go forward without the standard approval process. Each executive was able to get an experienced project manager from their group to manage their pet project.

At the first gate review meeting, both project managers stood up and recommended that their projects be cancelled and that the resources be assigned to other more promising projects. They both stated that the technical breakthrough needed could not be made in a timely manner. Under normal conditions, both of these project managers should have received medals for bravery in standing up and recommending that their project be cancelled. This certainly appeared as a recommendation in the best interest of the company.

But both executives were not willing to give up that easily. Cancelling both projects would be humiliating for the two executives that were sponsoring these projects. Instead, both executives stated that the projects were to continue on to the next gate review meeting at which time a decision would be made for possible cancellation of both projects.

At the second gate review meeting, both project managers once again recommended that their projects be cancelled. And, as before, both executives asserted that the project should continue to the next gate review meeting before a decision would be made.

As luck would have it, the necessary technical breakthrough was finally made, but six months late. That meant that the window of opportunity to sell the products and recover the R&D costs would be six months rather than one year. Unfortunately, the marketplace knew that these products might be obsolete in six months and no sales occurred of either product.

LESSON LEARNED Once again, failing to pull the plug can result in throwing good money after bad money while providing little value.

Both executives had to find a way to save face and avoid the humiliation of having to admit that they squandered a few million dollars on two useless R&D projects. This could very well impact their year-end bonuses. The solution they found was simple: Promote the project managers for having developed the products and then blame marketing and sales for not finding customers.

4.10 PROLOGUE TO THE DENVER INTERNATIONAL AIRPORT CASE STUDY

In the previous chapter we discussed the Iridium Project. The Iridium Project had a questionable business case and, when it became evident that the business case was no longer there, governance failed to take the appropriate steps. In the next two sections are two case studies involving Denver International Airport. The first case study creates the need for the airport and thus the business case. The second case study shows how the business case changed when the decision was made to have an automated baggage-handling system for the entire airport rather than for just one concourse.

These are the critical points to look for when reading the first case:

- Was there a need for Denver International Airport?
- What was the business case?
- Was the baggage-handling system part of the original business case?
- Who sat on the governance committee authorizing the automated baggage-handling system?
- Were the people on the governance committee capable of evaluating the technical complexity of including the automated baggage-handling system into the revised business case?

The first case study shows the history of Denver International Airport up to the day the new airport opened. The second case study shows what happened with the baggage-handling system from the day the airport opened to August 2005 when the automated baggage-handling system was removed from service. In the second case, look for the following critical points:

- Were there any tell-tale signs that the baggage-handling system might not work?
- Why were the critical signs ignored?
- Did the governance committee see the tell-tale signs?

4.11 DENVER INTERNATIONAL AIRPORT[6]

Background

How does one convert a $1.2 billion project into a $5.0 billion project? It's easy. Just build a new airport in Denver. The decision to replace Denver's

---

6. Copyright © 2013 by Harold Kerzner. All rights reserved. The case study also appears in *Project Management Case Studies*, 4th edition, Wiley, Hoboken, NJ, 2013, pp. 567–609.

Stapleton Airport with Denver International Airport (DIA) was made by well-intentioned city officials. The city of Denver would need a new airport eventually, and it seemed like the right time to build an airport that would satisfy Denver's needs for at least 50–60 years. DIA could become the benchmark for other airports to follow.

A summary of the critical events is listed below:

1985: Denver Mayor Federico Pena and Adams County officials agree to build a replacement for Stapleton International Airport. Project estimate: $1.2 billion.

1986: Peat Marwick, a consulting firm, is hired to perform a feasibility study including projected traffic. Their results indicate that, depending on the season, as many as 50% of the passengers would change planes. The new airport would have to handle this smoothly. United and Continental object to the idea of building a new airport, fearing the added cost burden.

May 1989: Denver voters pass an airport referendum. Project estimate: $1.7 billion.

March 1993: Denver Mayor Wellington Webb announces the first delay. Opening day would be postponed from October 1993 to December 1993. (Federico Pena becomes Secretary of Transportation under Clinton.) Project estimate: $2.7 billion.

October 1993: Opening day is to be delayed to March 1994. There are problems with the fire and security systems in addition to the inoperable baggage-handling system. Project estimate: $3.1 billion.

December 1993: The airport is ready to open, but without an operational baggage-handling system. Another delay is announced.

February 1994: Opening day is to be delayed to May 15, 1994, because of baggage-handling system.

May 1994: Airport misses the fourth deadline.

August 1994: DIA finances a backup baggage-handling system. Opening day is delayed indefinitely. Project estimate: $4 billion plus.

December 1994: Denver announces that DIA was built on top of an old Native American burial ground. An agreement is reached to lift the curse.

Airports and Airline Deregulation

Prior to the Airline Deregulation Act of 1978, airline routes and airfare were established by the Civil Aeronautics Board (CAB). Airlines were allowed to charge whatever they wanted for airfare, based on CAB approval. The cost of additional aircraft was eventually passed on to the consumer. Initially, the high cost for airfare restricted travel to the businessperson and the elite who could afford it.

Increases in passenger travel were moderate. Most airports were already underutilized and growth was achieved by adding terminals or runways on existing airport sites. The need for new airports was not deemed critical for the near term.

Following deregulation, the airline industry had to prepare for open market competition. This meant that airfares were expected to decrease dramatically. Airlines began purchasing hoards of planes, and most routes were "free game." Airlines had to purchase more planes and fly more routes in order to remain profitable. The increase in passenger traffic was expected to come from the average person who could finally afford air travel.

Deregulation made it clear that airport expansion would be necessary. While airport management conducted feasibility studies, the recession of 1979–1983 occurred. Several airlines, such as Braniff, filed for bankruptcy protection under Chapter 11 and the airline industry headed for consolidation through mergers and leveraged buyouts.

Cities took a wait-and-see attitude rather than risk billions in new airport development. Noise abatement policies, environmental protection acts and land acquisition were viewed as headaches. The only major airport built in the last 20 years was Dallas–Ft. Worth, which was completed in 1974.

Does Denver Need a New Airport?

In 1974, even prior to deregulation, Denver's Stapleton Airport was experiencing such rapid growth that Denver's Regional Council of Governments concluded that Stapleton would not be able to handle the necessary traffic expected by the year 2000. Modernization of Stapleton could have extended the inevitable problem to 2005. But were the headaches with Stapleton better cured through modernization or by building a new airport? There was no question that insufficient airport capacity would cause Denver to lose valuable business. Being 500 miles from other major cities placed enormous pressure upon the need for air travel in and out of Denver.

In 1988, Denver's Stapleton International Airport ranked as the fifth busiest in the country, with 30 million passengers. The busiest airports were Chicago, Atlanta, Los Angeles and Dallas–Ft. Worth. By the year 2000, Denver anticipated 66 million passengers, just below Dallas–Ft. Worth's 70 million and Chicago's 83 million estimates.

Delays at Denver's Stapleton Airport caused major delays at all other airports. By one estimate, bad weather in Denver caused up to $100 million in lost income to the airlines each year because of delays, rerouting, canceled flights, putting travelers into hotels overnight, employee overtime pay and passengers switching to other airlines.

Denver's United Airlines and Continental comprised 80% of all flights in and out of Denver. Table 4-2 shows the service characteristics of United and Continental between December 1993 and April 1994. Table 4-3 shows all of the airlines serving Denver as of June 1994. Figure 4-4 shows the cities that are serviced from Denver. It should be obvious that delays in Denver could cause delays in each of these cities. Table 4-4 shows

TABLE 4-2 Current Service Characteristics: United Airlines and Continental Airlines, December 1993 and April 1994

	ENPLANED PASSENGERS[a]	SCHEDULED SEATS[b]	BOARDING LOAD FACTOR	SCHEDULED DEPARTURES[b]	AVERAGE SEATS PER DEPARTURE
December 1993					
United Airlines	641,209	1,080,210	59%	7,734	140
United Express	57,867	108,554	53%	3,582	30
Continental Airlines	355,667	624,325	57%	4,376	143
Continental Express	52,680	105,800	50%	3,190	33
Other	236,751	357,214	66%	2,851	125
Total	1,344,174	2,276,103	59%	21,733	105
April 1994					
United Airlines	717,093	1,049,613	68%	7,743	136
United Express	44,451	92,880	48%	3,395	27
Continental Airlines	275,948	461,168	60%	3,127	147
Continental Express	24,809	92,733	27%	2,838	33
Other	234,091	354,950	66%	2,833	125
Total	1,296,392	2,051,344	63%	19,936	103

[a]Airport management records.
[b]Official Airline Guides, Inc. (online database), for periods noted.

the top 10 domestic passenger origin-destination markets from Denver Stapleton.

Stapleton was ranked as 1 of the 10 worst air traffic bottlenecks in the United States. Even low clouds at Denver Stapleton could bring delays of 30–60 minutes.

Stapleton has two parallel north-south runways that are close together. During bad weather where instrument landing conditions exist, the two runways are considered as only one. This drastically reduces the takeoffs and landings each hour.

The new airport would have three north-south runways initially with a master plan calling for eight eventually. This would triple or quadruple instrument flights occurring at the same time to 104 aircraft per hour.

TABLE 4-3 Airlines Serving Denver, June 1994

MAJOR/NATIONAL AIRLINES	REGIONAL/COMMUTER AIRLINES
America West Airlines	Air Wisconsin (United Express)[b]
American Airlines	Continental Express
Continental Airlines	GP Express Airlines
Delta Air Lines	Great Lakes Aviation (United Express)
Markair	Mesa Airlines (United Express)
Midway Airlines	Midwest Express[b]
Morris Air[a]	
Northwest Airlines	Cargo Airlines
TransWorld Airlines	
United Airlines	Airborne Express
USAir	Air Vantage
	Alpine Air
Charter Airlines	American International Airways
	Ameriflight
Aero Mexico	Bighorn Airways
American Trans Air	Burlington Air Express
Casino Express	Casper Air
Express One	Corporate Air
Great American	DHL Worldwide Express
Private Jet	Emery Worldwide
Sun Country Airlines	Evergreen International Airlines
	EWW Airline/Air Train
Foreign Flag Airlines (scheduled)	Federal Express
	Kitty Hawk
Martinair Holland	Majestic Airlines
Mexicana de Aviacion	Reliant Airlines
	United Parcel Service
	Western Aviators

Source: Airport management, June 1994.

[a]Morris Air was purchased by Southwest Airlines in December 1993. The airline announced that it would no longer serve Denver as of October 3, 1994.

[b]Air Wisconsin and Midwest Express have both achieved the level of operating revenues needed to qualify as a national airline as defined by the FAA. However, for purposes of this report, these airlines are referred to as regional airlines.

Figure 4-4 U.S. airports served nonstop from Denver. *Source:* Official Airline Guides, Inc. (On-line Database), June 1994.

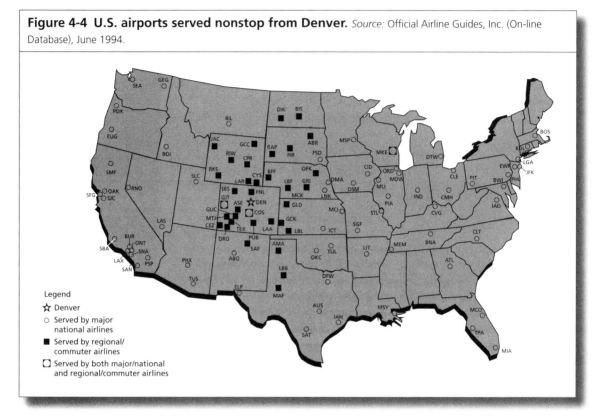

Legend
☆ Denver
○ Served by major national airlines
■ Served by regional/commuter airlines
☐ Served by both major/national and regional/commuter airlines

Currently, Stapleton can handle only 30 landings per hour under instrument conditions with a *maximum* of 80 aircraft per hour during clear weather.

The runway master plan called for ten 12,000-foot and two 16,000-foot runways. By opening day, three north-south and one east-west 12,000-foot runways would be in operation and one of the 16,000-foot north-south runways would be operational shortly thereafter.

The airfield facilities also included a 327-foot FAA air traffic control tower (the nation's tallest) and base building structures. The tower's height allowed controllers to visually monitor runway thresholds as much as 3 miles away. The runway/taxiway lighting system, with lights imbedded in the concrete pavement to form centerlines and stopbars at intersections, would allow air traffic controllers to signal pilots to wait on taxiways and cross active runways and to lead them through the airfield in poor visibility.

Due to shifting winds, runway operations were shifted from one direction to another. At the new airport, the changeover would require 4 minutes as opposed to the 45 minutes at Stapleton.

Sufficient spacing was provided for in the concourse design such that two FAA Class 6 aircraft (i.e., 747-XX) could operate back to back without impeding each other.

TABLE 4-4   Top Ten Domestic Passenger Origin-Destination Markets and Airline Service, Stapleton International Airport (for 12 months ending September 30, 1993)

CITY OF ORGIN OR DESTINATION[a]	AIR MILES FROM DENVER	PERCENTAGE OF CERTIFICATED AIRLINE PASSENGERS	AVERAGE DAILY NONSTOP DEPARTURES[b]
1. Los Angeles[c]	849	6.8	34
2. New York[d]	1,630	6.2	19
3. Chicago[e]	908	5.6	26
4. San Francisco[f]	957	5.6	29
5. Washington, D.C.[g]	1,476	4.9	12
6. Dallas–Forth Worth	644	3.5	26
7. Houston[h]	864	3.2	15
8. Phoenix	589	3.1	19
9. Seattle	1,019	2.6	14
10. Minneapolis	693	2.3	16
Cities listed		43.8	210
All others		56.2	241
Total		100.0	451

Sources: U.S. Department of Transportation/Air Transport Association of America, "Origin-Destination Survey of Airline Passenger Traffic, Domestic," third quarter 1993, except as noted.
[a]Top 10 cities based on total inbound and outbound passengers (on large certificated airlines) at Stapleton International Airport in 10% sample for the 12 months ending September 30, 1993.
[b]Official Airline Guides, Inc. (online database), April 1994. Includes domestic flights operated at least four days per week by major/national airlines and excludes the activity of foreign-flag and commuter/regional airlines.
[c]Los Angeles International, Burbank–Glendale–Pasadena, John Wayne (Orange County), Ontario International and Long Beach Municipal Airports.
[d]John F. Kennedy International, LaGuardia and Newark International Airports.
[e]Chicago-O'Hare International and Midway Airports.
[f]San Francisco, Metropolitan Oakland and San Jose International Airports.
[g]Washington Dulles International, Washington National and Baltimore/Washington International Airports.
[h]Houston Intercontinental and William P. Hobby Airports.

Even when two aircraft (one from each concourse) have pushed back at the same time, there could still exist room for a third FAA Class 6 aircraft to pass between them.

City officials believed that Denver's location, being equidistant from Japan and Germany, would allow twin-engine, extended range transports to reach both countries nonstop. The international opportunities were there. Between late 1990 and early 1991, Denver was entertaining four groups of leaders per month from Pacific Rim countries to look at DIA's planned capabilities.

In the long term, Denver saw the new airport as a potential hub for Northwest or USAir. This would certainly bring more business to Denver. Very few airports in the world can boast of multiple hubs.

Enplaned Passenger Market

Perhaps the most critical parameter that illustrates the necessity for a new airport is the enplaned passenger market. (An enplaned passenger is one who gets on a flight, either an origination flight or a connecting flight.)

Table 4-5 identifies the enplaned passengers for individual airlines servicing Denver Stapleton for 1992 and 1993.

Connecting passengers were forecast to decrease about 1 million between 1993 and 1995 before returning to a steady 3.0% per year growth, totaling 8,285,500 in 2000. As a result, the number of connecting passengers is forecast to represent a smaller share (46%) of total enplaned passengers

TABLE 4-5   Enplaned Passengers by Airline, Stapleton International Airport

ENPLANED PASSENGERS	1992	1993
United	6,887,936	7,793,246
United Express[a]	470,841	578,619
	7,358,777	8,371,865
Continental	5,162,812	4,870,861
Continental Express	514,293	532,046
	5,677,105	5,402,907
American Airlines	599,705	563,119
America West Airlines	176,963	156,032
Delta Air Lines	643,644	634,341
MarkAir	2,739	93,648
Northwest Airlines	317,507	320,527
TransWorld Airlines	203,096	182,502
USAir	201,949	197,095
Other	256,226	398,436
	2,401,829	2,545,700
Total	15,437,711	16,320,472

Source: Department of Aviation management records.
[a]Includes Mesa Airlines, Air Wisconsin, Great Lakes Aviation and Westair Airlines.

at the airport in 2000 than in 1993 (50%). Total enplaned passengers at Denver are forecast to increase from 16,320,472 in 1993 to 18,161,000 in 2000—an average increase of 1.6% per year (decreasing slightly from 1993 through 1995, then increasing 2.7% per year after 1995).

The increase in enplaned passengers will necessitate an increase in the number of aircraft departures. Since landing fees are based upon aircraft landed weight, more arrivals and departures will generate more landing fee revenue. Since airport revenue is derived from cargo operations as well as passenger activities, it is important to recognize that enplaned cargo is also expected to increase.

Land Selection[7]

The site selected was a 53-square-mile area 18 miles northeast of Denver's business district. The site would be larger than the Chicago O'Hare and Dallas–Ft. Worth airports combined. Unfortunately, a state law took effect prohibiting political entities from annexing land without the consent of its residents. The land was in Adams County. Before the vote was taken, Adams County and Denver negotiated an agreement limiting noise and requiring the creation of a buffer zone to protect surrounding residents. The agreement also included continuous noise monitoring, as well as limits on such businesses as airport hotels that could be in direct competition with existing services provided in Adams County. The final part of the agreement limited DIA to such businesses as airline maintenance, cargo, small package delivery and other such airport-related activities.

With those agreements in place, Denver annexed 45 square miles and purchased an additional 8 square miles for noise buffer zones. Denver rezoned the buffer area to prohibit residential development within a 65 LDN (level day/night) noise level. LDN is a weighted noise measurement intended to determine perceived noise in both day and night conditions. Adams County enacted even stiffer zoning regulations, calling for no residential development with an LDN noise level of 60.

Most of the airport land embodied two ranches. About 550 people were relocated. The site had overhead power lines and gas wells, which were relocated or abandoned. The site lacked infrastructure development and there were no facilities for providing water, power, sewage disposal or other such services.

Front Range Airport

Located 2.5 miles southeast of DIA is Front Range Airport, which had been developed to relieve Denver's Stapleton Airport of most nonairline traffic

---

7. Adapted from David A. Brown, "Denver Aims for Global Hub Status with New Airport Under Construction," *Aviation Week and Space Technology*, March 11, 1991, p. 44.

operations. As a satellite airport to DIA, Front Range Airport had been offering six aviation business services by 1991:

- Air cargo and air freight, including small-package services (in direct competition with DIA)
- Aircraft manufacturing
- Aircraft repair (in direct competition with DIA)
- Fixed-base operators to service general (and corporate) aviation
- Flight training
- Military maintenance and training

The airport was located on a 4800-acre site and was surrounded by a 12,000-acre industrial park. The airport was owned and operated by Adams County, which had completely different ownership than DIA. By 1991, Front Range Airport had two east-west runways: a 700-foot runway for general aviation use and an 8000-foot runway to be extended to 10,000 feet. By 1992, the general plans called for two more runways to be built, both north-south. The first runway would be 10,000 feet initially with expansion capability to 16,000 feet to support wide-body aircraft. The second runway would be 7000 feet to service general aviation.

Opponents of DIA contended that Front Range Airport could be enlarged significantly, thus reducing pressure on Denver's Stapleton Airport, and that DIA would not be necessary at that time. Proponents of DIA argued that Front Range should be used to relieve pressure on DIA if and when DIA became a major international airport as all expected. Both sides were in agreement that, initially, Front Range Airport would be a competitor to DIA.

Airport Design

The Denver International Airport was based upon a "Home-on-the-Range" design. The city wanted a wide-open entry point for visitors. In the spring of 1991, the city began soliciting bids.

To maintain a distinctive look that would be easily identified by travelers, a translucent tentlike roof was selected. The roof was made of two thicknesses of translucent, Teflon-coated glass fiber material suspended from steel cables hanging from the structural supports. The original plans for the roof called for a conventional design using 800,000 tons of structural steel. The glass fiber roof would require only 30,000 tons of structural steel, thus providing substantial savings on construction costs. The entire roof would permit about 10% of the sunlight to shine through, thus providing an open, outdoors-like atmosphere.

The master plan for the airport called for four concourses, each with a maximum of 60 gates. However, only three concourses would be built initially, and none would be full size. The first, concourse A, would have

32 airline gates and 6 commuter gates. This concourse would be shared by Continental and any future international carriers. Continental had agreed to give up certain gate positions if requested to do so in order to accommodate future international operations. Continental was the only long-haul international carrier, with one daily flight to London. Shorter international flights were to Canada and Mexico.

Concourses B and C would each have 20 gates initially for airline use plus 6 commuter gates. Concourse B would be the United concourse. Concourse C would be for all carriers other than Continental or United.

All three concourses would provide a total of 72 airline gates and 18 commuter gates. This would be substantially less than what the original master plan called for.

Although the master plan identified 60 departure gates for each concourse, cost became an issue. The first set of plans identified 106 departure gates (not counting commuter gates) and was then scaled down to 72 gates. United Airlines originally wanted 45 departure gates but settled for 20. The recession was having its effect.

The original plans called for a train running through a tunnel beneath the terminal building and the concourses. The train would carry 6000 passengers per hour. Road construction on and adjacent to the airport was planned to take one year. Runway construction was planned to take one year but was deliberately scheduled for two years in order to save on construction costs.

The principal benefits of the new airport compared to Stapleton were:

- A significantly *improved airfield configuration* that allowed for triple simultaneous instrument landings in all weather conditions, improved efficiency and safety of airfield operations and reduced taxiway congestion
- *Improved efficiency in the operation of the regional airspace*, which, coupled with the increased capacity of the airfield, was supposed to significantly reduce aircraft delays and airline operating costs both at Denver and systemwide
- *Reduced noise impacts* resulting from a large site that was situated in a relatively unpopulated area
- *A more efficient terminal/concourse/apron layout* that minimized passenger walking distance, maximized the exposure of concessions to passenger flows, provided significantly greater curbside capacity and allowed for the efficient maneuvering of aircraft in and out of gates
- *Improved international facilities* including longer runway lengths for improved stage length capability for international flights and larger Federal Inspection Services (FIS) facilities for greater passenger processing capability
- *Significant expansion capability* of each major functional element of the airport
- *Enhanced efficiency of airline operations* as a result of new baggage-handling, communications, deicing, fueling, mail sorting and other specialty systems

One of the problems with the airport design related to the high wind shears that would exist where the runways were placed. This could eventually become a serious issue.

Project Management

The city of Denver selected two companies to assist in the project management process. The first was Greiner Engineering, an engineering, architecture and airport planning firm. The second company was Morrison-Knudsen Engineering (MKE), a design-construct firm. The city of Denver and Greiner/MKE would function as the project management team (PMT) responsible for schedule coordination, cost control, information management and administration of approximately 100 design contracts, 160 general contractors and more than 2000 subcontractors.

In the selection of architects, it became obvious that there would be a split between those who would operate the airport and the city's aspirations. Airport personnel were more interested in an "easy-to-clean" airport and convinced the city to hire a New Orleans-based architectural firm with whom Stapleton personnel had worked previously. The city wanted a "thing of beauty" rather than an easy-to-clean venture.

In an unusual split of responsibilities, the New Orleans firm was contracted to create standards that would unify the entire airport and to take the design of the main terminal only through schematics and design development, at which point it would be handed off to another firm. This sharing of the wealth with several firms would later prove more detrimental than beneficial.

The New Orleans architectural firm complained that the direction given by airport personnel focused on operational issues rather than aesthetic values.

Furthermore, almost all decisions seemed to be made in reaction to maintenance or technical issues. This created a problem for the design team because the project's requirements specified that the design reflect a signature image for the airport, one that would capture the uniqueness of Denver and Colorado.

The New Orleans team designed a stepped-roof profile supported by an exposed truss system over a large central atrium, thus resembling the structure of train sheds. The intent was to bring the image of railroading, which was responsible for Denver's early growth, into the jet age.

The mayor, city council and others were concerned that the design did not express a $2 billion project. A blue-ribbon commission was formed to study the matter. The city council eventually approved the design.

Financial analysis of the terminal indicated that the roof design would increase the cost of the project by $48 million and would push the project off schedule. A second architectural firm was hired. The final design was a peaked roof with Teflon-coated fabric designed to bring out the image of the Rocky Mountains. The second architectural firm had the additional responsibility to take the project from design development through to construction. The cost savings from the new design was so substantial that the city upgraded the floor finish in the terminal and doubled the size of the parking structure to 12,000 spaces.

The effectiveness of the project management team was being questioned. The PMT failed to sort out the differences between the city's aspirations and the maintenance orientation of the operators. It failed to detect the cost and constructability issues with the first design even though both PMT partners had vast in-house expertise. The burden of responsibility was falling on the shoulders of the architects. The PMT also did not appear to be aware that the first design may not have met the project's standards.

Throughout the design battle, no one heard from the airlines. Continental and United controlled 80% of the flights at Stapleton. Yet the airlines refused to participate in the design effort, hoping the project would be canceled. The city ordered the design teams to proceed for bids without any formal input from the users.

With a recession looming in the wings and Continental fighting for survival, the city needed the airlines to sign on. To entice the airlines to participate, the city agreed to a stunning range of design changes while assuring the bond rating agencies that the 1993 opening date would be kept. Continental convinced Denver to move the international gates away from the north side of the main terminal to terminal A and to build a bridge from the main terminal to terminal A. This duplicated the function of a below-ground people-mover system. A basement was added the full length of the concourses. Service cores, located between gates, received a second level.

United's changes were more significant. It widened concourse B by 8 feet to accommodate two moving walkways in each direction. It added a second level of service cores and had the roof redesigned to provide a clerestory of natural light.

Most important, United wanted a destination-coded vehicle (DCV) baggage-handling system where bags could be transferred between gates in less than 10 minutes, thus supporting short turnaround times. The DCV was to be on concourse B (United) only. Within a few weeks thereafter, DIA proposed that the baggage-handling system be extended to the entire airport. Yet even with these changes in place, United and Continental *still* did not sign a firm agreement with DIA, thus keeping bond interest expense at a higher than anticipated level. Some people contended that United and Continental were holding DIA hostage.

From a project management perspective, there was no question that disaster was on the horizon. Nobody knew what to do about the DCV system. The risks were unknown. Nobody realized the complexity of the system, especially the software requirements. By one account, the launch date should have been delayed by at least two years. The contract for DCV hadn't been awarded yet, and terminal construction was already underway. Everyone wanted to know why the design (and construction) was not delayed until after the airlines had signed on. How could DIA install and maintain the terminal's baseline design without having a design for the baggage-handling system? Everyone felt that what they were now building would have to be ripped apart.

There were going to be massive scope changes. DIA management persisted in its belief that the airport would open on time. Work in process was now $130 million per month. Acceleration costs, because of the scope changes, would be $30–$40 million. Three shifts were running at DIA with massive overtime. People were getting burned out to the point where they couldn't continue.

To reduce paperwork and maintain the schedule, architects became heavily involved during the construction phase, which was highly unusual. The PMT seemed to be abdicating control to the architects who would be responsible for coordination. The trust that had developed during the early phases began evaporating.

Even the car rental companies got into the act. They balked at the fees for their in-terminal location and said that servicing within the parking structures was inconvenient. They demanded and finally received a separate campus. Passengers would now be forced to take shuttle buses out of the terminal complex to rent or return vehicles.

Baggage-Handling System

DIA's $200 million baggage-handling system was designed to be state of the art. Conventional baggage-handling systems are manual. Each airline operates its own system. DIA opted to buy a single system and lease it back to the airlines. In effect, it would be a one-baggage-system-fits-all configuration.

The system would contain 100 computers, 56 laser scanners, conveyor belts and thousands of motors. As designed, the system would contain 400 fiberglass carts, each carrying a single suitcase through 22 miles of steel tracks. Operating at 20 miles per hour, the system could deliver 60,000 bags per hour from dozens of gates. United was worried that passengers would have to wait for luggage since several of their gates were more than a mile from the main terminal. The system design was for the luggage to go from the plane to the carousel in 8–10 minutes. The luggage would reach the carousel before the passengers.

The baggage-handling system would be centered on track-mounted cars propelled by linear induction motors. The cars slow down, but don't stop, as a conveyor ejects bags onto their platform. During the induction process, a scanner reads the bar-coded label and transmits the data through a programmable logic controller to a radio frequency identification tag on a passing car. At this point, the car knows the destination of the bag it is carrying, as does the computer software that routes the car to its destination. To illustrate the complexity of the situation, consider 4000 taxicabs in a major city, all without drivers, being controlled by a computer through the streets of a city.

Early Risk Analysis

Construction began in 1989 without a signed agreement from Continental and United. By March 1991, the bidding process was in full swing for the main terminal, concourses and tunnel. Preliminary risk analysis involved three areas:

- **Cost:** The grading of the terminal area was completed at about $5 million under budget and the grading of the first runway was completed at about $1.8 million under budget. This led management to believe that the original construction cost estimates were accurate. Also, many of the construction bids being received were below the city's own estimates.
- **Human resources:** The economic recession hit Denver a lot harder than the rest of the nation. DIA was at that time employing about 500 construction workers. By late 1992, it was anticipated that 6000 construction workers would be needed. Although more than 3000 applications were on file, there remained the question of available, qualified labor. If the recession were to be prolonged, then the lack of qualified suppliers could be an issue as well.
- **Weather:** Bad weather, particularly in the winter, was considered the greatest risk to the schedule. Fortunately, the winters of 1989–1990 and 1990–1991 were relatively mild, which gave promise to future mild winters. Actually, more time was lost due to bad weather in the summer of 1990 than in either of the two previous winters.

March 1991

By early March 1991, Denver had already issued more than $900 million in bonds to begin construction of the new airport. Denver planned to issue another $500 million in bonds the following month. Standard & Poor's Corporation lowered the rating on the DIA bonds from BBB to BBB–, just a notch above the junk-grade rating. This could prove to be extremely costly to DIA because any downgrading in bond quality ratings would force DIA to offer higher yields on their new bond offerings, thus increasing their yearly interest expense.

Denver was in the midst of an upcoming mayoral race. Candidates were calling for the postponement of the construction, not only because of the lower ratings, but also because Denver *still* did not have a firm agreement with either Continental or United Airlines that they would use the new airport. The situation became more intense because three months earlier, in

December of 1990, Continental had filed for bankruptcy protection under Chapter 11. Fears existed that Continental might drastically reduce the size of its hub at DIA or even pull out altogether.

Denver estimated that cancelation or postponement of the new airport would be costly. The city had $521 million in contracts that could not be canceled. Approximately $22 million had been spent in debt service for the land, and $38 million in interest on the $470 million in bond money was already spent. The city would have to default on more than $900 million in bonds if it could not collect landing fees from the new airport. The study also showed that a two-year delay would increase the total cost by $2 billion to $3 billion and increase debt service to $340 million per year. It now appeared that the point of no return was at hand.

Fortunately for DIA, Moody's Investors Service, Inc. did *not* lower its rating on the $1 billion outstanding of airport bonds. Moody's confirmed its conditional BAA1 rating, which was slightly higher than the S & P rating of BBB–. Moody's believed that the DIA effort was a strong one and that even at depressed airline traffic levels, DIA would be able to service its debt for the scaled-back airport. Had both Moody's and S & P lowered their ratings together, DIA's future might have been in jeopardy.

April 1991

Denver issued $500 million in serial revenue bonds with a maximum yield of 9.185% for bonds maturing in 2023. A report by Fitch Investors Service estimated that the airport was ahead of schedule and 7% below budget. The concerns of the investor community seemed to have been tempered despite the bankruptcy filing of Continental Airlines. However, there was still concern that no formal agreement existed between DIA and either United Airlines or Continental Airlines.

May 1991

The city of Denver and United Airlines finally reached a tentative agreement. United would use 45 of the potential 90–100 gates at concourse B. This would be a substantial increase from the 26 gates DIA had originally thought that United would require. The 50% increase in gates would also add 2000 reservations jobs. United also expressed an interest in building a $1 billion maintenance facility at DIA employing 6000 people.

United stated later that the agreement did not constitute a firm commitment but was contingent upon legislative approval of a tax incentive package of $360 million over 30 years plus $185 million in financing and $23 million in tax exemptions. United would decide by the summer in which city the maintenance facility would be located. United reserved the right to renegotiate the hub agreement if DIA was not chosen as the site for the maintenance facility.

Some people believed that United had delayed signing a formal agreement until it was in a strong bargaining position. With Continental in bankruptcy and DIA beyond the point of no return, United was in a favorable position to demand tax incentives of $200 million in order to keep its hub in Denver and build a maintenance facility. The state legislature would have to be involved in approving the incentives. United Airlines ultimately located the $1 billion maintenance facility at the Indianapolis Airport.

August 1991

Hotel developers expressed concern about building at DIA, which is 26 miles from downtown compared to 8 miles from Stapleton to downtown Denver. DIA officials initially planned for a 1000-room hotel attached to the airport terminal, with another 300–500 rooms adjacent to the terminal. The 1000-room hotel had been scaled back to 500–700 rooms and was not likely to be ready when the airport was scheduled to open in October 1993. Developers had expressed resistance to building close to DIA unless industrial and office parks were also built near the airport. Even though ample land existed, developers were putting hotel development on the back burner until after 1993.

November 1991

Federal Express and United Parcel Service (UPS) planned to move cargo operations to the smaller Front Range Airport rather than to DIA. The master plan for DIA called for cargo operations to be at the northern edge of DIA, thus increasing the time and cost for deliveries to Denver. Shifting operations to Front Range Airport would certainly have been closer to Denver but would have alienated northern Adams County cities that counted on an economic boost in their areas. Moving cargo operations would have been in violation of the original agreement between Adams County and Denver for the annexation of the land for DIA.

The cost of renting at DIA was estimated at $0.75 per square foot, compared to $0.25 per square foot at Front Range. DIA would have higher landing fees of $2.68 per 1000 pounds compared to $2.15 for Front Range. UPS demanded a cap on landing fees at DIA if another carrier were to go out of business. Under the UPS proposal, area landholders and businesses would set up a fund to compensate DIA if landing fees were to exceed the cap. Cargo carriers at Stapleton were currently paying $2 million in landing fees and rental of facilities per year.

As the "dog fight" over cargo operations continued, the FAA issued a report calling for cargo operations to be colocated with passenger operations at the busier metropolitan airports. This included both full cargo carriers as well as passenger cargo (i.e., "belly cargo") carriers. Proponents of Front Range argued that the report didn't preclude the use of Front Range because of its proximity to DIA.

December 1991

United Airlines formally agreed to a 30-year lease for 45 gates at concourse B. With the firm agreement in place, the DIA revenue bonds shot up in price almost $30 per $1000 bond. Earlier in the year, Continental signed a five-year lease agreement.

Other airlines also agreed to service DIA. Table 4-6 sets forth the airlines that either executed use and lease agreements for, or indicated an interest in leasing, the 20 gates on concourse C on a first-preferential-use basis.

January 1992

BAE was selected to design and build the baggage-handling system. The airport had been under construction for three years before BAE was brought on board. BAE agreed to do eight years of work in two years to meet the October 1993 opening date.

June 1992

DIA officials awarded a $24.4 million contract for the new airport's telephone services to U.S. West Communication Services. The officials of DIA had considered controlling its own operations through shared tenant service, which would allow the airport to act as its own telephone company. All calls would be routed through an airport-owned computer switch. By grouping tenants together into a single shared entity, the airport would be in a position to negotiate discounts with long-distance providers, thus enabling cost savings to be passed on to the tenants.

TABLE 4-6   Airline Agreements

AIRLINE	TERM (YEARS)	NUMBER OF GATES
American Airlines	5	3
Delta Air Lines[a]	5	4
Frontier Airlines	10	2
MarkAir	10	5
Northwest Airlines	10	2
TransWorld Airlines	10	2
USAir[a]	5	2
Total		20

[a]The city has entered into Use and Lease Agreements with these airlines. The USAir lease is for one gate on concourse C and USAir has indicated its interest in leasing a second gate on concourse C.

By one estimate, the city would generate $3 million to $8 million annually in new, nontax net revenue by owning and operating its own telecommunication network. Unfortunately, DIA officials did not feel that sufficient time existed for them to operate their own system. The city of Denver was unhappy over this lost income.

September 1992

By September 1992, the city had received $501 million in FAA grants and $2.3 billion in bonds with interest rates of 9.0–9.5% in the first issue to 6% in the latest issue. The decrease in interest rates due to the recession was helpful to DIA. The rating agencies also increased the city's bond rating one notch.

The FAA permitted Denver to charge a $3 departure tax at Stapleton with the income earmarked for construction of DIA. Denver officials estimated that over 34 years the tax would generate $2.3 billion.

The cities bordering the northern edge of DIA (where the cargo operations were to be located) teamed up with Adams County to file lawsuits against DIA in its attempt to relocate cargo operations to the southern perimeter of DIA. This relocation would appease the cargo carriers and hopefully end the year-long battle with Front Range Airport. The Adams County commissioner contended that relocation would violate the Clean Air Act and the National Environmental Policy Act and would be a major deviation from the original airport plan approved by the FAA.

October 1992

The city issued $261 million of Airport Revenue Bonds for the construction of facilities for United Airlines. (See Appendix A at the end of this case.)

March 1993

The city of Denver announced that the launch date for DIA would be pushed back to December 18 rather than the original October 30 date in order to install and test all of the new equipment. The city wanted to delay the opening until late in the first quarter of 1994 but deemed it too costly because the airport's debt would have to be paid without an adequate stream of revenue. The interest on the bond debt was now at $500,000 per day.

The delay to December 18 angered the cargo carriers. This would be their busiest time of the year, usually twice their normal cargo levels, and a complete revamping of their delivery service would be needed. The Washington-based Air Freight Association urged the city to allow the cargo carriers to fly out of Stapleton through the holiday period.

By March 1993, Federal Express, Airborne Express and UPS (reluctantly) had agreed to house operations at DIA after the city pledged to build facilities for them at the south end of the airport. Negotiations were also underway with Emery Worldwide and Burlington Air Express. The "belly" carriers, Continental and United, had already signed on.

UPS had wanted to create a hub at Front Range Airport. If Front Range Airport were a cargo-only facility, it would free up UPS from competing with passenger traffic for runway access even though both Front Range and DIA were in the same air traffic control pattern. UPS stated that it would not locate a regional hub at DIA. This would mean the loss of a major development project that would have attracted other businesses that relied on UPS delivery.

For UPS to build a regional hub at Front Range would have required the construction of a control tower and enlargement of the runways, both requiring federal funds. The FAA refused to free up funds for Front Range, largely due to a lawsuit by United Airlines and environmental groups.

United's lawsuit had an ulterior motive. Adams County officials repeatedly stated that they had no intention of building passenger terminals at Front Range. However, once federal funds were given to Front Range, a commercial passenger plane could not be prevented from setting up shop in Front Range. The threat to United were the low-cost carriers such as Southwest Airlines. Because costs were fixed, fewer passengers traveling through DIA meant less profits for the airlines. United simply did not want any airline activities removed from DIA!

August 1993

Plans for a train to connect downtown Denver to DIA were underway. A $450,000 feasibility study and federal environmental assessment were being conducted, with the results due November 30, 1993. Union Pacific had spent $350,000 preparing a design for the new track, which could be constructed in 13–16 months.

The major hurdle would be the financing, which was estimated between $70 million and $120 million, based upon hourly trips or 20-minute trips. The more frequent the trips, the higher the cost.

The feasibility study also considered the possibility of baggage check-in at each of the stops. This would require financial support and management assistance from the airlines.

September 1993

Denver officials disclosed plans for transferring airport facilities and personnel from Stapleton to DIA. The move would be stage managed by Larry Sweat, a retired military officer who had coordinated troop movements for Operation Desert Shield. Bechtel Corporation would be responsible for directing the transport and setup of machinery, computer systems, furniture and service equipment, all of which had to be accomplished overnight since the airport had to be operational again in the morning.

October 1993

DIA, which was already $1.1 billion over budget, was to be delayed again. The new opening date would be March 1994. The city blamed the airlines for the delays, citing the numerous scope changes required. Even the fire safety system hadn't been completed.

Financial estimates became troublesome. Airlines would have to charge a $15- per-person tax, the largest in the nation. Fees and rent charged the airlines would triple from $74 million at Stapleton to $247 million at DIA.

January 1994

Front Range Airport and DIA were considering the idea of being designated as one system by the FAA. Front Range could legally be limited to cargo only. This would also prevent low-cost carriers from paying lower landing fees and rental space at Front Range.

February 1994

Southwest Airlines, being a low-cost no-frills carrier, said that it would not service DIA. Southwest wanted to keep its airport fees below $3 a passenger. Current projections indicated that DIA would have to charge between $15 and $20 per passenger in order to service its debt. This was based on a March 9 opening day.

Continental announced that it would provide a limited number of low-frill service flights in and out of Denver. Furthermore, Continental said that because of the high landing fees, it would cancel 23% of its flights through Denver and relocate some of its maintenance facilities.

United Airlines expected its operating cost to be $100 million more per year at DIA than at Stapleton. With the low-cost carriers either pulling out or reducing service to Denver, United was under less pressure to lower airfares.

March 1994

The city of Denver announced the fourth delay in opening DIA, from March 9 to May 15. The cost of the delay, $100 million, would be paid mostly by United and Continental. As of March, only concourse C, which housed the carriers other than United and Continental, was granted a temporary certificate of occupancy (TCO) by the city.

As the finger-pointing began, blame for this delay was given to the baggage-handling system, which was experiencing late changes, restricted access flow and a slowdown in installation and testing. A test by Continental Airlines indicated that only 39% of baggage was delivered to the correct location. Other problems also existed. As of December 31, 1993, there were 2100 design changes. The city of Denver had taken out insurance for construction errors and omissions. The city's insurance claims cited failure to coordinate design of the ductwork with ceiling and structure, failure to properly design the storm draining systems for the terminal to prevent freezing, failure to coordinate mechanical and structural designs of the terminal and failure to design an adequate subfloor support system.

Consultants began identifying potential estimating errors in DIA's operations. The runways at DIA were six times longer than the runways at Stapleton, but DIA had purchased only 25% more equipment. DIA's cost projections would be $280 million for debt service and $130 million for operating costs, for a total of $410 million per year. The total cost at Stapleton was $120 million per year.

April 1994

Denver International Airport began having personnel problems. According to DIA's personnel officer, Linda Rubin Royer, moving 17 miles away from its present site was creating serious problems. One of the biggest issues was the additional 20-minute drive that employees had to bear. To resolve this problem, she proposed a car/van pooling scheme and tried to get the city bus company to transport people to and from the new airport. There was also the problem of transferring employees to similar jobs elsewhere if they truly disliked working at DIA. The scarcity of applicants wanting to work at DIA was creating a problem as well.

May 1994

Standard and Poor's Corporation lowered the rating on DIA's outstanding debt to the noninvestment grade of BB, citing the problems with the baggage-handling system and no immediate cure in sight. Denver was currently paying $33.3 million per month to service debt. Stapleton was generating $17 million per month and United Airlines had agreed to pay $8.8 million in cash for the next three months only. That left a current shortfall of $7.5 million each month that the city would have to fund. Beginning in August 1994, the city would be burdened with $16.3 million each month.

BAE Automated Systems personnel began to complain that they were pressured into doing the impossible. The only other system of this type in the world was in Frankfurt, Germany. That system required six years to install and two years to debug. BAE was asked to do it all in two years.

BAE underestimated the complexity of the routing problems. During trials, cars crashed into one another, luggage was dropped at the wrong location, cars that were needed to carry luggage were routed to empty waiting pens and some cars traveled in the wrong direction. Sensors became coated with dirt, throwing the system out of alignment, and luggage was dumped prematurely because of faulty latches, jamming cars against the side of a tunnel. By the end of May, BAE was conducting a worldwide search for consultants who could determine what was going wrong and how long it would take to repair the system.

BAE conducted an end-of-month test with 600 bags. Outbound (terminal to plane), the sort accuracy was 94% and inbound the accuracy was 98%. The system had a zero downtime for both inbound and outbound testing. The specification requirements called for 99.5% accuracy.

BAE hired three technicians from Germany's Logplan, which helped solve similar problems with the automated system at Frankfurt, Germany. With no opening date set, DIA contemplated opening the east side of the airport for general aviation and air cargo flights. That would begin generating at least some revenue.

June 1994

The cost for DIA was now approaching $3.7 billion and the jokes about DIA appeared everywhere. One common joke was that when you fly to Denver, you will have to stop in Chicago to pick up your luggage. Other common jokes included the abbreviation DIA. Appendix B provides a list of 152 of the jokes.

The people who did not appear to be laughing at these jokes were the concessionaires, including about 50 food service operators, who had been forced to rehire, retrain and reequip at considerable expense. Several small businesses were forced to call it quits because of the eight-month delay. Red ink was flowing despite the fact that the $45/ft^2 rent would not have to be paid until DIA officially opened. Several of the concessionaires had requested that the rent be cut by $10/ft^2 for the first six months or so, after the airport opened. A merchant's association was formed at DIA to fight for financial compensation.

Project's Work Breakdown Structure (WBS)
The city had managed the design and construction of the project by grouping design and construction activities into seven categories, or *areas:*

Area 0	Program management/preliminary design
Area 1	Site development
Area 2	Roadways and on-grade parking
Area 3	Airfield
Area 4	Terminal complex
Area 5	Utilities and specialty systems
Area 6	Other

Note: Since the fall of 1992, the project budget had increased by $224 million (from $2700 million to $2924 million), principally as a result of scope changes.

- Structural modifications to the terminal buildings (primarily in the land-side terminal and concourse B) to accommodate the automated baggage system
- Changes in the interior configuration of concourse B
- Increases in the scope of various airline tenant finished, equipment and systems, particularly in concourse B
- Grading, drainage, utilities and access costs associated with the relocation of air cargo facilities to the south side of the airport
- Increases in the scope and costs of communication and control systems, particularly premises wiring
- Increases in the costs of runway, taxiway and apron paving and change orders as a result of changing specifications for the runway lighting system
- Increased program management costs because of schedule delays

Yet even with all of these design changes, the airport was ready to open except for the baggage-handling system.

July 1994

The Securities and Exchange Commission (SEC) disclosed that DIA was 1 of 30 municipal bond issuers that were under investigation for improper contributions to the political campaigns of Pena and his successor, Mayor Wellington Webb. Citing public records, Pena was said to have received $13,900 and Webb's campaign fund increased by $96,000. The SEC said that the contributions may have been in exchange for the right to underwrite DIA's municipal bond offerings. Those under investigation included Merrill Lynch, Goldman Sachs & Co. and Lehman Brothers, Inc.

August 1994

Continental confirmed that as of November 1, 1994, it would reduce its flights out of Denver from 80 to 23. At one time, Continental had 200 flights out of Denver.

Denver announced that it expected to sell $200 million in new bonds. Approximately $150 million would be used to cover future interest payments on existing DIA debt and to replenish interest and other money paid due to the delayed opening.

Approximately $50 million would be used to fund the construction of an interim baggage-handling system of the more conventional tug-and-conveyor type. The interim system would require 500–600 people rather than the 150–160 people needed for the computerized system. Early estimates said that the conveyor belt/tug-and-cart system would be at least as fast as the system at Stapleton and would be built using proven technology and off-the-shelf parts. However, modifications would have to be made to both the terminal and the concourses.

United Airlines asked for a 30-day delay in approving the interim system for fear that it would not be able to satisfy the requirements. The original lease agreement with DIA and United stipulated that on opening day there would be a fully operational automated baggage-handling system in place. United had 284 flights a day out of Denver and had to be certain that the interim system would support a 25-minute turnaround time for passenger aircraft.

The city's district attorney's office said it was investigating accusations of falsified test data and shoddy workmanship at DIA. Reports had come in regarding fraudulent construction and contracting practices. No charges were filed at that time.

DIA began repairing cracks, holes and fissures that had emerged in the runways, ramps and taxiways. Officials said that the cracks were part of the normal settling problems and might require maintenance for years to come.

United Airlines agreed to invest $20 million and act as the project manager to the baggage-handling system at concourse B. DIA picked February 28, 1995, as the new opening date as long as either the primary or secondary baggage-handling system was operational.

United Benefits from Continental's Downsizing

United had been building up its Denver hub since 1991, increasing its total departures 9% in 1992, 22% in 1993 and 9% in the first six months of 1994. Stapleton is United's second largest connecting hub after Chicago O'Hare (ORD), ahead of San Francisco (SFO), Los Angeles (LAX) and Washington Dulles (IAD) International Airports, as shown in Figure 4-5.

In response to the downsizing by Continental, United is expected to absorb a significant portion of Continental's Denver traffic by means of increased load factors and increased service (i.e., capacity), particularly in larger markets where significant voids in service might be left by Continental. United served 24 of the 28 cities served by Continental from Stapleton in June 1994, with about 79% more total available seats to those cities—23,937 seats provided by United compared with 13,400 seats provided by Continental. During 1993, United's average load factor from Denver was 63%, indicating that, with its existing service and available capacity, United had the ability to absorb many of the passengers abandoned by Continental. In addition, United had announced plans to increase service at Denver to 300 daily flights by the end of the calendar year.

As a result of its downsizing in Denver, Continental was forecasted to lose more than 3.9 million enplaned passengers from 1993 to 1995—a total decrease of 80%. However, this decrease was expected to be largely offset by the forecasted 2.2 million increase in enplaned passengers by United and 1.0 million by the other airlines, resulting in a total of 15,877,000 enplaned passengers at Denver in 1995. As discussed earlier, it was assumed that, in addition to a continuation of historical growth, United and the other airlines would pick up much of the traffic abandoned by Continental

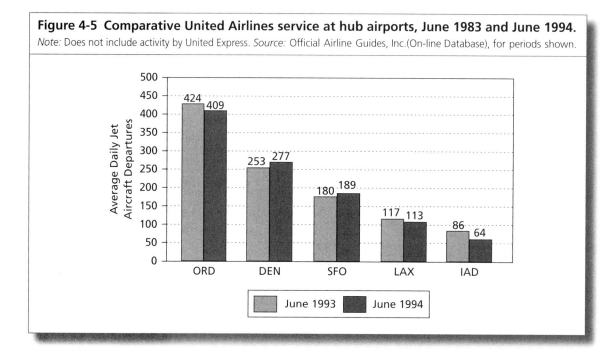

Figure 4-5 Comparative United Airlines service at hub airports, June 1983 and June 1994.

Note: Does not include activity by United Express. *Source:* Official Airline Guides, Inc.(On-line Database), for periods shown.

through a combination of added service, larger average aircraft size and increased load factors.

From 1995 to 2000, the increase in total enplaned passengers is based on growth rates of 2.5% per year in originating passengers and 3.0% per year in connecting passengers. Between 1995 and 2000, United's emerging dominance at the airport (with almost twice the number of passengers of all other airlines combined) should result in somewhat higher fare levels in the Denver markets and therefore may dampen traffic growth. As shown in Figure 4-6, of the 18.2 million forecasted enplaned passengers in 2000, United and United Express together are forecasted to account for 70% of total passengers at the airport—up from about 51% in 1993—while Continental's share, including GP Express, is forecasted to be less than 8%—down from about 33% in 1993.

Total connecting passengers at Stapleton increased from about 6.1 million in 1990 to about 8.2 million in 1993—an average increase of about 10% per year. The number of connecting passengers was forecast to decrease in 1994 and 1995 as a result of the downsizing by Continental and then return to steady growth of 3.0% per year through 2000, reflecting expected growth in passenger traffic nationally and a stable market share by United

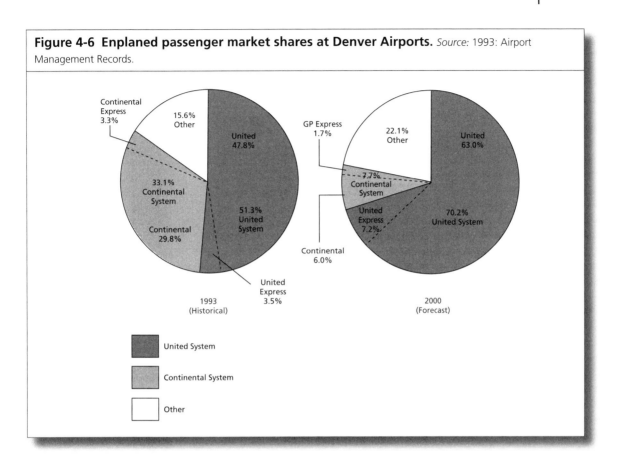

Figure 4-6 Enplaned passenger market shares at Denver Airports. *Source:* 1993: Airport Management Records.

in Denver. Airline market share of connecting passengers in 1993 and 1995 is shown in Figure 4-7.

September 1994

Denver began discussions with cash-strapped MarkAir of Alaska to begin service at DIA. For an undercapitalized carrier, the prospects of tax breaks, favorable rents and a $30 million guaranteed city loan were enticing.

DIA officials estimated an $18-per-person charge on opening day. Plans to allow only cargo carriers and general aviation to begin operations at DIA were canceled.

Total construction cost for the main terminal exceeded $455 million (including the parking structure and the airport office building). See Table 4-7.

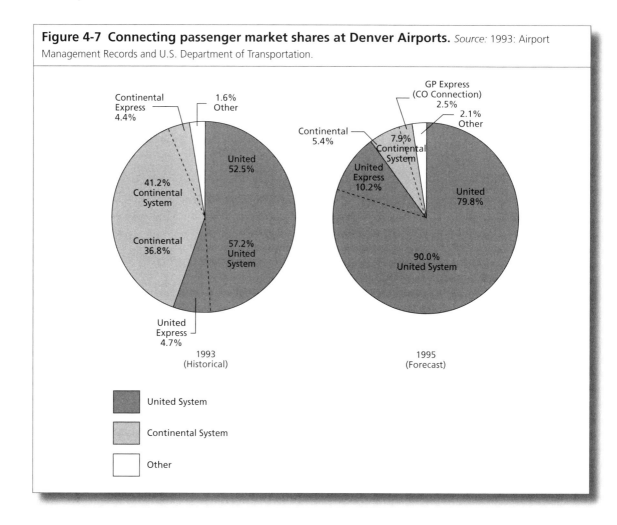

Figure 4-7 Connecting passenger market shares at Denver Airports. *Source:* 1993: Airport Management Records and U.S. Department of Transportation.

October 1994

A federal grand jury convened to investigate faulty workmanship and falsified records at DIA. The faulty workmanship had resulted in falling ceilings, buckling walls and collapsing floors.

November 1994

The baggage-handling system was working, but only in segments. Frustration still existed in not being able to get the whole system to work at the same time. The problem appeared to be with the software required to get computers to talk to computers. The fact that a mere software failure

TABLE 4-7   Total Construction Costs for Denver Airport

General site expenses, commission	$ 38,667,967
Sitework, building excavations	15,064,817
Concrete	89,238,296
Masonry	5,501,608
Metals	40,889,411
Carpentry	3,727,408
Thermal, moisture protection	8,120,907
Doors and windows	13,829,336
Finishes	37,025,019
Specialties	2,312,691
Building equipment	227,720
Furnishings	3,283,852
Special construction	39,370,072
Conveying systems	23,741,336
Mechanical	60,836,566
Electrical	73,436,575
Total	$455,273,581

could hold up Denver's new airport for more than a year put in question the project's risk management program.

Jerry Waddles was the risk manager for Denver. He left that post to become risk manager for the State of Colorado. Eventually the city found an acting risk manager, Molly Austin Flaherty, to replace Mr. Waddles, but for the most part, DIA construction over the previous several months had continued without a full-time risk manager.

The failure of the baggage-handling system had propelled DIA into newspaper headlines around the country. The SEC had launched a probe into whether Denver officials had deliberately deceived bondholders about how equipment malfunctions would affect the December 19, 1993, opening. The allegations were made by Denver's KCNC-TV. Internal memos indicated that in the summer of 1993 city engineers believed it would take at least until March 1994 to get the system working. However, Mayor Wellington Webb did not announce the delayed opening until October 1993. The SEC was investigating whether the last postponement misled investors holding $3 billion in airport bonds.

Under a new agreement, the city agreed to pay BAE an additional $35 million for modifications *if* the system was working for United Airlines by February 28, 1995. BAE would then have until August 1995 to complete the rest of the sys-tem for the other tenants. If the system was not operational by February 28, the city could withhold payment of the $35 million.

BAE lodged a $40 million claim against the city, alleging that the city caused the delay by changing the system's baseline configuration after the April 1, 1992, deadline. The city filed a $90 million counterclaim, blaming BAE for the delays.

The lawsuits were settled out of court when BAE agreed to pay $12,000 a day in liquidated damages dating from December 19, 1993, to February 28, 1995, or approximately $5 million. The city agreed to pay BAE $6.5 million to cover some invoices submitted by BAE for work already done to repair the system.

Under its DIA construction contract, BAE's risks were limited. BAE's liability for consequential damages resulting from its failure to complete the baggage-handling system on time was capped at $5 million. BAE had no intention of being held liable for changes to the system. The system as it was at the time was not the system that BAE had been hired to install.

Additional insurance policies also existed. Builder's risk policies generally pay damages caused by defective parts or materials, but so far none of the parts used to construct the system had been defective. BAE was also covered for design errors or omissions. The unknown risk at that point was who would be responsible if the system worked for concourse B (i.e., United) but then failed when it was expanded to cover all concourses.

A study was underway to determine the source of respiratory problems suffered by workers at the construction site. The biggest culprit appeared to be the use of concrete in a confined space.

The city and DIA were also protected from claims filed by vendors whose businesses were put on hold because of the delays under a hold-harmless agreement in the contracts. However, the city had offered to permit the concessionaires to charge higher fees and also to extend their leases for no charge to make up for lost income due to the delays.

December 1994

The designer of the baggage-handling system was asked to reexamine the number of bags per minute that the BAE system was required to accommodate as per the specifications. The contract called for departing luggage to concourse A to be delivered at a peak rate of 90 bags per minute. The designer estimated peak demand at 25 bags per minute. Luggage from concourse A was contracted for at 223 bags per minute but, again, the designer calculated peak demand at a lower rate of 44 bags per minute.

Airport Debt

By December 1994, DIA was more than $3.4 billion in debt, as shown in Table 4-8.

Airport Revenue

Airports generally have two types of contracts with their tenants. The first type is the residual contract where the carriers guarantee that the airport will remain solvent. Under this contract, the carriers absorb the majority of the risk. The airport maintains the right to increase rents and landing fees to cover operating expenses and debt coverage. The second type of contract is the compensatory contract where the airport is at risk. DIA has a residual contract with its carriers.

Airports generate revenue from several sources. The most common breakdown includes landing fees and rent from the following entities: airline carriers, passenger facilities, rental car agencies, concessionary stores, food and beverage services, retail shops and parking garages. Retail shops and other concessionary stores also pay a percent of sales.

Airline Costs per Enplaned Passenger

Revenues derived from the airlines are often expressed on a per-enplaned-passenger basis. The average airline cost per enplaned passenger at Stapleton in 1993 was $5.02. However, this amount excludes costs related to major investments in terminal facilities made by United Airlines in the mid-1980s and, therefore, understates the true historical airline cost per passenger.

TABLE 4-8 **Outstanding Debt at Denver Airport**	
Series 1984 bonds	$ 103,875,000
Series 1985 bonds	175,930,000
Series 1990A bonds	700,003,843
Series 1991A bonds	500,003,523
Series 1991D bonds	600,001,391
Series 1992A bonds	253,180,000
Series 1992B bonds	315,000,000
Series 1992C bonds	392,160,000
Series 1992D–G bonds	135,000,000
Series 1994A bonds	257,000,000
Total	$3,432,153,757

TABLE 4-9	Total Average Airline Costs per Enplaned Passenger	
YEAR	**CURRENT DOLLARS**	**1990 DOLLARS**
1995	18.15	14.92
2000	17.20	11.62

Average airline costs per enplaned passenger at the airport in 1995 and 2000 are forecast to be as shown in Table 4-9.

The forecasted airline costs per enplaned passenger at the airport are considerably higher than costs at Stapleton today and the highest of any major airport in the United States. (The cost per enplaned passenger at Cleveland Hopkins is $7.50.) The relatively high airline cost per passenger is attributable, in part, to:

1. The unusually large amount of tenant finishes, equipment and systems costs being financed as part of the project relative to other airport projects
2. Delayed costs incurred since the original opening date for purposes of the plan of financing (January 1, 1994)

The city estimates that, as a result of the increased capacity and efficiency of the airfield, operation of the airport will result in annual delay savings to the airlines of $50 million to $100 million per year (equivalent to about $3 to $6 per enplaned passenger) and other advanced technology and systems incorporated into the design of the airport will result in further operational savings. In the final analysis, the cost effectiveness of operating at the airport is a judgment that must be made by the individual airlines in deciding to serve the Denver market.

It is assumed for the purposes of this analysis that the city and the airlines will resolve the current disputes regarding cost allocation procedures and responsibility for delay costs and the airlines will pay rates generally in accordance with the procedures of the use and lease agreements as followed by the city and as summarized in the accompanying exhibits.

February 28, 1995

The airline opened as planned on February 28, 1995. However, several problems became apparent. First, the baggage-handling system did have "bad days." Passengers traveling to and from Denver felt more comfortable carrying bags than having them transferred by the computerized baggage-handling system. Large queues began to form at the end of the escalators in the main terminal going down to the concourse trains. The trains were not running frequently enough, and the number of cars in each train did not appear to be sufficient to handle the necessary passenger traffic.

The author flew from Dallas–Ft. Worth to Denver in 1 hour and 45 minutes. It then took 1 hour and 40 minutes to catch the airport shuttles (which stop at all the hotels) and arrive at the appropriate hotel in downtown Denver. Passengers began to balk at the discomfort of the remote rental car facilities, the additional $3 tax per day for each rental car and the fact that the nearest gas station was 15 miles away. How does one return a rental car with a full tank of gas?

Departing passengers estimated it would take 2 hours to drive to the airport from downtown Denver, unload luggage, park their automobile, check in and take the train to the concourse.

Faults in the concourse construction were becoming apparent. Tiles that were supposed to be 5/8 inches thick were found to be 1/2 inch thick. Tiles began to crack. During rainy weather, rain began seeping in through the ceiling.

APPENDIX A[8]

Municipal Bond Prospectus
$261,415,000
City and County of Denver, Colorado
6.875% Special Facilities Airport Revenue Bonds
(United Airlines Project)
Series 1992A
Date: October 1, 1992
Due: October 1, 2032
Rating: Standard & Poor's BBB–
Moody's BAA2

Introduction

This official statement is provided to furnish information in connection with the sale by the City and County of Denver, Colorado (the "City") of 6.875% Special Facilities Airport Revenue Bonds (United Airlines Project) series 1992A in the aggregate principle [sic] amount of $261,415,000 (the "Bonds"). The bonds will be dated, mature, bear interest and be subject to redemption prior to maturity as described herein.

The Bonds will be issued pursuant to an Ordinance of the City and County of Denver, Colorado (the "Ordinance").

The proceeds received by the City from the sale of the Bonds will be used to acquire, construct, equip, or improve (or a reimbursement of

---

8. Only excerpts from the prospectus are included here.

payments for the acquisition, construction, equipping, or improvement of) certain terminals, Concourse B, aircraft maintenance, ground equipment maintenance, flight kitchen, and air freight facilities (the "Facilities") at the new Denver International Airport (the "New Airport").

The City will cause such proceeds to be deposited, distributed, and applied in accordance with the terms of a Special Facilities and Ground Lease, dated as of October 1, 1992 (the "Lease") between United Airlines and the City. Under the Lease, United has agreed to make payments sufficient to pay the principal, premium, if any, and interest on the Bonds. Neither the Facilities nor the ground rental payments under the Lease are pledged as security for the payment of principal, premium, if any, and interest on the bonds.

Agreement between United and the City

On June 26, 1991, United and the City entered into an agreement followed by a second agreement on December 12, 1991, which, among other things, collectively pro-vide for the use and lease by United of certain premises and facilities at the New Airport. In the United Agreement, United agrees among other things, to (1) support the construction of the New Airport, (2) relocate its present air carrier operations from Stapleton to the New Airport, (3) occupy and lease certain facilities at the New Airport, including no less than 45 gates on Concourse B within two years of the date of beneficial occupancy as described in the United Agreement, and (4) construct prior to the date of beneficial occupancy, a regional reservation center at a site at Stapleton.

In conjunction with the execution of the United Agreement, United also executes a 30-year use and lease agreement. United has agreed to lease, on a preferential use basis, Concourse B, which is expected to support 42 jet aircraft with up to 24 commuter aircraft parking positions at the date of beneficial occupancy, and, on an exclusive use basis, certain ticket counters and other areas in the terminal complex of the New Airport.

The Facilities

The proceeds of the bonds will be used to finance the acquisition, construction, and equipping of the Facilities, as provided under the Lease. The Facilities will be located on approximately 100 acres of improved land located within the New Airport, which United will lease from the City. The Facilities will include an aircraft maintenance facility capable of housing ten jet aircraft, a ground equipment support facility with 26 maintenance bays, an approximately 55,500-square-foot air freight facility, and an approximately 155,000-square-foot flight kitchen. Additionally, the proceeds of the Bonds will be used to furnish, equip, and install certain facilities to be used by United in Concourse B and in the terminal of the New Airport.

Redemption of Bonds

The Bonds will be subject to optional and mandatory redemption prior to maturity in the amounts, at the times, at the prices, and in the manner as provided in the Ordinance. If less than all of the Bonds are to be redeemed, the particular Bonds to be called for redemption will be selected by lot by the Paying Agent in any manner deemed fair and reasonable by the Paying Agent.

The bonds are subject to redemption prior to maturity by the City at the request of United, in whole or in part, by lot, on any date on or after October 1, 2002, from an account created pursuant to the Ordinance used to pay the principal, premium, if any, and interest on the Bonds (the "Bond Fund") and from monies otherwise available for such purpose. Such redemptions are to be made at the applicable redemption price shown below as a percentage of the principal amount thereof, plus interest accrued to the redemption date:

REDEMPTION PERIOD	OPTIONAL REDEMPTION PRICE
October 1, 2002 through September 30, 2003	102%
October 1, 2003 through September 30, 2004	101%
October 1, 2004 and thereafter	100%

The Bonds are subject to optional redemption prior to maturity, in whole or in part by lot, on any date, upon the exercise by United of its option to prepay Facilities Rentals under the Lease at a redemption price equal to 100% of the principal amount thereof plus interest accrued to the redemption date, if one or more of the following events occurs with respect to one or more of the units of the Leased Property:

a. the damage or destruction of all or substantially all of such unit or units of the Leased Property to such extent that, in the reasonable opinion of United, repair and restoration would not be economical and United elects not to restore or replace such unit or units of the Leased Property; or,
b. the condemnation of any part, use, or control of so much of such unit or units of the Leased Property that such unit or units cannot be reasonably used by United for carrying on, at substantially the same level or scope, the business theretofore conducted by United on such unit or units.

In the event of a partial extraordinary redemption, the amount of the Bonds to be redeemed for any unit of the Leased Property with respect to which such prepayment is made shall be determined as set forth below (expressed as a percentage of the original principal amount of the Bonds) plus accrued interest on the Bonds to be redeemed to the redemption date of such Bonds provided that the amount of Bonds to be redeemed may be reduced by the aggregate principal amount (valued at par) of any Bonds purchased by or on behalf of United and delivered to the Paying Agent for cancelation:

TERMINAL CONCOURSE B FACILITY	AIRCRAFT MAINTENANCE FACILITY	GROUND EQUIPMENT MAINTENANCE FACILITY	FLIGHT KITCHEN	AIR FREIGHT FACILITY
20%	50%	10%	15%	5%

The Bonds shall be subject to mandatory redemption in whole prior to maturity, on October 1, 2023, at a redemption price equal to 100% of the principal amount thereof, plus accrued interest to the redemption date if the term of the Lease is not extended to October 1, 2032, in accordance with the provisions of the Lease and subject to the conditions in the Ordinance.

Limitations

Pursuant to the United Use and Lease Agreement, if costs at the New Airport exceed $20 per revenue enplaned passenger, in 1990 dollars, for the preceding calendar year, calculated in accordance with such agreement, United can elect to terminate its Use and Lease Agreement. Such termination by United would not, however, be an event of default under the Lease.

If United causes an event of default under the Lease and the City exercises its remedies thereunder and accelerates Facilities Rentals, the City is not obligated to relet the Facilities. If the City relets the Facilities, it is not obligated to use any of the payments received to pay principal, premium, if any, or interest on the Bonds.

Application of the Bond Proceeds

It is estimated that the proceeds of the sale of the Bonds will be applied as follows:

Cost of Construction	$226,002,433
Interest on Bonds During Construction	22,319,740
Cost of Issuance Including Underwriters' Discount	1,980,075
Original Issue Discount	11,112,742
Principal Amount of the Bonds	$261,415,000

Tax Covenant

Under the terms of the lease, United has agreed that it will not take or omit to take any action with respect to the Facilities or the proceeds of the bonds (including any investment earnings thereon), insurance, condemnation, or any other proceeds derived in connection with the Facilities, which would cause the interest on the Bonds to become included in the gross income of the Bondholder for federal income tax purposes.

Other Material Covenants

United has agreed to acquire, construct, and install the Facilities to completion pursuant to the terms of the Lease. If monies in the Construction Fund are insufficient to pay the cost of such acquisition, construction, and installation in full, then United shall pay the excess cost without reimbursement from the City, the Paying Agent, or any Bondholder.

United has agreed to indemnify the City and the Paying Agent for damages incurred in connection with the occurrence of certain events, including without limitation, the construction of the Facilities, occupancy by United of the land on which the Facilities are located, and violation by United of any of the terms of the Lease or other agreements related to the Leased Property.

During the Lease Term, United has agreed to maintain its corporate existence and its qualifications to do business in the state. United will not dissolve or otherwise dispose of its assets and will not consolidate with or merge into another corporation provided, however, that United may, without violating the Lease, consolidate or merge into another corporation.

Additional Bonds

At the request of United, the City may, at its option, issue additional bonds to finance the cost of special Facilities for United upon the terms and conditions in the Lease and the Ordinance.

The Guaranty

Under the Guaranty, United will unconditionally guarantee to the Paying Agent, for the benefit of the Bondholders, the full and prompt payment of the principal, premium, if any, and interest on the Bonds, when and as the same shall become due whether at the stated maturity, by redemption, acceleration, or otherwise. The obligations of United under the Guaranty are unsecured, but are stated to be absolute and unconditional, and the Guaranty will remain in effect until the entire principal, premium, if any, and interest on the Bonds has been paid in full or provision for the payment thereof has been made in accordance with the Ordinance.

APPENDIX B
JOKES ABOUT THE ABBREVIATION DIA

DENVER—The Denver International Airport, whose opening has been delayed indefinitely because of snafus, has borne the brunt of joke writers

Punsters in the aviation and travel community have done their share of work on one particular genre, coming up with new variations on the theme of DIA, the star-crossed airport's new and as-yet-unused city code.

Here's what's making the rounds on electronic bulletin boards; it originated in the May 15 issue of the Boulder (Colo.) Camera newspaper.

1. Dis Is Awful
2. Doing It Again
3. Dumbest International Airport
4. Dinosaur In Action
5. Debt In Arrival
6. Denver's Intense Adventure
7. Darn It All
8. Dollar Investment Astounding
9. Delay It Again
10. Denver International Antique
11. Date Is AWOL
12. Denver Intellects Awry
13. Dance Is Autumn
14. Dopes In Authority
15. Don't Ice Attendance
16. Drop In Asylum
17. Don't Immediately Assume
18. Don't Ignore Aspirin
19. Dittohead Idle Again
20. Doubtful If Atall
21. Denver In Action
22. Deces, l'Inaugural Arrivage (means "dead on arrival" in French)
23. Dummies In Action
24. Dexterity In Action
25. Display In Arrogance
26. Denver Incomplete Act
27. D'luggage Is A'coming
28. Defect In Automation
29. Dysfunctional Itinerary Apparatus
30. Dis Is Absurd
31. Delays In Abundance
32. Did It Arrive?

33. Denver's Infamous Air-or-port (sounds like "error")
34. Dopes In Action
35. Doubtful Intermittent Access
36. Don't Intend Atall
37. .. Damned Inconvenient Airport
38. Duped In Anticipation
39. Delay In Action
40. Delirious In Accounting
41. Date Indeterminate, Ah?
42. Denver's Indisposed Access
43. Detained Interphase Ahead
44. Denver's Interminably Aground
45. Deceit In Action
46. Delay Institute America
47. Denver's Intractable Airport
48. Delayed Indefinitely Again
49. Delayed Introduction Again
50. Disaster In Arrears
51. Denver International Amusementpark
52. Debacle In Action
53. Deadline (of) Incomprehensible Attainment
54. Duffel Improbable Arrival
55. Delay In America
56. Dying In Anticipation
57. Dazzling Inaccessible Absurdity
58. Damned Intractable Automation
59. Da Infamous Annoyance
60. Dare I Ask?
61. Done In Arrears
62. Done In Ancestral
63. Denver International Accident
64. Dumb Idea Anyway
65. Diversion In Accounting
66. Doesn't Include Airlines
67. Disparate Instruments in Action
68. Delay International Airport
69. Dumb Idea Askew
70. Delayed Indefinitely Airport
71. Delays In Arrival
72. Deja In Absentee
73. Done In Aminute
74. Done In August
75. Denver's Inordinate Airport
76. Denver's Imaginary Airport
77. Debentures In Arrears

78. Denver Isn't Airborne
79. Descend Into Abyss
80. Done In April 2000
81. Disaster In Aviation
82. Denver's Interminable Airport
83. Denver In Arrears
84. Dallying Is Aggravating
85. Don't In Angst
86. Distress Is Acute
87. Development Is Arrested
88. Darned Inevitable Atrocity
89. Debt In Airport
90. Devastation In Aviation
91. Debacle in Automation
92. Denver's Inconstructable Airport
93. Denver Is Awaitin'
94. DIsAster
95. Denver's Inoperable Airport
96. Delay, Impede, Await
97. Date Isn't Available
98. Delayed International Airport
99. Denver Irrational Airport
100. Denver Irate Association
101. Denver's Ignominious Atrocity
102. Daytrippers Invitational Airport
103. Delay Is Anticipated
104. Doofis, Interruptness, Accidentalis
105. Denver International Arrival
106. Denver's Interminable Apparition
107. Distance Is Astronomical
108. Doubtful It's Able
109. Dreadfully Ineffective Automation
110. Do It Again
111. Did it, Installed it, Ate it
112. Drowned In Apoplexy
113. Dodo International Airport (the dodo is an extinct, flightless bird)
114. Dead In the Air
115. Denouncement In Ambiguity
116. Deserted, Inactive Airport
117. Definitely Incapable of Activation
118. Democracy In Action
119. Dysfunction Imitating Art
120. Design In Alabaster
121. Desperately In Arrears
122. Dazzling, If Anything
123. Delays In Aeternum
124. Delighted If Actualized

APPENDIX B (*continued*)
JOKES ABOUT THE ABBREVIATION DIA

125. Destination: Imagine Arabia
126. Dumb Idea: Abandoned?
127. Deem It Apiary
128. Dollars In Action
129. Definitely Iffy Achievement
130. Dreadfully Incompetent Architects
131. Denver International Ain't
132. Delayed In Automation
133. Dragging Its Ass
134. Driving Is Advantageous
135. Dang It All

136. Druggies Installing Automation
137. Dumb Idea Approved
138. Didn't Invite Airplanes
139. Died In April
140. Deplane In Albuquerque
141. Departure Is Agonizing
142. Denver's Infuriating Abscess
143. Denver's Ill-fated Airport
144. Domestic International Aggravation

145. Duffels In Anchorage
146. Denver's Indeterminate Abomination
147. Damn It All
148. Darn Idiotic Airport
149. Delay Is Acceptable
150. Denver's Idle Airport
151. Does It Arrive?
152. Damned Inconvenient Anyway

Source: Reprinted from *Boulder* (Colorado) *Camera* newspaper (May 15, 1991).

REFERENCES (IN CHRONOLOGICAL ORDER)

David A. Brown, "Denver Aims for Global Hub Status with New Airport Under Construction," *Aviation Week & Space Technology* (March 11, 1991), pp. 42–45.

"Satellite Airport to Handle Corporate, General Aviation for Denver Area," *Aviation Week & Space Technology* (March 11, 1991), pp. 44–45.

"Denver to Seek Bids This Spring for Wide-Open Terminal Building," *Aviation Week & Space Technology* (March 11, 1991), p. 50.

"Denver City Council Supports Airport Despite Downgrade," *The Wall Street Journal* (March 20, 1991), p. A1D.

"Denver Airport Bonds' Rating Is Confirmed by Moody's Investors," *The Wall Street Journal* (March 22, 1991), p. C14.

"Bonds for Denver Airport Priced to Yield up to 9.185%," *New York Times* (April 10, 1991), p. D16.

Marj Charlier, "Denver Reports a Tentative Agreement with United over Hub at New Airport," *The Wall Street Journal* (May 3, 1991), p. B2.

Brad Smith, "New Airport Has Its Ups and Downs," *Los Angeles Times* (July 9, 1991), p. A5.

Christopher Wood, "Hotel Development at New Airport Not Likely Until After '93," *Denver Business Journal* (August 2, 1991), p. 8S.

Christopher Wood, "FAA: Link Air Cargo, Passengers," *Denver Business Journal* (November 1–7, 1991), p. 3.

Christopher Wood, "Airport May Move Cargo Operations, Offer Reserve Funds," *Denver Business Journal* (December 6–12, 1991), pp. 1, 34.

"UAL in Accord on Denver," *The New York Times* (December 7, 1991), p. 39L.

Thomas Fisher, "Projects Flights of Fantasy," *Progressive Architecture* (March 1992), p. 103.

Tom Locke, "Disconnected," *Denver Business Journal* (June 12–18, 1992), p. 19.

"Big Ain't Hardly the Word for It," *ENR* (September 7, 1992), pp. 28–29.

Christopher Wood, "Adams Seeks Action," *Denver Business Journal* (September 4–10, 1992), pp. 1, 13.

"Denver Airport Rises under Gossamer Roof," *The Wall Street Journal* (November 17, 1992), p. B1.

Mark B. Solomon, "Denver Airport Delay Angers Cargo Carriers," *Journal of Commerce* (March 17, 1993), p. 3B.

"Denver Airport Opening Delayed Until December," *Aviation Week & Space Technology* (May 10, 1993), p. 39.

Aldo Svaldi, "DIA Air Train Gathering Steam as Planners Shift Possible Route," *Denver Business Journal* (August 27–September 2, 1993), p. 74.

Dirk Johnson, "Opening of New Denver Airport is Delayed Again," *The New York Times* (October 26, 1993), p. A19.

"Denver's Mayor Webb Postpones Opening International Airport," *The Wall Street Journal* (October 26, 1993), p. A9.

"An Airport Comes to Denver," *Skiing* (December 1993), p. 66.

Ellis Booker, "Airport Prepares for Takeoff," *Computerworld* (January 10, 1994).

Aldo Svaldi, "Front Range, DIA Weigh Merging Airport Systems," *Denver Business Journal* (January 21–27, 1994), p. 3.

Don Phillips, "$3.1 Billion Airport at Denver Preparing for a Rough Takeoff," *The Washington Post* (February 13, 1994), p. A10.

"New Denver Airport Combines Several State-of-the-Art Systems," *Travel Weekly* (February 21, 1994) p. 20.

Steve Munford, "Options in Hard Surface Flooring," *Buildings* (March 1994), p. 58.

Mars Charles, "Denver's New Airport, Already Mixed in Controversy, Won't Open Next Week," *The Wall Street Journal* (March 2, 1994), pp. B1, B7.

"Denver Grounded for Third Time," *ENR* (March 7, 1994), p. 6.

Shannon Peters, "Denver's New Airport Creates HR Challenges," *Personnel Journal* (April 1994), p. 21.

Laura Del Rosso, "Denver Airport Delayed Indefinitely," *Travel Weekly* (May 5, 1994), p. 37.

"DIA Bond Rating Cut," *Aviation Week & Space Technology* (May 16, 1994), p. 33.

Robert Scheler, "Software Snafu Grounds Denver's High-Tech Airport," *PC Week* (May 16, 1994), p. 1.

John Dodge, "Architects Take a Page from Book on Denver Airport-Bag System," *PC Week* (May 16, 1994), p. 3.

Jean S. Bozman, "Denver Airport Hits Systems Layover," *Computerworld* (May 16, 1994), p. 30.

Richard Woodbury, "The Bag Stops Here," *Time* (May 16, 1994), p. 52.

"Consultants Review Denver Baggage Problems," *Aviation Week & Space Technology* (June 6, 1994), p. 38.

"Doesn't It Amaze? The Delay that Launched a Thousand Gags," *Travel Weekly* (June 6, 1994), p. 16.

Michael Romano, "This Delay Is Costing Business a Lot of Money," *Restaurant Business* (June 10, 1994), p. 26.

Scott Armstrong, "Denver Builds New Airport, Asks 'Will Planes Come?' " *The Christian Science Monitor* (June 21, 1994), p. 1.

Benjamin Weiser, "SEC Turns Investigation to Denver Airport Financing," *The Washington Post* (July 13, 1994), p. D1.

Bernie Knill, "Flying Blind at Denver International Airport," *Material Handling Engineering* (July 1994), p. 47.

Keith Dubay, "Denver Airport Seeks Compromise on Baggage Handling," *American Banker Washington Watch* (July 25, 1994), p. 10.

Dirk Johnson, "Denver May Open Airport in Spite of Glitches," *The New York Times* (July 27, 1994), p. A14.

Jeffrey Leib, "Investors Want a Plan," *The Denver Post* (August 2, 1994), p. A1.

Marj Charlier, "Denver Plans Backup Baggage System for Airport's Troubled Automated One," *The Wall Street Journal* (August 5, 1994), p. B2.

Louis Sahagun, "Denver Airport to Bypass Balky Baggage Mover," *Los Angeles Times* (August 5, 1994), p. A1.

Len Morgan, "Airports Have Growing Pains," *Flying* (August 1994), p. 104.

Adam Bryant, "Denver Goes Back to Basics for Baggage," *The New York Times* (August 6, 1994), pp. 5N, 6L.

"Prosecutors Scrutinize New Denver Airport," *The New York Times* (August 21, 1994), p. 36L.

Kevin Flynn, "Panic Drove New DIA Plan," *Rocky Mountain News* (August 7, 1994), p. 5A.

David Hughes, "Denver Airport Still Months from Opening," *Aviation Week & Space Technology* (August 8, 1994), p. 30.

"Airport May Open in Early '95," *Travel Weekly* (August 8, 1994), p. 57.

Michael Meyer, and Daniel Glick, "Still Late for Arrival," *Newsweek* (August 22, 1994), p. 38.

Andrew Bary, "A $3 Billion Joke," *Barron's* (August 22, 1994), p. MW10.

Jean Bozman, "Baggage System Woes Costing Denver Airport Millions," *Computerworld* (August 22, 1994), p. 28.

Edward Phillips, "Denver, United Agree on Baggage System Fixes," *Aviation Week & Space Technology* (August 29, 1994).

Glenn Rifkin, "What Really Happened at Denver's Airport," *Forbes* (August 29, 1994), p. 110.

Andrew Bary, "New Denver Airport Bond Issue Could Face Turbulence from Investors," *Barron's* (August 29, 1994), p. MW9.

Andrew Bary, "Denver Airport Bonds Take Off as Investors Line Up for Higher Yields," *Barron's* (August 29, 1994), p. MW9.

Susan Carey, "Alaska's Cash-Strapped MarkAir Is Wooed by Denver," *The Wall Street Journal* (September 1, 1994), p. B6.

Dana K. Henderson, "It's in the Bag(s)," *Air Transport World* (September 1994), p. 54.

Dirk Johnson, "Late Already, Denver Airport Faces More Delays," *The New York Times* (September 25, 1994), p. 26L.

Gordon Wright, "Denver Builds a Field of Dreams," *Building Design and Construction* (September 1994), p. 52.

Alan Jabez, "Airport of the Future Stays Grounded," *Sunday Times* (October 9, 1994), Features Section.

Jean Bozman, "United to Simplify Denver's Troubled Baggage Project," *Computerworld* (October 10, 1994), p. 76.

"Denver Aide Tells of Laxity in Airport Job," *The New York Times* (October 17, 1994), p. A12.

Brendan Murray, "In the Bags: Local Company to Rescue Befuddled Denver Airport," *Marietta Daily Journal* (October 21, 1994), p. C1.

Joanne Wojcik, "Airport in Holding Pattern, Project Is Insured, but Denver to Retain Brunt of Delay Costs," *Business Insurance* (November 7, 1994), p. 1.

James S. Russell, "Is This Any Way to Build an Airport?," *Architectural Record* (November 1994), p. 30.

4.12 DENVER INTERNATIONAL AIRPORT BAGGAGE-HANDLING SYSTEM: ILLUSTRATION OF INEFFECTIVE DECISION MAKING[9]

Synopsis

Dysfunctional decision making is the poison that kills technology projects and the Denver Airport Baggage System project in the 1990's is a classic example. Although several case studies have been written about the Denver project, the following paper reexamines the case by looking at the key decisions that set the project on the path to disaster and the forces behind those decisions.

Background

What was to be the world's largest automated airport baggage handling system, became a classic story in how technology projects can go wrong. Faced with the need for greater airport capacity, the city of Denver elected to construct a new state of the art airport that would cement Denver's position as an air transportation hub. Covering a land area of 140 Km^2, the airport was to be the largest in the United States and have the capacity to handle more than 50m passengers annually [1,2].

The airport's baggage handling system was a critical component in the plan. By automating baggage handling, aircraft turnaround time was to be reduced to as little as 30 minutes [1]. Faster turnaround meant more efficient operations and was a cornerstone of the airports competitive advantage.

System at a Glance

- 88 airport gates in 3 concourses
- 17 miles of track and 5 miles of conveyor belts
- 3,100 standard carts + 450 oversized carts
- 14 million feet of wiring
- Network of more than 100 PC's to control flow of carts
- 5,000 electric motors
- 2,700 photo cells, 400 radio receivers and 59 laser arrays

Despite the good intentions the plan rapidly dissolved as underestimation of the project's complexity resulted in snowballing problems and public humiliation for everyone involved. Thanks mainly to problems with the baggage system, the airport's opening was delayed by a full 16 months. Expenditure to maintain the empty airport and interest charges on construction loans cost the city of Denver $1.1M per day throughout the delay [3].

The embarrassing missteps along the way included an impromptu demonstration of the system to the media which illustrated how the system crushed bags, disgorged content and how two carts moving at high speed reacted when they crashed into each other [4]. When opening day finally arrived, the system was just a shadow of the original plan. Rather than automating all 3 concourses into one integrated system, the system was used in a single concourse, by a single airline and only for outbound flights [5]. All other baggage handling was performed using simple conveyor belts plus a manual tug and trolley system that was hurriedly built when it became clear that the automated system would never achieve its goals.

Although the remnants of the system soldiered on for 10 years, the system never worked well and in August 2005, United Airlines announced that they would abandon the system completely [6]. The $1 million per month maintenance costs exceeded the monthly cost of a manual tug and trolley system.

Chronology of Events

DENVER INTERNATIONAL AIRPORT (DIA) BAGGAGE SYSTEM DEVELOPMENT TIMELINE [1, 2, 3, 4, 5, 6]

- **Nov 1989** Work starts on the construction of the airport
- **Oct 1990** City of Denver engages Breier Neidle Patrone Associates to analyze feasibility of building an integrated baggage system. Reports advises [sic] that complexity makes the proposition unfeasible
- **Feb 1991** Continental Airlines signs on and plans on using Denver as a hub
- **Jun 1991** United Airlines signs on and plans on using Concourse A as a hub
- **Jun 1991** United Airlines engages BAE Systems to build an automated baggage system for Concourse A. BAE was a world leader in the supply, installation and operation of baggage handling equipment
- **Summer 1991** Airport's Project Management team recognizes that a baggage handling solution for the complete airport was required. Bids for an airport wide solution are requested
- **Fall 1991** Of the 16 companies included in the bidding process only 3 respond and review of proposals indicate [sic] none could be ready in time for the Oct 1993 opening. The 3 bids are all rejected
- **Early 1992** Denver Airport Project Management team approach BAE directly requesting a bid for the project

(Continued)

- **Apr 1992** Denver Airport contracts with BAE to expand the United Airlines baggage handling system into an integrated system handling all 3 concourses, all airlines, departing as well as arriving flights. In addition system is to handle transfer [of] baggage automatically. Contract is hammered out in 3 intense working sessions
- **Aug 1992** United Airlines changes their plans and cuts out plans for the system to transfer bags between aircraft. Resulting changes save $20m, but result in a major redesign of the United Airlines portion of the system. Change requests are raised to add automated handling of oversized baggage and for the creation of a dedicated ski equipment handling area
- **Sep 1992** Continental requests ski equipment handling facilities be added to their concourse as well
- **Oct 1992** Chief Airport Engineer, Walter Singer dies. Mr. Singer had been one of the driving forces behind the creation of the automated baggage system
- **Jan 1993** Change orders raised altering size of ski equipment claim area and adding maintenance tracks so carts could be serviced without having to be removed from the rails
- **Feb 1993** Target opening date shifted from 31 Oct 93 to 19 Dec 93 and soon thereafter to 9 Mar 94
- **Sep 1993** Target opening date is shifted again, new target date is 15 May 1994
- **31 Oct 1993** Original target for opening
- **19 Dec 1993** Second target for opening
- **Jan 1994** United Airlines requests further changes to the oversize baggage input area
- **9 Mar 1994** Third target for opening
- **Mar 1994** Problems establishing a clean electrical supply results in continual power outages that disrupt testing and development. Solution requires installation of industrial filters into the electrical system. Ordering and installation of the filters takes [sic] several months
- **Apr 1994** Airport authorities arrange a demonstration for the system for the media (without first informing BAE). Demonstration is a disaster as clothes are disgorged from crushed bags
- **Apr 1994** Denver Mayor cancels 15 May target date and announces an indefinite delay in opening
- **May 1994** Logplan Consulting engaged to evaluate the project
- **15 May 1994** Fourth target for opening
- **May 1994** BAE Systems denies system is malfunctioning. Instead they say many of the issues reported to date had been caused by the airport staff using the system incorrectly
- **Aug 1994** System testing continues to flounder. Scope of work is radically trimmed back and based on Logplan's recommendation airport builds a manual tug and trolley system instead
- **Aug 1994** City of Denver starts fining BAE $12K per day for further delays
- **28 Feb 1995** Actual opening
- **Aug 2005** In order to save costs the system is scrapped in favor of a fully manual system. Maintenance costs were running at $1M per month at the time.

Basic Mode of Failure

As with all failures the problems can be viewed from a number of levels. In its simplest form, the Denver International Airport (DIA) project failed because those making key decision underestimated the complexity involved. As planned, the system was the most complex baggage system ever attempted. Ten times larger than any other automated system, the increased size resulted in an exponential growth in complexity. At the heart of the complexity lay an issue know [sic] as "line balancing" [1]. To optimize system performance, empty carts had to be distributed around the airport ready to pick up new bags. With more than 100 pickup points (check in rows and arrival gates) each pickup needed to be fed with enough empty carts to meet its needs. The algorithms necessary to anticipate where empty carts should wait for new bags represented a nightmare in the mathematic modeling of queue behaviors. Failure to anticipate the number of carts correctly would result in delays in picking up bags that would undermine the system's performance goals.

Failure to recognize the complexity and the risk involved contributed to the project being initiated too late. The process of requesting bids for the design and construction of the system was not initiated until summer of 1991 [7]. Based on the original project schedule, this left a little over two years for the contracts to be signed and for the system to be designed, built, tested and commissioned. The closest analogous projects were the San Francisco system and one installed in Munich. Although much smaller and simpler, those systems took two years to implement [7]. Given the quantum leap in terms of size and complexity, completing the Denver system in two years was an impossible task. The underestimation of complexity led to a corresponding underestimation of the effort involved. That underestimation meant that without realizing it, the Project Management team had allowed the baggage system to become the airport's critical path. In order to meet the airport's planned opening date, the project needed to be completed in just two years. This clearly was insufficient time and that misjudgment resulted in the project being exposed to massive levels of schedule pressure. Many of the project's subsequent problems were likely a result of (or exacerbated by) shortcuts the team took and the mistakes they made as they tried to meet an impossible schedule.

Key Decisions That Led to Disaster

Although the basic mode of failure is fairly clear, to understand the root cause and what should have been done differently we need to examine how the critical decisions that triggered the failure were made. Project failures usually involve numerous flawed decisions, but within those many missteps, certain key decisions are the triggers that set in motion the sequence of events that lead to disaster.

Key Decision 1—A Change in Strategy

At the start of a project strategic decisions are made that set the project's direction. In the DIA case, a strategic error was made that resulted in "flip-flop" being made part way through the project.

Prior to requesting bids for an integrated system in the summer of 1991, the airport's Project Management team had assumed that individual airlines would make their own baggage handling arrangements [5]. United Airlines had indeed proceeded with their own plan by engaging BAE (Boeing Airport Equipment Automated Systems Incorporated) directly. Continental Airlines had however not made any arrangements and given that the airport was not yet fully leased out, other sections of the airport were not being addressed.

In the summer of 1991, the airport's Project Management team changed their strategy and realized that if an integrated system was to be built, they needed to take responsibility back from the individual airlines and run the project themselves. This change in strategy came a little more than two years prior to the airport's planned opening date and the timing of the decision was in large part the trigger behind the excessive schedule pressure the project was exposed to.

In one way the change in strategy made sense because an integrated system required centralized control and the airport's Project Management team was the only central group that could run the project. Clearly the timing of the decision was however extremely poor. Had the correct strategy been set at the outset, there would have been two additional years in which to develop the system. Those two years may well have been enough to allow designers to understand the complexity issue more deeply and to find ways to either overcome it or agree with the stakeholders on a simpler design.

The delay in setting the correct strategy is likely rooted in the history of how prior airport construction projects had been run. Because earlier generation baggage facilities were dedicated to individual airlines, airlines had historically built their own systems when a new airport was built [5]. The advent of the integrated airport wide system required a change in mindset. The integrated nature of the new systems meant that instead of airlines looking after their own facilities, airport's [sic] needed to take control.

The key point the airport's project management team failed to see was that the shift in technology required a corresponding shift in organizational responsibilities. The failure to recognize that shift represents a planning failure that dated back to the very start of the construction project. The public record does not detail how the original strategy was set or even if the topic had been directly considered. However, people typically see the world through the eyes of their prior experiences and given that almost all prior airport projects had left this responsibility to the airline, it is very likely that the question was simply never discussed.

In broader terms, the mistake made was a failure to link the airport's overall strategy (the goal of having one of the world's most efficient airports) with the substrategy of how to build the baggage system. The mode in which that failure occurred may well simply have been a failure to ask the critical question of where responsibility for development of the baggage system needed to be.

Key Decision 2—The Decision to Proceed

Although the change in strategy is somewhat understandable, what is less understandable is why both the airport Project Management team and BAE decided to proceed with the full scale project despite clear indications that there was insufficient time left for the project to be completed successfully. Prior to entering into the BAE contract, there were at least three indications that the project required more than two years or was simply not feasible;

1. The 1990 Breier Neidle Patrone Associates report indicated the complexity was too high for the system to be built successfully [1],
2. Analysis of the three bids received indicated that none of the vendors could build the system in time for the Oct 1993 opening [4],
3. Experts from Munich airport advised that the much simpler Munich system had taken 2 full years to build and that it had run 24/7 for 6 months prior to opening to allow bugs to be ironed out [5].

Reports indicate that the decision to proceed was based on the communications between the airport's chief engineer (Walter Slinger) and BAE's senior management team. While BAE had initially chosen not to bid for the airport wide contract, the rejection of the three official bids resulted in the airport team speaking directly to BAE about the possibility of expanding the United Airlines system that was already under development. Those discussions resulted in the preparation of a specification and the creation of a large scale prototype (reported to have filled up a 50,000 sq ft warehouse) [7]. Demonstration of the prototype is said to have been the factor that convinced Slinger that the system was feasible.

Despite the fact that BAE was talking directly to Slinger about the possibility of building the system, some reports indicate that within BAE several managers were voicing concern. Again the issues related to whether or not it was feasible to build such a large system in such a short period of time. Reports indicate that several managers advised the BAE senior management team that the project was at minimum a four year project, not a two year project [5].

The failure by both Slinger and BAE's senior management team to heed the advice they were receiving and the failure of the airport's Project Management team to have the BAE proposal and prototype independently reviewed is the epicenter of the disaster.

Although published reports do not indicate why the expert advice was ignored, it is clear that both Slinger and BAE's senior management team underestimated the complexity of the project and ignored information that may have corrected their positions. Many factors may have led them into that trap and likely issues that may have influenced the decision making include;

1. From Slinger's perspective
   a. Denver was to be a state of the art airport and as such the desire to have the most advanced baggage system would likely have been a factor behind Slinger's willingness to proceed,

b. Slinger's prior experiences with baggage handling will have been based on simple conveyor belts combined with manual tug and trolley systems. Those prior experiences may have led Slinger to underestimate the complexity of moving to a fully automated system,

c. As a civil engineer, Slinger was used to the development of physical buildings and structures rather than complex technology systems, [and] this may have predisposed him to underestimate the mathematical complexity associated with an issue such as "line balancing",

d. Slinger is reported to have been a hands-on leader who liked to solve problems himself. As such Slinger may have been inclined to make decisions on his own rather than seeking independent advice,

e. Slinger dealt with the discussions with BAE personally, [and] given that he was responsible for the complete airport, he will have had considerable other duties that would have limited the amount of time he had to focus on the baggage system,

f. On the surface the prototype may well have made it look as if BAE had overcome the technical challenges involved in building the system and as such Slinger may have been lured into a false sense of security.

2. From BAE's perspective

a. The project was a big revenue opportunity and represented a chance to grow the business,

b. The prestige of securing the DIA contract would position BAE to secure other large contracts around the world. New airports or terminals were planned for Bangkok, Hong Kong, Singapore, London and Kuala Lumpur and BAE would be a strong contender if they could win the DIA project.

3. Other factors

a. Both BAE and Slinger will have recognized that they were working within a tight timeframe and the pressure to move quickly may have caused them to put due diligence to one side.

b. The belief that due to the airport's size, a manual system would not be fast enough to meet aircraft turnaround requirements. Note however that this belief was unfounded as the airport functions happily today using a manual system.

Key Decision 3—Schedule, Scope and Budget Commitments

The schedule, budget and scope commitments a team enter into are amongst the most critical decisions they will make. The seeds of project success or failure often lie in the analysis that goes into making those decisions and the way such commitments are structured.

In the DIA case, BAE committed to deliver the complete system under a fixed scope, schedule and budget arrangement. The decision to give a firm commitment to scope, schedule and budget transferred considerable risk onto BAE's shoulders. This move indicates strongly that those in the highest level of BAE's management structure had completely failed to recognize the level of risk they were entering into. Had they been more aware, they almost certainly would have taken steps to limit the risk and to find ways to limit the scope to something that was more achievable in the time available.

Again the finger prints of excessive schedule pressure can be seen in the commitments BAE entered into. The contractual conditions for the agreement and the scope of work were hammered out in just three *"intense"* working sessions [7]. Although BAE had some level of understanding because of their contract with United Airlines, clearly the three working sessions will not have provided sufficient time for the different parties to develop an in-depth understanding of what was involved or for them to fully understand the risks they were taking.

BAE and the airport project management team made another major mistake during the negotiations. Although the airlines were key stakeholders in the system they were excluded from the discussions. Excluding stakeholders from discussions in which key project decisions are made is always a losing strategy. When previously excluded stakeholders are finally engaged, they usually ask for significant changes that can negate much of the previous work done on the project.

Key Decision 4—Acceptance of Change Requests

Not surprisingly, as the project progressed the airlines did indeed ask for a number of significant changes. Although in the original negotiations, BAE had made it a condition that no changes would be made, the pressure to meet stakeholder needs proved to be too strong and BAE and the airport's Project Management team were forced into accepting them. Among the major changes were; the adding of ski equipment racks, the addition of maintenance tracks to allow carts to be serviced without being removed from the rails and changes to the handling of oversized baggage. Some of the changes made required significant redesign of portions of work already completed.

Accepting these changes into a project that was already in deep trouble raises some further troubling questions. Did the team fail to understand the impact the changes might have? Did they fail to recognize how much trouble the project was already in? Although answers to those questions are not available from the public record, the acceptance of the change requests again hints at the communications disconnects that were occurring inside the project. Clearly some of the people involved will have understood the implications, but those voices appear not to have connected with those who were making the overall decisions.

Key Decision 5—Design of the Physical Building Structure

Rather than being separate entities, the baggage system and the physical building represented a single integrated system. Sharing the physical space and services such as the electrical supply the designers of the physical building and the designers of the baggage system needed to work as one integrated team.

Largely because the design of the building was started before the baggage system design was known, the designers of the physical building only made general allowances for where they thought the baggage system would go. When the baggage system design was eventually started, the baggage system design team was forced to work within the constraints left to them by the designers of the physical building (estimates to change the physical structure to suit the needs of the baggage system are reported to have been up to $100M).

The resulting design meant that the baggage system had to accommodate sharp turns that were far from optimal and increased the physical loads placed on the system [1]. Those stresses were key contributors to the system's reliability problems. In particular, navigating sharp turns is reported to have been one of the major problems that lead to bags being ejected from their carts. These problems ultimately proved so severe that the speed of the system was halved from 60 cars per minute to 30 cars in order to reduce the physical forces when negotiating tight turns. That quick fix however had the side affect [sic] that it began to undermine the performance goals the system was trying to meet.

Although the designers of the physical building likely did their best to make allowance for the baggage system, this portion of the story once again illustrates a breakdown in the overall planning of the project. The allowance of spaces in which the baggage system would operate represented a key interface between the design of the physical building and the baggage system. To make effective decisions about how to design the physical building, the designers of the physical building needed to be working alongside people who had expertise in designing baggage systems. Clearly this did not happen.

What is not clear is if the designers of the physical building requested such expertise be provided or if they just went ahead in isolation. In either case, the project management team should have recognized the significance of the interface between the baggage system and the physical building and arranged for the appropriate people to work together.

Key Decision 6—The Decision to Seek a Different Path

Following the embarrassing public demonstration to the press in Apr 1994, the Mayor of Denver recognized that the project was in deep trouble. The demonstration had been an unmitigated disaster and pressure was building from various sources pushing the Mayor to intercede. When the Mayor did step in, Mattias Franz of Logplan Consulting of Germany (a specialist in the design and construction of baggage handling systems) was called in to review the situation [9]. Despite United Airlines insistence that the automated system be finished, based on Logplan's recommendation the Mayor slashed the project and ordered that a manual trolley system [be] built at an additional cost of $51M [8].

While the Mayor was correct in taking action, the timing of the intervention again reveals something about the internal dynamics of the project. By the time the Mayor took action, the airport was already 6 months behind schedule and four opening dates had already been missed. In addition the disastrous demonstration of the system had shown to the world how bad the state of the project really was.

The four missed opening dates and the disastrous demonstration indicate that those at the highest level really had little idea what the true status of the project was. Bringing in an external consultant to review the project was certainly a good decision, but again it was a decision that was made far too late. A project of this size, complexity and risk should have had a number of such reviews along the way and independent expert assessment should have been a continual part of the project.

Other Failure Points

While the underestimation of complexity, lack of planning, ineffective communications and poor management oversight drove the failure, the project suffered many other difficulties that compounded the problems. Some of those issues were unavoidable, but others were likely a result of the schedule pressure the project was working under. Among the other issues that affected the project;

Risk Management Failures

The project encountered a number of major technical problems for which no allowances had been made. One of the most significant was caused by the fact that the electrical system suffered from power fluctuations that crashed the system. The resolution to the problem required filters to be built into the electrical power system to eliminate surges. Delivery and installation of the filters took several months, during which time testing was severely constrained. Such issues were likely predictable had the team focused on risk management activities. Again possibly as a result of the schedule pressure under which they were working, appropriate risk management strategies appear not to have been developed.

Leadership Change

In October of 1992 Walter Slinger died. Slinger was the system's de facto sponsor and his death left the project without much needed leadership. According to reports, Mr. Slinger's replacement lacked the in-depth engineering knowledge required to understand the system. In addition the replacement manager retained their [sic] prior responsibilities and hence was stretched to the limit.

Architectural and Design Issues

A number of reports indicate that the design the team chose to use was particularly complex and error prone. Among the issues noted;

1. The system had more than 100 individual PCs that were networked together. Failure of any one of the PCs could result in an outage as there was no automatic backup for failed components,

2. The distributed nature of the design (with PCs dotted around the different concourses) added to the difficulty of resolving problems when they arose,
3. The system was unable to detect jams and as a result when a jam occurred, the system simply kept piling up more and more bags making the jam that much worse.

Again schedule pressure may well have been a factor in the design problems. When under excessive schedule pressure teams often settle for the first design they think of. In addition schedule pressure often forces teams to focus on the "happy path" design while spending little time thinking through how to deal with problems and how to make the system fault tolerant.

Conclusion

The Denver debacle is a template for failure that many other projects have followed. As with so many other failures, Denver suffered from;

1. The underestimation of complexity
2. A lack of planning resulting in subsequent changes in strategy
3. Excessive schedule pressure
4. Lack of due diligence
5. Making firm commitments in the face of massive risks and uncertainty
6. Poor stakeholder management
7. Communications breakdowns
8. People working in silos
9. Poor design
10. Failure to perform risk management
11. Failure to understand the implication change requests might have
12. Lack of management oversight

While the above points represent contributors to the failure, there is one central problem that triggered the fiasco. Successful projects are projects in which people make effective decisions and making effective decisions requires a number of ingredients. Chief among those ingredients are knowledge and expertise. Walter Slinger, the airport's project management team and even the BAE's Senior Managers did not have prior experience of a system of this scale. In addition, given that automated baggage systems were relatively new, even BAE's senior management team only had a limited understanding of what was involved. That lack of knowledge, combined with the fact that expert advice was routinely ignored, is the epicenter of the failure.

The initial planning decisions, the decision to proceed with one airport wide integrated system (despite the fact that it was too late to do so) and the firm contractual commitments to scope, schedule and budget all represented decisions that were made by people who lacked the necessary knowledge. The misjudgments resulting from those decisions were the sparks that ignited the fire.

We are often faced with situations in which we lack the prior experience to know how to proceed with certainty. The way in which we respond to those situations can spell the difference between success and failure. The first step lies in recognizing the situation and Slinger, The project management team and BAE's Senior Manager seem to have fallen at that first hurdle. Had they recognized their lack of knowledge and the uncertainty they were facing, they could have taken a number of steps that would have reduced the risk. Chief among those steps would have been listening to those who did have the necessary prior knowledge.

The bright side of the story is that in Feb 1995 DIA did eventually open and despite using a largely manual trolley based system the airport proved to be an operational success [10]. Fears that a manual system would be too slow to service an airport the size of DIA proved to be unfounded.

REFERENCES

1. The Baggage System at Denver: Prospects and Lessons—Dr. R. de Neufville—Journal of Air Transport Management, Vol. 1, No. 4, Dec., pp. 229–236, 1994
2. Denver International website (www.FlyDenver.com)
3. Software's Chronic Crisis, Trends in Computing—W. Gibbs—Scientific American—Sep 1994, P86
4. The Denver International Airport Baggage Handling System—Papers from the Information Systems Foundations: Constructing and Criticizing Workshop at the Australian National University from 16 to 17 July 2004 S. Lukaitis, J. Cybulski, School of Information Systems, Deakin University
5. The Denver International Airport automated baggage handling system—Cal Poly—M. Schloh—Feb 16, 1996
6. Denver airport to mangle last bag—K. Johnson—International Herald Tribune—Aug 27, 2005
7. Software Forensics Centre Technical Report TR 2002-01—A Case Narrative of the Project Problems with the Denver Airport Baggage Handling System (DABHS) —A.J.M. Donaldson—Middlesex University, School of Computing Science
8. New Denver Airport: Impact of the Delayed Baggage System—Briefing Report (GAO/RCED-95-35BR, Oct 14, 1994.
9. Wellington Webb: The Man, The Mayor, and the Making of Modern Denver—Fulcrum Publishing – 2007
10. Denver Airport Nestles Into Its Lair—New York Times—Mar 6, 1996

4.13 SUMMARY OF LESSONS LEARNED

Project managers do not necessarily have the authority to make all of the decisions on a project. Effective governance is required. Project managers must understand their limitations.

TABLE 4-10 *PMBOK® Guide* **Alignment to Lessons Learned**

LESSONS LEARNED	PMBOK® GUIDE SECTIONS
The larger and more complex the project, the greater the likelihood that governance will be by committee rather than a single sponsor.	1.5.1.2, 2.2, 2.2.1, 2.2.2
Project managers must know who the stakeholders are.	1.5.1.2, 2.2, 2.2.1, 2.2.2
Project managers must know their limitations on authority and decision making.	2.2, 2.2.1, 2.2.2
Project managers must recognize the tell-tale signs of governance failure.	2.2
Project managers must know when to say, "I give up! The business case cannot be achieved."	4.1.1.1, 4.1.1.2

A checklist of techniques for effective project governance might include:

☐ Identify all of the stakeholders, especially those that sit on the project governance committee.

☐ Work with the client and the stakeholders to identify the business case.

☐ Identify how involved the governance committee want to be in decision making.

☐ Understand your limitations and the governance committee's limitations on authority and decision making.

☐ Determine the power and influence of the members of the governance committee.

☐ Try to identify if the members of the governance committee have hidden agendas.

☐ After project initiation, see if a collective belief exists on the project.

☐ Make sure there are decision points for determining of the project should continue or be cancelled.

Table 4-10 provides a summary of the lessons learned and alignment to various sections of the *PMBOK® Guide* where additional or supporting information can be found. In some cases, these sections of the *PMBOK® Guide* simply provide supporting information related to the lesson learned. There are numerous sections of the *PMBOK® Guide* that could be aligned for each lesson learned. For simplicity sake, only a few are listed.

5 PROJECT POLITICS AND FAILURE

5.0 INTRODUCTION

The completion of a project requires people. But simply because people are assigned to the project doesn't necessarily mean that they will always make decisions for what is in the best interest of the project. When people are first assigned to a new project, they ask themselves, "What's in it for me? How will my career benefit from this assignment?"

This type of thinking can permeate all levels of management on a project, including those responsible for the governance of the project. People tend to play politics to get what they want and this gamesmanship creates barriers that the project manager must overcome. People in governance positions may play politics to get what they want even if it means that the project might fail.

People are motivated by the rewards they can receive from the formal structure of the company and also from the informal political power structure that exists. Barriers are created when an individual's rewards from either structure are threatened. The barriers lead to conflicts and can involve how the project will be planned, who will be assigned to specific activities, especially those activities that may receive high level-visibility, which approach to take to solve a problem and other such items that are often hidden agenda items. Some people may even want to see the project fail if it benefits them. This can occur even if the failure of the project may result in the loss of lives.

Political savvy is an essential skill for today's project manager. One can no longer rely solely upon technical or managerial competence when managing a project. You must understand the political nature of the people and organizations you must deal with. You must understand that politics and conflicts are inevitable and are a way of life in project management. Project managers of the future must become politically astute. Unfortunately, even though there are some books published on politics in project management,[1] there has been limited research conducted on project management politics compared to other areas of the *PMBOK® Guide*.

---

1. See Jeffrey K. Pinto, *Power & Politics in Project Management*, The Project Management Institute, Newtown Square, PA, 1996, and Brian Irwin, *Managing Politics and Conflicts in Projects, Management Concepts*, Vienna, VA, 2008.

5.1 POLITICAL RISKS

On large and complex projects, politics are often treated as a political risk, especially when the project is being conducted in the host's country and subjected to government interference or political violence. The factors often considered as part of political risks include:

- Political change such as a new party elected into power
- Changes in the host country's fiscal policy, procurement policy and labor policy
- Nationalization or unlawful seizure of project assets and/or intellectual property
- Civil unrest resulting from a coup, acts of terrorism, kidnapping, ransom, assassinations, civil war and insurrection
- Significant inflation rate changes resulting in unfavorable monetary conversion policies
- Contract failure such as license cancellation and payment failure

We tend to include many of these risks within the scope of enterprise environmental factors that are the responsibility of the project sponsor or the governance committee. But when the project is being conducted within the host's country, it is usually the project manager that has to deal with the political risks.

The larger and more complex the project, the larger the cost overrun. And the larger the cost overrun, the greater the likelihood of political intervention. In some countries, such as in the United States, escalating problems upward usually implies that the problem ends up in the hands of the project sponsor. But in other countries, especially emerging market nations, problems may rise beyond the project's governance committee and involve high-level government officials. This is particularly true for megaprojects that are susceptible to large cost overruns.

5.2 REASONS FOR PLAYING POLITICS

There are numerous reasons why people play political games. Some of the common reasons are:

- Wanting to maintain control over scarce resources
- Seeking rewards, power or recognition
- Maintaining one's image and personal values
- Having hidden agendas
- Fear of the unknown
- Control over who gets to travel to exotic locations
- Control over important information since information is a source of power

- Getting others to do one's work
- Seeing only what one wants to see
- Refusing to accept or admit defeat or failure
- Viewing bad news as a personal failure
- Fearful of exposing mistakes to others
- Viewing failure as a sign of weakness
- Viewing failure as damage to one's reputation
- Viewing failure as damage to one's career

All of these are reasons that may benefit you personally. There are also negative politics where political games are played with the intent of hurting others, which in turn may end up benefiting you personally. Some examples would be:

- Wanting to see the project fail
- Fearful of change if the project succeeds
- Wanting to damage someone else's image or reputation, especially if they stand in the way of your career advancement
- Berating the ideas of others to strengthen your position

5.3 SITUATIONS WHERE POLITICAL GAMES WILL OCCUR

While politics can exist on any project and during any project life-cycle phase, there are some specific situations where history has shown us that politics are most likely to occur:

- Trying to achieve project management maturity within a conservative culture
- During mergers and acquisitions where the "landlord" and the "tenant" are at different levels of project management maturity
- Trying to get an entire organization to accept a project management methodology that was created by one functional area rather than a committee composed of members from all functional areas (i.e., the not invented here syndrome)
- Not believing that the project can be completed successfully and wanting to protect oneself
- Having to change one's work habits and do things differently if the project is a success
- When problems occur, not knowing where they will end up for resolution
- Believing that virtual teams are insulated from project politics
- The larger and more complex the project, the greater the chances of political interference
- The larger the size of the governance committee, the greater the chance for disagreements and political issues to appear

- Failing to understand stakeholder effective relations management practices
- The more powerful the people are on the project, the greater the chance that they will be involved in project politics
- Employees that are recognized as prima donnas are more prone to play political games that the average worker
- The project is in trouble and tradeoffs are needed to recover a possibly failing project
- Implementing a project that requires organizational change

5.4 GOVERNANCE COMMITTEE

Project politics usually ends up pushing the project in a direction different from the original statement of work (SOW). The push can originate within your own senior management, some of your project team members, the customer and even some of the stakeholders. Each may want a slightly different project outcome and your job is to try to find a way to appease everyone.

On the surface, the simplest solution appears to be the creation of a governance committee composed of senior managers from your company, representation from the customer's company and representatives from various stakeholder groups. Now, it seems that you can let the governance committee resolve all of the conflicts among themselves and give you a unified direction for the project. Gaining support from a higher power certainly seems like the right thing to do. Unfortunately, there is still the possibility that the committee cannot come to an agreement, and even if they appear to be in agreement, certain members of the committee may still try to play politics behind the scenes. The existence of the governance committee does not eliminate the existence of project politics. People that serve on a governance committee often play the political game in order to enhance their power base.

Most companies have limited funds available for projects. The result is an executive level competition for project funding that may serve the best interest of one functional area but not necessarily the best interest of the entire company. Executives may play political games to get their projects approved ahead of everyone else, viewing this as an increase to their power base. But the governance committee may include executives from those functional areas that lost out in the battle for project funding, and these executives may try to exert negative political influence on the project even so far as to hope that the project would fail. The result often occurs when a project manager is assigned to such a project and brought on board after the project is approved, never fully understanding until well into the project the politics that were played during project approval and initiation.

5.5 FRIENDS AND FOES

It is often difficult to identify quickly which people are friends or foes. Not all people that have political agendas are enemies. Some people may be playing the political game for your best interest. It is therefore beneficial to identify if possible from the personal agendas that people have whether they are friends or foes. This implies that you must communicate with them, perhaps more informally than formally, to understand their agendas. Reading body language is often a good way to make a first guess if someone is a friend or foe.

One possible way to classify people might be:

- **True supporters:** These are people that openly demonstrate their willingness to support you and your position on the project.
- **Fence sitters:** These are people that you believe will support you down the road as long as you prove to them that you are deserving of their trust and support. You may need to spend extra time with them to show them your position and to gain their support.
- **True unknowns:** Unlike fence sitters that may be won over to your way of thinking, these people are true unknowns. They may have hidden agendas that are not in your best interest, but they are relatively quiet and may have not yet expressed their concerns. These people could pose a serious threat if they are adamantly opposed to the direction in which the project is proceeding.
- **True enemies:** These are people that have made it quite clear that they are unlikely to support your views. You understand their position and probably are quite sure how they will respond to you and the direction the project is taking.

5.6 ATTACK OR RETREAT

When people play political games on projects, there are two facts that we seem to take for granted. First, these people are most likely experienced in playing such games, and second they expect to win. Based upon whom the conflict is with, you must then decide whether to aggressively attack them or retreat. Simply taking no action is a form of withdrawal and you are sure to lose the battle.

The first rule in battle is to gather as much intelligence as you can about your enemy. As an example, as part of stakeholder relations management, we can map project stakeholders according to Figure 5-1. Stakeholder mapping is most frequently displayed on a grid comparing their power and their level of interest in the project.

Manage closely: These are high-power, interested people that can make or break your project. You must put forth the greatest effort to satisfy

Figure 5-1 Stakeholder mapping.

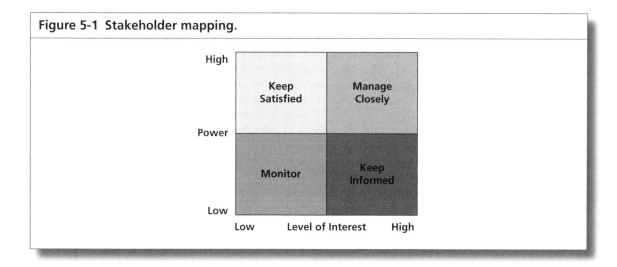

them. Be aware that there are factors that can cause them to change quadrants rapidly.

Keep satisfied: These are high-power, less interested people that can also make or break your project. You must put forth some effort to satisfy them but not with excessive detail that can lead to boredom and total disinterest. They may not get involved until the end of the project approaches.

Keep informed: These are people with limited power but keenly interested in the project. They can function as an early warning system of approaching problems and may be technically astute to assist with some technical issues. These are the stakeholders that often provide hidden opportunities.

Monitor only: These are people with limited power and may not be interested in the project unless a disaster occurs. Provide them with some information but not with too much detail such that they will become disinterested or bored.

When you go on offense and attack the people playing politics, you must have not only ammunition but also backup support if necessary. You must be prepared to show how the political decision might impact the constraints on the project as well as the accompanying baselines. Based upon the power and influence level of your opponent according to Figure 5-1, you may need other stakeholders to help you plead your case. It is highly beneficial to have supporters at the same level of position power or higher than the people playing the political game.

Not all political battles need to be won. People that play politics and possess a great deal of power may also have the authority to cancel the project or assist in the recovery process. In such cases where people possess the power to cancel the project, retreating from a political battle may be the only viable option. If you truly alienate the people playing power games, the situation can deteriorate even further. There is always the chance that you may have to work with the same people in the future. In any case, the best approach is to try to understand the people playing politics, the reason why they are playing politics and how much power and influence they have over the final decision.

5.7 NEED FOR EFFECTIVE COMMUNICATIONS

While it is not always possible to tell when someone is playing or intends to play the political game on your project, there are some tell-tale signs that this may be happening. Some of the signs are:

- People do not care about your feelings.
- People avoid discussing critical issues.
- People never ask you about your feeling on the matter.
- People procrastinate making decisions.
- People have excuses for not completing action items.
- People discuss only those items that may benefit them personally.

While project managers may not have any control over these tell-tale signs, project managers can make the situation worse through ineffective communications. To minimize the political impact on a project, the project manager should consider using the following practices:

- Listen carefully before speaking and do not jump at conclusions.
- Make sure you understand what others are saying and try to see the issue from their point of view.
- All informal communications should be followed up with a memo outlining what was discussed and to make sure that there were no misunderstandings.
- Before stating your point of view, make sure that you have gathered all of the necessary supporting information.
- Make sure that you have a clear understanding of how culture impacts the way that people are communicating with you.
- If you must provide criticism, make sure that it is constructive rather than personal criticism.
- When resolving political issues, there will be winners and losers. It is not a matter of just picking a winner. You must also explain to everyone why you selected this approach and likewise why the other approaches were not considered. This must be done tactfully.

- If the situation cannot be managed effectively, do not be embarrassed to ask senior management for advice and assistance.
- Ineffective communications encourages lying, which, in turn, generates additional political games to be played accompanied by a great deal of mistrust.

Project managers must be careful when discussing politics with team members, the client and stakeholders. The information could be misunderstood or filtered, especially if people hear what they want to hear. The result could be additional politics that were unexpected, and friends could easily turn into foes.

5.8 POWER AND INFLUENCE

Effective communication skills alone cannot resolve all political situations. To understand why, we must look at how project management generally works. If all projects stayed within the traditional hierarchy, someone would have the ultimate authority to resolve political issues. But since most projects are managed outside the traditional hierarchy, the burden for the resolution of conflicts and political issues usually falls upon the shoulders of the project manager even if a governance committee is in place. The governance committee may very well be the cause of the conflict.

On the surface, it seems like the simplest solution would be to give the project manager sufficient authority to resolve political issues. But projects are usually executed outside of the traditional hierarchy, thus limiting the authority that the project manager will possess. This lack of formal authority makes the project manager's job difficult. While project charters do give project managers some degree of authority for a given project, most project managers still have limitations because:

- The project managers must negotiate with functional managers for qualified resources.
- The project managers may not be able to remove employees from a project without the functional manager's concurrence.
- The project managers generally have no direct responsibility for wage and salary administration.
- The project managers may possess virtually no reward or punishment power.
- If employees are assigned to multiple projects, the project managers may not be able to force the employees to work on their projects in a timely manner.

With a lack of position power which comes from the traditional hierarchy, and without the ability to reward or punish, the project manager must rely upon other forms of power and the ability to influence people.

Behavioral skills such as effective communications, motivation techniques, conflict management, bargaining and negotiations are essential to resolve political disputes. Unfortunately most project managers lack political savvy and have poor conflict resolution skills.

5.9 MANAGING PROJECT POLITICS

While project politics are inevitable, there are actions the project manager can take to minimize or control political issues. Some of these actions are:

- Gather as much information as you can about the political situation.
- Make sure that everyone fully understands the impact of the political situation upon the project's baselines.
- Try to see the picture through the eyes of the person playing politics.
- Try to form a coalition with the people playing politics.
- See if your sponsor or the governance committee can insulate you from the political games.
- Having a structured decision-making process as part of your project management methodology can reduce some of the political games.
- Try to determine one's political position by reading their body language.
- If the political situation cannot be resolved quickly, demonstrate a willingness to compromise as long as the integrity of the project is not sacrificed.

Power breeds politics and politics in turn breeds power. Expecting to manage a project without any political interference is wishful thinking rather than reality. We cannot predict customer and stakeholder behavior. Sometimes the political situation occurs without any early warning signs.

Nobody can agree on a definition of organizational or project politics. Politics can appear in many shapes, forms and sizes. Therefore the project manager must develop superior behavioral skills to deal with political situations. The danger in not being able to manage political situations correctly is redirection or misdirection of the project.

5.10 PROLOGUE TO THE SPACE SHUTTLE *CHALLENGER* DISASTER CASE STUDY

More than 25 years ago, seven astronauts were killed when the space shuttle *Challenger* exploded shortly after liftoff. When projects fail, especially when there is a loss of life, people quickly look for someone or something to blame for the catastrophe. Politics often become prevalent in deciding where the blame may fall. Politics may be used to help identify where the blame exists or political intervention may hinder the actual investigation and try to guide it down the wrong path.

Shortly after the disaster, everyone pointed the finger at the infamous O-rings that supposedly failed to perform correctly. The subject that was avoided during the investigation following the accident was, given the technology at that time that indicated that there were severe risks with the launch, who ordered the launch? Was politics the real reason for the death of seven astronauts?

Whenever a disaster occurs, it usually takes 10–20 years after the disaster for the truth to come out. People that knew the truth at that time were afraid to speak up for fear of retribution and/or loss of employment. But after they retire, they usually write books about what really happened, and that's when all of the pieces begin to fit together.

When reading over the case study in Section 5.11, look at the following key points:

- From a technical point of view, was there any evidence that indicated that the launch was a high risk?
- Who made the decision to launch?
- Was the decision to launch made using the normal chain of command or was the launch decision made elsewhere, such as by the governance committee?
- Were there political reasons to launch given the risks?
- Who most likely made the launch decision?

5.11 SPACE SHUTTLE *CHALLENGER* DISASTER[2]

On January 28, 1986, the space shuttle *Challenger* lifted off the launch pad at 11:38 a.m., beginning the flight of mission 51-L.[3] Approximately 74 seconds into the flight, the *Challenger* was engulfed in an explosive burn and all communication and telemetry ceased. Seven brave crewmembers lost their lives. On board the *Challenger* were Francis R. (Dick) Scobee (commander), Michael John Smith (pilot), Ellison S. Onizuka (mission specialist one), Judith Arlene Resnik (mission specialist two), Ronald Erwin McNair (mission specialist three), S. Christa McAuliffe (payload specialist one), and Gregory Bruce Jarvis (payload specialist two). A faulty seal, or O-ring, on one of the two solid rocket boosters, caused the accident.

Following the accident, significant energy was expended trying to ascertain whether or not the accident was predictable. Controversy arose from

---

3. The first digit indicates the fiscal year of the launch (i.e., "5" means 1985). The second number indicates the launch site (i.e., "1" is the Kennedy Space Center in Florida, "2" is Vandenberg Air Force Base in California). The letter represents the mission number (i.e., "C" would be the third mission scheduled). This designation system was implemented after space shuttle flights one through nine, which were designated STS-XX. STS is the Space Transportation System and XX would indicate the flight number.

the desire to assign, or avoid, blame. Some publications called it a management failure, specifically in risk management, while others called it a technical failure.

Whenever accidents occurred in the past at NASA, an internal investigation team was formed. But in this case, perhaps because of the visibility, the White House took the initiative in appointing an independent commission. There did exist significant justification for the commission. NASA was in a state of disarray, especially in the management ranks. The agency had been without a permanent administrator for almost four months. The turnover rate at the upper echelons of management was significantly high, and there seemed to be a lack of direction from the top down.

Another reason for appointing a presidential commission was the visibility of this mission. This mission was highly publicized as the Teacher in Space mission with Christa McAuliffe, a Concord, New Hampshire, schoolteacher selected from a list of over 10,000 applicants. The nation knew the names of all of the crewmembers on board *Challenger*. The mission was highly publicized for months stating that Christa McAuliffe would be teaching students from the *Challenger* on day 4 of the mission.

The Presidential Commission on the Space Shuttle *Challenger* Accident consisted of the following members:

- **William P. Rogers**, Chairman: Former Secretary of State under President Nixon and Attorney General under President Eisenhower
- **Neil A. Armstrong**, Vice Chairman: former astronaut and spacecraft commander for Apollo 11
- **David C. Acheson**: former Senior Vice President and General Counsel, Communications Satellite Corporation (1967–1974), and a partner in the law firm of Drinker Biddle & Reath
- **Dr. Eugene E. Covert**: Professor and Head, Department of Aeronautics and Astronautics at Massachusetts Institute of Technology
- **Dr. Richard P. Feynman**: Physicist and Professor of Theoretical Physics at California Institute of Technology; Nobel Prize winner in Physics, 1965
- **Robert B. Hotz**: Editor-in-Chief of *Aviation Week & Space Technology* magazine (1953-1980)
- **Major General Donald J. Kutyna, USAF**: Director of Space Systems and Command, Control, Communications
- **Dr. Sally K. Ride**: Astronaut and mission specialist on STS-7, launched on June 18, 1983, becoming the first American woman in space. She also flew on mission 41-G, launched October 5, 1984. She holds a Doctorate in Physics from Stanford University (1978) and was still an active astronaut.
- **Robert W. Rummel**: Vice President of Trans World Airlines and President of Robert W. Rummel Associates, Inc., of Mesa, Arizona
- **Joseph F. Sutter**: Executive Vice President of the Boeing Commercial Airplane Company

- **Dr. Arthur B. C. Walker, Jr.:** Astronomer and Professor of Applied Physics, formerly Associate Dean of the Graduate Division at Stanford University, and consultant to Aerospace Corporation, Rand Corporation and the National Science Foundation
- **Dr. Albert D. Wheelon:** Executive Vice President, Hughes Aircraft Company
- **Brigadier General Charles Yeager, USAF (Retired):** Former experimental test pilot. He was the first person to penetrate the sound barrier and the first to fly at a speed of more than 1600 miles an hour.
- **Dr. Alton G. Keel, Jr.:** Executive Director; detailed to the commission from his position in the Executive Office of the President, Office of Management and Budget, as Associate Director for National Security and International Affairs; formerly Assistant Secretary of the Air Force for Research, Development and Logistics, and Senate Staff

The commission interviewed more than 160 individuals, and more than 35 formal panel investigative sessions were held generating almost 12,000 pages of transcript. Almost 6300 documents totaling more than 122,000 pages, along with hundreds of photographs, were examined and made a part of the commission's permanent database and archives. These sessions and all the data gathered added to the 2800 pages of hearing transcript generated by the commission in both closed and open sessions. Unless otherwise stated, all of the quotations and memos in this case study come from the direct testimony cited in the *Report by the Presidential Commission* (*RPC*).

Background to Space Transportation System

During the early 1960s, NASA's strategic plans for post-Apollo manned space exploration rested upon a three-legged stool. The first leg was a reusable space transportation system, the space shuttle, which could transport people and equipment to low Earth orbits and then return to Earth in preparation for the next mission. The second leg was a manned space station that would be resupplied by the space shuttle and serve as a launch platform for space research and planetary exploration. The third leg would be planetary exploration to Mars. But by the late 1960s, the United States was involved in the Vietnam War. The war was becoming costly. In addition, confidence in the government was eroding because of civil unrest and assassinations. With limited funding due to budgetary cuts and the lunar landing missions coming to an end, prioritization of projects was necessary. With a Democratic Congress continuously attacking the cost of space exploration and minimal support from President Nixon, the space program was left standing on one leg only, the space shuttle.

President Nixon made it clear that funding for all programs would be impossible and that funding for any program on the order of the

Apollo Program was likewise not possible. President Nixon seemed to favor the space station concept, but this required the development of a reusable space shuttle. Thus, NASA's Space Shuttle Program became the near-term priority.

One of the reasons for the high priority given to the Space Shuttle Program was a 1972 study completed by Dr. Oskar Morgenstern and Dr. Klaus Heiss of the Princeton-based Mathematica organization. The study showed that the space shuttle could orbit payloads for as little as $100 per pound based on 60 launches per year with payloads of 65,000 pounds. This provided tremendous promise for military applications such as reconnaissance and weather satellites as well as scientific research.

Unfortunately, the pricing data was somewhat tainted. Much of the cost data was provided by companies that were hopeful of becoming NASA contractors and therefore provided unrealistically low cost estimates in hopes of winning future bids. The actual cost per pound was more than 20 times the original estimate. Furthermore, the main engines never achieved the 109% of thrust that NASA desired, thus limiting the payloads to 47,000 pounds instead of the predicted 65,000 pounds. In addition, the European Space Agency began successfully developing the capability to place satellites into orbit and began competing with NASA for the commercial satellite business.

NASA Succumbs to Politics and Pressure

To retain shuttle funding, NASA was forced to make a series of major concessions. First, facing a highly constrained budget, NASA sacrificed the research and development necessary to produce a truly reusable shuttle and instead accepted a design that was only partially reusable, eliminating one of the features that made the shuttle attractive in the first place. Solid rocket boosters (SRBs) were used instead of safer liquid-fueled boosters because they required a much smaller research and development effort and were less costly to maintain. Numerous other design changes were made to reduce the level of research and development required.

Second, to increase its political clout and to guarantee a steady customer base, NASA enlisted the support of the United States Air Force. The Air Force could provide the considerable political clout of the Defense Department and had many satellites that required launching. However, Air Force support did not come without a price. The shuttle payload bay was required to meet Air Force size and shape requirements, which placed key constraints on the ultimate design. Even more important was the Air Force requirement that the shuttle be able to launch from Vandenburg Air Force Base in California. This constraint required a larger cross range than the Florida site, which in turn decreased the total allowable vehicle weight. The weight reduction required the elimination of the design's air breathing engines, resulting in a single-pass unpowered landing. This greatly limited the safety and landing versatility of the vehicle.[4]

As the year 1986 began, there was extreme pressure on NASA to "Fly out the Manifest." From its inception, the Space Shuttle Program had been plagued by exaggerated expectations, funding inconsistencies and political pressure. The ultimate vehicle and mission designs were shaped almost as much by politics as by physics. President Kennedy's declaration that the United States would land a man on the moon before the end of the decade had provided NASA's Apollo Program with high visibility, a clear direction and powerful political backing. The Space Shuttle Program was not as fortunate; it had neither a clear direction nor consistent political backing.

Cost containment became a critical issue for NASA. In order to minimize cost, NASA designed a space shuttle system that utilized both liquid and solid propellants. Liquid propellant engines are more easily controllable than solid propellant engines. Flow of liquid propellant from the storage tanks to the engine can be throttled and even shut down in case of an emergency. Unfortunately, an all-liquid-fuel design was prohibitive because a liquid fuel system is significantly more expensive to maintain than a solid fuel system.

Solid fuel systems are less costly to maintain. However, once a solid propellant system is ignited, it cannot be easily throttled or shut down. Solid propellant rocket motors burn until all of the propellant is consumed. This could have a significant impact on safety, especially during launch, at which time the solid rocket boosters are ignited and have maximum propellant loads. Also, solid rocket boosters can be designed for reusability whereas liquid engines are generally a one-time use.

The final design that NASA selected was a compromise of both solid and liquid fuel engines. The space shuttle would be a three-element system composed of the orbiter vehicle, an expendable external liquid fuel tank carrying liquid fuel for the orbiter's engines, and two recoverable solid rocket boosters.[5] The orbiter's engines were liquid fuel because of the necessity for throttle capability. The two solid rocket boosters would provide the added thrust necessary to launch the space shuttle into or close to its orbiting altitude.

In 1972, NASA selected Rockwell as the prime contractor for building the orbiter. Many industry leaders believed that other competitors who had actively participated in the Apollo Program had a competitive advantage. Rockwell, however, was awarded the contract. Rockwell's proposal did not include an escape system. NASA officials decided against the launch escape

---

4. Kurt Hoover and Wallace T. Fowler (The University of Texas at Austin and The Texas Space Grant Consortium), "Studies in Ethics, Safety and Liability for Engineers," http://www.tsgc. utexas.edu/archive/general/ethics/shuttle.html, p. 2.

5. The terms "solid rocket booster" (SRB) and "solid rocket motor" (SRM) will be used interchangeably.

system since it would have added too much weight to the shuttle at launch and was very expensive. There was also some concern on how effective an escape system would be if an accident occurred during launch while all of the engines were ignited. Thus, the space shuttle became the first U.S. manned spacecraft without a launch escape system for the crew.

In 1973, NASA went out for competitive bidding for the solid rocket boosters. The competitors were Morton-Thiokol, Inc. (MTI) (henceforth called Thiokol), Aerojet General, Lockheed, and United Technologies. The contract was eventually awarded to Thiokol because of its low cost, $100 million lower than the nearest competitor. Some believed that other competitors who ranked higher in technical design and safety should have been given the contract. NASA believed that Thiokol-built solid rocket motors would provide the lowest cost per flight.

Solid Rocket Boosters

Thiokol's solid rocket boosters had a height of approximately 150 feet and a diameter of 12 feet. The empty weight of each booster was 192,000 pounds and the full weight was 1,300,000 pounds. Once ignited, each booster provided 2.65 million pounds of thrust, which is more than 70% of the thrust needed to reach orbit.

Thiokol's design for the boosters was criticized by some of the competitors and even NASA personnel. The boosters were to be manufactured in four segments and then shipped by rail from Utah to the launch site where the segments would be assembled into a single unit. The Thiokol design was largely based upon the segmented design of the Titan III solid rocket motor produced by United Technologies in the 1950s for Air Force satellite programs. Satellite programs were unmanned efforts.

The four solid rocket sections made up the case of the booster, which essentially encased the rocket fuel and directed the flow of the exhaust gases. This is shown in Figure 5-2. The cylindrical shell of the case is protected from the propellant by a layer of insulation. The mating sections of the field joint are called the tang and the clevis. One hundred and seventy seven pins spaced around the circumference of each joint hold the tang and the clevis together. The joint is sealed in three ways. First, zinc chromate putty is placed in the gap between the mating segments and their insulation. This putty protects the second and third seals, which are rubber-like rings, called O-rings. The first O-ring is called the primary O-ring and is lodged in the gap between the tang and the clevis. The last seal is called the secondary O-ring and is identical to the primary O-ring except it is positioned further downstream in the gap. Each O-ring is 0.280 inches in diameter. The placement of each O-ring can be seen in Figure 5-3. Another component of the field joint is called the leak check port, which is shown in Figure 5-4. The leak check port is designed to allow technicians to check the status of the two O-ring seals. Pressurized air is inserted through the leak

Figure 5-2 Solid rocket booster.

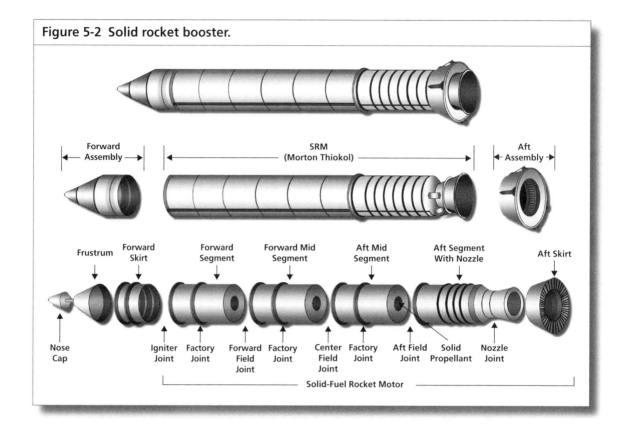

check port into the gap between the two O-rings. If the O-rings maintain the pressure and do not let the pressurized air past the seal, the technicians know the seal is operating properly.[6]

In the Titan III assembly process, the joints between the segmented sections contained one O-ring. Thiokol's design had two O-rings instead of one. The second O-ring was initially considered as redundant but was included to improve safety. The purpose of the O-rings was to seal the space in the joints such that the hot exhaust gases could not escape and damage the case of the boosters.

Both the Titan III and shuttle O-rings were made of Viton rubber, which is an elastomeric material. For comparison, rubber is also an elastomer. The elastomeric material used is a fluoroelastomer, which is an elastomer that contains fluorine. This material was chosen because of its resistance to high temperatures and its compatibility with the surrounding materials. The Titan III O-rings were molded in one piece whereas the shuttle's SRB

6. "The Challenger Accident: Mechanical Causes of the Challenger Accident," University of Texas, http://www.me.utexas.edu/~uer/challenger/chall2.html, pp. 1–2.

Figure 5-3 Location of O-rings.

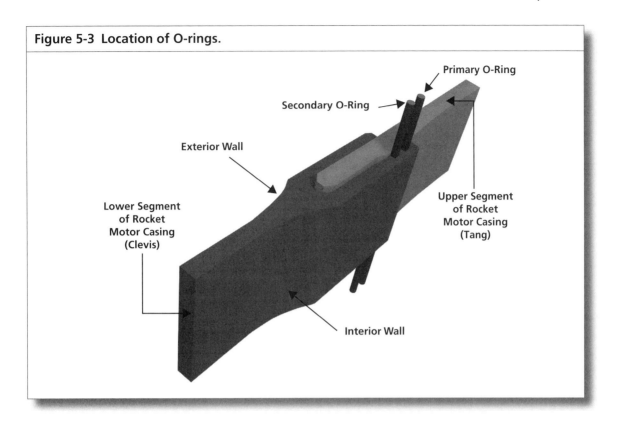

O-rings would be manufactured in five sections and then glued together. Routinely, repairs would be necessary for inclusions and voids in the rubber received from the material suppliers.

Blowholes

The primary purpose of the zinc chromate putty was to act as a thermal barrier that protected the O-rings from the hot exhaust. As mentioned before, the O-ring seals were tested using the leak check port to pressurize the gap between the seals. During the test, the secondary seal was pushed down into the same, seated position as it occupied during ignition pressurization. However, because the leak check port was between the two O-ring seals, the primary O-ring was pushed up and seated against the putty. The position of the O-rings during flight and their position during the leak check test are shown in Figure 5-4.

During early flights, engineers worried that, because the putty above the primary seal could withstand high pressures, the presence of the putty would prevent the leak test from identifying problems with the primary O-ring seal. They contended that the putty would seal the gap during testing

Figure 5-4 Cross section showing leak test port.

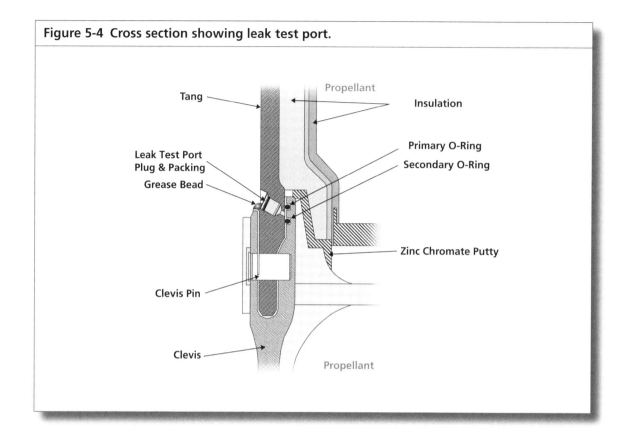

regardless of the condition of the primary O-ring seal. Since the proper operation of the primary O-ring seal was essential, engineers decided to increase the pressure used during the test to above the pressure that the putty could withstand. This would insure that the primary O-ring was properly sealing the gap without the aid of the putty. Unfortunately, during this new procedure, the high test pressures blew holes through the putty before the primary O-ring could seal the gap.

Since the putty was on the interior of the assembled solid rocket booster, technicians could not mend the blowholes in the putty. As a result, this procedure left small, tunneled holes in the putty. These holes would allow focused exhaust gases to contact a small segment of the primary O-ring during launch. Engineers realized that this was a problem but decided to test the O-ring seals at the high pressure despite the formation of blowholes rather than risking a launch with a faulty primary O-ring seal.

The purpose of the putty was to prevent the hot exhaust gases from reaching the O-rings. For the first nine successful shuttle launches, NASA and Thiokol used asbestos-bearing putty manufactured by the Fuller-O'Brien

Company of San Francisco. However, because of the notoriety of products containing asbestos and the fear of potential lawsuits, Fuller-O'Brien stopped manufacturing the putty that had served the shuttle so well. This created a problem for NASA and Thiokol.

The new putty selected came from Randolph Products of Carlstadt, New Jersey. Unfortunately, with the new putty, blowholes and O-ring erosion were becoming more common to a point where the shuttle engineers became worried. Yet the new putty was still used on the boosters. Following the *Challenger* disaster, testing showed that, at low temperatures, the Randolph putty became much stiffer than the Fuller-O'Brien putty and lost much of its stickiness.[7]

O-Ring Erosion

If the hot exhaust gases penetrate the putty and contact the primary O-ring, the extreme temperatures would break down the O-ring material. Because engineers were aware of the possibility of O-ring erosion, the joints were checked after each flight for evidence of erosion. The amount of O-ring erosion found on flights before the new high-pressure leak check procedure was around 12%. After the new high-pressure leak test procedure the percentage of O-ring erosion was found to increase by 88%. High percentages of O-ring erosion in some cases allowed the exhaust gases to pass the primary O-ring and begin eroding the secondary O-ring. Some managers argued that some O-ring erosion was "acceptable" because the O-rings were found to seal the gap even if they were eroded by as much as one-third their original diameter.[8] The engineers believed that the design and operation of the joints were an acceptable risk because a safety margin could be identified quantitatively. This numerical boundary would become an important precedent for future risk assessment.

Joint Rotation

During ignition, the internal pressure from the burning fuel applies approximately 1000 pounds per square inch on the case wall, causing the walls to expand. Because the joints are generally stiffer than the case walls, each section tends to bulge out. The swelling of the solid rocket sections causes the tang and the clevis to become misaligned; this misalignment is called joint rotation. A diagram showing a field joint before and after joint rotation is shown in Figure 5-5. The problem with joint rotation is that it increases the gap size near the O-rings. This increase in size is extremely fast, which makes it difficult for the O-rings to follow the increasing gap and keep the seal.[9]

---

7. Ibid., p. 3.

8. Ibid., p. 4.

9. Ibid., p. 4.

Figure 5-5 Field joint rotation.

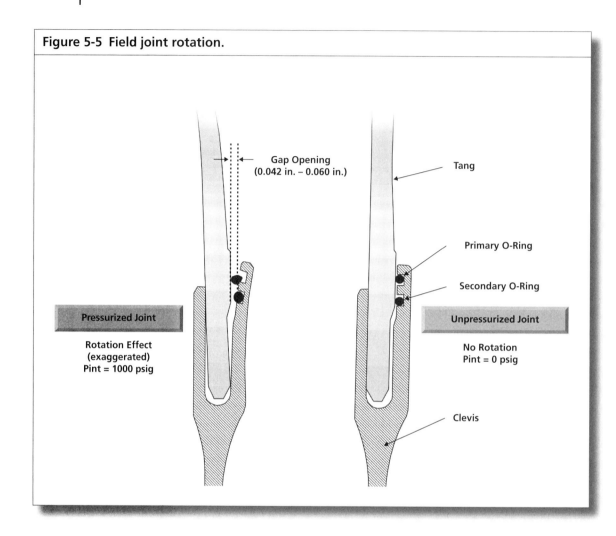

Prior to ignition, the gap between the tang and the clevis is approximately 0.004 inches. At ignition, the gap will enlarge to between 0.042 and 0.060 inches, *but for a maximum of 0.60 second,* and then return to its original position.

O-Ring Resilience

The term O-ring resilience refers to the ability of the O-ring to return to its original shape after it has been deformed. This property is analogous to the ability of a rubber band to return to its original shape after it has been stretched. As with a rubber band, the resiliency of an O-ring is directly related to its temperature. As the temperature of the O-ring gets lower, the O-ring material becomes stiffer. Tests have shown that an O-ring at 75°F is five times more responsive in returning to its original shape than an O-ring at 30°F. This decrease in O-ring resiliency during a cold-weather launch would make the O-ring much less likely to follow the increasing gap size during joint rotation. As a result of poor O-ring resiliency the O-ring would not seal properly.[10]

External Tank

The solid rockets are each joined forward and aft to the external liquid fuel tank.

They are not connected to the orbiter vehicle. The solid rocket motors are mounted first, and the external liquid fuel tank is put between them and connected. Then the orbiter is mounted to the external tank at two places in the back and one place forward, and those connections carry all of the structural loads for the entire system at liftoff and through the ascent phase of flight. Also connected to the orbiter, under the orbiter's wing, are two large propellant lines 17 inches in diameter. The one on the port side carries liquid hydrogen from the hydrogen tank in the back part of the external tank.

The line on the right side carries liquid oxygen from the oxygen tank at the forward end, inside the external tank (RPC, p. 50).

The external tank contains about 1.6 million pounds of liquid cryogenic propellant, or about 526,000 gallons. The orbiter's three engines burn the liquid hydrogen and liquid oxygen at a ratio of 6:1 and at a rate equivalent to emptying out a family swimming pool every 10 seconds! Once ignited, the exhaust gases leave the orbiter's three engines at approximately 6000 miles per hour. After the fuel is consumed, the external tank separates from the orbiter, falls to Earth and disintegrates in the atmosphere on reentry.

Spare Parts Problem

In March 1985, NASA's administrator, James Beggs, announced that there would be one shuttle flight per month for all of fiscal year 1985. In actuality, there were only six flights. Repairs became a problem. Continuous repairs were needed on the heat tiles required for reentry, the braking system and the main engines' hydraulic pumps. Parts were routinely borrowed from other shuttles. The cost of spare parts was excessively high, and NASA was looking for cost containment.

Risk Identification Procedures

The necessity for risk management was apparent right from the start. Prior to the launch of the first shuttle in April of 1981, hazards were analyzed and subjected to a formalized hazard reduction process as described in NASA Handbook, NHB5300.4. The process required that the credibility and

---

10. Ibid., pp. 4–5.

TABLE 5-1 Risk Classification System

LEVEL	DESCRIPTION
Criticality 1 (C1)	Loss of life and/or vehicle if the component fails
Criticality 2 (C2)	Loss of mission if the component fails
Criticality 3 (C3)	All others
Criticality 1R (C1R)	Redundant components exist. The failure of both could cause loss of life and/or vehicle.
Criticality 2R (C2R)	Redundant components exist. The failure of both could cause loss of mission.

probability of the hazards be determined. A Senior Safety Review Board was established for overseeing the risk assessment process. For the most part, the risks assessment process was qualitative. The conclusion reached was that no single hazard or combination of hazards should prevent the launch of the first shuttle *as long as the aggregate risk remains acceptable.*

NASA used a rather simplistic Safety (Risk) Classification System. A quantitative method for risk assessment was not in place at NASA because the data needed to generate statistical models would be expensive and labor intensive. If the risk identification procedures were overly complex, NASA would have been buried in paperwork due to the number of components on the space shuttle. The risk classification system selected by NASA is illustrated in Table 5-1.

In 1982, the O-ring seals were labeled criticality 1. By 1985, there were 700 components identified as criticality 1.

Teleconferencing

The Space Shuttle Program involves a vast number of people at both NASA and the contractors. Because of the geographical separation between NASA and the contractors, it became impractical to have continuous meetings. Travel between Thiokol in Utah and the Cape in Florida was one day's travel each way. Therefore, teleconferencing became the primary method of communication and a way of life. Interface meetings were still held, but the emphasis was on teleconferencing. All locations could be linked together in one teleconference and data could be faxed back and forth as needed.

Paperwork Constraints

With the rather optimistic flight schedule provided to the news media, NASA was under scrutinization and pressure to deliver. For fiscal 1986, the mission manifest called for 16 flights. The pressure to meet schedule was about to take its toll. Safety problems had to be resolved quickly.

As the number of flights scheduled began to increase, so did the requirements for additional paperwork. The majority of the paperwork had to be completed prior to NASA's flight readiness review (FRR) meetings. Prior to every flight (approximately one week), flight operations and cargo managers were required to endorse the commitment of flight readiness to the NASA associate administrator for space flight at the FRR meetings. The responsible project/element managers would conduct pre-FRR meetings with their contractors, center managers and the NASA level II manager. The content of the FRR meetings included:

- Overall status, plus establishing the baseline in terms of significant changes since the last mission
- Review of significant problems resolved since the last review and significant anomalies from the previous flight
- Review of all open items and constraints remaining to be resolved before the mission
- Presenting all new waivers since the last flight

NASA personnel were working excessive overtime, including weekends, to fulfill the paperwork requirements and prepare for the required meetings. As the number of space flights increased, so did the paperwork and overtime.

The paperwork constraints were affecting the contractors as well. Additional paperwork requirements existed for problem solving and investigations. On October 1, 1985, an interoffice memo was sent from Scott Stein, space booster project engineer at Thiokol, to Bob Lund, vice president for engineering at Thiokol, and to other selected managers concerning the O-ring Investigation Task Force:

> We are currently being hog-tied by paperwork every time we try to accomplish anything. I understand that for production programs, the paperwork is necessary. However, for a priority, short schedule investigation, it makes accomplishment of our goals in a timely manner extremely difficult, if not impossible. We need the authority to bypass some of the paperwork jungle. As a representative example of problems and time that could easily be eliminated, consider assembly or disassembly of test hardware by manufacturing personnel. . . . I know the established paperwork procedures can be violated if someone with enough authority dictates it. We did that with the DR system when the FWC hardware "Tiger Team" was established. If changes are not made to allow us to accomplish work in a reasonable amount of time, then the O-ring investigation task force will never have the potency necessary to resolve problems in a timely manner.

Both NASA and the contractors were now feeling the pressure caused by the paperwork constraints.

Politics and O-Rings

Scott Stein's memo clearly indicated that many of the engineers at Thiokol (and also at NASA) had serious concerns about the performance of the O-rings. Yet it was apparent that neither Thiokol nor NASA was committing sufficient resources to resolve the issues. There were several rumors for why this was happening. First, if serious design or operational flaws were found, the space shuttle flights could be shut down for two to three years during the redesign and requalification efforts. Second, there would be no guarantee that Thiokol would still have the contract. Third, the Reagan administration was using 25% of the shuttle flights for military purposes. The shuttle cargo bay could carry military satellites and weaponry to support Reagan's desire to promote the arms race. Shutting down the shuttle for redesign efforts would not please the Reagan administration. Fourth, both NASA and the Reagan administration wanted approximately 24 flights per year and that would put pressure on Thiokol's resources. NASA was considering qualifying a second source supplier for some of the boosters. There were rumors that Thiokol would not put forth an effort to redesign the boosters as long as NASA eliminated the need for a second source supplier. The second source supplier efforts were then cancelled, but the concerns over the O-rings still remained.

Issuing Waivers

One quick way of reducing paperwork and meetings was to issue a waiver. Historically a waiver was a formalized process that allows an exception to a rule, specification, technical criterion or risk. Waivers were ways to reduce excessive paperwork requirements. Project managers and contract administrators had the authority to issue waivers, often with the intent of bypassing standard protocols in order to maintain a schedule. Engineers did not have the authority to issue waivers. The use of waivers had been in place well before the manned space program even began. What is important here was **NOT** NASA's use of the waiver, but the **JUSTIFICATION** for the waiver given the risks. For example, were waivers being issued based upon sound technical judgment and common sense or because of pressure from the client or political pressure to launch and maintain a schedule?

NASA had issued waivers on both criticality 1 status designations and launch constraints. In 1982, the solid rocket boosters were designated C1 by the Marshall Space Flight Center because failure of the O-rings could have caused loss of the crew and the shuttle. This meant that the secondary O-rings were not considered redundant. The SRB project manager at Marshall, Larry Mulloy, issued a waiver just in time for the next shuttle launch to take place as planned. Later, the O-ring designation went from C1 to C1R (i.e., a redundant process), thus partially avoiding the need for a waiver. The waiver was a necessity to keep the shuttle flying according to the original manifest. Later, during the Congressional testimony, This document became known as the "Death Document," implying that sooner or later we would lose a shuttle and its crew.

But having a risk identification of C1 was not regarded as a sufficient reason to cancel a launch. It simply meant that component failure could be disastrous. It implied that this might be a potential problem that needed attention. If the risks were acceptable, NASA could still launch. A more serious condition was the issuing of launch constraints. Launch constraints were official NASA designations for situations in which mission safety was a serious enough problem to justify a decision not to launch. An example would be the temperature prior to launch. But once again, a launch constraint did not imply that the launch should be delayed. It meant that this was an important problem and needed to be addressed.

Following the 1985 mission that showed O-ring erosion and exhaust gas blow-by, a launch constraint was imposed. Yet on each of the next five shuttle missions, NASA's Mulloy issued a launch constraint waiver allowing the flights to take place on schedule without any changes to the O-rings.

Were the waivers a violation of serious safety rules just to keep the shuttle flying? The answer is NO! NASA had protocols such as policies, procedures and rules for adherence to safety. Waivers were also protocols but for the purpose of deviating from other existing protocols. Neither Larry Mulloy, his colleagues at NASA nor the contractors had any intentions of doing evil. Waivers were simply a way of saying that we believe that the risk is an *acceptable risk*.

The lifting of launch constraints and the issuance of waivers became the norm or standard operating procedure. Waivers became a way of life. If waivers were issued and the mission was completed successfully, then the same waivers would exist for the next flight and did not have to be brought up for discussion at the FRR meeting. This is an extremely important point. Without waivers, all critical issues, including C1 risks, would be brought up to the senior levels of management for review. Now, using waivers, senior management at NASA were insulated from possible bad news.

The justification for the waivers seemed to be the similarity between flight launch conditions, temperature, etc. Launching under similar conditions seemed to be important for the engineers at NASA and Thiokol because it meant that the forces acting on the O-rings were within their region of experience and could be correlated to existing data. The launch temperature effect on the O-rings was considered predictable and therefore constituted an acceptable risk to both NASA and Thiokol, thus perhaps eliminating costly program delays in having to redesign the O-rings. The completion of each shuttle mission added another data point to the region of experience, thus guaranteeing the same waivers on the next launch. Flying with acceptable risk became the norm in NASA's culture and senior management was insulated from knowledge concerning the acceptable risks.

Waivers meant that NASA could launch regardless of the risks and launch conditions such as temperature. NASA could launch even if launch conditions were outside of the range of their specifications. Simply stated, all problems were treated as anomalies. We will fly "as is" and fix all of the problems or anomalies sometime in the future.

Launch Liftoff Sequence Profile: Possible Aborts

During the countdown to liftoff, the launch team closely monitors weather conditions, not only at the launch site, but also at touchdown sites should the mission need to be prematurely aborted.

Dr. Frynman: Would you explain why we are so sensitive to the weather?
Mr. Moore: (NASA's Deputy Administrator for Space Flight): Yes, there are several reasons. I mentioned the return to the landing site. We need to have visibility if we get into a situation where we need to return to the landing site after launch, and the pilots and the commanders need to be able to see the runway and so forth. So, you need a ceiling limitation on it [i.e., weather].

We also need to maintain specifications on wind velocity so we don't exceed crosswinds. Landing on a runway and getting too high of a crosswind may cause us to deviate off of the runway and so forth, so we have a crosswind limit. During assent, assuming a nominal flight, a chief concern is damage to tiles due to rain. We have had experiences in seeing what the effects of a brief shower can do in terms of the tiles. The tiles are thermal insulation blocks, very thick. A lot of them are very thick on the bottom of the Orbiter. But if you have a raindrop and you are going at a very high velocity, it tends to erode the tiles, pock the tiles, and that causes us a grave concern regarding the thermal protection.

In addition to that, you are worried about the turn-around time of the Orbiters as well, because with the kind of tile damage that one could get in rain, you have an awful lot of work to do to go back and replace tiles back on the system. So, there are a number of concerns that weather enters into, and it is a major factor in our assessment of whether or not we are ready to launch.

(RPC, p. 18)

Approximately 6–7 seconds prior to the liftoff, the shuttle's main engines (liquid fuel) ignite. These engines consume one half million gallons of liquid fuel. It takes 9 hours prior to launch to fill the liquid fuel tanks. At ignition, the engines are throttled up to 104% of rated power. Redundancy checks on the engines' systems are then made. The launch site ground complex and the orbiter's onboard computer complex check a large number of details and parameters about the main engines to make sure that everything is proper and that the main engines are performing as planned.

If a malfunction is detected, the system automatically goes into a shutdown sequence and the mission is scrubbed. The primary concern at this point is to make the vehicle "safe." The crew remains on board and performs a number of functions to get the vehicle into a safe mode. This includes making sure that all propellant and electrical systems are properly safed. Ground crews at the launch pad begin servicing the launch pad. Once the launch pad is in a safe condition, the hazard and safety teams begin draining the remaining liquid fuel out of the external tank.

If no malfunction is detected during this 6-second period of liquid fuel burn, then a signal is sent to ignite the two solid rocket boosters and liftoff occurs. For the next 2 minutes, with all engines ignited, the shuttle goes through a maximum-Q, or high-dynamic-pressure, phase that exerts maximum pressure loads on the orbiter vehicle. Based upon the launch profile, the main engines may be throttled down slightly during the maximum-Q phase to lower the loads.

After 128 seconds into the launch sequence, all of the solid fuel is expended and the SRB staging occurs. The SRB parachutes are deployed. The SRBs then fall back to Earth 162 miles from the launch site and are recovered for examination, cleaning and reuse on future missions. The main liquid fuel engines are then throttled up to maximum power. After 523 seconds into the liftoff, the external liquid fuel tanks are essentially expended of fuel. The main engines are shut down. Ten to 18 seconds later, the external tank is separated from the orbiter and disintegrates on reentry into the atmosphere.

From a safety perspective, the most hazardous period is the first 128 seconds when the SRBs are ignited. According to Arnold Aldrich, Manager, NASA's STS Program, Johnson Space Center:

Mr. Alrich: Once the Shuttle System starts off the launch pad, there is no capability in the system to separate these [solid propellant] rockets until they reach burnout. They will burn for two minutes and eight or nine seconds, and the system must stay together. There is not a capability built into the vehicle that would allow these to separate. There is a capability available to the flight crew to separate at this interface the Orbiter from the tank, but that is thought to be unacceptable during the first stage when the booster rockets are on and thrusting. So, essentially the first two minutes and a little more of flight, the stack is intended and designed to stay together, and it must stay together to fly successfully.

Mr. Hotz:	Mr. Aldrich, why is it unacceptable to separate the Orbiter at that stage?
Mr. Aldrich:	It is unacceptable because of the separation dynamics and the rupture of the propellant lines. You cannot perform the kind of a clean separation required for safety in the proximity of these vehicles at the velocities and the thrust levels they are undergoing, [and] the atmosphere they are flying through. In that regime, it is the design characteristic of the total system.

(RPC, p. 51)

If an abort is deemed necessary during the first 128 seconds, the actual abort will not begin until *after* SRB staging has occurred, which is after 128 seconds into the launch sequence. Based upon the reason and timing of an abort, options include those shown in Table 5-2.

Arnold Aldrich commented on different abort profiles:

Chairman Rogers:	During the two-minute period, is it possible to abort through the Orbiter?
Mr. Aldrich:	You can abort for certain conditions. You can start an abort, but the vehicle won't do anything yet, and the intended aborts are build [sic] around failures in the main engine system, the liquid propellant systems and their controls. If you have a failure of a main engine, it is well detected by the crew and by the ground support, and you can call for a return-to-launch-site abort. That would be logged in the computer. The computer would be set up to execute it, but everything waits until the solids take you to altitude. At that time, the solids will separate in the sequence I described, and then the vehicle flies downrange some 400 miles, maybe 10 to 15 additional minutes, while all of the tank propellant is expelled through these engines.
	As a precursor to setting up the conditions for this return-to-launch-site abort to be successful towards the end of that burn downrange, using the propellants and the thrust of the main engines, the vehicle turns and actually points heads up back towards Florida. When the tank is essentially depleted, automatic signals are sent to close off the [liquid] propellant lines and to separate the Orbiter, and the Orbiter then does a similar approach to the one we are familiar with with orbit back to the Kennedy Space Center for approach and landing.
Dr. Walker:	So, the propellant is expelled but not burned?

TABLE 5-2 Abort options for the shuttle

TYPES OF ABORT	LANDING SITE
Once-around abort	Edwards Air Force Base
Transatlantic abort	DaKar
Transatlantic abort	Casablanca
Return-to-landing-site (RTLS)	Kennedy Space Center

Mr. Aldrich: No, it is burned. You burn the system on two engines all the way down-range until it is gone, and then you turn around and come back because you don't have enough to burn to orbit. That is the return-to-launch-site abort, and it applies during the first 240 seconds of—no, 240 is not right. It is longer than that—the first four minutes, either before or after separation you can set that abort up, but it will occur after the solids separate, and if you have a main engine anomaly after the solids separate, at that time you can start the RTLS, and it will go through that same sequence and come back.

Dr. Ride: And you can also only do an RTLS if you have lost just one main engine. So if you lose all three main engines, RTLS isn't a viable abort mode.

Mr. Aldrich: Once you get through the four minutes, there's a period where you now don't have the energy conditions right to come back, and you have a forward abort, and Jesse mentioned the sites in Spain and on the coast of Africa. We have what is called a trans-Atlantic abort, and where you can use a very similar sequence to the one I just described. You still separate the solids, you still burn all the propellant out of the tanks, but you fly across and land across the ocean.

Mr. Hotz: Mr. Aldrich, could you recapitulate just a bit here? Is what you are telling us that for two minutes of flight, until the solids separate, there is not practical abort mode?

Mr. Aldrich: Yes, sir.

Mr. Hotz: Thank you.

Mr. Aldrich: A trans-Atlantic abort can cover a range of just a few seconds up to about a minute in the middle where the across-the-ocean sites are effective, and then you reach this abort once-around capability where you go all the way around and land in California or back to Kennedy by going around the earth. And finally, you have abort-to-orbit where you have enough propulsion to make orbit but not enough to achieve the exact orbital parameters that you desire. That is the way that the abort profiles are executed.

There are many, many nuances of crew procedure and different conditions and combinations of sequences of failures that make it much more complicated than I have described it.

(RPC, pp. 51–52)

O-Ring Problem

There were two kinds of joints on the Shuttle—field joints that were assembled at the launch site connecting together the SRB's cylindrical cases and nozzle joints that connected the aft end of the case to the nozzle. During the pressure of ignition, the field joints could become bent such that the secondary O-ring could lose contact within an estimated 0.17–0.33 second after ignition. If the primary O-ring failed to seal properly before the gap within the joints opened up and the secondary seal failed, the results could be disastrous.

When the solid propellant boosters are recovered after separation, they are disassembled and checked for damage. The O-rings could show evidence of coming into contact with heat. Hot gases from the ignition sequence could blow by the primary O-ring briefly before sealing. This "blow-by" phenomenon could last for only a few milliseconds before sealing and result in no heat damage to the O-ring. If the actual sealing process takes longer than expected, then charring and erosion of the O-rings can occur. This would be evidenced by gray or black soot and erosion to the O-rings. The terms used are impingement erosion and "by-pass" erosion with the latter identified also as sooted "blow-by."

Roger Boisjoly of Thiokol describes blow-by erosion and joint rotation as follows:

> O-ring material gets removed from the cross section of the O-ring much, much faster than when you have bypass erosion or blow-by, as people have been terming it. We usually use the characteristic blow-by to define gas past it, and we use the other term [bypass erosion] to indicate that we are eroding at the same time. And so you can have blow-by without erosion, [and] you [can] have blow-by with erosion.
>
> —(RPC, pp. 784–785)

> At the beginning of the transient cycle [initial ignition rotation, up to 0.17 second] . . . [the primary O-ring] is still being attacked by hot gas, and it is eroding at the same time it is trying to seal, and it is a race between, will it erode more than the time allowed to have it seal.
>
> —(RPC, p. 136)

On January 24, 1985, STS 51-C (flight no. 15) was launched at 51 °F, which was the lowest temperature of any launch up to that time. Analyses of the joints showed evidence of damage. Black soot appeared between the primary and secondary O-rings. The engineers concluded that the cold weather had caused the O-rings to harden and move more slowly. This allowed the hot gases to blow by and erode the O-rings. This scorching effect indicated that low-temperature launches could be disastrous.

On July 31, 1985, Roger Boisjoly of Thiokol sent an interoffice memo to R. K. Lund, Vice President for Engineering, at Thiokol:

> This letter is written to insure that management is fully aware of the seriousness of the current O-ring erosion problem in the SRM joints from an engineering standpoint.
>
> The mistakenly accepted position on the joint problem was to fly without fear of failure and to run a series of design evaluations which would ultimately lead to a solution or at least a significant reduction of the erosion problem. This position is now drastically changed as a result of the SRM 16A nozzle joint erosion which eroded a secondary O-ring with the primary O-ring never sealing.
>
> If the same scenario should occur in a field joint (and it could), then it is a jump ball as to the success or failure of the joint because the secondary O-ring cannot respond to the clevis opening rate and may not be capable of pressurization. The result would be a catastrophe of the highest order—loss of human life.
>
> An unofficial team (a memo defining the team and its purpose was never published) with [a] leader was formed on 19 July 1985 and was tasked with solving the problem for both the short and long term. This unofficial team is essentially nonexistent at this time. In my opinion, the team must be officially given the responsibility and the authority to execute the work that needs to be done on a non-interference basis (full time assignment until completed).
>
> It is my honest and very real fear that if we do not take immediate action to dedicate a team to solve the problem with the field joint having the number one priority, then we stand in jeopardy of losing a flight along with all the launch pad facilities.
>
> —(RPC, pp. 691–692)

On August 9, 1985, a letter was sent from Brian Russell, manager of the SRM Ignition System, to James Thomas at the Marshall Space Flight Center. The memo addressed the following:

> Per your request, this letter contains the answers to the two questions you asked at the July Problem Review Board telecon.
>
> 1. Question: If the field joint secondary seal lifts off the metal mating surfaces during motor pressurization, how soon will it return to a position where contact is re-established?

Answer: Bench test data indicates that the O-ring resiliency (its capability to follow the metal) is a function of temperature and rate of case expansion. MTI [Thiokol] measured the force of the O-ring against Instron plattens, which simulated the nominal squeeze on the O-ring and approximated the case expansion distance and rate.

At 100°F, the O-ring maintained contact. At 75°F, the O-ring lost contact for 2.4 seconds. At 50°F, the O-ring did not re-establish contact in 10 minutes at which time the test was terminated.

The conclusion is that secondary sealing capability in the SRM field joint cannot be guaranteed.

2. Question: If the primary O-ring does not seal, will the secondary seal seat in sufficient time to prevent joint leakage?

Answer: MTI has no reason to suspect that the primary seal would ever fail after pressure equilibrium is reached; i.e., after the ignition transient. If the primary O-ring were to fail from 0 to 170 milliseconds, there is a very high probability that the secondary O-ring would hold pressure since the case has not expanded appreciably at this point. If the primary seal were to fail from 170 to 330 milliseconds, the probability of the secondary seal holding is reduced. From 330 to 600 milliseconds the chance of the secondary seal holding is small. This is a direct result of the O-ring's slow response compared to the metal case segments as the joint rotates.

—(RPC, pp. 1568–1569)

At NASA, the concern for a solution to the O-ring problem became not only a technical crisis but also a budgetary crisis. In a July 23, 1985, memorandum from Richard Cook, program analyst, to Michael Mann, chief of the STS Resource Analysis Branch, the impact of the problem was noted:

Earlier this week you asked me to investigate reported problems with the charring of seals between SRB motor segments during flight operations. Discussions with program engineers show this to be a potentially major problem affecting both flight safety and program costs.

Presently three seals between SRB segments use double O-rings sealed with putty. In recent Shuttle flights, charring of these rings has occurred. The O-rings are designed so that if one fails, the other will hold against the pressure of firing. However, at least in the joint between the nozzle and the aft segment, not only has the first O-ring been destroyed, but the second has been partially eaten away.

Engineers have not yet determined the cause of the problem. Candidates include the use of a new type of putty (the putty formerly in use was removed from the market by EPA because it contained asbestos), failure of the second ring to slip into the groove which must engage it for it to work properly, or new, and as yet unidentified, assembly procedures at Thiokol. MSC is trying to identify the cause of the problem, including on-site investigation at Thiokol, and OSF hopes to have some results from their analysis within 30 days. There is little question, however, that flight safety has been and is still being compromised by potential failure of the seals, and it is acknowledged that failure during launch would certainly be catastrophic. There is also indication that staff personnel knew of this problem sometime in advance of management's becoming apprised of what was going on.

The potential impact of the problem depends on the as yet undiscovered cause. If the cause is minor, there should be little or no impact on budget or flight rate. A worst case scenario, however, would lead to the suspension of Shuttle flights, redesign of the SRB, and scrapping of existing stockpiled hardware. The impact on the FY 1987-8 budget could be immense.

It should be pointed out that Code M management [NASA's Associate Administrator for Space Flight] is viewing the situation with the utmost seriousness. From a budgetary standpoint, I would think that any NASA budget submitted this year for FY 1987 and beyond should certainly be based on a reliable judgment as to the cause of the SRB seal problem and a corresponding decision as to budgetary action needed to provide for its solution.

—(RPC, pp. 391–392)

On October 30, 1985, NASA launched flight STS 61-A (flight no. 22) at 75°F. This flight also showed signs of sooted blow-by, but the color was significantly blacker. Although there was some heat effect, there was no measurable erosion observed on the secondary O-ring. Since blow-by and erosion now occurred at a higher launch temperature, the original premise that launches under cold temperatures were a problem was now being questioned. Table 5-3 shows the temperature at launch of all the shuttle flights up to this time and the O-ring damage, if any.

Management at both NASA and Thiokol wanted *concrete* evidence that launch temperature was directly correlated to blow-by and erosion. Other than simply a "gut feel," engineers were now stymied on how to show the direct correlation. NASA was not ready to cancel a launch simply due to an engineer's "gut feel".

William Lucas, director of the Marshall Space Center, made it clear that NASA's manifest for launches would be adhered to. Managers at NASA were pressured to resolve problems internally rather than to escalate them up the chain of command. Managers became afraid to inform anyone higher up that they had problems, even though they knew that one existed.

Richard Feynman, Nobel laureate and member of the Rogers Commission, concluded that a NASA official altered the safety criteria so that flights could be certified on time under pressure imposed by the leadership of William Lucas. Feynman commented:

. . . They, therefore, fly in a relatively unsafe condition with a chance of failure of the order of one percent. Official management claims to believe that the probability of failure is a thousand times less.

TABLE 5-3 Erosion and Blow-by History (temperature in ascending order from coldest to warmest)

FLIGHT	DATA	TEMPERATURE, °F	EROSION INCIDENTS	BLOW-BY INCIDENTS	COMMENTS
51-C	01/24/85	53	3	2	Most erosion any flight; blow-by; secondary O-rings heated up
41-B	02/03/84	57	1		Deep, extensive erosion
61-C	01/12/86	58	1		O-ring erosion
41-C	04/06/84	63	1		O-rings heated but no damage
1	04/12/81	66			Coolest launch without problems
6	04/04/83	67			
51-A	11/08/84	67			
51-D	04/12/85	67			
5	11/11/82	68			
3	03/22/82	69			
2	11/12/81	70	1		Extent of erosion unknown
9	11/28/83	70			
41-D	08/30/84	70	1		
51-G	06/17/85	70			
7	06/18/83	72			
8	08/30/83	73			
51-B	04/29/85	75			
61-A	10/20/85	75		2	No erosion but soot between O-rings
51-I	08/27/85	76			
61	11/26/85	76			
41-G	10/05/84	78			
51-J	10/03/85	79			
4	06/27/82	80			
51-F	07/29/85	81			

Without concrete evidence of the temperature effect on the O-rings, the secondary O-ring was regarded as a redundant safety constraint and the criticality factor was changed from C1 to C1R. Potentially serious problems were treated as anomalies peculiar to a given flight. Under the guise of anomalies, NASA began issuing waivers to maintain the flight schedules. Pressure was placed upon contractors to issue closure reports. On December 24, 1985, L. O. Wear (NASA's SRM Program office manager) sent a letter to Joe Kilminster, Thiokol's vice president for the Space Booster Program:

> During a recent review of the SRM Problem Review Board open problem list I found that we have 20 open problems, 11 opened during the past 6 months, 13 open over 6 months, 1 three years old, 2 two years old, and 1 closed during the past six months. As you can see our closure record is very poor. You are requested to initiate the required effort to assure more timely closures and the MTI personnel shall coordinate directly with the S&E personnel the contents of the closure reports.
>
> —(RPC, p. 1554)

Pressure, Paperwork and Waivers

To maintain the flight schedule, critical issues such as launch constraints had to be resolved or waived. This would require extensive documentation. During the Rogers Commission investigation, there seemed to be a total lack of coordination between NASA's Marshall Space Center and Thiokol. Joe Kilminster, Thiokol's vice president for the Space Booster Program, testified:

Mr. Kilminster: Mr. Chairman, if I could, I would like to respond to that. In response to the concern that was expressed—and I had discussions with the team leader, the task force team leader, Mr. Don Kettner, and Mr. Russell and Mr. Ebeling. We held a meeting in my office and that was done in the October time period where we called the people who were in a support role to the task team, as well as the task force members themselves.

In that discussion, some of the task force members were looking to circumvent some of our established systems. In some cases, that was acceptable; in other cases, it was not. For example, some of the work that they had recommended to be done was involved with full-scale hardware, putting some of these joints together with various putty layup configurations; for instance, taking them apart and finding out what we could from that inspection process.

Dr. Sutter: Was that one of these things that was outside of the normal work, or was that accepted as a good idea or a bad idea?

Mr. Kilminster:	A good idea, but outside the normal work, if you will.
Dr. Sutter:	Why not do it?
Mr. Kilminster:	Well, we were doing it. But the question was, can we circumvent the system, the paper system that requires, for instance, the handling constraints on those flight hardware items? And I said no, we can't do that. We have to maintain our handling system, for instance, so that we don't stand the possibility of injuring or damaging a piece of flight hardware.
	I asked at that time if adding some more people, for instance, a safety engineer—that was one of the things we discussed in there. The consensus was no, we really didn't need a safety engineer. We had the manufacturing engineer in attendance who was in support of that role, and I persuaded him that, typical of the way we normally worked, that he should be calling on the resources from his own organization, that is, in Manufacturing, in order to get this work done and get it done in a timely fashion.
	And I also suggested that if they ran across a problem in doing that, they should bubble that up in their management chain to get help in getting the resources to get that done. Now, after that session, it was my impression that there was improvement based on some of the concerns that had been expressed, and we did get quite a bit of work done. For your evaluation, I would like to talk a little bit about the sequence of events for this task force.
Chairman Rogers:	Can I interrupt? Did you know at that time it was a launch constraint, a formal launch constraint?
Mr. Kilminster:	Not an overall launch constraint as such. Similar to the words that have been said before, each Flight Readiness Review had to address any anomalies or concerns that were identified at previous launches and in that sense, each of those anomalies or concerns were established in my mind as launch constraints unless they were properly reviewed and agreed upon by all parties.
Chairman Rogers:	You didn't know there was a difference between the launch constraint and just considering it an anomaly? You thought they were the same thing?
Mr. Kilminster:	No, sir. I did not think they were the same thing.
Chairman Rogers:	My question is: Did you know that this launch constraint was placed on the flights in July 1985?
Mr. Kilminster:	Until we resolved the O-ring problem on that nozzle joint, yes. We had to resolve that in a fashion for the subsequent flight before we would be okay to fly again.

Chairman Rogers: So you did know there was a constraint on that?

Mr. Kilminster: On a one flight per one flight basis; yes, sir.

Chairman Rogers: What else would a constraint mean?

Mr. Kilminster: Well, I get the feeling that there's a perception here that a launch constraint means all launches, whereas we were addressing each launch through the Flight Readiness Review process as we went.

Chairman Rogers: No, I don't think—the testimony that we've had is that a launch constraint is put on because it is a very serious problem and the constraint means don't fly unless it's fixed or taken care of, but somebody has the authority to waive it for a particular flight. And in this case, Mr. Mulloy was authorized to waive it, which he did, for a number of flights before 51-L. Just prior to 51-L, the papers showed the launch constraint was closed out, which I guess means no longer existed. And that was done on January 23, 1986. Now, did you know that sequence of events?

Mr. Kilminster: Again, my understanding of closing out, as the term has been used here, was to close it out on the problem actions list, but not as an overall standard requirement. We had to address these at subsequent Flight Readiness Reviews to insure that we were all satisfied with the proceeding to launch.

Chairman Rogers: Did you understand the waiver process, that once a constraint was placed on this kind of a problem, that a flight could not occur unless there was a formal waiver?

Mr. Kilminster: Not in the sense of a formal waiver, no, sir.

Chairman Rogers: Did any of you? Didn't you get the documents saying that?

Mr. McDonald: I don't recall seeing any documents for a formal waiver.

(RPC, pp. 1577–1578)

Mission 51-L

On January 25, 1986, questionable weather caused a delay of mission 51-L to January 27. On January 26, the launch was reconfirmed for 9:37 A.M. on the 27th. However, on the morning of January 27, a malfunction with the hatch, combined with high crosswinds, caused another delay. All preliminary procedures had been completed and the crew had just boarded when the first problem appeared. A microsensor on the hatch indicated that the hatch was not shut securely. It turned out that the hatch was shut securely but the sensor had malfunctioned. Valuable time was lost in determining the problem.

After the hatch was finally closed, the external handle could not be removed. The threads on the connecting bolt were stripped and, instead of cleanly disengaging when turned, simply spun around. Attempts to use a portable drill to remove the handle failed. Technicians on the scene asked mission control for permission to saw off the bolt. Fearing some form of structural stress to the hatch, engineers made numerous time-consuming calculations before giving the go-ahead to cut off the bolt. The entire process consumed almost 2 hours before the count-down resumed.

However, the misfortunes continued. During the attempts to verify the integrity of the hatch and remove the handle, the wind had been steadily rising. Chief astronaut John Young flew a series of approaches in the shuttle training aircraft and confirmed the worst fears of mission control. The crosswinds at the Cape were in excess of the level allowed for the abort contingency. The opportunity had been missed. The mission was then reset to launch the next day, January 28, at 9:38 A.M. Everyone was quite discouraged since extremely cold weather was forecast for Tuesday that could further postpone the launch.

Weather conditions indicated that the temperature at launch could be as low as 26°F. This would be much colder and well below the temperature range at which the O-rings were designed to operate. This was well outside of the range where data existed. The components of the solid rocket motors were qualified only to 40°F at the lower limit. Undoubtedly, when the sun would come up and launch time approached, both the air temperature and vehicle would warm up, but there was still concern. Would the ambient temperature be high enough to meet the launch requirements? NASA's Launch Commit Criteria stated that no launch should occur at temperatures below 31°F. There were also worries over any permanent effects on the shuttle due to the cold overnight temperatures. NASA became concerned and asked Thiokol for their recommendation on whether or not to launch. NASA admitted under testimony that if Thiokol had recommended not launching, then the launch would not have taken place.

On all previous shuttle launches, Larry Mulloy, solid rocket booster project manager, would verbally ask his contractors if they are ready for launch. If the contractors responded "yes," Larry would sign the launch document. For this launch, Larry wanted Alan McDonald, director for the Solid Rocket Motor Project, to provide in writing his ok to launch. McDonald refused to sign the letter citing the risks.

At 5:45 P.M. eastern standard time, a teleconference was held between the Kennedy Space Center, Marshall Space Flight Center and Thiokol. Bob Lund, vice president for engineering, summarized the concerns of the Thiokol engineers that in Thiokol's opinion the launch should be delayed until noontime or even later such that a launch temperature of at least 53°F could be achieved. Thiokol's engineers were concerned that no data was available for launches at this temperature of 26°F. This was the first time in 14 years that Thiokol had recommended not to launch.

The design validation tests originally done by Thiokol covered only a narrow temperature range. The temperature data did not include any temperatures below 53°F. The O-rings from flight 51-C, which had been launched under cold conditions the previous year, showed very significant erosion. This was the only data available on the effects of cold, but all of the Thiokol engineers agreed that the cold weather would decrease the elasticity of the synthetic rubber O-rings, which in turn might cause them to seal slowly and allow hot gases to surge through the joint.[11]

NASA's Larry Mulloy stated that this decision was not acceptable to NASA and wanted another meeting. Another teleconference was set up for 8:45 P.M. to invite more parties to be involved in the decision. Meanwhile, Thiokol was asked to fax all relevant and supporting charts to all parties involved in the 8:45 P.M. teleconference.

The following information was included in the pages that were faxed:

Blow-by History

SRM-15 Worst Blow-by

- Two case joints (80°, 110° Arc)
- Much worse visually than SRM-22
- SRM-22 blow-by
- Two case joints (30-40°)
- SRM-13A, 15, 16A, 18, 23A, 24A
- Nozzle blow-by

Field Joint Primary Concerns—SRM-25

- A temperature lower than the current database results in changing primary O-ring sealing timing function
- SRM-15A—80° arc black grease between O-rings
- SRM-15B—110° arc black grease between O-rings
- Lower O-ring squeeze due to lower temperature
- Higher O-ring shore hardness
- Thicker grease viscosity
- Higher O-ring pressure activation time
- If activation time increases, threshold of secondary seal pressurization capability is approached
- If threshold is reached, then secondary seal may not be capable of being pressurized

---

11. Ibid., p. 4.

Conclusions

- Temperature of O-ring is not the only parameter controlling blow-by:
  - SRM-15 with blow-by had an O-ring temperature of 53°F.
  - SRM-22 with blow-by had an O-ring temperature of 75°F.
  - Four development motors with no blow-by were tested at O-ring temperature of 47–52°F.
  - Development motors had putty packing which resulted in better performance.
- At about 50°F blow-by could be experienced in case joints.
- Temperature for SRM-25 on January 28, 1986, launch will be 29°F 9 A.M., 38°F 2 P.M.
- Have no data that that would indicate SRM-25 is different than SRM-15 other than temperature.

Recommendations

- O-ring temperature must be ≥ 53°F at launch.
- Development motors at 47–52°F with putty packing had no blow-by.
- SRM-15 (the best simulation) worked at 53°F.
- Project ambient conditions (temperature and wind) to determine launch time.

From NASA's perspective, the launch window was from 9:30 A.M. to 12:30 P.M. on January 28. This was based upon weather conditions and visibility, not only at the launch site but also at the landing sites, should an abort be necessary. An additional consideration was the fact that the temperature might not reach 53°F prior to the launch window closing. Actually, the temperature at the Kennedy Space Center was not expected to reach 50°F until two days later. NASA was hoping that Thiokol would change their minds and recommend launch.

Second Teleconference

At the second teleconference, Bob Lund once again asserted Thiokol's recommendation not to launch below 53°F. NASA's Mulloy then burst out over the teleconference network:

> My God, Morton Thiokol! When do you want me to launch—next April?

NASA challenged Thiokol's interpretation of the data and argued that Thiokol was inappropriately attempting to establish a new launch commit criterion just prior to launch. NASA asked Thiokol to reevaluate their conclusions. Crediting NASA's comments with some validity, Thiokol then requested a 5-minute off-line caucus. In the room at Thiokol were 14 engineers, namely:

- Jerald Mason, senior vice president, Wasatch Operations
- Calvin Wiggins, vice president and general manager, Space Division
- Joe C. Kilminster, vice president, Space Booster Programs
- Robert K. Lund, vice president, Engineering
- Larry H. Sayer, director, Engineering and Design
- William Macbeth, manager, Case Projects, Space Booster Project
- Donald M. Ketner, supervisor, Gas Dynamics Section and Head Seal Task Force
- Roger Boisjoly, member, Seal Task Force
- Arnold R. Thompson, supervisor, Rocket Motor Cases
- Jack R. Kapp, manager, Applied Mechanics Department
- Jerry Burn, associate engineer, Applied Mechanics
- Joel Maw, associate scientist, Heat Transfer Section
- Brian Russell, manager, Special Projects, SRM Project
- Robert Ebeling, manager, Ignition System and Final Assembly, SRB Project

There were no safety personnel in the room because nobody thought to invite them. The caucus lasted some 30 minutes. Thiokol (specifically Joe Kilminster) then returned to the teleconference stating that they were unable to sustain a valid argument that temperature affects O-ring blow-by and erosion. Thiokol then reversed its position and was now recommending launch.

NASA stated that the launch of the *Challenger* would not take place without Thiokol's approval. But when Thiokol reversed its position following the caucus and agreed to launch, NASA interpreted this as an acceptable risk. The launch would now take place.

Mr. McDonald (Thiokol): The assessment of the data was that the data was not totally conclusive, that the temperature could affect everything relative to the seal. But there was data that indicated that there were things going in the wrong direction, and this was far from our experience base.

The conclusion being that Thiokol was directed to reassess all the data because the recommendation was not considered acceptable at that time of [waiting for] the 53 degrees [to occur]. NASA asked us for a reassessment and some more data to show that the temperature in itself can cause this to be a more serious concern than we had said it would be. At that time Thiokol in Utah said that they would like to go off-line and caucus for about five minutes and reassess what data they had there or any other additional data.

And that caucus lasted for, I think, a half hour before they were ready to go back on. When they came back on they said they had reassessed all the data and had come to the conclusions that the temperature influence, based on the data they had available to them, was inconclusive and therefore they recommended a launch.

(RPC, p. 300)

During the Rogers Commission testimony, NASA's Mulloy stated his thought process in requesting Thiokol to rethink its position:

General Kutyna:	You said the temperature had little effect?
Mr. Mulloy:	I didn't say that. I said I can't get a correlation between O-ring erosion, blow-by and O-ring, and temperature.
General Kutyna:	51-C was a pretty cool launch. That was January of last year.
Mr. Mulloy:	It was cold before then but it was not that much colder than other launches.
General Kutyna:	So it didn't approximate this particular one?
Mr. Mulloy:	Unfortunately, that is one you look at and say, aha, is it related to a temperature gradient and the cold. The temperature of the O-ring on 51-C, I believe, was 53 degrees. We have fired motors at 48 degrees.

(RPC, p. 290)

Mulloy asserted he had not pressured Thiokol into changing its position. Yet, the testimony of Thiokol's engineers stated they believed they were being pressured.

Roger Boisjoly, one of Thiokol's experts on O-rings, was present during the caucus and vehemently opposed the launch. During testimony, Boisjoly described his impressions of what occurred during the caucus:

> The caucus was started by Mr. Mason stating that a management decision was necessary. Those of us who were opposed the launch continued to speak out, and I am specifically speaking of Mr. Thompson and myself because in my recollection, he and I were the only ones who vigorously continued to oppose the launch. And we were attempting to go back and rereview and try to make clear what we were trying to get across, and we couldn't understand why it was going to be reversed.
>
> So, we spoke out and tried to explain again the effects of low temperature. Arnie actually got up from his position which was down the table and walked up the table and put a quad pad down in front of the table, in front of the management folks, and tried to sketch out once again what his concern was with the joint, and when he realized he wasn't getting through, he just stopped.
>
> I tried one more time with the photos. I grabbed the photos and I went up and discussed the photos once again and tried to make the point

that it was my opinion from actual observations that temperature was indeed a discriminator, and we should not ignore the physical evidence that we had observed.

And again, I brought up the point that SRM-15 had a 110 degree arc of black grease while SRM-22 had a relatively different amount, which was less and wasn't quite as black. I also stopped when it was apparent that I could not get anybody to listen.

Dr. Walker: At this point did anyone else [i.e. engineers] speak up in favor of the launch?

Mr. Boisjoly: No, sir. No one said anything, in my recollection. Nobody said a word. It was then being discussed amongst the management folks. After Arnie and I had our last say, Mr. Mason said we have to make a management decision. He turned to Bob Lund and asked him to take off his engineering hat and put on his management hat. From this point on, management formulated the points to base their decision on. There was never one comment in favor, as I have said, of launching by any engineer or other nonmanagement person in the room before or after the caucus. I was not even asked to participate in giving any input to the final decision charts.

I went back on the net with the final charts or final chart, which was the rationale for launching, and that was presented by Mr. Kilminster. It was handwritten on a notepad, and he read from that notepad. I did not agree with some of the statements that were being made to support the decision. I was never asked nor polled, and it was clearly a management decision from that point.

I must emphasize, I had my say, and I never take any management right to take the input of an engineer and then make a decision based upon that input, and I truly believe that. I have worked at a lot of companies, and that has been done from time to time, and I truly believe that, and so there was no point in me doing anything any further [other] than [what] I had already attempted to do.

I did not see the final version of the chart until the next day. I just heard it read. I left the room feeling badly defeated, but I felt I really did all I could to stop the launch. I felt personally that management was under a lot of pressure to launch, and they made a very tough decision, but I didn't agree with it.

One of my colleagues who was in the meeting summed it up best. This was a meeting where the determination was to launch, and it was up to us to prove beyond a shadow of a doubt that it was not safe to do so. This is in total reverse to what the position usually is in a preflight conversation or a Flight Readiness Review. It is usually exactly opposite that.

Dr. Walker: Do you know the source of the pressure on management that you alluded to?

Mr. Boisjoly: Well, the comments made over the net are what I felt. I can't speak for them, but I felt it. I felt the tone of the meeting exactly as I summed up, that we were being put in a position to prove that we should not launch rather than being put in the position and prove that we had enough data to launch.

(RPC, pp. 793–794)

General Kutyna: What was the motivation driving those who were trying to overturn your opposition?

Mr. Boisjoly: They felt that we had not demonstrated, or I had not demonstrated, because I was the prime mover in SRM-15. Because of my personal observations and involvement in the Flight Readiness Reviews, they felt that I had not conclusively demonstrated that there was a tie-in between temperature and blow-by.

My main concern was if the timing function changed and that seal took longer to get there, then you might not have any seal left because it might be eroded before it seats. And then, if that timing function is such that it pushes you from the 170 millisecond region into the 330 second region, you might not have a secondary seal to pick up if the primary is gone. That was my major concern.

I can't quantify it. I just don't know how to quantify that. But I felt that the observations made were telling us that there was a message there telling us that temperature was a discriminator, and I couldn't get that point across. I basically had no direct input into the final recommendation to launch, and I was not polled.

I think Astronaut Crippin hit the tone of the meeting exactly right on the head when he said that the opposite was true of the way the meetings were normally conducted. We normally have to absolutely prove beyond a shadow of a doubt that we have the ability to fly, and it seemed like we were trying to prove, have proved that we had data to prove that we couldn't fly at this time, instead of the reverse. That was the tone of the meeting, in my opinion.

(RPC, p. 676)

Jerald Mason, senior vice president at Thiokol's Wasatch Division directed the caucus at Thiokol. Mason continuously asserted that a management decision was needed and instructed Bob Lund, vice president for engineering, to take off his engineering hat and put on his management hat. During testimony, Mason commented on his interpretation of the data:

Dr. Ride: [a member of the Commission]:: You know, what we've seen in the charts so far is that the data was inconclusive and so you said go ahead.

Mr. Mason: . . . I hope I didn't convey that. But the reason for the discussion was the fact that we didn't have enough data to quantify the effect of the cold, and that was the heart of our discussion . . . We have had blow-by on earlier flights. We had not had any reason to believe that we couldn't experience it again at any temperature. . . .

(RPC, p. 764)

At the end of the second teleconference, NASA's Hardy at Marshall Space Flight Center requested that Thiokol put its recommendation to launch in writing and fax it to both Marshall Space Flight Center and Kennedy Space Center. The memo (shown below) was signed by Joe Kilminster, vice president for Thiokol's Space Booster Program, and faxed at 11:45 p.m. the night before the launch.

- Calculations show that SRM-25 O-rings will be 20° colder than SRM-15 O-rings
- Temperature data not conclusive on predicting primary O-ring blow-by
- Engineering assessment is that:
  - Colder O-rings will have increased effective durometer ("harder")
  - "Harder" O-rings will take longer to "seat"
    - More gas may pass primary O-ring before the primary seal seats (relative to SRM-15)
    - Demonstrated sealing threshold is 3 times greater than 0.038″ erosion experienced on SRM-15
- If the primary seal does not seat, the secondary seal will seat
  - Pressure will get to secondary seal before the metal parts rotate
  - O-ring pressure leak check places secondary seal in outboard position which minimizes sealing time
- MTI recommends STS-51L launch proceed on 28 January 1986
- SRM-25 will not be significantly different from SRM-15

Ice Problem

At 1:30 A.M. on the day of the launch, NASA's Gene Thomas, launch director, ordered a complete inspection of the launch site due to cold weather and severe ice conditions. The prelaunch inspection of the *Challenger* and the launch pad by the ice team was unusual to say the least. The ice team's responsibility was to remove any frost or ice on the vehicle or launch structure. What they found during their inspection looked like something out of a science fiction movie. The freeze protection plan implemented by Kennedy personnel had gone very wrong. Hundreds of icicles, some up to 16 inches long, clung to the launch structure. The handrails and walkways near the shuttle entrance were covered in ice, making them extremely dangerous if the crew had to make an emergency evacuation. One solid sheet of ice stretched from the 195-foot level to the 235- foot level on the gantry. However, NASA continued to cling to its calculations that there would be no damage due to flying ice shaken loose during the launch.[12] A decision was then made to delay the launch from 9:38 A.M. to 11:30 A.M. so that the ice on the launch pad could melt. The delay was still within the launch window of 9:30 A.M.–12:30 P.M.

At 8:30 A.M., a second ice inspection was made. Ice was still significantly present at the launch site. Robert Glaysher, vice president for Orbital Operations at Rockwell, stated that the launch was unsafe. Rockwell's concern was that falling ice could damage the heat tiles on the orbiter. This could have a serious impact during reentry.

At 10:30 A.M., a third ice inspection was made. Though some of the ice was beginning to melt, there was still significant ice on the launch pad. The temperature of the left solid rocket booster was measured at 33°F and the right booster was measured at 19°F. Even though the right booster was 34 degrees colder than Thiokol's original recommendation for a launch temperature (i.e., 53°F), no one seemed alarmed. Rockwell also agreed to launch even though their earlier statement was that the launch was unsafe.

Arnold Aldrich, manager of the STS Program at the Johnson Space Center, testified on the concern over the ice problem:

Mr. Aldrich: Kennedy facility people at that meeting, everyone in that meeting, voted strongly to proceed and said they had no concern, except for Rockwell. The comment to me from Rockwell, which was not written specifically to the exact words, and either recorded or logged, was that they had some concern about the possibility of ice damage to the Orbiter. Although it was a minor concern, they felt that we had no experience base launching in this exact configuration before, and therefore they thought we had some additional risk of Orbiter damage from ice than we had on previous meetings, or from previous missions.

Chairman Rogers: Did they sign off on it or not?

---

12. RPC, p. 5.

Mr. Aldrich:	We don't have a sign-off at that point. It was not—it was not maybe 20 minutes, but it was close to that. It was within the last hour of launch.
Chairman Rogers:	But they still objected?
Mr. Aldrich:	They issued what I would call a concern, a less than 100 percent concurrence in the launch. They did not say we do not want to launch, and the rest of the team overruled them. They issued a more conservative concern. They did not say don't launch.
General Kutyna:	I can't recall a launch that I have had where there was 100 percent certainty that everything was perfect, and everyone around the table would agree to that. It is the job of the launch director to listen to everyone, and it's our job around the table to listen and say there is this element of risk, and you characterize this as 90 percent, or 95, and then you get a consensus that that risk is an acceptable risk, and then you launch. So I think this gentleman is characterizing the degree of risk, and he's honest, and he had to say something.
Dr. Ride:	But one point is that their concern is a specific concern, and they weren't concerned about the overall temperature or damage to the solid rockets or damage to the external tank. They were worried about pieces of ice coming off and denting the tile.

(RPC, pp. 237-238)

Following the accident, the Rogers Commission identified three major concerns about the ice-on-the-pad issue:

1. An analysis of all of the testimony and interviews established that Rockwell's recommendation on launch was ambiguous. The commission found it difficult, as did Mr. Aldrich, to conclude that there was a no-launch recommendation. Moreover, all parties were asked specifically to contact Aldrich or Moore about launch objections due to weather. Rockwell made no phone calls or further objections to Aldrich or other NASA officials after the 9:00 A.M. mission management team meeting and subsequent to the resumption of the countdown.

2. The commission was also concerned about the NASA response to the Rockwell position at the 9:00 A.M. meeting. While it was understood that decisions have to be made in launching a shuttle, the commission was not convinced levels I and II (of NASA's management) appropriately considered Rockwell's concern about the ice. However ambiguous Rockwell's position was, it was clear that they did tell NASA that the ice was an unknown condition. Given the extent of the ice on the pad, the admitted

unknown effect of the solid rocket motor and space shuttle main engine ignition on the ice, as well as the fact that debris striking the orbiter was a potential flight safety hazard, the commission found the decision to launch questionable under those circumstances. In this situation, NASA appeared to be requiring a contractor to prove that it was not safe to launch, rather than proving it was safe. Nevertheless, the commission had determined that the ice was not a cause of the 51-L accident and did not conclude that NASA's decision to launch specifically overrode a no-launch recommendation by an element contractor.

3. The commission concluded that the freeze protection plan for launch pad 39B was inadequate. The commission believed that the severe cold and presence of so much ice on the fixed service structure made it inadvisable to launch on the morning of January 28 and that margins of safety were whittled down too far.

It became obvious that NASA's management knew of the ice problem, but did they know of Thiokol's original recommendation not to launch and then their reversal. Larry Mulloy, the SRB project manager for NASA, and Stanley Reinartz, NASA's manager of the Shuttle Office, both admitted that they told Arnold Aldrich, manager of the STS program, Johnson Space Center, about their concern for the ice problem but there was no discussion about the teleconferences with Thiokol over the O-rings. It appeared that Mulloy and Reinartz considered the ice as a potential problem whereas the O-rings constituted an acceptable risk. Therefore, only potential problems went up the chain of command, not the components of the "aggregate acceptable launch risk." It became common practice in FRR documentation to use the term "acceptable risk." This became the norm at NASA and resulted in insulating senior management from certain potential problems. It was the culture that had developed at NASA that created the flawed decision-making process rather than an intent by individuals to withhold information and jeopardize safety.

The Accident

Just after liftoff at 0.678 second into the flight, photographic data showed a strong puff of gray smoke spurting from the vicinity of the aft field joint on the right solid rocket booster. The two pad 39B cameras that would have recorded the precise location of the puff were inoperative. Computer graphic analysis of film from other cameras indicated the initial smoke came from the 270°–310°-sector of the circumference of the aft field joint of the right solid rocket booster. This area of the solid booster faced the external tank. The vaporized material streaming from the joint indicated there was incomplete sealing action within the joint.

Eight more distinctive puffs of increasingly blacker smoke were recorded between 0.836 and 2.500 seconds. The smoke appeared to puff upward from the joint. While each smoke puff was being left behind by the upward flight of the shuttle, the next fresh puff could be seen near the level of the joint. The multiple smoke puffs in this sequence occurred about four times per second, approximating the frequency of the structural load dynamics and resultant joint flexing. Computer graphics applied to NASA photos from a variety of cameras in this sequence again placed the smoke puffs' origin in the 270°–310° sector of the original smoke spurt.

As the shuttle *Challenger* increased its upward velocity, it flew past the emerging and expanding smoke puffs. The last smoke was seen above the field joint at 2.733 seconds.

The black color and dense composition of the smoke puffs suggested that the grease, joint insulation and rubber O-rings in the joint seal were being burned and eroded by the hot propellant gases.

At approximately 37 seconds, *Challenger* encountered the first of several high-altitude wind shear conditions that lasted about 64 seconds. The wind shear created forces of relatively large fluctuations on the vehicle itself. These were immediately sensed and countered by the guidance, navigation and control systems.

The steering system (thrust vector control) of the solid rocket booster responded to all commands and wind shear effects. The wind shear caused the steering system to be more active than on any previous flight.

Both the *Challenger*'s main engines and the solid rockets operated at reduced thrust approaching and passing through the area of maximum dynamic pressure of 720 pounds per square foot. Main engines had been throttled up to 104% thrust and the solid rocket boosters were increasing their thrust when the first flickering flame appeared on the right solid rocket booster in the area of the aft field joint. This first very small flame was detected on image-enhanced film at 58.788 seconds into the flight. It appeared to originate at about 305° around the booster circumference at or near the aft field joint.

One film frame later from the same camera, the flame was visible without image enhancement. It grew into a continuous, well-defined plume at 59.262 seconds. At approximately the same time (60 seconds), telemetry showed a pressure differential between the chamber pressures in the right and left boosters. The right booster chamber pressure was lower, confirming the growing leak in the area of the field joint.

As the flame plume increased in size, it was deflected rearward by the aerodynamic slipstream and circumferentially by the protruding structure of the upper ring attaching the booster to the external tank. These deflections directed the flame plume onto the surface of the external tank. This sequence of flame spreading is confirmed by analysis of the recovered wreckage. The growing flame also impinged on the strut attaching the solid rocket booster to the external tank.

The first visual indication that swirling flame from the right solid rocket booster breached the external tank was at 64.660 seconds when there was an abrupt change in the shape and color of the plume. This indicated that it was mixing with leaking hydrogen from the external tank. Telemetered changes in the hydrogen tank pressurization confirmed the leak. Within 45 milliseconds of the breach of the external tank, a bright, sustained glow developed on the black tiled underside of the *Challenger* between it and the external tank.

Beginning around 72 seconds, a series of events occurred extremely rapidly that terminated the flight. Telemetered data indicated a wide variety of flight system actions that supported the visual evidence of the photos as the shuttle struggled futilely against the forces that were destroying it.

At about 72.20 seconds, the lower strut linking the solid rocket booster and the external tank was severed or pulled away from the weakened hydrogen tank permitting the right solid rocket booster to rotate around the upper attachment strut. This rotation was indicated by divergent yaw and pitch rates between the left and right solid rocket boosters.

At 73.124 seconds, a circumferential white vapor pattern was observed blooming from the side of the external tank bottom dome. This was the beginning of the structural failure of the hydrogen tank that culminated in the entire aft dome dropping away. This released massive amounts of liquid hydrogen from the tank and created a sudden forward thrust of about 2.8 million pounds, pushing the hydrogen tank upward into the intertank structure. About the same time, the rotating right solid rocket booster impacted the intertank structure and the lower part of the liquid oxygen tank. These structures failed at 73.137 seconds as evidenced by the white vapors appearing in the intertank region.

Within milliseconds there was massive, almost explosive, burning of the hydrogen streaming from the failed tank bottom and the liquid oxygen breach in the area of the intertank.

At this point in its trajectory, while traveling at a Mach 1.92 at an altitude of 46,000 feet, the *Challenger* was totally enveloped in the explosive burn. The *Challenger*'s reaction control system ruptured, and a hypergolic burn of its propellants occurred producing the oxygen-hydrogen flames. The reddish brown colors of the hypergolic fuel burn were visible on the edge of the main fireball. The orbiter, under severe aerodynamic loads, broke into several large sections which emerged from the fireball. Separate sections that can be identified on film include the main engine/tail section with the engines still burning, one wing of the orbiter and the forward fuselage trailing a mass of umbilical lines pulled loose from the payload bay.

The consensus of the commission and participating investigative agencies was that the loss of the space shuttle *Challenger* was caused by a failure in the joint between the two lower segments of the right solid rocket motor. The specific failure was the destruction of the seals that were intended to prevent hot gases from leaking through the joint during the propellant burn of the rocket motor. The evidence assembled by the commission indicates that no other element of the space shuttle system contributed to this failure.

In arriving at this conclusion, the commission reviewed in detail all available data, reports and records; directed and supervised numerous tests, analyses and experiments by NASA, civilian contractors and various government agencies; and then developed specific failure scenarios and the range of most probable causative factors.

The failure was due to a faulty design unacceptably sensitive to a number of factors. These factors were the effects of temperature, physical dimensions, the character of materials, the effects of reusability, processing and the reaction of the joint to dynamic loading.

NASA and Media

Following the tragedy, many believed that NASA's decision to launch was an attempt to minimize further ridicule by the media. Successful shuttle flights were no longer news because they were almost ordinary. However, launch aborts and delayed landings were more newsworthy because they were less common. The *Columbia* launch, which immediately preceded the *Challenger* mission, was delayed seven times. The *Challenger* launch had gone through four delays already. News anchor personnel were criticizing NASA. Some believed that NASA had to do something quickly to dispel its poor public image.

The *Challenger* mission had more media coverage and political ramifications than other missions. This would be the launch of the Teacher in Space Project. The original launch date of the *Challenger* was just before President Reagan's State of the Union message that was scheduled for the evening of January 28. Some believed that the president would publicly praise NASA for the Teacher in Space Project and possibly even talk to her live during his address. This would certainly enhance NASA's image.

Following the tragedy, there were questions as to whether or not the White House had pressured NASA into launching the shuttle because of President Reagan's (and NASA's) love of favorable publicity. The commission found no evidence of White House intervention in the decision to launch.

Findings of Commission

Determining the cause of an engineering disaster can take years of investigation. The *Challenger* disaster arose from many factors, including launch conditions, mechanical failure, communication and decision making. In the end, the last-minute decision to launch put all possible factors into a lethal action.

The commission concluded that the accident was rooted in history. The space shuttle's solid rocket booster problem began with the faulty design of its joint and increased as both NASA and contractor management first failed to recognize it as a problem, then failed to fix it and finally treated it as an acceptable flight risk.

Morton Thiokol, Inc., the contractor, did not accept the implication of tests early in the program that the design had a serious and unanticipated flaw. NASA did not accept the judgment of its engineers that the design was unacceptable, and as the joint problems grew in number and severity, NASA minimized them in management briefings and reports. Thiokol's stated position was that "the condition is not desirable but is acceptable."

Neither Thiokol nor NASA expected the rubber O-rings sealing the joints to be touched by hot gases of motor ignition, much less to be partially burned. However, as tests and then flights confirmed damage to the sealing rings, the reaction by both NASA and Thiokol was to increase the amount of damage considered "acceptable." At no time did management either recommend a redesign of the joint or call for the shuttle's grounding until the problem was solved.

The genesis of the *Challenger* accident—the failure of the joint of the right solid rocket motor—began with decisions made in the design of the joint and in the failure by both Thiokol and NASA's Solid Rocket Booster Project Office to understand and respond to facts obtained during testing.

The commission concluded that neither Thiokol nor NASA responded adequately to internal warnings about the faulty seal design. Furthermore, Thiokol and NASA did not make a timely attempt to develop and verify a new seal after the initial design was shown to be deficient. Neither organization developed a solution to the unexpected occurrences of O-ring erosion and blow-by, even though this problem was experienced frequently during the shuttle flight history. Instead, Thiokol and NASA management came to accept erosion and blow-by as unavoidable and an acceptable flight risk. Specifically, the commission found that:

1. The joint test and certification program was inadequate. There was no requirement to configure the qualifications test motor as it would be in flight, and the motors were static tested in a horizontal position, not in the vertical flight position.
2. Prior to the accident, neither NASA nor Thiokol fully understood the mechanism in which the joint sealing action took place.
3. NASA and Thiokol accepted escalating risk apparently because they "got away with it last time." As Commissioner Feynman observed, the decision making was:

   a kind of Russian roulette. . . . [The Shuttle] flies [with O-ring erosion] and nothing happens. Then it is suggested, therefore, that the risk is no longer so high for the next flights. We can lower our standards a little bit because we got away with it last time. . . . You got away with it, but it shouldn't be done over and over again like that.

4. NASA's system for tracking anomalies for flight readiness reviews failed in that, despite a history of persistent O-ring erosion and blow-by,

flight was still permitted. It failed again in the strange sequence of six consecutive launch constraint waivers prior to 51-L, permitting it to fly without any record of a waiver, or even of an explicit constraint. Tracking and continuing only anomalies that are "outside the data base" of prior flight allowed major problems to be removed from and lost by the reporting system.

5. The O-ring erosion history presented to level I at NASA headquarters in August 1985 was sufficiently detailed to require corrective action prior to the next flight.

6. A careful analysis of the flight history of O-ring performance would have revealed the correlation of O-ring damage and low temperature. Neither NASA nor Thiokol carried out such an analysis; consequently, they were unprepared to properly evaluate the risks of launching the 51-L mission in conditions more extreme than they had encountered before.

The commission also identified a concern for the "silent" safety program. The commission was surprised to realize after many hours of testimony that NASA's safety staff was never mentioned. No witness related the approval or disapproval of the reliability engineers, and none expressed the satisfaction or dissatisfaction of the quality assurance staff. No one thought to invite a safety representative or a reliability and quality assurance engineer to the January 27, 1986, teleconference between Marshall and Thiokol. Similarly, there was no safety representative on the mission management team that made key decisions during the countdown on January 28, 1986.

The unrelenting pressure to meet the demands of an accelerating flight schedule might have been adequately handled by NASA if it had insisted upon the exactingly thorough procedures that were its hallmark during the Apollo Program. An extensive and redundant safety program comprising interdependent safety, reliability and quality assurance functions existed during the lunar program to discover any potential safety problems. Between that period and 1986, however, the safety program became ineffective. This loss of effectiveness seriously degraded the checks and balances essential for maintaining flight safety.

On April 3, 1986, Arnold Aldrich, the space shuttle program manager, appeared before the commission at a public hearing in Washington. D.C. He described five different communication or organization failures that affected the launch decision on January 28, 1986. Four of those failures related directly to faults within the safety program. These faults included a lack of problem reporting requirements, inadequate trend analysis, misrepresentation of criticality and lack of involvement in critical discussions. A robust safety organization that was properly staffed and supported might well have avoided these faults and thus eliminated the communication failures.

NASA had a safety program to ensure that the communication failures to which Mr. Aldrich referred did not occur. In the case of mission 51-L, that program fell short.

The commission concluded that there were severe pressures placed on the launch decision-making system to maintain a flight schedule. These pressures caused rational men to make irrational decisions.

With the 1982 completion of the orbital flight test series, NASA began a planned acceleration of the space shuttle launch schedule. One early plan contemplated an eventual rate of a mission a week, but realism forced several downward revisions. In 1985, NASA published a projection calling for an annual rate of 24 flights by 1990. Long before the *Challenger* accident, however, it was becoming obvious that even the modified goal of two flights a month was overambitious.

In establishing the schedule, NASA had not provided adequate resources. As a result, the capabilities of the launch decision-making system were strained by the modest nine-mission rate of 1985, and the evidence suggested that NASA would not have been able to accomplish the 15 flights scheduled for 1986. These were the major conclusions of a commission examination of the pressures and problems attendant upon the accelerated launch schedule:

1. The capabilities of the launch decision-making system were stretched to the limit to support the flight rate in winter 1985/1986. Projections into the spring and summer of 1986 showed a clear trend; the system, as it existed, would have been unable to deliver crew training software for scheduled flights by the designated dates. The result would have been an unacceptable compression of the time available for the crews to accomplish their required training.

2. Spare parts were in critically short supply. The shuttle program made a conscious decision to postpone spare parts procurements in favor of budget items of perceived higher priority. Lack of spare parts would likely have limited flight operations in 1986.

3. Stated manifesting policies were not enforced. Numerous late manifest changes (after the cargo integration review) have been made to both major payloads and minor payloads throughout the shuttle program:

- Late changes to major payloads or program requirements required extensive resources (money, manpower, facilities) to implement.
- If many late changes to "minor" payloads occurred, resources were quickly absorbed.
- Payload specialists frequently were added to a flight well after announced deadlines.
- Late changes to a mission adversely affect the training and development of procedures for subsequent missions.

4. The scheduled flight rate did not accurately reflect the capabilities and resources:

- The flight rate was not reduced to accommodate periods of adjustment in the capacity of the work force. There was no margin for error in the system to accommodate unforeseen hardware problems.

- Resources were primarily directed toward supporting the flights and thus not enough were available to improve and expand facilities needed to support a higher flight rate.

5. Training simulators may have been the limiting factor on the flight rate: the two current simulators could not train crews for more than 12–15 flights per year.

6. When flights come in rapid succession, current requirements did not ensure that critical anomalies occurring during one flight are identified and addressed appropriately before the next flight.

Chain-of-Command Communication Failure

The commission also identified a communication failure within the reporting structure at both NASA and Thiokol. Part of the problem with the chain of command structure was the idea of the proper reporting channel. Engineers report only to their immediate managers, while those managers report only to their direct supervisors. Engineers and managers believed in the chain-of-command structure; they felt reluctant to go above their superiors with their concerns. Boisjoly at Thiokol and Powers at Marshall felt that they had done all that they could as far as voicing their concerns. Anything more could have cost them their jobs. When questioned at the Rogers Commission hearing about why he did not voice his concerns to others, Powers replied, "That would not be my reporting channel." The chain-of-command structure dictated the only path which information could travel at both NASA and Thiokol. If information was modified or silenced at the bottom of the chain, there was not an alternate path for it to take to reach high-level officials at NASA. The Rogers Commission concluded that there was a breakdown in communication between Thiokol engineers and top NASA officials and faulted the management structure for not allowing important information about the SRBs to flow to the people who needed to know it. The commission reported that the "fundamental problem was poor technical decision-making over a period of several years by top NASA and contractor personnel."

Bad news does not travel well in organizations like NASA and Thiokol. When the early signs of problems with the SRBs appeared, Thiokol managers did not believe that the problems were serious. Thiokol did not want to accept the fact that there could be a problem with their boosters. When Marshall received news of the problems, they considered it Thiokol's problem and did not pass the bad news upward to NASA headquarters. At Thiokol, Boisjoly described his managers as shutting out the bad news. He claims that he argued about the importance of the O-ring seal problems until he was convinced that "no one wanted to hear what he had to say." When Lund finally decided to recommend delay of the launch to Marshall, managers at Marshall rejected the bad news and refused to accept the recommendation not to launch. As with any information going up the chain of command at these two organizations, bad news could often be modified so that it had less impact, perhaps skewing its importance.[13]

On January 31, 1986, President Ronald Reagan stated:

The future is not free: the story of all human progress is one of a struggle against all odds. We learned again that this America, which Abraham Lincoln called the last, best hope of man on Earth, was built on heroism and noble sacrifice. It was built by men and women like our seven star voyagers, who answered a call beyond duty, who gave more than was expected or required and who gave it little thought of worldly reward.

Epilogue

Following the tragic accident, virtually every senior manager that was involved in the space shuttle *Challenger* decision-making processes, at both NASA and Thiokol, accepted early retirement. Whether this was the result of media pressure, peer pressure, fatigue or stress we can only postulate. The only true failures are the ones from which nothing is learned. Lessons on how to improve the risk management process were learned, unfortunately at the expense of human life.

On January 27, 1967, astronauts Gus Grissom, Edward White and Roger Chaffee were killed on board a test on Apollo-Saturn 204. James Webb, NASA's administrator at that time, was allowed by President Johnson to conduct an internal investigation of the cause. The investigation was primarily a technical investigation. NASA was fairly open with the media during the investigation. As a result of the openness, the credibility of the agency was maintained.

With the *Challenger* accident, confusion arose as to whether it was a technical failure or management failure. There was no question in anyone's mind that the decision-making process was flawed. NASA and Thiokol acted independently in their response to criticism. Critical information was withheld from both the media and the presidential commission, at least temporarily, and this undermined people's confidence in NASA. The media, as expected, began a vengeful attack on NASA and Thiokol.

Following the Apollo-Saturn 204 fire, there were few changes made in management positions at NASA. Those changes that did occur were the result of a necessity for improvement and where change was definitely warranted. Following the *Challenger* accident, almost every top management position at NASA underwent a change of personnel.

How an organization fares after an accident is often measured by how well it interfaces with the media. Situations such as the Tylenol tragedy and the Apollo-Saturn 204 fire bore this out.

---

13. "The *Challenger* Accident: Administrative Causes of the Challenger Accident", http://www.me.utexas.edu/~uer/challenger/chall3.html, pp. 8–9.

Following the accident, and after critical data was released, papers were published showing that the O-ring erosion data and temperature correlation was indeed possible. In one such paper, Lighthall[14] showed that not only was a correlation possible, but the real problem may be a professional weakness shared by many people, but especially engineers, who have been required to analyze technical data. Lighthall's argument was that engineering curriculums might not provide engineers with strong enough statistical education, especially in covariance analysis. The Rogers Commission also identified this conclusion when they found that there were no engineers at NASA trained in statistical sciences. This implied that certain critical risks could not be effectively mitigated.

Almost all scientific achievements require the taking of risks. The hard part is deciding which risk is worth taking and which is not. Every person who has ever flown in space, whether military or civilian, was a volunteer. They were all risk takers who understood that safety in space can never be guaranteed with 100% accuracy.

Potential Cover-Up

The commission did an admirable job discovering and reporting the facts, but did the commission report all of the facts? Was there a cover-up? Was the commission part of the cover-up? Was there any involvement by the White House and the Reagan administration in the cover-up as well as in the decision to launch? Sometimes, it takes more than 20 years after a disaster occurs for the entire truth to appear. People that were active participants in the project have retired over the past several years and have written books giving their account of what actually happened. The remainder of this case study come from information within these two books: Alan J. McDonald and James R. Hansen, *Truth, Lies and O-rings*, University Press of Florida, Gainesville, FL, 2009, and Richard C. Cook, *Challenger Revealed: An Inside Account of How the Reagan Administration Caused the Greatest Tragedy of the Space Age*, Thunder's Mouth Press, New York, 2006.

One of the highlights of the Reagan presidency was the escalation of the arms race and the Strategic Defense Initiative (SDI). The concept behind SDI was to place weapons in space that could shoot down and destroy any missiles directed at the United States. Historians believe that the SDI had forced the ailing Russian economy to commit additional funds to counter the SDI by taking funds from their economic programs to support their additional military efforts, thus worsening economic conditions. Some people contend that this was one of the main reasons why the Iron Curtain eventually fell.

14. Frederick F. Lighthall, "Launching the Space Shuttle Challenger: Disciplinary Deficiencies in the Analysis of Engineering Data," *IEEE Transactions on Engineering Management*, Vol. 38, No. 1, February 1991, pp. 63–74.

The Reagan presidency saw the space program as a military space program. Approximately 25% of NASA's budget was for military projects. SDI experiments were planned on two shuttle missions a year. To support the SDI, Reagan created a Committee on Present Danger. Out of the 182 members on the committee, 32 members eventually ended up in government positions, many in senior positions. James Beggs, head of NASA, was indicted for alleged procurement fraud and placed on administrative leave. William Graham, one of the 32 members of the Committee on Present Danger to receive government positions, became the acting head of NASA.

The Reagan administration could now use NASA for military purposes easily.

In the presidential race of 1984, Walter Mondale attacked Reagan as being antieducation, resulting in the National Education Association endorsing Mondale. To make sure this would not become an issue in the next election, Reagan initiated the Teacher in Space Project. Reagan had planned to extensively promote this project by talking to her directly in space during his State-of-the-Union speech on January 29, 1986. Some people believe that the only thing that was important on the *Challenger* mission was getting Christa McAuliffe into space prior to the State-of-the-Union speech. Christa had commented to one of her friends that she thought that she was being used by the Reagan administration. Also, the night before the fatal launch, Christa called one of her friends and stated that "NASA would launch the next day, no matter what."

There were also concerns as to why a presidential commission was needed. For all previous disasters, NASA handled the investigation themselves. The news media was now questioning whether NASA or the contractors had something to hide and if the commission was actually formed to insulate the White House from any involvement or pressure to launch. Even after the commission completed its report, there were still issues open for discussion:

- The members of the commission were selected by the White House.
- William Rogers, commission chairman, was good friends with the White House.
- Rogers stated that NASA and the commission were working together; this is a form of whitewashing.
- MTI's personnel were sworn in prior to providing testimony but many of NASA's personnel, especially the senior levels of management, were not sworn in, thus limiting the chance that they could later be held liable for perjury.
- Rogers was telling NASA personnel what to say and how to release information to the public.
- The commission was not asking the right questions, thus allowing the people providing testimony to list many possible causes for the tragedy other than the O-rings. Could this have been the commission's plan

to create as much distance as possible from involvement by the White House?

- NASA's Bill Cook was in the audience and heard that the wrong questions were being asked. He then went to Phil Boffey, a reporter at the *New York Times*, and gave him information showing that the real problem was most likely the O-rings.

- MTI's Alan McDonald was in the audience when the O-rings were being discussed. McDonald defied MTI's gag order and informed the commission about the two teleconferences the night before the launch and how vigorously MTI's technical community were opposed to the launch at these temperatures.

- The media was now doing more investigation than the commission and the public began believing that the commission was hiding information.

- Rogers could no longer apologize for NASA.

- MTI's Boisjoly, one of the experts on O-rings, also defies the gag order and reiterates Alan McDonald's information about the two teleconferences and his concern over the performance of the O-rings at low temperatures.

- Boisjoly and McDonald are reassigned to other positions at MTI not related to the space shuttle.

- Two House of Representatives members prepare a bill stating that, if Boisjoly or McDonald are demoted or given a cut in pay, NASA will cancel contracts with MTI.

- To keep the White House out of the picture, the commission comes up with a plan; Alan McDonald will be painted as an American hero, and MTI's senior management and Larry Mulloy at NASA will be the scapegoats.

- William Graham, acting administrator for NASA, announces that the Teacher in Space Project will continue with Barbara Morgan, who was Christa McAuliffe's backup.

Senate Hearing

Several senators began questioning why the presidential commission never asked if anyone at NASA had talked to Reagan's office the night before the launch. NASA personnel were asked, "Were you under any pressure?" And the answer was always the same; "No." The subject was then dropped. Senator Hollings (Democrat from South Carolina) headed up the Senate hearing and began wondering why the White House was never interviewed by the commission. The following information was discovered by the Senate hearing:

- Reagan refused to release the draft of his State-of-the-Union speech which would have clearly shown the importance of the Teacher in Space Project. Instead, the senators were provided with a modified version which had, on the last page of the speech, words related to just a "thank you" to

Christa McAuliffe. There was no mention of talking with her during the State-of-the-Union speech. Later it was discovered that Reagan did in fact plan to talk with her during the speech.

- Reagan's White House chief of staff ordered his staff to say to NASA personnel the night before the launch, "Tell them to get that thing up."
- The night before the launch, several of NASA's senior managers, all of whom testified that they knew nothing about the two teleconferences where MTI vigorously opposed the launch, met in Graham's hotel room. There were 161 phone calls that evening from the hotel room to the White House and staff members.
- The Republican-controlled Senate decided to prevent the bashing of NASA and the White House. Hollings was pressured to end his investigation for fear that the Senate would cancel all federal government contracts in the State of South Carolina.

5.12 SUMMARY OF LESSONS LEARNED

Project politics are inevitable. Good project managers are able to cope with project politics without sacrificing the integrity of the project.

A checklist of techniques for effective management of project politics might include:

- ☐ Identify all of the stakeholders, especially those that sit on the project governance committee.
- ☐ Work with the client and the stakeholders to identify the business case.
- ☐ Identify how involved the governance committee want to be in decision making and whether or not politics appears in the discussions and decisions.

TABLE 5-4 *PMBOK® Guide* **Alignment to Lessons Learned**

LESSONS LEARNED	PMBOK® GUIDE SECTIONS
The greater the number of people on the governance committee, the more likely it is that politics will become important.	1.5.1.2, 2.2, 2.2.1, 2.2.2
There will be hidden agendas on projects that are not recognized by the project manager until it is too late.	11.1.1.4, 11.1.1.9, 11.1.1.12
The two *PMBOK® Guide* knowledge areas probably most critical for managing project politics are risk management and project communications management.	10.1.1.2, 10.2.1.3, 10.3.1.3
Project managers must recognize the tell-tale signs that politics may be damaging the project.	2.1.5, 5.4.1.4, 6.1.1.3, 7.1.1.3

☐ Understand your limitations with the governance committee when addressing political issues.
☐ Determine the power and influence of the members of the governance committee.
☐ Understand the importance of risk management and effective communications when dealing with political situations.

Table 5-4 provides a summary of the lessons learned and alignment to various sections of the *PMBOK® Guide* where additional or supporting information can be found. In some cases, these sections of the *PMBOK® Guide* simply provide supporting information related to the lesson learned. There are numerous sections of the *PMBOK® Guide* that could be aligned for each lesson learned. For simplicity sake, only a few are listed.

6

SOFTWARE FAILURES

6.0 INTRODUCTION

The literature abounds with projects that fail. The greater the failure, the greater the amount of publicity. While failures can exist in any industry, IT failures seem to dominate the literature.

IT failures can run into the hundreds of millions of dollars. Sometimes, the failures do not appear until postimplementation where bugs appear. On large IT projects, it is impossible to test for every scenario that can exist on a project.

6.1 IT'S BIGGEST FAILURES[1]

You'll notice that many of the failures are government projects. That's not necessarily because government fails more often than the private sector, but because regulations and oversight make it harder for governments to cover up their mistakes. Private enterprise, on the other hand, is a bit better at making sure fewer people know of its failures.

So here, in chronological order, are *Computerworld*'s favorite IT boondoggles.

IBM's Stretch Project

In 1956, a group of computer scientists at IBM set out to build the world's fastest supercomputer. Five years later, they produced the IBM 7030—also called Stretch— the company's first transistorized supercomputer, and delivered the first unit to the Los Alamos National Laboratory in 1961. Capable of handling a half-million instructions per second, Stretch was the fastest computer in the world and would remain so through 1964.

Nevertheless, the 7030 was considered a failure. IBM's original bid to Los Alamos was to develop a computer 100 times faster than the system it was meant to replace, and the Stretch came in only at 30–40 times faster. Because it failed to meet its goal, IBM had to drop Stretch's price to

---

1. This section has been adapted from Jake Widman, "Lessons Learned: IT's Biggest Failures," *Computerworld*, October 9, 2008.

$7.8 million from the planned $13.5 million, which meant the system was priced below cost. The company stopped offering the 7030 for sale, and only nine were ever built.

That wasn't the end of the story, however. "A lot of what went into that effort was later helpful to the rest of the industry," said Turing Award winner and Stretch team member Fran Allen at a recent event marking the project's 50th anniversary. Stretch introduced pipelining, memory protection, memory interleaving and other technologies that have shaped the development of computers as we know them.

LESSON LEARNED Don't throw the baby out with the bathwater. Even if you don't meet your project's main goals, you may be able to salvage something of lasting value from the wreckage.

Knight-Ridder's Viewtron Service

The Knight-Ridder media giant was right to think that the future of home information delivery would be via computer. Unfortunately, this insight came in the early 1980s, and the computer they had in mind was an expensive dedicated terminal.

Knight-Ridder launched its Viewtron version of videotex—the in-home information retrieval service—in Florida in 1983 and extended it to other U.S. cities by 1985. The service offered banking, shopping, news and ads delivered over a custom terminal with color graphics capabilities beyond those of the typical PC of the time. But Viewtron never took off: It was meant to be the "McDonald's of videotex" and at the same time cater to upmarket consumers, according to a Knight-Ridder representative at the time who apparently didn't notice the contradictions in that goal.

A Viewtron terminal cost $900 initially (the price was later dropped to $600 in an attempt to stimulate demand); by the time the company made the service available to anyone with a standard PC, videotex's moment had passed.

Viewtron only attracted 20,000 subscribers, and by 1986, it was canceled, but not before it cost Knight-Ridder $50 million. *The New York Times* business section wrote, with admirable understatement, that Viewtron "tried to offer too much to too many people who were not overly interested."

Nevertheless, *BusinessWeek* concluded at the time, "Some of the nation's largest media, technology and financial services companies . . . remain convinced that someday, everyday life will center on computer screens in the home." Can you imagine?

LESSON LEARNED Sometimes you can be so far ahead of the curve that you fall right off the edge.

DMV Projects—California and Washington

Two Western states spent the 1990s attempting to computerize their departments of motor vehicles, only to abandon the projects after spending millions of dollars. First was California, which in 1987 embarked on a five-year, $27 million plan to develop a system for keeping track of the state's 31 million drivers' licenses and 38 million vehicle registrations. But the state solicited a bid from just one company and awarded the contract to Tandem Computers. With Tandem supplying the software, the state was locked into buying Tandem hardware as well, and in 1990, it purchased six computers at a cost of $11.9 million.

That same year, however, tests showed that the new system was slower than the one it was designed to replace. The state forged ahead, but in 1994, it was finally forced to abandon what the *San Francisco Chronicle* described as "an unworkable system that could not be fixed without the expenditure of millions more." In that May 1994 article, the *Chronicle* described it as a "failed $44 million computer project." In an August article, it was described as a $49 million project, suggesting that the project continued to cost money even after it was shut down. A state audit later concluded that the DMV had "violated numerous contracting laws and regulations."

LESSON LEARNED Regulations are there for a reason, especially ones that keep you from doing things like placing your future in the hands of one supplier.

Meanwhile, the state of Washington was going through its own nightmare with its License Application Mitigation Project (LAMP). Begun in 1990, LAMP was supposed to cost $16 million over five years and automate the state's vehicle registration and license renewal processes. By 1992, the projected cost had grown to $41.8 million; a year later, $51 million; by 1997, $67.5 million. Finally, it became apparent that not only was the cost of installing the system out of control, but it would also cost six times as much to run every year as the system it was replacing. Result: plug pulled, with $40 million spent for nothing.

LESSON LEARNED When a project is obviously doomed to failure, get out sooner rather than later.

Apple's Copland Operating System

It's easy to forget these days just how desperate Apple Computer was during the 1990s. When Microsoft Windows 95 came out, it arrived with multitasking and dynamic memory allocation, neither of which was available in the existing Mac System 7. *Copland* was Apple's attempt to develop a new operating system (OS) in-house; actually begun in 1994, the new OS was intended to be released as System 8 in 1996.

Copland's development could be the poster child for feature creep. As the new OS came to dominate resource allocation within Apple, project managers began protecting their fiefdoms by pushing for their products to be incorporated into System 8. Apple did manage to get one developers' release out in late 1996, but it was wildly unstable and did little to increase anyone's confidence in the company.

Before another developer release could come out, Apple made the decision to cancel Copland and look outside for its new operating system; the outcome, of course, was the purchase of NeXT, which supplied the technology that became OS X.

Copland did not die in vain. Some of the technology seen in demos eventually turned up in OS X. And even before that, some Copland features wound up in System 8 and 9, including a multithreaded Finder that provided something like true preemptive multitasking.

LESSON LEARNED Project creep is a killer. Keep your project's goals focused.

Sainsbury's Warehouse Automation

Sainsbury's, the British supermarket giant, was determined to install an automated fulfillment system in its Waltham Point distribution center in Essex. Waltham Point was the distribution center for much of London and southeast England, and the barcode-based fulfillment system would increase efficiency and streamline operations. If it worked, that is.

Installed in 2003, the system promptly ran into what were then described as "horrendous" barcode-reading errors. Regardless, in 2005 the company claimed the system was operating as intended. Two years later, the entire project was scrapped, and Sainsbury's wrote off £150 million in IT costs. (That's $265,335,000 calculated by today's exchange rate, enough to buy a lot of groceries.)

LESSON LEARNED A square peg in a round hole won't fit any better as time goes on. Put another way—problems that go unaddressed at rollout will only get worse, not better, over time.

Canada's Gun Registration System

In June 1997, Electronic Data Systems and U.K.-based SHL Systemhouse started work on a Canadian national firearm registration system. The original plan was for a modest IT project that would cost taxpayers only $2 million—$119 million for implementation, offset by $117 million in licensing fees.

But then politics got in the way. Pressure from the gun lobby and other interest groups resulted in more than 1000 change orders in just the first two years. The changes involved having to interface with the computer systems of more than 50 agencies, and since that integration wasn't part of the original contract, the government had to pay for all the extra work. By 2001, the costs had ballooned to $688 million, including $300 million for support.

But that wasn't the worst part. By 2001, the annual maintenance costs alone were running $75 million a year. A 2002 audit estimated that the program would wind up costing more than $1 billion by 2004 while generating revenue of only $140 million, giving rise to its nickname "the billion-dollar boondoggle."

The registry is still in operation and still a political football. Both the Canadian Police Association and the Canadian Association of Chiefs of Police have spoken in favor of it, while opponents argue that the money would be better spent otherwise.

Three Current Projects in Danger

At least Canada managed to get its project up and running. Our final three projects, courtesy of the U.S. government, are still in development—they have failed in many ways already but can still fail more. Will anyone learn anything from them? After reading these other stories, we know how we'd bet.

> **LESSON LEARNED** Define your project scope and freeze specifications before the requests for changes get out of hand.

FBI Virtual Case File

In 2000, the FBI finally decided to get serious about automating its case management and forms processing, and in September of that year, Congress approved $379.8 million for the Information Technology Upgrade Project. What started as an attempt to upgrade the existing Automated Case Support System became, in 2001, a project to develop an entirely new system, the Virtual Case File (VCS), with a contract awarded to Science Applications International Corp. (SAIC).

That sounds reasonable until you read about the development time allotted (a mere 22 months), the rollout plans (a "flash cutover," in which the new system would come online and the old one would go offline over a single weekend) and the system requirements (an 800-page document specifying details down to the layout of each page).

By late 2002, the FBI needed another $123.2 million for the project. And change requests started to take a toll: According to SAIC, those totaled about 400 by the end of 2003. In April 2005, SAIC delivered 700,000 lines of code that the FBI considered so bug ridden and useless that the agency decided to scrap the entire VCS project. A later audit blamed factors such as poorly defined design requirements, an overly ambitious schedule and the lack of an overall plan for purchases and deployment.

The FBI did use some of what it learned from the VCF disaster in its current Sentinel project. Sentinel, now scheduled for completion in 2012, should do what VCS was supposed to do using off-the-shelf, Web-based software.

Homeland Security's Virtual Fence

The U.S. Department of Homeland Security (DHS) is bolstering the U.S. Border Patrol with a network of radar, satellites, sensors and communication links—what's commonly referred to as a "virtual fence." In September 2006, a contract for this Secure Border Initiative Network (SBInet, not to be confused with Skynet) was awarded to Boeing, which was given $20 million to construct a 28-mile pilot section along the Arizona-Mexico border.

But early in 2008 Congress learned that the pilot project was being delayed because users had been excluded from the process and the complexity of the project had been underestimated. (Sound familiar?) In February 2008, the Government Accountability Office (GAO) reported that the radar meant to detect aliens coming across the border could be set off by rain and other weather, and the cameras meant to zoom in on subjects were sending back images of uselessly low resolution for objects beyond 3.1 miles. Also, the pilot's communications system interfered with local residents' WiFi networks—not good PR.

In April, DHS announced that the surveillance towers of the pilot fence did not meet the Border Patrol's goals and were being replaced—a story picked up by the Associated Press and widely reported in the mainstream media. But the story behind the story is less clear. The DHS and Boeing maintained the original towers were only temporary installations for demonstration purposes. Even so, the project was already experiencing delays and cost overruns, and in April, SBInet program manager Kirk Evans resigned, citing lack of a system design as just one specific concern. Not an auspicious beginning.

Census Bureau's Handheld Units

Back in 2006, the U.S. Census Bureau made a plan to use 500,000 handheld devices—purchased from Harris Corp. under a $600 million contract—to help automate the 2010 census. However, the cost more than doubled, and their use was curtailed in 2010—but the Census Bureau is moving ahead with the project anyway.

During a rehearsal for the census conducted in the fall of 2007, according to the GAO, field staff found that the handheld devices froze or failed to retrieve mapping coordinates (see Hard questions needed to save projects for details). Furthermore, multiple devices had the same identification number, which meant they would overwrite one another's data.

After the rehearsal, a representative of Mitre Corp., which advises the bureau on IT matters, brought notes to a meeting with the bureau's representative that read, "It is not clear that the system will meet Census' operational needs and quality goals. The final cost is unpredictable. Immediate, significant changes are required to rescue the program. However, the risks are so large considering the available time that we recommend immediate development of contingency plans to revert to paper operations."

There you have it; handheld computers that don't work as well as pencil and paper, new systems that are slower and less capable than the old ones they're meant to replace. Perhaps the overarching lesson is one that project managers should have learned at their mothers' knees: Don't bite off more than you can chew.

6.2 SOFTWARE BUGS

Software bugs most frequently appear during postimplementation. When they do occur, the delay can cause significant financial damage. When the bugs cause delays in the financial markets, billions of dollars can be lost, and quickly. When a false rumor about possible explosions at the White House was reported on April 23, 2012, the S&P briefly wiped out $136 billion from the S&P 500 in approximately 2 minutes. Eventually, the S&P recovered. Some examples of the devastating results of software bugs include:

- July 28, 1962: Mariner 1 space probe: Shortly after launch, mission control destroyed the rocket over the Atlantic. A formula that was written on a piece of paper was improperly rewritten in software code, causing an erroneous flight trajectory for the rocket.
- Intel, the manufacturer of Pentium chips, suffered an embarrassing moment resulting in a product recall. A mathematics professor, while performing prime number calculations on 10-digit numbers, discovered significant round-off errors using Pentium chips. Intel believed that the errors were insignificant and would show up only in every few billion calculations. But the mathematician was performing billions of calculations and the errors were now significant.

    The professor informed Intel of the problem. Intel refused to take action on the problem, stating that these errors were extremely rare and would affect a very small percentage of Pentium users. The professor went public with the disclosure of the error.

    Suddenly the small percentage of the people discovering the error was not as small as originally thought. Intel still persisted in its belief that the error affected only a small percentage of the population. Intel put the burden of responsibility on the user to show that his or her applications necessitated a replacement chip. Protests from consumers grew stronger. Finally, the company agreed to replace all chips, no questions asked, after IBM announced it would no longer use Pentium chips in its personal computers.

    Intel created its own public relations nightmare. Its response was slow and insincere. Intel tried to solve the problem solely through technical channels and completely disregarded the human issue of the crisis. Telling people who work in hospitals or air traffic control that there is a flaw in their computer but it is insignificant is not an acceptable response. Intel spent more than a half billion dollars in the recall, significantly more than the cost of an immediate replacement.
- In August, 1999, MCI Worldcom upgraded its infrastructure. The result was unexpected instability of its systems. When efforts to fix the problem repeatedly failed, MCI was forced to shut down its system for 24 hours. MCI has 3000 customers, one of which was the Chicago Board of Trade (CBOT). The failure disabled the CBOT system that controls the trades leading to a loss of some 180,000 trades. Since most of the trades range from $10,000 to $100,000 per trade, the total loss was quite large and difficult to calculate.
- On May 18, 2012, Facebook eagerly anticipated its initial public offering to raise $16 billion. The Nasdaq computer system had a technical

glitch and stopped working for some 30 minutes. Nasdaq then decided to use a secondary system which resulted in delays in placing orders and confirmations. As the price of the new stock dropped after its initial high, investors were unable to complete their orders promptly. According to some estimates, investors, banks and brokers lost more than $500 million because of the glitch. Nasdaq has regulations that limits its losses paid to customers to be $3 million per month. Nasdaq has offered to pay $62 million, which is significantly more that their regulations state. The people that lost money, however, want to be made whole and recover all of their losses.

- On April 26, 2013, the Chicago Board Options Exchange (CBOE) opened three and a half hours late because of a software malfunction that caused an outage. The financial damage to investors is yet to be determined.

6.3 CAUSES OF FAILURE IN SOFTWARE PROJECTS

In Section 2.2, we listed many of the possible causes that lead to project failure. In this section, we list the causes that are more appropriate for the failure of large software projects such as those related to enterprise resource planning (ERP) projects. They include:

- Failure to prepare a robust business case
- Lack of agreement on objectives
- Failure of governance
- Inexperienced sponsor
- No clear definition of success or failure
- Wishful thinking, believing the budgets can be controlled and optimistic deadlines achieved
- Stating that we do not want to hear bad news
- Poor link between project objectives and strategic business objectives
- No project ownership
- Poor engagement with stakeholders
- Establishing project based upon initial price rather than long-term value that can be achieved
- Failing to capture and understand lessons learned from previous projects
- Failing to choose the alternative based upon the best estimate
- Failing to understand that alternative analysis must be based upon value and human behavior rather than just technology
- We ignore behavioral concerns
- Not looking at all alternatives, tradeoffs and consequences
- The greater the technology, the greater the impact on organizational change
- No change management strategy; poor testing and employee training; users not prepared to do their jobs

- Bad go-live timing; unrealistic timing set by executives
- Inexperienced or incompetent consultants
- Multiple enterprise-wide software projects at the same time
- No disaster recovery plans
- Not understanding the impact of business process changes
- Poor risk management
- Poor metrics
- Managing legacy replacement
- Poor vendor management
- Judgments by stakeholders about success (and failure) often made too early in the project's life cycle
- Many project managers actually plan for failure rather than success
- For political reasons, risk management is not performed and written down (relate this to early days of project management in government). It may be discussed behind closed doors only.
- No risk management strategy
- Must understand institutional conditions; how will employees work with or work around a new system
- Organizational change management
- Sometimes we intentionally underestimate to get it approved; and then, as we get into it, we increase budgets.
- Albert Einstein once said, "The definition of insanity is doing the same thing over and over again and expecting different results."
- No matter how hard we try, system requirements cannot be fully defined up front because the users cannot predict them in advance; then we establish budgets and schedules based upon partial information.

6.4 LARGE-SCALE IT FAILURE

We usually do not hear much about the mistakes made on small IT projects even though the financial damage can be severe. But large IT projects with order-of-magnitude cost overruns make good headlines. One such example is Maine's Medicaid mistakes that turned a $25 million investment into a $300 million backlog in six short months.[2] This is a lesson in how to not run a Web services project.

Reader ROI

- The importance of having a contingency plan
- The consequences of skipping end-to-end testing
- Ten rules for successful project management

---

2. The remainder of this section has been adapted from Allan Holmes, "Massive Project, Massive Mistakes: Maine's Medicaid Mistakes Turned a $25 Million Investment into a $300 Million Backlog, *CIO*, May 3, 2006.

On Friday, January 21, 2005, the state of Maine cut the ribbon on its new, Web-based Maine Medicaid Claims System for processing $1.5 billion in annual Medicaid claims and payments. The new $25 million program, which replaced the state's old Honeywell mainframe, was hailed as a more secure system that would clear claims faster, track costs better and give providers more accurate information on claims status.

But within days of turning on the new system, Craig Hitchings, director of information technology for Maine's Department of Human Services (DHS), knew that something was seriously wrong.

There had been problems right from the start—an unusually high rate of rejected claims—but Hitchings had assumed they were caused by providers using the wrong codes on the new electronic claim forms. By the end of the month, he wasn't so sure. The department's Bureau of Medical Services, which runs the Medicaid program, was being deluged with hundreds of calls from doctors, dentists, hospitals, health clinics and nursing homes, angry because their claims were not being paid. The new system had placed most of the rejected claims in a "suspended" file for forms that contained errors.

Tens of thousands of claims representing millions of dollars were being left in limbo.

Hitchings's team—about 15 IT staffers and about four dozen employees from CNSI, the contractor hired to develop the system—were working 12-hour days, writing software fixes and performing adjustments so fast that Hitchings knew that key project management guidelines were beginning to fall by the wayside. And nothing seemed to help.

Day after day, the calls kept coming. The bureau's call center was so backed up that many providers could not get through. And when they did, they had to wait on the phone for a half hour to speak to a human.

By the end of March, the number of Medicaid claims in the suspended bin had reached approximately 300,000, and the state was falling further and further behind in its ability to process them. With their bills unpaid, some of Maine's 262,000 Medicaid recipients were turned away from their doctors' offices, according to the Maine Medical Association. Several dentists and therapists were forced to close their doors, and some physicians had to take out loans to stay afloat. With the Medicaid program accounting for one-third of the entire state budget, Maine's finances were in shambles, threatening the state's financial stability and its credit rating. Yet Hitchings was at a loss to explain what was causing all the suspensions.

And every day brought hundreds more.

More than a year later, it's fair to say that the Maine Medicaid Claims System project was a disaster of major proportions. Since the new system went live, it had cost the state of Maine close to $30 million. The fallout was broad and deep. In December 2005, Jack Nicholas, the commissioner of DHS who oversaw the project, resigned.

As of press time, Maine was the only state in the union not in compliance with the U.S. Health Insurance Portability and Accountability Act of

1996 (HIPAA)—a striking irony given that the new system was designed to facilitate that compliance. Although U.S. federal authorities had said they would work with the state in extending the deadline, the failure was a black eye on Maine's ability to manage the health of hundreds of thousands of its residents. And it became an issue in that year's race for governor.

State IT officials say they have fixed most of the bugs in the new Web services system and that it is now processing 85% of claims (although physician groups dispute this). With 20/20 hindsight, they can now look back and see where the project went wrong. Hiring a vendor, CNSI, that had no experience in developing Medicaid claims systems was the first mistake. And that was compounded by the decision to build a new and relatively unproven technology platform for the entire system rather than, as other U.S. states have done, integrating a Web-based portal with back-end legacy systems. Third, IT switched over to the new system overnight with no backup system in case something went wrong. And making matters worse, no end-to-end testing or training was conducted before the switch-over. Indeed, the story of the Maine Medicaid Claims System is a classic example of how not to develop, deploy and manage an advanced Web services system.

"By the first of March, it was clear that we were missing any sort of basic management of this project and were in complete defensive mode," recalls Dick Thompson, then head of procurement for the state of Maine and now its CIO. "We could not see our way out of this."

Out with the Old

In the late 1990s, states were moving fast to overhaul their Medicaid claims processing systems. Driving the transformation was HIPAA, which required numerous changes in managing patient health and records, the most significant of which was protecting patient privacy. Maine, like other states, had to upgrade its systems to better secure Medicaid patient records. Under HIPAA, the state had until October 1, 2002, to have a system in place that would secure and limit access to that information.

At the same time, the federal Medicaid program was becoming more complex. As additional health services were added, the number of codes and subcodes for services grew, and payments to doctors and hospitals were parsed accordingly. Maine also needed to give providers a way to check the eligibility of Medicaid patients and the status of their claims. Making this information available online, they hoped, would cut down on the number of calls to the state Bureau of Medical Services, thereby saving the state money.

State officials knew that upgrading the old system would be a Herculean task. Maine processes more than 120,000 Medicaid claims per week, and the existing claims processing system—a 1970s vintage Honeywell mainframe—was not up to the job, nor could it meet HIPAA's demands or provide online access. The state's IT managers reasoned that a new end-to-end system would be easier and cheaper to maintain. (Other states reached different conclusions. Massachusetts, for example, decided to build a new front-end Web portal for providers and Medicaid patients that could be integrated with the state's existing legacy systems.)

The development of the new system was assigned to the IT staff in the DHS, which decided it wanted a system built on a rules-based engine so that as Medicaid rules changed, the changes could be programmed easily into the system.

Some service providers, such as EDS, offered states the opportunity to outsource claims processing systems. But the DHS staff believed building its own system would give it more flexibility. The staff also believed it could manage the system better than an outsourcer. "We had a track record of running the old system for 25 years," Thompson explained.

In April 2001, the state of Maine issued an RFP for the new system. But by the end of the year, the state had received only two proposals: one from Keane (for $30 million) and another from CNSI (for $15 million).

Typically, agencies like to see several bids within a close range. That way, procurement officials are confident that the requirements are doable and the bids realistic. In this case, the low bidder, CNSI, had no experience in building Medicaid claims processing systems. In contrast, Keane had some experience in developing Medicaid systems, and the company had worked on the Maine system for Medicaid eligibility.

The paucity of bidders and the 100% difference in price between the two bids should have been red flags, said J. Davidson Frame, dean of the University of Management and Technology. "Only two bidders is a dangerous sign," he said, adding that the low response rate indicated that potential bidders knew the requirements of the RFP were unreasonable. "Thompson should have realized immediately something was wrong with the solicitation, and redone it," Frame said. "Even if they missed the [HIPAA] deadline, it would have saved time and money in the long run."

Seeds of Failure

CNSI proposed building the new system with the J2EE software language, arguing that it was needed to get the scalability state officials were asking for, according to Hitchings. J2EE is a powerful programming language, the Ferrari of software code, which some of the largest corporations are now using to run their global operations. Experts said deploying such advanced technology, especially in state government, increased the risk in an already risky project. Most Medicaid claims systems contain bundles of code that have been tinkered with for decades to adjust rates, services and rules. Attempting to translate all of that human intelligence, gathered over thousands of person-years, into a system built from the ground up, was, at best, problematic. "It was a big misstep," Frame said.

But Thompson argued that the state was in a corner. Maine's budget was tight. State revenue was dropping, and saving money was critical. Also, the deadline to become compliant with HIPAA was looming, and Thompson decided that the six months that would have been needed to redo the RFP was too much. "We had a requirement to get something in place soon," Thompson said.

In October 2001, the state awarded the contract to CNSI, giving the company 12 months to build and deploy a new high-end processing system by the HIPAA deadline of October 1, 2002. As head of procurement, Thompson signed off on the contract.

Almost immediately, it became evident that the state was not going to meet the deadline. To begin with, the 65-person team composed of DHS IT staffers and CNSI representatives assigned to the project had difficulty securing time with the dozen of Medicaid experts in the Bureau of Medical Services to get detailed information about how to code for Medicaid rules. As a result, the contractors had to make their own decisions on how to meet Medicaid requirements. And then they had to reprogram the system after consulting with a Medicaid expert, further slowing development.

The system also was designed to look at claims in more detail than the old system in order to increase the accuracy of payments and comply with HIPAA security requirements. The legacy system checked three basic pieces of information: that the provider was in the system, the eligibility of the patient and whether the service was covered. The new system checked 13 pieces, such as making sure the provider was authorized to perform that service on the date the service was provided and the provider's license. "There were a lot more moving parts," Thompson explained.

Looking back, Thompson said the DHS team was seriously understaffed. But Thompson said he was afraid to ask for more resources. "That is a significant problem in government," Thompson said. "If I say I need 60 to 70 percent more staff because we need to work this project for two years, the response would be: 'What, are you crazy?' So, we just couldn't make the turnaround times."

In late 2002, just months away from the HIPAA deadline, the DHS team got a reprieve. The federally run Center for Medicare and Medicaid Services pushed back the deadline to October 1, 2003.

For the next two years, CNSI and Maine's DHS IT shop worked long hours writing code. Errors kept cropping up as programmers had to reprogram the system to accept Medicaid rule changes at the federal and state levels. The changes created integration problems. The developers also had to add more storage capacity and computing power to accommodate the increase in information generated by the new rules, and that further delayed the development.

In January 2003, John Baldacci was inaugurated governor. One of Baldacci's campaign promises was to streamline state government, and part of the plan called for merging Maine's Department of Behavioral and Developmental Services with the Department of Human Services to create the Department of Health and Human Services (HHS). That meant consolidating systems and databases that had resided in both departments and creating new business processes, diverting crucial resources from the development of the claims system. Thompson said the merger also diverted executives' attention. Meanwhile, the cost of the project rose, increasing 50% to more than $22 million.

The IT staff could not meet the extended HIPAA deadline. In an attempt to catch up, they began to cut corners. For example, testing the system from end to end was dismissed as an option. The state did conduct a pilot with about 10 providers and claims clearinghouses, processing a small set of claims. But the claims were not run through much of the system because it was not ready for testing. Beyond a few fliers announcing the new system and new provider ID codes, HHS offered little or no guidance to providers on the use of the system. And there was no training for the staff who would have to answer providers' questions.

"We kept saying: 'Gosh, let's keep our head down; we can work through this'," Thompson recalled. Instead, he acknowledged, he and other top officials should have taken a step back and analyzed the risks that the new system might pose for the state's Medicaid providers and their patients.

Early Warnings

Hitchings and his staff made the decision to go live in January 2005. The switch to the new system would be made in a flash cutover in which the legacy system would be shut down for good and the new system would take over. Codes identifying providers (tax identifier numbers) and Medicaid patients (Social Security numbers) had to be changed to meet HIPAA guidelines, and the legacy system would not be able to recognize the new numbers. Nor could it read the new electronic claim forms. HHS dismissed the idea of running a parallel system as too costly and complicated.

Maine officials did have one contingency plan: They would pay providers for two to four weeks if the new system failed. Under the interim payment plan, if a provider's claims were not being processed in a timely manner, the provider would receive a payment based on the average monthly payment the provider had received the five weeks prior to the new system coming on.

On January 21, Hitchings arrived at his office to find the claims system up and running. The initial reports from the contractor and his staff were that the system was humming along, quickly moving through Medicaid claims.

But the following Monday morning, Hitchings sat down with CNSI contractors to go over the file statistics for the system's first three days. Something wasn't right. The system had sent about 50% of the claims—24,000 in the first week alone—into a "suspended" file, a dumping ground for claims that have an error that is not significant enough to reject the claim outright but that are not accurate enough for payment. Typically, the error can be fixed fairly quickly by a claims processor. But the 50% rate was very high; the legacy system had suspended only about 20% of claims.

By the end of the month, angry calls from providers were mounting. One of the calls came from Kevin Flanigan, the only internist and pediatrician in Pittsfield, a town of 4000 people in south central Maine. Early one morning at the end of January, Dr. Flanigan sat down with his business manager to go over the Medicaid payments that had arrived in that day's mail. Flanigan sliced open an envelope, pulled out the statement, and read "rejected." In the amount paid column, he saw 0.00. His manager opened a statement. Zero amount paid. "One after the other it said zero, zero, zero," Flanigan recalls. "My first reaction was that the state blew it, and it was no big deal. I could just call them up, straighten it out, and they'll send me a check."

Flanigan called HHS. He was told the problem was a computer glitch. The state would have it fixed in one or two weeks.

Flanigan went back to seeing his patients.

The glitch, however, kept sending tens of thousands of claims to the suspended file. Hitchings discovered that the system was suspending duplicate claims—claims from the same provider who had filed the claim a second time after learning the first had been suspended. The system was programmed to reject the second claim if it was identical to one already in suspension. With the capacity to work off only 1000 claims a week, it would take the Bureau of Medical Services more than six months to clear all of them.

Hitchings and CNSI began to look at the code and the design of the system. They found numerous problems. For example, without adequate guidance from Medicaid experts, the system had been designed to accept files with up to 1000 lines of claim data. But many claims were much larger, some containing up to 10,000 lines, and the server was rejecting them automatically. The Medical Bureau staff asked providers to submit smaller files. In the meantime, the IT staff would try to rewrite the software.

At the same time, other errors began popping up. The state now owed health care providers as much as $50 million in Medicaid payments, and the backlog of claims had reached almost 100,000. Providers couldn't get through to HHS. When they didn't get a busy signal, the wait to talk to a staff person at MaineCare (formerly the Bureau of Medical Services) was a half hour or more. Providers began calling state legislators. A press conference was held on the steps of the state capitol on February 16, declaring a financial crisis for Maine health care providers.

The calls were coming in so fast that Hitchings decided to man the phones himself. One call was from a woman in a provider's billing office. She was frustrated because the system would not accept her claim, no matter what she did. Hitchings walked her through the process, making sure she had the correct billing and file name conventions. After 45 minutes, the system still wouldn't accept the claim. Hitchings had to admit defeat.

"That was just so frustrating," Hitchings said. "I just couldn't fix the problem. I didn't know what more we could do."

In Pittsfield, Flanigan opened more claim statements with no checks. He began to make plans to draw on a line of credit that used his office building as equity.

Over the next nine months, Flanigan would take out $30,000 in loans to pay his bills.

Call for Help

By early March 2005, Hitchings's staff and CNSI were overwhelmed. For $860,000, the department hired XWave, an integrator and project management consultant, to take over the project. More people were hired to take phone calls. Governor Baldacci, saying "enough is enough," ordered Commissioner Nicholas to have the claims system operable and running smoothly by the end of March.

But March came and went and nothing changed. Desperate, state officials decided to change the program's management, and Rebecca Wyke, head of Maine's financing department, appointed Thompson as CIO in late March, replacing Harry Lanphear, who is now CEO of the Kennebec Valley YMCA. Thompson was put in charge of the project and ordered to right the system as quickly as possible. (Lanphear could not be reached for comment.)

By the end of the summer, 647,000 claims were clogging the suspended claims database, representing about $310 million in back payments. Interim payments were being made, but reconciling those payments with the claims was an accounting nightmare. Wyke hired the accounting firm Deloitte & Touche to audit the state books to determine if Maine would have enough money to pay Medicaid bills by the June 30 end of the fiscal year. The $7 million contract also called for Deloitte to consult on how to reconcile the Medicaid bills.

XWave set up a project management office and steering committee that met weekly to establish priorities and monitor the progress of system software fixes. The goal was to get the new system to process claims at the same rate that the legacy system had, sending 20% into a suspended or rejection file. Thompson hired Jim Lopatosky, an Oracle database specialist in the state's Bureau of Information Services, as operations manager to act as a calming influence on the department's battered IT division. When Lopatosky took over in June, he encountered a staff "running at 100 miles per hour" trying to fix every software bug, with little direction on what was most important. "They couldn't see the forest for the trees," he recalls.

Lopatosky soon realized, as XWave had, that the system's problems could be laid at the door of poor project management and worse communication among the HHS IT staff, contractors and business users. For instance, programmers for the state and those working for CNSI would work on parts of the system without telling each other what they were doing. Lopatosky prioritized tasks. He acted as a liaison between teams working on different functions. He directed the programmers to fix those software bugs that would resolve the largest number of suspended claims and postponed work on the portal through which providers could check on the status of claims. That could wait.

But the intricacies of the Medicaid program continued to thwart progress. Thompson needed a business owner who could clarify Medicaid business processes for the IT staff. The previous October, Dr. Laureen Biczak, the medical director for MaineCare, had agreed to take on that responsibility.

"This is what brought it all together," Thompson said. "It was something we should have done from the start: have someone who knew the business [of Medicaid] working full-time on the project."

With Biczak's assistance, the Bureau of Information Services set up a triage process for the help desk. Medicaid business process questions would be sent to the Medicaid specialists; software and hardware questions would be sent to IT program specialists. The triage process was implemented in January. By the end of the month, Thompson claimed the new system could process 85% of claims as either pay or deny. "I can now see the light at the end of the tunnel," he said.

For the provider community, however, that light was still the headlamps of an oncoming train. Gordon Smith, head of the Maine Medical Association, said the new claims system was still far from what was promised: an advanced system that would clear claims faster, track costs better and give providers more accurate information on claims status. Smith disputed Thompson's claim, saying the new system still rejected 20% of the total claims, most of which met accepted standards for payment. "Why are we comparing this system to a legacy system that wasn't good enough in the first place?" he asked. "Why spend $US25 million on a new system that isn't any better?"

For doctors like Flanigan, the entire ordeal—the postponed payments, the lack of communication with providers, the system's continued fallibility—will not easily be forgotten. Or forgiven. And it was certainly on Flanigan's mind when he and others like him went to the polls to vote for the governor in November.

"They are supposed to be protecting the most-at-risk people in the state," Flanigan said. "It goes beyond shock and dismay how utterly disrespectful the state has been to providers and patients."

---

10 STEPS TO A SUCCESSFUL PROJECT

1. **Scope out a detailed plan.** Describe what the system must do for users and how you will measure the performance of the system and its output.
2. **Watch out for bad RFP bids.** A low number of bids or bids that are not within an acceptable range suggest that the requirements have not been properly communicated or are unrealistic.

(Continued)

3. **Plan ahead**. Line up subject matter experts who know the business processes for the new system and can provide guidance to developers and programmers during buildout. Assign a business expert full time, or nearly full time, to the implementation. Create a steering committee that includes subject matter experts and developers and meet frequently.

4. **Find the bottleneck**. You can develop a system only as fast as it takes to build the most complicated component. Many times the delay is not from writing code, but rather something else, such as finding time with a subject matter expert. So, resist hiring more programmers to speed up the development process until you analyze what is slowing down the project and focus resources there.

5. **Do not cut corners on testing**. The last thing you want to do is ignore critical pilot tests and end-to-end tests. Ultimately, such corner cutting will result in longer delays later. If you need more time, ask for it, and defend why you need it.

6. **Develop a backup system**. If replacing a legacy system, make sure the users can fall back to the old system if the new system fails and needs to be reworked.

7. **Prepare other contingency plans**. As part of your backup plan, be prepared to communicate with system users so that they can use the backup system and know what is expected of them.

8. **Train, train and train**. Provide frequent training for internal staff on new business processes and system requirements, including what must be done in case of a system failure. Train call center staff on how to manage users' questions. Train users on how to use the system and what they should do in case of failure.

9. **Honesty is your best policy**. In case of failure, provide honest answers to users and staff. Do not make promises that you do not know you can keep.

10. **Triage fixes**. In fixing a flawed system, prioritize fixing those requirements that have the biggest impact on users and that provide basic, needed functionality. Come back to the bells and whistles later.

6.5 WORST POSSIBLE FAILURE: FOXMEYER DRUGS

We read about massive IT failures in the hundreds of millions of dollars. Companies can take a financial hit and still remain solvent. The worst case is when the software package is an absolute necessity for ongoing business and the system fails to work properly. If all of your eggs are in one basket, such as in an ERP system, and it does not work, hemorrhaging cash can lead to bankruptcy.

Case Study: FoxMeyer Drugs' Bankruptcy: Was It a Failure of ERP?[3]

Abstract

This interpretive case study of FoxMeyer Drugs' ERP implementation is based on empirical frameworks and models of software project risks and project escalation.

Implications of the study offer suggestions on how to avoid ERP failure.

Introduction

FoxMeyer Drugs was a $5 billion company and the nation's fourth largest distributor of pharmaceuticals before the fiasco. With the goal of using technology to increase efficiency, the Delta III project began in 1993. FoxMeyer conducted market research and product evaluation and purchased SAP R/3 in December of that year. FoxMeyer also purchased warehouse-automation from a vendor called Pinnacle, and chose Andersen Consulting to integrate and implement the two systems. Implementation of the Delta III project took place during 1994 and 1995.

According to Christopher Cole, chief operating officer at Pinnacle, the FoxMeyer mess was "not a failure of automation. It was not a failure of commercial software per se. It was a management failure" (Jesitus, 1997). Perhaps management had unrealistic expectations. Did management expect technology to be a "magic bullet"? (Markus and Benjamin 1997a, 1997b). In reality, it was the opposite. FoxMeyer was driven to bankruptcy in 1996, and the trustee of FoxMeyer announced in 1998 that he is suing SAP, the ERP vendor, as well as Andersen Consulting, its SAP integrator, for $500 million each (Caldwell 1998, Stein 1998).

Project Risks

The Delta III project at FoxMeyer Drugs was at risk for several reasons. Using a framework developed for identifying software project risks (Keil, Cule, Lyytinen and Schmidt 1998), this study classifies the project risks at FoxMeyer into (1) customer mandate, (2) scope and requirements, (3) execution and (4) environment. First, the customer mandate relies on commitment from both top management and users. At FoxMeyer, although senior management commitment was high, reports reveal that some users were not as committed. In fact, there was a definite morale problem among the warehouse employees. This was not surprising, since the project's Pinnacle warehouse automation integrated with SAP R/3 threatened their jobs. With the closing of three warehouses, the transition to the first automated warehouse was a disaster. Disgruntled workers damaged inventory, and orders were not filled, and mistakes occurred as the new system struggled with the volume of transactions. $34 million worth of inventory were lost (Jesitus 1997).

---

3. The FoxMeyer Drugs Case Study was prepared by Judy Scott. Copyright © 2013 by Judy E. Scott, Associate Professor at the University of Colorado Denver. judy.scott@ucdenver.edu.

Second, the scope of the project was risky. FoxMeyer was an early adopter of SAP R/3. After the project began, FoxMeyer signed a large contract to supply University HealthSystem Consortium (UHC). This event exacerbated the need for an unprecedented volume of R/3 transactions. Although, prior to the contract, testing seemed to indicate that R/3 on HP9000 servers would be able to cope with the volume of transactions, in 1994 R/3 could process only 10,000 customer orders per night, compared with 420,000 under FoxMeyer's original mainframe system (Jesitus 1997).

Third, the execution of the project was an issue due to the shortage of skilled and knowledgeable personnel. FoxMeyer did not have the necessary skills in-house and was relying on Andersen Consulting to implement R/3 and integrate the ERP with an automated warehouse system from Pinnacle. Although at the height of the project there were over 50 consultants at FoxMeyer, many of them were inexperienced and turnover was high (Computergram International 1998).

Finally, the environment quadrant of the risk framework includes issues over which project management has little or no control (Keil, Cule, Lyytinen and Schmidt 1998). Although FoxMeyer must have realized the project was in trouble, its perceived dependence on consultants and vendors prevented it from seeing how it could gain control. Since FoxMeyer was competing on price, it needed a high volume of transactions to be profitable. Yet with the UHC contract "the focus of the project dramatically changed", contributing to rising project costs (eventually over $100 million), lowering FoxMeyer's already narrow margins and erasing its profitability.

Given the high level of risk, why did FoxMeyer initiate the project? Furthermore, why was the project allowed to escalate to the extent of contributing to FoxMeyer's bankruptcy?

Project Escalation

FoxMeyer's mainframe systems were becoming inadequate for its growing volume of business. Moreover, its Unisys system was being phased out by the vendor and needed to be replaced. The Delta project was envisaged as a client/server R/3 solution integrated with automated warehouses to accommodate future company growth. A model of factors that promote project escalation suggests that (1) project factors, (2) psychological factors, (3) social factors and (4) organizational factors all contributed to the continuation of the project despite negative information (Keil 1995). The *implementation appeared troubled almost from the start.* Despite warnings from Woltz Consulting, during the early stages of the project, that a schedule for the entire implementation to be completed in 18 months was totally unrealistic, FoxMeyer's Delta project went ahead (Jesitus 1997).

Project Factors

Escalation is more likely when there is perceived evidence that continued investment could produce a large payoff. FoxMeyer expected the Delta project to save $40 million annually. Andersen Consulting and SAP were also motivated to continue the project. According to FoxMeyer, Andersen used trainees (Caldwell 1998) and used the Delta project as a "training ground" for "consultants who were very inexperienced"(Computergram International 1998).

Similarly, FoxMeyer claimed that SAP treated it like "its own research and development guinea pig" (Financial Times 1998). Furthermore, project setbacks appeared temporary. For example, there was some measurement evidence that these systems could perform at FoxMeyer's required volume of transactions.

Psychological Factors

Andersen and SAP had a prior history of success that encouraged them to continue the project. Andersen stated "we delivered an effective system, just as we have for thousands of other clients" (Computergram International 1998). FoxMeyer CIO Robert Brown felt a high degree of personal responsibility saying, "We are betting our company on this." (Cafasso 1994). Moreover, he expressed his emotional attachment to the project when he boasted about how an integrated $65 million computer system built on SAP R/3 would radically improve the company's critical operations. However, FoxMeyer overspent and bit off more than they could chew, since they lacked available users on staff with the sophistication to handle a fast-track installation. Also, the decision to go with two different vendors for two of the company's most important business systems was "an error in information processing" (Keil 1995). This added still greater complexity to an already challenging situation (Jesitus1997).

Social Factors

It is likely that Andersen Consulting and SAP needed to externally justify the Delta project. They probably did not consider de-escalating the project since abandonment would not be good publicity. Moreover their "norms for consistency" (Keil 1995) were such that perseverance with project problems usually paid off for them.

Organizational Factors

Both FoxMeyer's CEO and CIO were strong advocates of the project. However in February 1996, Thomas Anderson, FoxMeyer Health's president and CEO (and champion of the company's integration /warehouse-automation projects) was asked to resign due to delays in the new warehouse and realizing the SAP system's projected savings. A change in management is often needed for de-escalation (Montealegre and Keil 1998). But it was too late for FoxMeyer.

Reports seem to indicate that FoxMeyer had loose management controls, shown by the fact that management did not control the scope of the Delta project. For example, originally, FoxMeyer expected Andersen to design a system that could "ship in X number of hours". Although Andersen designed a system that could do that, FoxMeyer later, wanted to be able to ship in one-third to one-half that time (Jesitus 1997). Also, with the UHC contract, the throughput capacity of the SAP project had to be increased substantially. Furthermore, FoxMeyer did not have adequate change management policies and procedures. For example, its labor problems exploded when workers began leaving their jobs en masse from three Ohio warehouses, which were scheduled to be replaced by the automated Washington Court House center. Because of a "debilitating morale problem among departing workers, a lot of merchandise was dumped into trucks and arrived at Washington Court House with packages damaged or broken open or otherwise unsalable as new product, [resulting in] a huge shrinkage in inventory" (Jesitus 1997).

Implications

There are high risks involved when adopting new technologies, especially in a unique situation that vendors cannot adequately test prior to actual use. On the other hand, customers should be aware of the risks and be compensated with discounts or other incentives for early adoption. FoxMeyer should have realized the risk in adopting R/3 in its early years and negotiated with the consultants to share the project risks by tying their compensation to project results. The contract with the consultants should have specified experienced personnel by name and no billing for "rookies." Also, FoxMeyer should have made an effort to become less dependent on the consultants. For example, knowledge transfer should have been written into the consulting contract. FoxMeyer needed to ensure that project knowledge was transferred to them from the consultants so that they could develop in-house skills for maintenance of the system after the consultants had left.

In hindsight, it is obvious that FoxMeyer should not have "bet the company" (Cafasso 1994) and should have de-escalated the project. To do that, it could have reduced the scope of the project (Montealegre and Keil 1998)—perhaps foregoing the UHC contract, or postponing it to a later phase in the project. A phased implementation would have been less risky and would have given the implementation team a chance to test transaction throughput more thoroughly. The pre-implementation testing was inadequate, partly because the UHC contract was added afterwards. Also, if FoxMeyer had not reduced their prices as much, then they would not have been as dependent on such a high volume of transactions. In other words, FoxMeyer should have reengineered its business practices to be compatible with the capabilities of the technology at that time. Using just one vendor in the first phase would have reduced the risks and complexity of the project. The warehouse automation multiplied the project risk and interactions between R/3 and Pinnacle's automation took FoxMeyer into uncharted waters. Control of the project scope, costs and progress should have been tighter. An objective audit of the project progress might have saved FoxMeyer. Finally, FoxMeyer should have avoided the morale problem in the warehouses by training the employees, helping them develop new skills, putting some of them on the implementation team and using other change management techniques. Although a lack of management commitment can result in project failure, management over-commitment can be even more disastrous. It can cause errors in judgment and lead to project escalation. Overall, the expected payoff from the Delta III project was probably overestimated, given that benefits are often intangible. But regardless of expectations, for FoxMeyer it was not worth taking the risks it did. In conclusion, FoxMeyer's experiences provide valuable lessons on how to avoid ERP failure.

REFERENCES

Cafasso, R. "Success strains SAP support", *Computerworld*, 28(36), September 5, 1994.

Caldwell, B. "Andersen Sued On R/3", *InformationWeek*, July 6, 1998.

Computergram International. "FoxMeyer Plus TwoSue Andersen for SAP Snafus", *Computergram International*, July 20, 1998.

Financial Times. "SAP in $500m US lawsuit", *Financial Times*, Surveys, September 2, 1998, 2.

Jesitus, J. "Broken Promises?; FoxMeyer 's Project was a Disaster. Was the Company Too Aggressive or Was It Misled?", *Industry Week*, November 3, 1997, 31–37.

Keil, M., Cule, P. E., Lyytinen, K., and Schmidt, R. C. "A framework for identifying software project risks", *Communications of the ACM*, 41(11), November 1998,76–83.

Keil, M. "Pulling the plug: Software project management and the problem of project escalation", *MIS Quarterly*, 19(4), December 1995, 421–447.

Markus, M. L. and Benjamin, R. I. "The magic bullet theory in IT-enabled transformation", *Sloan Management Review*, 38(2), Winter 1997a, 55–68.

Markus, M. L. and Benjamin, R. I. "Are you gambling on a magic bullet?", *Computerworld*, 31(42), October 20 1997b, C1–C11.

Montealegre, R. and Keil, M. "Denver International Airport's Automated Baggage Handling system: A Case Study of De-escalation of Commitment", *Academy of Management Proceedings*, August 1998.

Stein T. "SAP Sued Over R/3", *Information Week*, August 31, 1998.

6.6 LONDON HEATHROW TERMINAL[4]

London Heathrow Terminal 5 is an airport terminal at London Heathrow Airport, serving the U.K. capital city of London. Opened in 2008, the main building in the complex is the largest free-standing structure in the United Kingdom. Terminal 5 is currently used exclusively as one of the three global hubs of International Airlines Group, served by British Airways (BA) and Iberia, with the others being London Gatwick North and Madrid Barajas Terminal 4. Prior to March 2012, the terminal was used exclusively by

---

4. Part of this case has been adapted from London Heathrow Terminal 5, *Wikipedia, the Free Encyclopedia*.

British Airways. The terminal is designed to ultimately handle 35 million passengers a year.

The building's lead architects were from the Richard Rogers Partnership and production design was completed by aviation architects Pascall and Watson. The engineers for the structure were Arup and Mott MacDonald. The building cost £4.3 billion ($8.5 billion, which included $346 million for IT) and took 19 years from conception to completion, including the longest public inquiry in British history.

History

The possibility of a fifth terminal at Heathrow emerged as early as 1982, when there was debate over whether the expansion of Stansted or the expansion of Heathrow (advocated by BA) was the way forward for the U.K. aviation industry.[5] Planning studies for the terminal commenced in February 1988 and Richard Rogers was selected to design the terminal in 1989. BAA formally announced its proposal for T5 in May 1992, submitting a formal planning application on February 17, 1993.[6] A public inquiry into the proposals began on May 16, 1995, and lasted nearly four years, finally ending on March 17, 1999, after sitting for 525 days. The inquiry, based at the Renaissance Hotel Heathrow, was the longest planning inquiry ever held in the United Kingdom.[7] Finally, more than eight years after the initial planning application, then-transport minister Stephen Byers announced on November 20, 2001 the British government's decision to grant planning permission for the building of a fifth passenger terminal at Heathrow.

Construction

Construction began in September 2002, with earthworks for the construction of the buildings' foundation. A preparatory archaeological dig at the site found more than 80,000 artifacts.[8] In November of the following year, work started on the steel superstructure of the main terminal building. By January 2005 the nine tunnels needed to provide road and rail access and drainage were completed. In March of the same year, the sixth and final section of the main terminal roof was lifted into position, and in December the building was made weatherproof. This roof could not have been lifted with conventional cranes because it would have penetrated vertically into the

---

5. Michael Donne, "The Battle of Heathrow," *Financial Times*. January 12, 1982, p. 16.

6. Mary Fagan, "BAA Presses on with Heathrow Fifth Terminal," *The Independent* (Newspaper Publishing), May 13, 1992, p. 5; Roger Bray, "Plans Are Ready for Huge Fifth Heathrow Terminal," *Evening Standard* (Associated Newspapers), February 17, 1993, p. 5.

7. "Heathrow Terminal 5 Inquiry". archived from the original on December 24, 2007, retrieved November 2, 2007.

8. Archaeology at Heathrow Terminal 5

airport's radar field. Therefore, the roof was assembled on the ground using smaller cranes, then lifted into place by eight custom-built towers, each fitted with two hydraulic jacks to pull the roof up. At peak there were around 8000 people working on the construction site, while over the life of the project over 60,000 people have been involved.[9] Over 15,000 volunteers were recruited for a total of 68 trials lasting from September 2007 until March 2008 to test the operational readiness of terminal 5 prior to its opening.

Main Terminal Building

The main terminal building is 396 meters (1299 feet) long, 176 meters (577 feet) wide and 40 meters (130 feet) tall. It is the largest building in the terminal 5 complex and is the biggest free-standing building in the United Kingdom. Its four stories are covered by a single-span undulating steel frame roof, with glass façades angled at 6.5° to the vertical. The area covered by the roof is the size of five football pitches, and each section weighs 2200 tons.

T5A contains a check-in hall, a departure lounge with retail stores and other passenger services and a baggage reclaim hall. T5A contains the bulk of the terminal's baggage-handling system. This baggage-handling system is the largest in the world with 8 kilometers (5.0 miles) of high-speed track and 18 kilometers (11 miles) of regular conveyor belts. It is designed to handle 4000 bags per hour and also has an "early bag store" which can temporarily store up to 4000 bags.

Departing passengers enter the departures level on the third floor by lift or escalator from the interchange plaza. Upon entering the departures concourse, passengers see views across Heathrow and the surrounding area and are in a space that is unobstructed to the rising roof above. After check-in and security screening, the airside departure lounge also provides views across the airport, its runways and beyond.

In 2011 terminal 5 handled 26.3 million passengers on 184,616 flights.

Satellite Terminal Buildings

Terminal 5B was the first satellite building to be built. Terminal 5B measures 442 meters (1450 feet) long by 52 meters (171 feet) wide and 19.5 meters (64 feet) high and contains 37 lifts and 29 escalators.

Terminal 5C is the second satellite building, opening unofficially on May 20, 2011, with official opening on June 1, 2011, in conjunction with the relaunch of British Airways service to San Diego. There is also the potential for an additional satellite building, T5D, to be located to the east of T5C, as displayed in Heathrow's Capital Investment Plan for 2009.

---

9. "The Making of Terminal 5". BAA, retrieved November 3, 2008 ; "Press Room / Highlights / T5 Heathrow / T5 Making Off," Grupo Ferrovial, retrieved Novermber 5, 2008.

An underground automated people mover (APM) system is used to transport passengers between terminal 5A, terminal 5B and terminal 5C. The APM system is located air side and is thus only available to passengers and other authorized personnel. The system can accommodate up to 6800 passengers per hour and the trains run at 50 km/h (31 miles per hour) with a journey time of 45 seconds. Passengers descend to the station via the longest open design escalator in Europe.

New Heathrow Control Tower

At the time of its design terminal 5's proposed height was so tall that it would have blocked runway views from Heathrow Airport's then control tower. Therefore, before construction began on the terminal building, a new taller air traffic control tower was constructed. Costing £50 million ($99 million) it was assembled off-site before being maneuvered into position within the central terminal area near Heathrow terminal 3 during 2004. This new control tower weighs nearly 1000 tons and is 87 meters (285 feet) in height, making it one of the tallest in Europe. It became operational in April 2007.

Opening Day

Queen Elizabeth II officially opened terminal 5 in a ceremony on March 14, 2008. Used exclusively by British Airways [and now IAG (Iberia)], the terminal opened for passenger use on March 27, 2008, with flight BA26 from Hong Kong, its first arrival at 04:50 GMT.

On the day of opening it quickly became apparent that the new terminal was not operating smoothly, and British Airways cancelled 34 flights and was later forced to suspend baggage check-in.[10] Over the following 10 days some 42,000 bags failed to travel with their owners, and over 500 flights were cancelled. British Airways was not able to operate its full schedule from terminal 5 until April 8, 2008 and had to postpone the transfer of its long-haul flights from terminal 4 to terminal 5.[11] The difficulties were later blamed on a number of problems with the terminal's IT systems, coupled with car parking.[12]

The software system created the biggest headache. The IT portion of terminal 5 involved 180 IT suppliers, 163 IT systems, and 2100 PCs.[13] The baggage-handling system, which was designed to handle 70,000 bags each day, had technical issues that were still unresolved by opening day. The software said that the planes had taken off, which was not the case, and the bags were then returned to the concourse.

---

10. "Air Travel: Terminal 5 Still Losing 900 Bags Every Day," *The Guardian*, July 10, 2008; "Baggage Halted at New £4.3bn T5," BBC News, retrieved March 27, 2008.

11. "BA Postpones Long-Haul Move to T5,". BBC News, April 11, 2011, retrieved May 17, 2008.

12. "British Airways Reveals What Went Wrong with Terminal 5," *Computer Weekly*, May 14, 2008, retrieved May 17, 2008.

13. Michael Krigsman, "Beyond IT Failure," zdnet, April 7, 2008.

British Airways launched an advertising campaign to assure the public that things were working normally again. Unfortunately, significant damage was done to the reputations of many of the major participants as well as government officials due to the unfavorable publicity.

6.7 SUMMARY OF LESSONS LEARNED

Software projects are known for having the greatest failure rate of projects within any industry. Although there are many reasons, the real problem appears to be the software bugs that become evident during project implementation.

A checklist of techniques for possibly reducing the number of software failures might include:

- ☐ Clearly understand the requirements for the project.
- ☐ Stay focused on the business case.
- ☐ Make absolutely sure you have user involvement.
- ☐ Minimize the number of scope changes.
- ☐ If changes must be made, make the corrections as quickly as possible.
- ☐ Understand the causes of failure and establish metrics for common causes.
- ☐ Understand that not all software projects will be successful.
- ☐ If failure appears imminent, be prepared to pull the plug on the project.

Table 6-1 provides a summary of the lessons learned and alignment to various sections of the *PMBOK® Guide* where additional or supporting information can be found. In some cases, these sections of the *PMBOK® Guide* simply provide supporting information related to the lesson learned. There are numerous sections of the *PMBOK® Guide* that could be aligned for each lesson learned. For simplicity sake, only a few are listed.

TABLE 6-1 *PMBOK® Guide* **Alignment to Lessons Learned**

LESSONS LEARNED	PMBOK® GUIDE SECTIONS
The larger the project, the greater the number of software bugs that will appear during implementation.	4.5, 4.5.1.3, 4.5.2.3
Establish metrics for causes of failure and track them using the PMIS.	1.4.3, 1.6, 3.6, 3.8
Maintain a rigid change control process.	4.1.1.1, 5.2, 5.2.3.1
When success is not possible, be prepared to cancel the project.	1.3, 1.4, 2.2.3, 3.3

7
SAFETY CONSIDERATIONS

7.0 IMPORTANCE OF SAFETY

There are many forms of safety. On IT projects, safety protocols are installed to make sure that proprietary data is not compromised. Food and health care product manufacturers worry about product tampering and safety protection for the consumers. Manufacturers worry about consumers using their products in a safe manner. Companies like Disney have safety as the number one constraint for rides and attractions at the theme parks. Most companies would rather allow projects to intentionally fail or be cancelled before risking lawsuits over violations of safety. This is particularly true if the there is a chance for loss of human life.

In the airline industry, significantly more than a decade and perhaps as much as $15 billion are spent in designing a new commercial aircraft. But even in the design and manufacturing phases, safety issues and problems can still exist but remain hidden. The only real way to verify that safety issues have been addressed is in the commercial use of the plane.

Companies like Boeing and Airbus may end up spending billions of dollars after the planes are put in use to resolve any and all safety issues. This is what consumers expect from them. And Boeing and Airbus comply as seen in the literature with the problems with the batteries on the 787 Dreamliner and the A380.

7.1 BOEING 787 DREAMLINER BATTERY PROBLEMS[1]

In the Boeing 787 Dreamliner's first year of service, at least four aircraft suffered from electrical system problems stemming from its lithium-ion batteries. Teething problems are common within the first year of any new aircraft design's life:

- November 1, 2011: Landing gear failed to deploy
- July 23, 2012: Corrosion risk identified in an engine component
- December 4, 2012: Leakage in fuel line connectors

---

1. Adapted from "Boeing 787 Dreamliner Battery Problems," *Wikipedia, the Free Encyclopedia.*

- December 4, 2012: A power generator failed
- January 7, 2013: Smoke in the cockpit during an inspection
- January 8, 2013: Faulty left wing surge tank vent
- January 9, 2013: Indicator falsely reported brake problems
- January 11, 2013: Engine oil leak
- January 11, 2013: Crack developed on the cockpit wide screen

But after a number of incidents, including an electrical fire aboard an All Nippon Airways 787 and a similar fire found by maintenance workers on a landed Japan Airlines 787 at Boston's Logan International Airport, the U.S. Federal Aviation Administration (FAA) ordered a review into the design and manufacture of the Boeing 787 Dreamliner, following five incidents in five days involving the aircraft, mostly involved with problems with the batteries and electrical systems. This was followed with a full grounding of the entire Boeing 787 fleet, the first such grounding since that of DC-10s following the American Airlines flight 191 disaster in 1979.[2] It is reported that the plane has had two major battery thermal runaway events in 100,000 flight hours, which substantially exceeded the 10 million flight hours predicted by Boeing, and had done so in a dangerous manner.[3]

In December 2012, Boeing CEO James McNerney told media outlets that the problems were no greater than those experienced by the company with the introduction of other new models, such as the Boeing 777.[4] However, on January 7, 2013, a battery overheated and started a fire in an empty 787 operated by Japan Airlines (JAL) at Boston's Logan International Airport.[5] On January 9, United Airlines reported a problem in one of its six 787s with the wiring in the same area as the battery fire on JAL's airliner; subsequently, the U.S. National Transportation Safety Board opened a safety probe.[6]

On January 11, 2013, the FAA announced a comprehensive review of the 787's critical systems, including the design, manufacture and assembly of the aircraft. U.S. Department of Transportation secretary Ray LaHood stated the administration was "looking for the root causes" behind the recent issues. The head of the FAA, Michael Huerta, said that so far nothing

---

2. "Dreamliner: Boeing 787 Planes Grounded on Safety Fears," BBC News, retrieved January 17, 2013.

3. "Accident: ANA B787 Near Takamatsu on Jan 16th 2013, Battery Problem and Burning Smell on Board," *Aviation Herald*, retrieved February 8, 2013.

4. "Boeing: Problems with 787 Dreamliner 'Normal,'" *Frequent Business Traveler*, December 16, 2012, retrieved December 16, 2012.

5. "Fire Aboard Empty 787 Dreamliner Prompts Investigation," CNN, January 8, 2013 ; "Second Faulty Boeing Dreamliner in Boston," BBC, retrieved January 8, 2013.

6. "U.S. Opens Dreamliner Safety Probe," *The Wall Street Journal*, retrieved January 9, 2013.

found "suggests [the 787] is not safe."[7] Japan's transport ministry also launched an investigation in response.[8]

On January 16, 2013, an All Nippon Airways (ANA) 787 made an emergency landing at Takamatsu Airport on Shikoku Island after the flight crew received a computer warning that there was smoke inside one of the electrical compartments.[9] ANA said that there was an error message in the cockpit citing a battery malfunction. Passengers and crew were evacuated using the emergency slides.[10] According to *The Register*, there are no fire suppression systems in the electrical compartments holding batteries, only smoke detectors.[11]

U.S.-based aviation regulators' oversight into the 2007 safety approval and FAA certification of the 787 has now come under scrutiny, as a key U.S. Senate committee prepares for a hearing into the procedures of aviation safety certification "in coming weeks." However, an FAA spokesperson defended their 2007 safety certification of the 787 by saying, "the whole aviation system is designed so that if the worst case happens, there are systems in place to prevent that from interfering with other systems on the plane."[12]

On February 12, 2013, the *Wall Street Journal* reported that "Aviation safety investigators are examining whether the formation of microscopic structures known as dendrites inside the Boeing Co. 787's lithium-ion batteries played a role in twin incidents that prompted the fleet to be grounded nearly a month ago."[13]

On January 16, 2013, both major Japanese airlines ANA and JAL announced that they were voluntarily grounding or suspending flights for their fleets of 787s after multiple incidents involving different 787s, including emergency landings. These two carriers operate 24 of the 50 Dreamliners delivered to date.[14] The grounding could cost ANA over $1.1 million a day.[15]

---

7. "Boeing 787 Dreamliner to be Investigated by US Authorities," *The Guardian*, retrieved January 11, 2013.

8. Anna Mukai, "Japan to Investigate Boeing 787 Fuel Leak as FAA Reviews," Bloomberg, January 15, 2013, retrieved January 20, 2013.

9. "Top Japan Airlines Ground Boeing 787s after Emergency," BBC, retrieved January 16, 2013.

10. "A Boeing 787 Plane Makes an Emergency Landing in Japan," BBC, retrieved January 16, 2013.

11. Iain Thomson, "Boeing 787 Fleet Grounded Indefinitely as Investigators Stumped," *The Register*, January 25, 2013, retrieved February 8, 2013.

12. "Boeing 787's Battery Woes Put US Approval under Scrutiny," *Business Standard*, retrieved February 22, 2013.

13. Friday, Feb 22, 2013 (2013-01-23). "Boeing 787's Battery Woes Put US Approval under Scrutiny,". *Business Standard*, January 23, 2013, retrieved February 22, 2013.

14. "Japanese Airlines Ground Boeing 787s after Emergency Landing," Reuters, retrieved January 16, 2013 ; "787 Emergency Landing: Japan Grounds Entire Boeing Dreamliner Fleet," *The Guardian*, retrieved January 16, 2013.

15. "Boeing Dreamliners Grounded Worldwide on Battery Checks," Reuters, January 17, 2013, retrieved January 21, 2013.

On January 16, 2013, the FAA issued an emergency airworthiness directive ordering all U.S.-based airlines to ground their Boeing 787s until yet-to-be-determined modifications were made to the electrical system to reduce the risk of the battery overheating or catching fire.[16] This is the first time that the FAA had grounded an airliner type since 1979. The FAA also announced plans to conduct an extensive review of the 787's critical systems. The focus of the review would be on the safety of the lithium-ion batteries made of lithium cobalt oxide ($LiCoO2$). The 787 battery contract was signed in 2005[17] when $LiCoO2$ batteries were the only type of lithium aerospace battery available, but since then newer and safer[18] types (such as LiFePO), which provide less reaction energy during thermal runaway, have become available.[19] The FAA approved a 787 battery in 2007 with nine "special conditions."[20] A battery approved by the FAA (through Mobile Power Solutions) was made by Rose Electronics using Kokam cells,[21] but the batteries installed in the 787 were made by Yuasa.[22]

On January 20, the National Transportation Safety Board (NTSB) declared that overvoltage was not the cause of the Boston incident, as voltage did not exceed the battery limit of 32 V,[23] and the charging unit passed tests. The battery had signs of short circuiting and thermal runaway.[24] Despite this, on January 24 the NTSB announced that it had not yet pinpointed the cause of the Boston fire; the FAA did not allow U.S.-based Dreamliners to fly again until the problem is found and corrected. In a press briefing that day, NTSB Chairwoman Deborah Hersman said that the NTSB had found evidence of

---

16. FAA Press Release, Federal Aviation Administration, January 16, 2013, retrieved January 17, 2013.

17. "Thales Selects GS Yuasa for Lithium Ion Battery System in Boeing's 787 Dreamliner," GS Yuasa, retrieved January 18, 2013.

18. Brier Dudley, "Lithium-Ion Batteries Pack a Lot Of Energy—and Challenges," *The Seattle Times*, January 17, 2013, retrieved January 24, 2013. "iron phosphate "has been known to sort of be safer."

19. Per Erlien Dalløkken, "Her er Dreamliner-problemet" (in Norwegian), Teknisk Ukeblad, retrieved January 17, 2013; "Energy Storage Technologies—Lithium," Securaplane, retrieved January 24, 2013.

20. "Special Conditions: Boeing Model 787– 8 Airplane; Lithium Ion Battery Installation," FAA / Federal Register, October 11, 2007, retrieved January 30, 2013. "NM375 Special Conditions No. 25–359–SC";;
Alwyn Scott and Mari Saito. "FAA Approval of Boeing 787 Battery under Scrutiny," NBC News / Reuters, retrieved January 24, 2013.

21. Supko / Iverson (2011), "Li Battery UN Test Report Applicability," NextGov, retrieved January 23, 2013.

22. Bob Brewin, "A 2006 Battery Fire Destroyed Boeing 787 Supplier's Facility," NextGov, January 22, 2013, retrieved January 23, 2013.

23. Kelly Nantel, "NTSB Provides Third Investigative Update on Boeing 787 Battery Fire in Boston," NTSB. January 20, 2013, retrieved January 21, 2013.

24. NTSB Press Release, retrieved January 26, 2013.

failure of multiple safety systems designed to prevent these battery problems and stated that fire must never happen on an airplane.[25] The Japan Transport Safety Board (JTSB) had said on January 23 that the battery in ANA jets in Japan reached a maximum voltage of 31 V (lower than the 32-V limit in the Boston JAL 787), but had a sudden unexplained voltage drop to near zero.[26] All cells had signs of thermal damage before thermal runaway.[27] ANA and JAL had replaced several 787 batteries before the mishaps. As of January 29, 2013, JTSB approved the Yuasa factory quality control while the American NTSB continued to look for defects in the Boston battery.[28]

Industry experts disagree on consequences of the grounding: Airbus is confident that Boeing will resolve the issue[29] and that no airlines will switch plane type,[30] while other experts see the problem as "costly"[31] and "could take upwards of a year."[32]

The only U.S.-based airline that operates the Dreamliner is United Airlines, which has six.[33] Chile's Directorate General of Civil Aviation (DGAC) grounded LAN Airlines' three 787s.[34] The Indian Directorate General of Civil Aviation (DGCA) directed Air India to ground its six Dreamliners. The Japanese Transport Ministry made the ANA and JAL groundings official and indefinite following the FAA announcement.[35] The European Aviation Safety Agency has also followed the FAA's advice

25. Matthew Weld and Jad Mouwad, "Protracted Fire Inquiry Keeping 787 on Ground," *New York Times*, January 25, 2013, retrieved January 26, 2013.

26. Sofia Mitra-Thakur, "Japan Says 787 Battery Was Not Overcharged," *Engineering & Technology*, retrieved January 23, 2013.; Christopher Drew, Hiroko Tabuchi, and Jad Mouawad,, "Boeing 787 Battery Was a Concern Before Failure," *The New York Times*, January 29, 2013, retrieved January 30, 2013.

27. Simon Hradecky, "ANA B788 Near Takamatsu On Jan 16th 2013, Battery Problem and Burning Smell On Board," *Aviation Herald*, February 5, 2013, retrieved February 6, 2013.

28. Hiroko Tabuchi, "No Quality Problems Found at Battery Maker for 787," *The New York Times*, January 28, 2013, retrieved January 30, 2013.; Chris Cooper and Kiyotaka Matsuda, "GS Yuasa Shares Surge as Japan Ends Company Inspections," *BusinessWeek*, January 28, 2013, retrieved January 29, 2013.; Peter Knudson, "NTSB Issues Sixth Update On JAL Boeing 787 Battery Fire Investigation," NTSB, retrieved January 29, 2013.

29. "Airbus CEO 'Confident' Boeing Will Find Fix for 787," Bloomberg, January 17, 2013.

30. Robert Wall and Andrea Rothman, "Airbus Says A350 Design Is 'Lower Risk' Than Troubled 787," Bloomberg, retrieved January 17, 2013. ""I don't believe that anyone's going to switch from one airplane type to another because there's a maintenance issue," Leahy said. "Boeing will get this sorted out.""

31. "'Big Cost' Seen for Boeing Dreamliner Grounding," Bloomberg, January 17, 2013.

32. Martha C. White, "Is the Dreamliner Becoming a Financial Nightmare for Boeing?" *Time*, January 17, 2013.

33. "FAA Grounding All Boeing 787s," KIRO TV. retrieved January 16, 2013.

34. "LAN suspende de forma temporal la operación de flota Boeing 787 Dreamliner," *La Tercera*, retrieved January 16, 2013.

35. "DGCA Directs Air India to Ground All Six Boeing Dreamliners on Safety Concerns," *The Economic Times*, retrieved January 17, 2013.

and grounded the only two European 787s operated by LOT Polish Airlines.[36] Qatar Airways has announced that they are grounding their five Dreamliners.[37] Ethiopian Air was the final operator to announce temporary groundings of its four Dreamliners.[38]

As of January 17, 2013, all 50 of the aircraft delivered to date had been grounded.[39] On January 18, Boeing announced that it was halting 787 deliveries until the battery problem is resolved.[40] On February 4, 2013, the FAA said it would permit Boeing to conduct test flights of 787 aircraft to gather additional data.[41]

On April 19, 2013, the FAA approved Boeing's new design for the Boeing 787 battery. This would allow the eight airlines that maintained a fleet of 50 787 planes to begin making repairs. The repairs would include a containment and venting system for the batteries.[42] The new design would add more protection and would also increase the weight of the plane by more than 150 pounds. This was considered a necessity to ensure safety. The cost of the repairs would be $465,000 per plane. Boeing committed more than 300 people on ten teams to make the repairs, which would take about five days per plane.[43]

ANA, which operated 17 Dreamliner jets, estimated that it was losing $868,300 per plane over a two-week period and would be talking with Boeing about compensation for losses. Other airlines were also expected to seek some compensation.

7.2 AIRBUS A380 PROBLEMS[44]

The Airbus A380 is a double-deck, wide-body, four-engine jet airliner manufactured by the European corporation Airbus. It is the world's largest passenger airliner. Many airports have had to upgrade their facilities to

36. "European Safety Agency to Ground 787 in Line with FAA," Reuters, January 16, 2013, retrieved January 17, 2013.

37. "Qatar Airways Grounds Boeing Dreamliner Fleet," Reuters, retrieved January 17, 2013.

38. "U.S., Others Ground Boeing Dreamliner Indefinitely," Reuters, January 16, 2013, retrieved January 17, 2013.

39. "U.S., Others Ground Boeing Dreamliner Indefinitely," Reuters, January 16, 2013, retrieved January 17, 2013; "Boeing's 787 Dreamliner," Reuters, retrieved January 16, 2013; "Boeing 787 Dreamliner: The Impact of Safety Concerns," BBC News, retrieved January 17, 2013.

40. "BBC News—Dreamliner Crisis: Boeing Halts 787 Jet Deliveries," Bbc.co.uk, January 1, 1970, retrieved January 20, 2013.

41. "FAA Approves Test Flights for Boeing 787," Seattle PI, retrieved February 7, 2013.

42. " FAA Approves Fix for Boeing 787 Battery," Los Angeles Times, April 20, 2013.

43. "ANA's Dreamliner Test Flight Seen as Step in Regaining Customers," Bloomberg News, April 27, 2013.

44. Adapted from "Airbus A380," Wikipedia, the Free Encyclopedia.

properly accommodate it because of its size. Initially named Airbus A3XX, the aircraft was designed to challenge Boeing's monopoly in the large-aircraft market. The A380 made its first flight on April 27, 2005 and began commercial service in October 2007 with Singapore Airlines.

The A380 provides seating for 525 people in a typical three-class configuration or up to 853 people in all-economy class configurations. The A380-800 has a design range of 9800 miles, sufficient to fly from New York to Hong Kong, and a cruising speed of Mach 0.85, about 560 mph at cruising altitude.

Configurations

The initial purchasers of the A380 typically configured their aircrafts for three-class service, while adding extra features for passengers in premium cabins. Launch customer Singapore Airlines debuted partly enclosed first-class suites on its A380s in 2007, each featuring a leather seat with a separate bed[45]; center suites could be joined to create a double bed. A year later, Qantas debuted a new first-class seat-bed and a sofa lounge at the front of the upper deck on its A380s.[46] In late 2008, Emirates introduced "shower spas" in first class on its A380s, along with a bar lounge and seating area on the upper deck, and in 2009 Air France unveiled an upper deck electronic art gallery. In addition to lounge areas, some A380 operators have installed amenities consistent with other aircraft in their respective fleets, including self-serve snack bars, premium economy sections, and redesigned business class seating.

Brief History

In January 1993, Boeing and several companies in the Airbus consortium started a joint feasibility study of an aircraft known as the Very Large Commercial Transport (VLCT), aiming to form a partnership to share the limited market. This joint study was abandoned two years later, Boeing's interest having declined because analysts thought that such a product was unlikely to cover the projected $15 billion development cost. Despite the fact that only two airlines had expressed public interest in purchasing such a plane, Airbus was already pursuing its own large-plane project. Analysts suggested that Boeing instead would pursue stretching its 747 design and that air travel was already moving away from the hub-and-spoke system

---

45. "Seat Map Singapore Airlines Airbus A380," Seat Guru, archived from the original on February 25, 2009, retrieved February 19, 2009; "Singapore Airlines A380," Singapore Airlines, archived from the original on October 17, 2007, retrieved October 28, 2007; "Singapore Airlines Suites," Singapore Airlines, retrieved September 29, 2012.

46. "Qantas and the A380," Qantas, archived from the original on December 14, 2007, retrieved December 15, 2007; "SeatGuru Seat Map Qantas Airways Airbus A380-800 (388):".

that consolidated traffic into large planes and toward more nonstop routes that could be served by smaller planes.[47]

A380 Production and Delivery Delays

Initial production of the A380 was troubled by delays attributed to the 330 miles of wiring in each aircraft. Airbus cited as underlying causes the complexity of the cabin wiring (98,000 wires and 40,000 connectors), its concurrent design and production, the high degree of customization for each airline and failures of configuration management and change control.[48] The German and Spanish Airbus facilities continued to use the computer-aided design system CATIA version 4, while British and French sites migrated to version 5.[49] This caused overall configuration management problems, at least in part because wiring harnesses manufactured using aluminum rather than copper conductors necessitated special design rules including nonstandard dimensions and bend radii; these were not easily transferred between versions of the software.[50]

Airbus announced the first delay in June 2005 and notified airlines that deliveries would be delayed by six months.[51] This reduced the total number of planned deliveries by the end of 2009 from about 120 to 90–100. On June 13, 2006, Airbus announced a second delay, with the delivery schedule slipping an additional six to seven months.[52] Although the first delivery was still planned before the end of 2006, deliveries in 2007 would drop to only 9 aircraft, and deliveries by the end of 2009 would be cut to 70–80 aircraft. The announcement caused a 26% drop in the share price of Airbus' parent, EADS,[53] and led to the departure of EADS CEO, Noël Forgeard.

On May 13, 2008, Airbus announced reduced deliveries for the years 2008 (12) and 2009 (21).[54] After further manufacturing setbacks, Airbus

47. "Boeing, Partners Expected to Scrap Super-Jet Study," *Los Angeles Times*, July 10, 1995, retrieved December 30, 2011.

48. Mario Heinen, "The A380 Programme" (PDF), EADS, October 19, 2006, archived from the original on November 3, 2006, retrieved December 30, 2011; Max Kingsley-Jones, "The Race to Rewire the Airbus A380," Flight International, July 18, 2006, retrieved December 30, 2011.

49. Nicola Clark, "The Airbus Saga: Crossed Wires and a Multibillion-Euro Delay," *International Herald Tribune*, November 6, 2006, retrieved December 30, 2011.

50. Kenneth Wong, "What Grounded the Airbus A380?" *Catalyst Manufacturing*, December 6, 2006, retrieved December 30, 2011.

51. Nicola Clark, "The Airbus Saga: Crossed Wires and a Multibillion-Euro Delay," *International Herald Tribune*, November 6, 2006, retrieved December 30, 2011.

52. Mary Crane, "Major Turbulence for EADS on A380 Delay," *Forbes*, June 6, 2006, archived from the original on August 12, 2010, retrieved December 30, 2011.

53. Nicola Clark, "Airbus Delay on Giant Jet Sends Shares Plummeting," *International Herald Tribune*, June 5, 2006, retrieved December 30, 2011.

54. "A380 Production Ramp-Up Revisited," *Airbus*, May 13, 2008, archived from the original on May 17, 2008, retrieved December 30, 2011.

announced its plan to deliver 14 A380s in 2009, down from the previously revised target of 18.[55] A total of 10 A380s were delivered in 2009. In 2010 Airbus delivered only 18 of the expected 20 A380s, due to Rolls-Royce engine availability problems. Airbus planned to deliver "between 20 and 25" A380s in 2011 before ramping up to three a month in 2012.[56] In the event, Airbus delivered 26 units, thus outdoing its predicted output for the first time. As of July 2012[update], production was 3 aircraft per month. Among the production problems were challenging interiors, interiors being installed sequentially rather than concurrently as in smaller planes and union/government objections to streamlining.[57] As of March 2013[update], there had been 262 firm orders for the A380, of which 101 had been delivered. The largest order, for 90 aircraft, was from Emirates. The 100th A380 was delivered to Malaysia Airlines.

Problems Develop

In the summer of 2008, after a roughly two-year delay, the Arab airline took delivery on the first of 58 A380s it had ordered. In mid-February 2009, senior executives from Airbus and the airline Emirates, the biggest customer for Airbus's A380, attended a crisis meeting in Toulouse to discuss the super-jumbo. The 46-slide presentation identified serious issues. Snapshots were shown of singed power cables, partially torn-off paneling and defective parts of thrust nozzles. On one of the slides, the experts provide a detailed list of the prestigious plane's various breakdowns. They stated that the A380 had already been grounded nine times, which represented a loss of close to 500 operating hours. In 23 cases, said the Emirates managers, replacement aircraft had to be obtained at short notice. Minor glitches, the critique continues, happen in Emirates' A380 fleet about once every two days.[58]

Incidents and Accidents

On November 4, 2010, Qantas Flight 32, en route from Singapore Changi Airport to Sydney Airport, suffered an uncontained engine failure, resulting in a series of related problems and forcing the flight to return to Singapore. There were no injuries to the passengers, crew or people on the ground

55. "Airbus Expects Sharp Order Drop in 2009," *Aviation Week and Space Technology*, January 15, 2009, retrieved December 30, 2011.

56. Andrea Rothman, "Airbus Beats Boeing on 2010 Orders, Deliveries as Demand Recovery Kicks In," Bloomberg, January 17, 2011, retrieved December 30, 2011.

57. Daniel Michaels, "Airbus Wants A380 Cost Cuts," *Wall Street Journal*, July 13, 2012, retrieved July 15, 2012.

58. Adapted from Dinah Deckstein, "Stormy Skies: Emirates Slams Airbus over A380 Defects," *Der Spiegel*, August 12, 2009.

despite debris falling onto the Indonesian island of Batam.[59] The A380 was damaged sufficiently for the event to be classified as an accident.[60] Qantas subsequently grounded all of its A380s that day subject to an internal investigation taken in conjunction with the engine manufacturer Rolls-Royce plc. Engine Alliance GP7000 powered A380s were unaffected but other operators of Rolls-Royce Trent 900 powered A380s were also affected. Investigators later determined the cause of the explosion to be an oil leak in the Trent 900 engine.[61] Repairs cost an estimated $145 million.[62] As other Rolls-Royce Trent 900 engines also showed problems with the same oil-leak, Rolls-Royce ordered many engines to be changed, including about half of the engines in the Qantas A380 fleet.[63]

During repairs following the Qantas Flight 32 engine failure incident, cracks were discovered in fittings within the wings. As a result of the discovery, EASA issued an Airworthiness Directive in January 2012 affecting 20 A380 aircraft that had accumulated over 1300 flights.[64] A380s with under 1800 flight hours were to be inspected within 6 weeks or 84 flights; aircraft with over 1800 flight hours were to be examined within four days or 14 flights.[65] Fittings found to be cracked were being replaced following the inspections to maintain structural integrity.[66] On February 8, 2012, the checks were extended to cover all 68 A380 aircraft in operation. The problem was considered to be minor and was not expected to affect operations.[67] EADS acknowledged that the cost of repairs would be over $130 million, to be borne by Airbus. The company said the problem was traced

---

59. "Indonesians Collect Debris from Qantas Plane Engine," Australian Broadcasting Corporation, November 6, 2010, retrieved April 3, 2011.

60. "Inflight Engine Failure—Qantas, Airbus A380, VH-OQA, Overhead Batam Island, Indonesia, 4 November 2010," Australian Transport Safety Bureau, May 18, 2011.

61. Peter Walker, "Qantas A380 Landing: Airlines Were Warned in August over Engine Safety," Airportwatch.org.uk, November 5, 2010, retrieved April 3, 2011.

62. Jordan Chong, "Qantas A380 Back in the Air, 'as Good As New'," *Herald-Sun*, April 20, 2012, retrieved April 21, 2012.

63. "Qantas Replaces RR Engines," *The Guardian*, November 18, 2010, retrieved June 25, 2012.

64. "EASA Mandates Prompt Detailed Visual Inspections of the Wings of 20 A380s," EASA, retrieved January 20, 2012.

65. Simon Hradecky, "Airworthiness Directive Regarding Airbus A380 Wing Cracks," *The Aviation Herald*, January 21, 2012; "EASA AD No.:2012-0013," EASA, January 20, 2012, retrieved January 22, 2012; Rob Waugh, "World's Biggest Super-Jumbos Must Be GROUNDED, Say Engineers after Cracks Are Found in the Wings of Three Airbus A380s," London: *The Daily Mail* (UK), January 9, 2012.

66. "Airbus Adjusts A380 Assembly Process," *Aviation Week*, January 26, 2012, retrieved 29 January 2012.

67. "Airbus to Inspect All A380 Superjumbos for Wing Cracks," BBC News Online, retrieved February 8, 2012.

to stress and material used for the fittings.[68] Additionally, major airlines were seeking compensation from Airbus for revenue lost as a result of the cracks and subsequent grounding of fleets.[69] Airbus has switched to a different type of aluminum alloy so aircraft delivered from 2014 onward will not have this issue.[70]

Importance of Confidence

Both Airbus and Boeing understand the importance of customer confidence. If the aircraft customers lose confidence in the aircraft manufacturer's ability to deliver a safe aircraft, significant business will be lost. Aircrafts can have more than 100,000 components. In the cabin area alone on the A380 are more than 23,000 parts. Given the fact that it takes at least 10 years and billions of dollars to design and test these planes, it is impossible to prevent some of these teething problems to have been simulated. Dry runs cannot simulate every possible scenario that could happen. The reliability of every part and every system can be proven only when the aircraft is in operation. As an example, Emirates installed two showers in its first-class cabin. A female passenger was unable to operate the showerhead and tore out the entire fixture, resulting in some flooding of the first-class section.

The A380 has undergone more testing than any other jet. Yet despite the testing, it may be some time until all of the problems are resolved. Because lives may be at stake, Airbus will be spending billions to correct all of the potential problems.

7.3 SUMMARY OF LESSONS LEARNED

Safety may very well be the most important constraint, especially if human lives are at stake. Unfortunately we often perform tradeoffs and accept scope changes without fully realizing the impact on safety.

A checklist of techniques for possibly reducing the number of software failures might include:

- ☐ Clearly understand the safety requirements for the project.
- ☐ Make sure the business case identifies safety requirement.
- ☐ Establish safety metrics if possible.

---

68. "A380 Repairs to Cost Airbus 105 Million Pounds," *Air Transport World*, March 14, 2012, retrieved May 5, 2012.

69. http://www.defenceweb.co.za/index.php?option=com_content&view=article&id=28338: air-france-seeks-airbus-compensation-for-a380-glitches-report&catid=113:international-news&Itemid=248.

70. http://www.bbc.co.uk/news/business-18397398.

TABLE 7-1 *PMBOK® Guide* Alignment to Lessons Learned

LESSONS LEARNED	*PMBOK® GUIDE* SECTIONS
Safety metrics can be established on projects.	1.3, 1.4, 5.3.3.1, 12.1.2.1
Make sure that the project's requirements clearly define the required safety levels.	5.2, 5.2.3.1, 5.3.3.1
Discussions involving the approval of scope changes must consider the impact on safety.	1.6, 2.2.3, 5.3.3.2, 5.5
Governance committees must consider the impact on safety, especially when political decisions are made.	2.2, 2.2.1, 2.2.2, 4.1.1.2
Safety and risk management are inseparable.	11.1.1.4, 11.1.1.4
All assumptions that impact safety must be clearly identified.	11.2.2.4, 11.3.3.1, 11.5.3.2

☐ Periodically review safety protocols to make sure safety has not been compromised.

☐ Maintain clear and up-to-date documentation for all changes and the impact on safety.

Table 7-1 provides a summary of the lessons learned and alignment to various sections of the *PMBOK® Guide* where additional or supporting information can be found. In some cases, these sections of the *PMBOK® Guide* simply provide supporting information related to the lesson learned. There are numerous sections of the *PMBOK® Guide* that could be aligned for each lesson learned. For simplicity sake, only a few are listed.

8

SCOPE CREEP

8.0 UNDERSTANDING SCOPE CREEP

There are three things that most project managers know will happen with almost certainty: death, taxes and scope creep. Scope creep is the continuous enhancement of the project's requirements as the project's deliverables are being developed. Scope creep is viewed as the growth in the project's scope. The larger and more complex the project, the greater the chances of significant scope creep.

Although scope creep can occur in any project in any industry, it is most frequently associated with information systems development projects. Scope changes can occur during any project life-cycle phase. Scope changes occur because it is the nature of humans not to be able to completely describe the project or the plan to execute the project at the start. This is particularly true on large, complex projects. As a result, we gain more knowledge as the project progresses, and this leads to creeping scope and scope changes.

Scope creep is a natural occurrence for project managers. We must accept the fact that this will happen. Some people believe that there are magical charms, potions and rituals that can prevent scope creep. This is certainly not true. Perhaps the best we can do is to establish processes, such as configuration management systems or change control boards, to get some control over scope creep. However, these processes are designed not so much to prevent scope creep but to prevent unwanted scope changes from taking place.

Therefore, we can argue that scope creep isn't just allowing the scope to change, but an indication of how well we manage changes to the scope, whether to add value or reduce value. If all of the parties agree that a scope change is needed, then perhaps we can argue that the scope simply changed rather than creeped. Some people view scope creep as scope changes not approved by the sponsor or the change control board.

Scope creep is often viewed as being detrimental to the success of a project because it increases the cost and elongates the schedule. While this is true, scope creep can also produce favorable results such as add-ons that give your product a competitive advantage. Scope creep can also please the customer if the scope changes are seen as additional value for the final deliverable.

8.1 CREEPING FAILURE

Some projects fail because the growth in the requirements drives up the cost and elongates the schedule to a point where executives look for other alternatives. There are two types of creep:

- Scope creep
- Feature creep

Scope creep occurs when the client is unsure about his or her actual needs or the project team works on a project without fully understanding what the customer really wants. Feature creep, also known as "featuritis," occurs when bells and whistles are added into the project to embellish the deliverables even though the additional features may be unnecessary.

Most people seem to underestimate the seriousness of scope and feature creep. Creep is like looking at the tip of the iceberg; it is what's beneath the surface that is the real danger. Adding in scope and adding in features tie people up in meetings, many of which result in action items for future meetings because decisions cannot be made quickly. Projects end up getting delayed and the costs increase significantly due to development of new time, cost and scope baselines. And what may make matters worse is that many of the changes can be accompanied by additional risks that were not planned for.

Sometimes people have hidden agendas for wanting the scope to intentionally increase.

This happens when the increase will benefit them personally. As an example:

Situation: A senior manager in IT was fearful that the design and implementation of a new software program could make his position unnecessary. When the project was added to the portfolio of projects, he volunteered to serve as the project sponsor. He was the only member of the portfolio selection committee that had IT literacy and IT experience. He was a few years away from retirement and wanted to guarantee that his position and salary would not change. To do so, he had to find a way to sabotage the project.

Acting as the project sponsor, he encouraged the team to bring forth scope changes and bells and whistles. Many of the people on the team viewed the project as a means by which they could exhibit their true creativity. The sponsor tried to minimize user involvement stating that he could handle everything himself. All changes were made initially in small increments until all of the slack in the schedule was consumed and all of the management reserve had been expended.

Finally there came a point where the information had to be reported to the portfolio selection committee. By this time, the schedule began to slip and the costs increased to the point where the projected cost at the completion of the project would be almost twice the original cost. This meant that other more important projects may have to be delayed due to a lack of funding. The schedule slippage was more critical than the cost overrun because there were other projects in the queue that were waiting for these resources to be released for assignment on their projects. This would delay the start date for several projects. The portfolio selection committee then decided to delay continuation of this project in lieu of other more important projects in the queue. The project was finally completed right before the sponsor retired from the company.

> **LESSONS LEARNED** There are always reasons behind scope creep. Many times, the scope changes requested may be for personal reasons.

8.2 DEFINING SCOPE

Perhaps the most critical step in the initiation phase of a project is the defining of the scope. The first attempt at scope definition may occur as early as the proposal or competitive bidding stage. At this point, sufficient time and effort may not be devoted to an accurate determination or understanding of the scope and customer requirements. And to make matters worse, all of this may be done well before the project manager is brought on board.

Once the project manager is brought on board, he or she she must either familiarize themselves with and validate the scope requirements if they have already been prepared or interview the various stakeholders and gather the necessary information for a clear understanding of the scope. In doing so, we prepare a list of what is included and excluded from our understanding of the requirements. Yet no matter how meticulous the project manager attempts to do this, clarity in the scope is never known with 100% certainty. This was clearly evident in the Denver International Airport case study where an entire airport was built before having leases signed by the two primary tenants, thereby not knowing what requirements they had. Another mistake was agreeing to an all-airport automated baggage-handling system without understanding the complexity of the scope.

The project manager's goal is to establish the boundaries of the scope. To do this, the project manager's vision of the project and each stakeholder's vision of the project must be aligned. There must also be an alignment with corporate business objectives because there must be a valid business reason for undertaking this project. If the alignments do not occur, then the boundary for the project will become dynamic or constantly changing rather than stationary.

Figure 8-1 shows the boundaries of the project. The project's boundary is designed to satisfy both business objectives established by your company as well as technical/scope objectives established by your customer, assuming it is an external client. The project manager and the various

Figure 8-1 Project boundary.

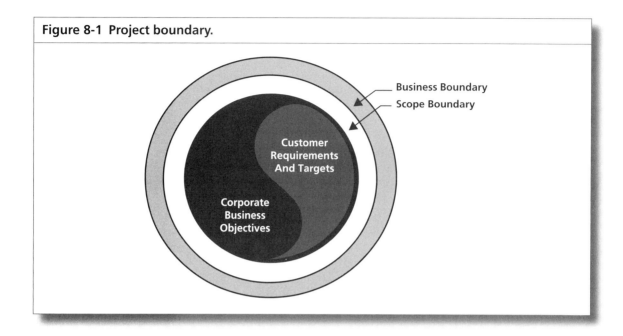

stakeholders, including the customer, can have a different interpretation of the scope boundary and the business boundary. Also, the project manager may focus heavily on the technology that the customer needs rather than the business value that the project manager's company desires. Simply stated, the project manager may seek to exceed the specifications whereas the stakeholders and your company want to meet the minimum specification levels in the shortest amount of time. The Sydney, Australia, Opera House, discussed later in this chapter, is a perfect example of this.

When scope creep occurs and scope changes are necessary, the scope boundary can move. However, the scope boundary may not be able to move if it alters the business boundary and corporate expectations. As an example, a scope change to add value to a product might not be approved if it extends the launch date of the product or overprices the product in the marketplace.

It is important to understand that the project scope is not what the customer asked for but what we agree to deliver. What we agree to can have inclusions and exclusions from what the customer asked for.

There are certain facts that we now know:

- The scope boundary is what the project manager commits to delivering.
- The boundary is usually never clearly defined at the start of the project.
- Sometimes the boundary may not be clearly defined until we are well into the project.

- We may need to use progressive or rolling wave planning to clearly articulate the scope.
- Sometimes the scope isn't fully known until the deliverables are completed and tested.
- Finally, even after stakeholders' acceptance of the deliverables, the interpretation of the scope boundary can still be up for debate.

The scope boundary can drift during the implementation of the project because, as we get further into the project and more knowledge is gained, we identify unplanned additions to the scope. This scope creep phenomenon is then accompanied by cost increases and schedule elongations. But is scope creep really evil? Perhaps not; it is something we must live with as a project manager. Some projects may be fortunate to avoid scope creep. In general, the larger the project, the greater the likelihood that scope creep will occur. The question, of course, is whether or not it adds value to the project.

The length of the project also impacts scope creep. If the business environment is highly dynamic and continuously changing, products and services must be developed to satisfy existing or future market needs. The case study discussed later in this chapter on terminal 5 at London Heathrow Airport is an example of this. Therefore, on long-term projects, scope creep may be seen as a necessity for keeping up with customer demands, and project add-ons may be required to obtain customer acceptance.

8.3 SCOPE CREEP DEPENDENCIES

Oftentimes, scope changes are approved without evaluating the downstream impact that the scope change can have on work packages that have not started yet. As an example, making a scope change early on in the project to change the design of a component may result in a significant cost overrun if long lead raw materials that were ordered and paid for are no longer needed. Also, there could be other contractors that have begun working on their projects assuming that the original design was finalized. Now, a small scope change by one contractor could have a serious impact on other downstream contractors. Dependencies must be considered when approving a scope change because the cost of reversing a previous decision can have a severe financial impact on the project

8.4 CAUSES OF SCOPE CREEP

In order to prevent scope creep from occurring, one must begin by understanding the causes of scope creep. The causes are numerous and it is wishful thinking to believe that all of these causes can be prevented. Many of the causes are well beyond the control of the project manager. Some causes are related to business scope creep, and others are part of technical scope creep.

Poor understanding of requirements: This occurs when we accept or rush into a project without fully understanding what must be done.

Poorly defined requirements: Sometimes the requirements are so poorly defined that we must make numerous assumptions, and as we get into the later stages of the project, we discover that some of the assumptions are no longer valid.

Complexity: The more complex the project, the greater the impact of scope creep. Being too ambitious and believing that we can deliver more than we can offer on a complex project can be disastrous.

Failing to "drill down": When a project is initiated using only high-level requirements, scope creep can be expected when we get involved in the detailed activities in the work breakdown structure.

Poor communication: Poor communication between the project manager and the stakeholders can lead to ill-defined requirements and misinterpretation of the scope.

Misunderstanding expectations: Regardless of how the scope is defined, stakeholders and customers have expectations of the outcome of the project. Failure to understand these expectations up front can lead to costly downstream changes.

Featuritis: This is also called gold plating a project and occurs when the project team adds in their own often unnecessary features and functionality in the form of "bells and whistles."

Perfectionism: This occurs when the project team initiates scope changes in order to exceed the specifications and requirements rather than just meeting them. Project teams may see this as a chance for glory.

Career advancement: Scope creep may require additional resources, thus perhaps making the project manager more powerful in the eyes of senior management. Scope creep also elongates projects and provides team members with a much longer temporary home if they are unsure about their next assignment.

Time-to-market pressure: Many projects start out with an optimistic point of view. If the business exerts pressure on the project manager to commit to an unrealistic product launch date, then the project manager may need to reduce functionality. This could be less costly or even more costly based upon where the descoping takes place.

Government regulations: Compliance with legislation and regulatory changes can cause costly scope creep.

Deception: Sometimes we know well in advance that the customer's statement of work has "holes" in it. Rather than inform the customer about the additional work that will be required, we underbid the job based upon the original scope and, after contract award, we push through profitable scope changes.

Penalty clauses: Some contracts have penalty clauses for late delivery. By pushing through (perhaps unnecessary) scope changes that will elongate the schedule, the project manager may be able to avoid penalty clauses.

Placating the customer: Some customers will request "nice to have but not necessary" scope changes after the contract begins. While it may appear nice to placate the customer, always saying "yes" does not guarantee follow-on work.

Poor change control: The purpose of a change control process is to prevent unnecessary changes. If the change control process is merely a rubber stamp that approves all of the project manager's requests, then continuous scope creep will occur.

8.5 NEED FOR BUSINESS KNOWLEDGE

Scope changes must be properly targeted prior to approval and implementation, and this is the weakest link because it requires business knowledge as well as technical knowledge. As an example, scope changes should not be implemented at the expense of risking exposure to product liability lawsuits or safety issues. Likewise, scope changes exclusively for the sake of enhancing image or reputation should be avoided if it could result in an unhappy client. Also, scope changes should not be implemented if the payback period for the product is drastically extended in order to capture the recovery costs of the scope change.

Scope changes should be based upon a solid business foundation. For example, developing a very high quality product may seem nice at the time, but there must be customers willing to pay the higher price. The result might be a product that nobody wants or can afford.

There must exist a valid business purpose for a scope change. This includes the following factors at a minimum:

- An assessment of the customers' needs and the added value that the scope change will provide
- An assessment of the market needs, including the time required to make the scope change, the payback period, return on investment and whether the final product selling price will be overpriced for the market
- An assessment on the impact on the length of the project and product life cycle
- An assessment on the competition's ability to imitate the scope change
- An assessment on product liability associated with the scope change and the impact on the company's image

8.6 WAYS TO MINIMIZE SCOPE CREEP

Some people believe that scope creep should be prevented at all costs. But not allowing necessary scope creep to occur can be dangerous and possibly detrimental to business objectives. Furthermore, it may be impossible to prevent scope creep. Perhaps the best we can do is to control scope creep by minimizing the amount and extent of the scope creep. Some of the activities that may be helpful include:

Realize that scope creep will happen: Scope creep is almost impossible to prevent. Rather, attempts should be made to control scope creep.

Know the requirements: You must fully understand the requirements of the project and you must communicate with the stakeholders to make sure you both have the same understanding.

Know the client's expectations: Your client and the stakeholders can have expectations that may not be in alignment with your interpretation of the requirements on scope. You must understand the expectations and continuous communication is essential.

Eliminate the notion that the customer is always right: Constantly saying "yes" to placate the customer can cause sufficient scope creep such that a good project becomes a distressed project. Some changes could probably be clustered together and accomplished later as an enhancement project.

Act as the devil's advocate: Do not take for granted that all change requests are necessary even if they are internally generated by the project team. Question the necessity for the change. Make sure that there is sufficient justification for the change.

Determine the effect of the change: Scope creep will affect the schedule, cost, scope/requirements and resources. See whether some of the milestone dates can or cannot be moved. Some dates are hard to move while others are easy. See if additional resources are needed to perform the scope change and if the resources will be available.

Get user involvement early: Early user involvement may prevent some scope creep or at least identify the scope changes early enough such that the effects of the changes are minimal.

Add in flexibility: It may be possible to add some flexibility into the budget and schedule if a large amount of scope creep is expected. This could appear as a management/contingency monetary reserve for cost issues and a "reserve" activity built into the project schedule for timing issues.

Know who has signature authority: Not all members of the scope change control board possess signature authority to approve a scope change. You must know who possesses this authority.

In general, people that request scope changes do not attempt to make your life miserable. It is a desire to "please," through a need for perfection, to add functionality or to increase the value in the eyes of the client. Some scope changes are necessary for business reasons, such as add-ons for increased competitiveness. Scope creep is a necessity and cannot be eliminated. But it can be controlled.

8.7 SYDNEY OPERA HOUSE[1]

The Sydney Opera House is a multivenue performing arts center in New South Wales, Australia. It was conceived and largely built by Danish architect Jørn Utzon, opening in 1973 after a long gestation that began with his competition-winning design in 1957. Joseph Cahill's New South Wales Government gave the go-ahead for work to begin in 1958. The government's bold decision to select Utzon's design is often overshadowed by the scandal that followed.[2] It is on Bennelong Point in Sydney Harbor, close to the Sydney Harbor Bridge. It sits at the northeastern tip of the Sydney central business district (the CBD), surrounded on three sides by the harbor (Sydney Cove and Farm Cove) and inland by the Royal Botanic Gardens.

Contrary to its name, it houses multiple performance venues. It is among the busiest performing arts centers in the world, hosting over 1500 performances each year attended by some 1.2 million people. It provides a venue for many performing arts companies, including the four key resident companies Opera Australia, The Australian Ballet, the Sydney Theatre Company and the Sydney Symphony Orchestra, and presents a wide range of productions on its own account. It is also one of the most popular visitor attractions in Australia, with more than seven million people visiting each year, 300,000 of whom take a guided tour.[3]

It is administered by the Sydney Opera House Trust, under the New South Wales Ministry of the Arts. On June 28, 2007, it was made a UNESCO World Heritage Site.[4] It is one of the 20th century's most distinctive buildings and one of the most famous performing arts centers in the world.[5]

It is a modern expressionist design, with a series of large precast concrete "shells," each composed of sections of a sphere of 75.2 meters (246 feet 8.6 inches) radius, forming the roofs of the structure, set on a monumental podium. The building covers 1.8 hectares (4.4 acres) of land and is 183 meters (600 feet) long and 120 meters (394 feet) wide at its widest point. It is supported on 588 concrete piers sunk as much as 25 meters (82 feet) below sea level.

---

1. Adapted from Sydney Australia Opera House, *Wikipedia, the Free Encyclopedia.*

2. Tobias Faber "Jørn Utzon," Kunstindekx Danmark & Weilbachskunstnerleksikon (in Danish), retrieved September 18, 2011.

3. "Sydney Opera House 2011 Annual Report—Vision and Goals," retrieved January 25, 2013; "Sydney Opera House 08/09 Annual Report," retrieved June 20, 2010.

4. David Braithwaite, "Opera House Wins Top Status," *The Sydney Morning Herald*, retrieved June 28, 2007.

5. Statement of Values for Sydney Opera House National Heritage Listing; Nick Carbone, "World Landmarks Go Dark in Honor of Earth Hour," *Time*, March 26, 2011, retrieved January 28, 2013; "3D Illuminations Light Up the Sydney Opera House for Vivid Sydney," *The Independent*, May 9, 2011, retrieved January 28, 2013.

Although the roof structures are commonly referred to as "shells" (as in this discussion), they are precast concrete panels supported by precast concrete ribs, not shells in a strictly structural sense. The shells are covered in a subtle chevron pattern with 1,056,006 glossy white- and matte-cream-colored Swedish-made tiles from Höganäs AB, a factory that generally produced stoneware tiles for the paper-mill industry, though, from a distance, the shells appear a uniform white.

Apart from the tile of the shells and the glass curtain walls of the foyer spaces, the building's exterior is largely clad with aggregate panels composed of pink granite quarried at Tarana. Significant interior surface treatments also include off-form concrete, Australian white birch plywood supplied from Wauchope in northern New South Wales, and brush box glulam.

Of the two larger spaces, the Concert Hall is in the western group of shells, the Joan Sutherland Theatre in the eastern group. The scale of the shells was chosen to reflect the internal height requirements, with low entrance spaces, rising over the seating areas up to the high stage towers. The smaller venues (the Drama Theatre, the Playhouse and The Studio) are within the podium, beneath the Concert Hall. A smaller group of shells set to the western side of the Monumental Steps houses the Bennelong Restaurant. The podium is surrounded by substantial open public spaces, and the large stone-paved forecourt area with the adjacent monumental steps is regularly used as a performance space.

Performance Venues and Facilities

It houses the following performance venues:

- The Concert Hall, with 2679 seats, the home of the Sydney Symphony Orchestra and used by a large number of other concert presenters. It contains the Sydney Opera House Grand Organ, the largest mechanical tracker action organ in the world, with over 10,000 pipes.
- The Joan Sutherland Theatre, a proscenium theatre with 1507 seats, the Sydney home of Opera Australia and The Australian Ballet.
- The Drama Theatre, a proscenium theatre with 544 seats, used by the Sydney Theatre Company and other dance and theatrical presenters.
- The Playhouse, an end-stage theatre with 398 seats.
- The Studio, a flexible space with a maximum capacity of 400, depending on configuration.
- The Utzon Room, a small multipurpose venue, seating up to 210.
- The Forecourt, a flexible open-air venue with a wide range of configuration options, including the possibility of utilizing the Monumental Steps as audience seating, used for a range of community events and major outdoor performances. The Forecourt will be closed to visitors and performances in 2011–2014 to construct a new entrance tunnel to a rebuilt loading dock for the Joan Sutherland Theatre.

Other areas (for example the northern and western foyers) are also used for performances on an occasional basis. Venues are also used for conferences, ceremonies and social functions.

The building also houses a recording studio, cafes, restaurants and bars and retail outlets. Guided tours are available, including a frequent tour of the front-of-house spaces and a daily backstage tour that takes visitors backstage to see areas normally reserved for performers and crew members.

Construction History

Planning began in the late 1940s, when Eugene Goossens, the Director of the NSW State Conservatorium of Music, lobbied for a suitable venue for large theatrical productions. The normal venue for such productions, the Sydney Town Hall, was not considered large enough. By 1954, Goossens succeeded in gaining the support of NSW Premier Joseph Cahill, who called for designs for a dedicated opera house.

A design competition was launched by Cahill on September 13, 1955, and received 233 entries, representing architects from 32 countries. The criteria specified a large hall seating 3000 and a small hall for 1200 people, each to be designed for different uses, including full-scale operas, orchestral and choral concerts, mass meetings, lectures, ballet performances and other presentations. The winner, announced in 1957, was Jørn Utzon, a Danish architect. According to legend the Utzon design was rescued from a final cut of 30 "rejects" by the noted Finnish architect Eero Saarinen. The prize was £5000.[6] Utzon visited Sydney in 1957 to help supervise the project.[7] His office moved to Sydney in February 1963.

Utzon received the Pritzker Prize, architecture's highest honor, in 2003.[8] The Pritzker Prize citation stated:

> There is no doubt that the Sydney Opera House is his masterpiece. It is one of the great iconic buildings of the 20th century, an image of great beauty that has become known throughout the world—a symbol for not only a city, but a whole country and continent.

(a) Design and Construction

The Fort Macquarie Tram Depot, occupying the site at the time of these plans, was demolished in 1958 and construction began in March 1959. It was built in three stages: stage I (1959–1963) consisted of building the

---

6. "Millennium Masterwork: Jorn Utzon's Sydney Opera House," *Hugh Pearman*, Gabion, retrieved June 28, 2007.

7. Eric Ellis interview with Utzon, *Sydney Morning Herald Good Weekend*, October 31, 1992, Ericellis.com, retrieved December 2, 2008.

8. *Sydney Morning Herald* – his death.

upper podium; stage II (1963–1967) the construction of the outer shells; stage III (1967–1973) interior design and construction.

Stage I: Podium Stage I commenced on March 2, 1959. The government had pushed for work to begin early, fearing that funding, or public opinion, might turn against them. However, Utzon had still not completed the final designs. Major structural issues still remained unresolved. By January 23, 1961, work was running 47 weeks behind,[9] mainly because of unexpected difficulties (inclement weather, unexpected difficulty diverting stormwater, construction beginning before proper construction drawings had been prepared, changes of original contract documents). Work on the podium was finally completed in February 1963. The forced early start led to significant later problems, not least of which was the fact that the podium columns were not strong enough to support the roof structure and had to be rebuilt.[10]

Stage II: Roof The shells of the competition entry were originally of undefined geometry,[11] but, early in the design process, the "shells" were perceived as a series of parabolas supported by precast concrete ribs. However, engineers Ove Arup and Partners were unable to find an acceptable solution to constructing them. The formwork for using in situ concrete would have been prohibitively expensive, but, because there was no repetition in any of the roof forms, the construction of precast concrete for each individual section would possibly have been even more expensive.

From 1957 to 1963, the design team went through at least 12 iterations of the form of the shells trying to find an economically acceptable form (including schemes with parabolas, circular ribs and ellipsoids) before a workable solution was completed. The design work on the shells involved one of the earliest uses of computers in structural analysis, in order to understand the complex forces to which the shells would be subjected.[12] In mid-1961, the design team found a solution to the problem: the shells all being created as sections from a sphere. This solution allows arches of varying length to be cast in a common mold and a number of arch segments of common length to be placed adjacent to one another to form a spherical section. With whom exactly this solution originated has been the subject of some controversy. It was originally credited to Utzon. Ove Arup's letter to Ashworth, a member of the Sydney Opera House Executive Committee, states: "Utzon came up with an idea of making all the shells of uniform curvature throughout in both directions."[13] Peter Jones, the author of Ove

9. *Sydney Architecture*, retrieved November 1, 2008.

10. Peter Murray, *The Saga of the Sydney Opera House*, Spon Press, London, 2004.

11. Ove Arup and G. J. Zunz, *Structural Engineer*, Vol. 47, March 1969.

12. Peter Jones, *Ove Arup: Masterbuilder of the Twentieth Century*, Yale University Press, 2006.

13. Ibid., p. 199.

Arup's biography, states that "the architect and his supporters alike claimed to recall the precise eureka moment . . . ; the engineers and some of their associates, with equal conviction, recall discussion both in central London and at Ove's house."

Ove Arup and Partners' site engineer supervised the construction of the shells, which used an innovative adjustable steel-trussed "erection arch" to support the different roofs before completion. On April 6, 1962, it was estimated that the Opera House would be completed between August 1964 and March 1965.

Stage III: Interiors Stage III, the interiors, started with Utzon moving his entire office to Sydney in February 1963. However, there was a change of government in 1965, and the new Robert Askin government declared the project under the jurisdiction of the Ministry of Public Works. This ultimately led to Utzon's resignation in 1966 (see below).

The cost of the project so far, even in October 1966, was still only $22.9 million,[14] less than a quarter of the final $102 million cost. However, the projected costs for the design were at this stage much more significant.

The second stage of construction was progressing toward completion when Utzon resigned. His position was principally taken over by Peter Hall, who became largely responsible for the interior design. Other persons appointed that same year to replace Utzon were E. H. Farmer as government architect, D. S. Littlemore and Lionel Todd.

Following Utzon's resignation, the acoustic advisor, Lothar Cremer, confirmed to the Sydney Opera House Executive Committee (SOHEC) that Utzon's original acoustic design allowed for only 2000 seats in the main hall and further stated that increasing the number of seats to 3000 as specified in the brief would be disastrous for the acoustics. According to Peter Jones, the stage designer, Martin Carr, criticized the "shape, height and width of the stage, the physical facilities for artists, the location of the dressing rooms, the widths of doors and lifts, and the location of lighting switchboards."[15]

(b) Significant Changes to Utzon's Design
The final constructions were modified from Utzon's original designs:

- The major hall, which was originally to be a multipurpose opera/concert hall, became solely a concert hall, called the Concert Hall. The minor hall, originally for stage productions only, had the added function of opera and ballet to deal with and was called the Opera Theatre, later renamed the Joan Sutherland Theatre. As a result, the Joan Sutherland Theatre is inadequate to stage large-scale opera and ballet. A theater, a

---

14. *Sydney Architecture*, retrieved December 1, 2008.

15. Jones, p. 203.

cinema and a library were also added. These were later changed to two live drama theaters and a smaller theater "in the round." These now comprise the Drama Theatre, the Playhouse, and the Studio, respectively. These changes were primarily because of inadequacies in the original competition brief, which did not make it adequately clear how the Opera House was to be used. The layout of the interiors was changed, and the stage machinery, already designed and fitted inside the major hall, was pulled out and largely thrown away.

- Externally, the cladding to the podium and the paving (the podium was originally not to be clad down to the water, but to be left open.
- The construction of the glass walls (Utzon was planning to use a system of prefabricated plywood mullions, but a different system was designed to deal with the glass).
- Utzon's plywood corridor designs and his acoustic and seating designs for the interior of both major halls were scrapped completely. His design for the Concert Hall was rejected as it only seated 2000, which was considered insufficient. Utzon employed the acoustic consultant Lothar Cremer, and his designs for the major halls were later modeled and found to be very good. The subsequent Todd, Hall and Littlemore versions of both major halls have some problems with acoustics, particularly for the performing musicians. The orchestra pit in the Joan Sutherland Theatre is cramped and dangerous to musicians' hearing.[16] The Concert Hall has a very high roof, leading to a lack of early reflections onstage—perspex rings (the "acoustic clouds") hanging over the stage were added shortly before opening in an (unsuccessful) attempt to address this problem.

(c) Completion and Cost

The Opera House was formally completed in 1973, having cost $102 million.[17] H. R. "Sam" Hoare, the Hornibrook director in charge of the project, provided the following approximations in 1973: Stage I: podium Civil & Civic Pty Ltd approximately $5.5m. Stage II: roof shells M. R. Hornibrook (NSW) Pty Ltd approximately $12.5m. Stage III: completion The Hornibrook Group $56.5m. Separate contracts: stage equipment, stage lighting and organ $9.0m. Fees and other costs $16.5m.

The original cost estimate in 1957 was £3,500,000 ($7 million). The original completion date set by the government was January 26, 1963 (Australia Day).[18] Thus, the project was completed 10 years late and over-budget by more than 14 times.

---

16. Joyce Morgan "The Phantoms That Threaten the Opera House," *The Sydney Morning Herald*, November 2006, retrieved March 13, 2007.

17. New South Wales Government, Department of Commerce, NSW.gov.au, accessed December 1, 2008.

18. Peter Jones, *Ove Arup: Masterbuilder of the Twentieth Century*, Yale University Press, 2006.

Jørn Utzon and His Resignation Before the Sydney Opera House competition, Jørn Utzon had won 7 of the 18 competitions he had entered but had never seen any of his designs built. Utzon's submitted concept for the Sydney Opera House was almost universally admired and considered groundbreaking. The Assessors Report of January 1957 stated:

> The drawings submitted for this scheme are simple to the point of being diagrammatic. Nevertheless, as we have returned again and again to the study of these drawings, we are convinced that they present a concept of an Opera House which is capable of becoming one of the great buildings of the world.

For the first stage, Utzon worked very successfully with the rest of the design team and the client, but, as the project progressed, the Cahill government insisted on progressive revisions. They also did not fully appreciate the costs or work involved in design and construction. Tensions between the client and the design team grew further when an early start to construction was demanded despite an incomplete design. This resulted in a continuing series of delays and setbacks while various technical engineering issues were being refined. The building was unique, and the problems with the design issues and cost increases were exacerbated by commencement of work before the completion of the final plans.

After the election of Robert Askin as Premier of New South Wales in 1965, the relationship of client, architect, engineers and contractors became increasingly tense. Askin had been a "vocal critic of the project prior to gaining office."[19] His new Minister for Public Works, Davis Hughes, was even less sympathetic. Elizabeth Farrelly, Australian architecture critic, has written:

> At an election night dinner party in Mosman, Hughes's daughter Sue Burgoyne boasted that her father would soon sack Utzon. Hughes had no interest in art, architecture or aesthetics. A fraud, as well as a philistine, he had been exposed before Parliament and dumped as Country Party leader for 19 years of falsely claiming a university degree. The Opera House gave Hughes a second chance. For him, as for Utzon, it was all about control; about the triumph of homegrown mediocrity over foreign genius.[20]

Differences ensued. One of the first was that Utzon believed the clients should receive information on all aspects of the design and construction through his practice, while the clients wanted a system (notably drawn in

---

19. Elizabeth Farrelly, "High Noon at Bennelong Point,"' *Canberra Times*, Canberratimes.com .au, retrieved December 1, 2008.
20. Ibid.

sketch form by Davis Hughes) where architect, contractors and engineers each reported to the client directly and separately. This had great implications for procurement methods and cost control, with Utzon wishing to negotiate contracts with chosen suppliers (such as Ralph Symonds for the plywood interiors) and the New South Wales government insisting contracts be put out to tender.[21]

Utzon was highly reluctant to respond to questions or criticism from the client's Sydney SOHEC. However, he was greatly supported throughout by a member of the committee and one of the original competition judges, Professor Harry Ingham Ashworth. Utzon was unwilling to compromise on some aspects of his designs that the clients wanted to change.

Utzon's ability was never in doubt, despite questions raised by Davis Hughes, who attempted to portray Utzon as an impractical dreamer. Ove Arup actually stated that Utzon was "probably the best of any I have come across in my long experience of working with architects" and:

> The Opera House could become the world's foremost contemporary masterpiece if Utzon is given his head.

In October 1965, Utzon gave Hughes a schedule setting out the completion dates of parts of his work for stage III. Utzon was at this time working closely with Ralph Symonds, a manufacturer of plywood based in Sydney and highly regarded by many, despite an Arup engineer warning that Ralph Symonds's "knowledge of the design stresses of plywood, was extremely sketchy" and that the technical advice was "elementary to say the least and completely useless for our purposes." In any case, Hughes shortly after withheld permission for the construction of plywood prototypes for the interiors, and the relationship between Utzon and the client never recovered. By February 1966, Utzon was owed more than $100,000 in fees.[22] Hughes then withheld funding so that Utzon could not even pay his own staff. The government minutes record that following several threats of resignation, Utzon finally stated to Davis Hughes: "If you don't do it, I resign." Hughes replied: "I accept your resignation. Thank you very much. Goodbye."

Utzon left the project on February 28, 1966. He said that Hughes's refusal to pay him any fees and the lack of collaboration caused his resignation and later famously described the situation as "Malice in Blunderland". In March 1966, Hughes offered him a subordinate role as "design architect" under a panel of executive architects, without any supervisory powers over the House's construction, but Utzon rejected this. Utzon left the country never to return.

---

21. Peter Murray, *The Saga of the Sydney Opera House*, Spon Press, London, 2004.

22. "High Noon at Bennelong Point—National News—National—General," *The Canberra Times*, December 1, 2008, retrieved July 9, 2010.

Following the resignation, there was great controversy about who was in the right and who was in the wrong. The Sydney Morning Herald initially reported: "No architect in the world has enjoyed greater freedom than Mr. Utzon. Few clients have been more patient or more generous than the people and the government of NSW. One would not like history to record that this partnership was brought to an end by a fit of temper on the one side or by a fit of meanness on the other." On March 17, 1966, it reported: "It was not his fault that a succession of Governments and the Opera House Trust should so signally have failed to impose any control or order on the project . . . his concept was so daring that he himself could solve its problems only step by step . . . his insistence on perfection led him to alter his design as he went along."

The Sydney Opera House opened the way for the immensely complex geometries of some modern architecture. The design was one of the first examples of the use of computer-aided design to design complex shapes. The design techniques developed by Utzon and Arup for the Sydney Opera House have been further developed and are now used for architecture, such as works of Gehry and blobitecture, as well as most reinforced concrete structures. The design is also one of the first in the world to use araldite to glue the precast structural elements together and proved the concept for future use.

Opening Day

The Opera House was formally opened by Elizabeth II, Queen of Australia, on October 20, 1973. A large crowd attended. Utzon was not invited to the ceremony, nor was his name mentioned. The opening was televised and included fireworks and a performance of Beethoven's Symphony No. 9.

8.8 SUMMARY OF LESSONS LEARNED

Regardless of how hard we try, scope creep is inevitable. We must recognize that it will happen and do our best to minimize unwanted changes from being approved.

A checklist of techniques for possibly reducing the number of software failures might include:

- ☐ Clearly understand the requirements for the project.
- ☐ Establish freeze points after which no further scope change can be allowed.
- ☐ Establish a well-structured process for approving and rejecting scope change requests.
- ☐ Make sure that there is a valid reason for the scope change and that the result will be added business value.

TABLE 8-1 *PMBOK® Guide* Alignment to Lessons Learned

LESSONS LEARNED	PMBOK® GUIDE SECTIONS
Scope creep will happen.	5.6
Feature creep will happen on some projects, especially IT projects.	5.6
You must understand the reasons for the scope creep before the approval process begins.	4.5, 4.5.1.3, 5.5.3.2, 5.6.3.2
It is essential to understand the impact that scope creep will have on safety.	3.6
If possible, do not allow politics to dictate scope changes.	4.5.1.3
Well defined requirements can minimize the need for scope creep.	4.1.1.1, 4.1.1.2, 5.2, 5.2.3.1, 5.3.3.1, 5.5
There must be a rigid change control process in place.	4.5.2, 4.5.3.1, 4.5.3.2, 4.5.3.4

Table 8-1 provides a summary of the lessons learned and alignment to various sections of the *PMBOK® Guide* where additional or supporting information can be found. In some cases, these sections of the *PMBOK® Guide* simply provide supporting information related to the lesson learned. There are numerous sections of the *PMBOK® Guide* that could be aligned for each lesson learned. For simplicity sake, only a few are listed.

9 PROJECT HEALTH CHECKS

9.0 NEED FOR PROJECT HEALTH CHECKS

Projects seem to progress quickly until they are about 60–70% complete. During that time, everyone applauds that work is progressing as planned. Then, perhaps without warning, the truth comes out, possibly due to significant scope creep, and we discover that the project is in trouble. This occurs because of:

- Our disbelief in the value of using the project's metrics correctly
- Selecting the wrong metrics
- Our fear of what project health checks may reveal

Some project managers have an incredible fixation with project metrics and numbers, believing that metrics are the Holy Grail in determining status. Most projects seem to focus on only two metrics: time and cost. These are the primary metrics in all earned value measurement systems (EVMSs). While these two metrics "may" give you a reasonable representation of where you are today, using these two metrics to provide forecasts into the future are "grey" areas and may not indicate future problem areas that could prevent a successful and timely completion of the project. At the other end of the spectrum we have managers that have no faith in the metrics and therefore focus on vision, strategy, leadership and prayers.

Rather than relying on metrics alone, the simplest solution might be to perform periodic health checks on the project. In doing this, three critical questions must be addressed:

- Who will perform the health check?
- Will the interviewees be honest in their responses?
- Will management and stakeholders overreact to the truth?

The surfacing of previously unknown or hidden issues could lead to loss of employment, demotions or project cancellation. Yet project health checks offer the greatest opportunity for early corrective action to save a potentially failing project. It is a lot easier to take corrective action when problems are small. You also have more alternatives from which to select.

Health checks can discover future opportunities as well, especially opportunities to add value to the project.

9.1 UNDERSTANDING PROJECT HEALTH CHECKS

People tend to use audits and health checks synonymously. Both are designed to ensure successful, repeatable project outcomes, and both must be performed on projects that appear to be heading for a successful outcome as well as those that seem destined to fail. There are lessons learned and best practices that can be discovered from both successes and failures. Also, detailed analysis of a project that appears to be successful at the moment might bring to the surface issues that show that the project is really in trouble.

Table 9-1 shows some of the differences between audits and health checks. Although some of the differences may be subtle, we will focus our attention on health checks.

During a team meeting, a project manager asked the team, "How's the work progressing?" The response was:

> We're doing reasonable [sic] well. We're just a little bit over budget and a little behind schedule, but we think we've solved both issues by using lower salaried resources for the next month and having them work overtime. According to our enterprise project management methodology, our unfavorable cost and schedule variances are still within the threshold limits and the generation of an exception report for management is not necessary. The customer should be happy with our results thus far.

These comments are representative of a project team that has failed to acknowledge the true status of the project because they are too involved in

TABLE 9-1   Audit vs. Health Checks

VARIABLE	AUDIT	HEALTH CHECKS
Focus	On the present	On the future
Intent	Compliance	Execution effectiveness and deliverables
Timing	Generally scheduled and infrequent	Generally unscheduled and when needed
Items to be searched	Best practices	Hidden, possible destructive issues and possible cures
Interviewer	Usually someone internal	External consultant
How interview is led	With entire team	One-on-one sessions
Time frame	Short term	Long term
Depth of analysis	Summary	Forensic review

the daily activities of the project. There may even exist a collective belief that discourages the truth from coming out. Likewise, we have project managers, sponsors and executives that are caught up in their own daily activities and readily accept these comments with blind faith, thus failing to see the big picture. If an audit had been conducted, the conclusion might have been the same, namely that the project is successfully following the enterprise project management methodology and that the time and cost metrics are within the acceptable limits. A forensic project health check, on the other hand, may disclose the seriousness of the issues. However, as discussed previously, several of the more serious issues may not become apparent until after implementation.

Just because a project is on time and/or within the allotted budget does not guarantee success. Software bugs may not become apparent until much later. The end result could be that the deliverable has poor quality such that it is unacceptable to the customer. In addition to time and cost, project health checks focus on quality, resources, benefits and requirements, just to name a few. The true measure of the project's future success is the value that the customers see at the completion of the project. Health checks must therefore be value focused. Audits, on the other hand, usually do not focus on value.

Health checks can function as an ongoing tool by being performed randomly when needed or periodically throughout various life-cycle stages. However, there are specific circumstances that indicate that a health check should be accomplished quickly. These include:

- Significant scope creep
- Escalating costs accompanied by a deterioration in value and benefits
- Schedule slippages that cannot be corrected
- Missed deadlines
- Poor morale accompanied by changes in key project personnel

Periodic health checks, if done correctly, eliminate ambiguity such that true status can be determined. The benefits of health checks include:

- Determining the current status of the project
- Identifying problems early enough such that sufficient time exists for corrective action to be taken
- Identifying the critical success factors that will support a successful outcome or the critical issues that can prevent successful delivery
- Identifying lessons learned, best practices and critical success factors that can be used on future projects
- Evaluating compliance to and improvements for the enterprise project management methodology
- Identifying which activities may require or benefit from additional resources
- Identifying present and future risks as well as possible risk mitigation strategies

- Determining if the benefits and value will be there at completion
- Determining if euthanasia is required to put the project out of its misery
- The development of or recommendations for a fix-it plan

There are misconceptions about project health checks. Some of these are:

- The person doing the health check does not understand the project or the corporate culture, thus wasting time.
- The health check is too costly for the value we will get by performing it.
- The health check ties up critical resources in interviews.
- By the time we get the results from the health check, either it is too late to make changes or the nature of the project may have changed.

9.2 WHO PERFORMS HEALTH CHECKS?

One of the challenges facing companies is whether the health check should be conducted by internal personnel or by external consultants. The risk with using internal personnel is that they may have loyalties or relationships with people on the project team and therefore may not be totally honest in determining the true status of the project or in deciding who was at fault.

Using external consultants or facilitators professionally trained in performing health checks is often the better choice. External facilitators can bring to the table:

- A multitude of forms, guidelines, templates and checklists used in other companies and similar projects
- A promise of impartiality and confidentiality
- A focus on only the facts and hopefully free of politics
- An environment where people can speak freely and vent their personal feelings
- An environment that is relatively free from other day-to-day issues

9.3 HEALTH CHECK LIFE-CYCLE PHASES

There are three life-cycle phases for project health checks:

- Review of the business case and the project's history
- Research and discovery of the facts
- Preparation of the health check report

Reviewing the business case and project's history may require the health check leader to have access to proprietary knowledge and financial information. The leader may have to sign nondisclosure agreements and also noncompete clauses before being allowed to perform the health check.

Review of the business case is essential to verify that the business case has not changed. The Iridium Project was a classical example where health checks would have identified that the business case was no longer valid.

In the research and discovery phase, the leader prepares a list of questions that need to be answered. The list can be prepared from the *PMBOK® Guide's* domain areas or areas of knowledge. The questions can also come from the knowledge repository in the consultant's company and may appear in the form of templates, guidelines, checklists or forms. The questions can change from project to project and industry to industry.

Some of the critical areas that must be investigated are:

- Performance against baselines
- Ability to meet forecasts
- Benefits and value analyses
- Governance
- Stakeholder involvement
- Risk mitigation
- Contingency planning

If the health check requires one-on-one interviews, the health check leader must be able to extract the truth from interviewees that have different interpretations or conclusions about the status of the project. Some people will be truthful whereas others will either say what they believe the interviewer wants to hear or distort the truth as a means of self-protection.

The final phase is the preparation of the report. This should include:

- A listing of the issues
- Root cause analyses, possibly including identification of individuals that created the problems
- Gap analysis
- Opportunities for corrective action
- A get-well or fix-it plan

Project health checks are not "Big Brother is Watching You" activities. Rather, they are part of project oversight. Without these health checks, the chances for project failure are significantly increased. Project health checks also provide us with insight on how to keep risks under control. Performing health checks and taking corrective action early are certainly better than having to manage a distressed project.

9.4 PROJECT MANAGEMENT FAILURE WARNING SIGNS

Sometimes, the words that people speak, the way they act and how they go about doing their job serve as early warning indicators that failure is possible and a health check may be necessary. The remainder of this section comes from Patrick D. Shediack's paper.[1]

I've been a project manager since 1983 and a supervisor or manager since 1977, so I've had a little bit of time to observe project related issues. For your use or amusement, I've put together a list of project failure warning signs that seem to be, in no particular order of priority, pretty common. Judging from the constant stream of e-mails I get from around the world, these warning signs seem to pop up in numerous countries, projects and industries!

For simplification, I included a few items which also apply to financial, sales organization or program management failure warning signs.

"Instant Amnesia" and "Da Nial Ain't In Egypt"

People suddenly can't remember anything or want to own anything.

- WARNING SIGN: Executives can remember every detail of their "big idea" the PM is trying to execute, but conveniently forget when reminded about problems like "there's not enough money" to pay for that big idea!
- WARNING SIGN: Executives say "I don't remember that" when told "we briefed this before" (you don't need to go to WebMD to diagnose this problem as "instant amnesia", a tragic disease which strikes hesitant decision makers).
- WARNING SIGN: Executives and middle managers trying not to look at problems and mistaking "denial" for "da Nile."
- Let me explain it to those folks one more time:
  - "Da Nile" has three pyramids and a sphinx sitting next to it;
  - "Denial" is the curtain managers like to pull over the truth about their project's problems
- WARNING SIGN: Executives stop calling it "my project" and start referring to it as "your project" or "(PM)'s project"
- WARNING SIGN: "You're now in charge of it" is your new term of address from management

Project Cost

The proposal writer uses a reality-defying "magic calculator"

How do you decide on a project price during the sales cycle without asking for a PM or analyst "reality check" to see if the work can actually be done as proposed within the price? You can't and expect the project to be on time or on budget.

- WARNING SIGN: No PERT estimate completed prior to giving the price quotation to the customer

---

1. Copyright © 2013 by Patrick D. Shediack, PMP®. "Project Management Failure Warning Signs." Reproduced with permission of Patrick D. Shediack, PMP®, and Bluejeans Place, www.bluejeansplace.com.

- WARNING SIGN: Heavy discounting by sales or executives to get the project with no outside (read no PM) validation
- WARNING SIGN: Sales representative gives you a blank look, argues, walks away or outright refuses when you ask for his calculations which support his price

The Lone Ranger Rides Again!

Even the customer knows when you're running the hide off your labor force. The Lone Ranger had Tonto, Yogi Bear had Boo-Boo, Quick Draw McGraw had Baba-Looey, so why do so many PMs run projects without adequate staff to help track issues, research solutions to problems, conduct risk analyses, mark up schedules on a daily basis and so forth?

- WARNING SIGN: PM working alone with no dedicated resources
- WARNING SIGN: PM does not have an analyst to complete analytical or testing tasks
- WARNING SIGN: PM tasked to use a matrix staff, but multiple managers or executives can divert project team members to other tasks regardless of project impact
- WARNING SIGN: No project expediters (read "grunts") to do low-level project tasks, even on a billable basis!
- WARNING SIGN: The customer observes the resource issues and tells executives they need to fix the problem.

No Sale!

Have you ever seen a CEO or sales staff who can't sell?

Very few PMs receive commissions on the project statements of work or change orders, so why are they expected to bring in the sales for the company?

- WARNING SIGN: PM asked to make sales pitch to client instead of sale representative
- WARNING SIGN: PM asked to sell change order to client without sales support
- WARNING SIGN: Rapid turnover of sales people
- WARNING SIGN: Staff notices executives are not closing deals to bring in sales themselves, but relying totally on sales staff. (Shorthand: What's so wrong that the CEO can't bring in new business?)
- WARNING SIGN: Previous customers won't see sales people even when offering to bring the PM along
- WARNING SIGN: Sales people do not stop in at clients just to THANK them for the current work; they only visit the customer to make sales calls

Arrogance Rules!

Look out for the backbiting and sniping all around you.
Tact and diplomacy seem to be found only at the State Department.

- WARNING SIGN: The client staff argues amongst themselves in front of vendors
- WARNING SIGN: The client staff publicly ridicules its sponsors and decision makers
- WARNING SIGN: People who enter and leave the project sporadically are seen as "all knowing"
  - aka "The seagulls who fly in out of nowhere, [commit an act which creates manure] half-baked solutions, and fly out again to nowhere, leaving you with nothing useful" *(credit for the warning sign: a very wise chief master sergeant at Edwards AFB CA circa 1991 who shall remain anonymous)*
  - aka "Why aren't you just doing _____?"
  - aka "Well, that doesn't sound hard..."
- WARNING SIGNS: Weekly reports and meetings upon meetings abound to satisfy disengaged managers' sudden and directed interest
- WARNING SIGN: In state and local consulting, the (governor's) (commissioner's)(some other grand poo-bah's) name is mentioned often for emphasis
- WARNING SIGN: Someone who's not a project manager recommends discarding PM practices and using a task list on a Post-It or something similar, often called "PM Light"
- WARNING SIGN: You receive e-mail(s) from someone not on your project telling you how to run your project

2 + 2 = 17!

The numbers do not add up even if you use a child's abacus!
A lot of folks pay lip service to resource management, but have no idea what they're talking about or doing.

- WARNING SIGN: No one listens or responds positively when the PM notes the price or estimate is unrealistic
- WARNING SIGN: Nothing is reserved in the pricing or resources for contingency costs
- WARNING SIGN: Nothing is reserved in the pricing or resources for risk mitigation
- WARNING SIGN: No one accepts the concept of a 40 hour work week or 2080 hour man-year or even the concept that people get sick, take vacations, have to run their baby to the doctor or are otherwise not available full-time every week

- WARNING SIGN: The basic elements of the pricing equation are not used on each and every task:

  Price = (direct cost + indirect cost + overhead + profit)

Mao Didn't Have the Only "Long March"

The project has to get done no matter what so long as the profit margin is preserved.

Management underestimated the cost of a project, misstated the technical difficulties or failed to accept risk mitigation, so a "death march" is used to get the job done.

- WARNING SIGN: Additional resources are unavailable for the life of the project
- WARNING SIGN: Overtime is out of control, exceeding fifteen per cent of the average worker's 40 hour work week
- WARNING SIGN: Management has no idea how to get overtime under control
- WARNING SIGN: Management dictates continued overtime for more than three weeks to make up for lack of resources
- WARNING SIGN: Management rejects any effort to bring overtime under control
- WARNING SIGN: Multiple employees from organizations participating in your project are exploring or participating in union organization activities of the workplace due to uncontrolled overtime (No offense meant— I come from a union organizer's family!)
- WARNING SIGN: Management screams and curses at workers despite "hostile work environment" litigation potential

What Risk? There's No Risk Here!

Due diligence keeps you out of trouble and lawsuits!

This problem area is just one of the reasons why I believe project managers should be licensed professionally just like civil engineers, architects, surveyors, pharmacists, doctors, nurses, certified public accountants and lawyers.

- WARNING SIGN: Client dictates solution based on emotion or advertising
- WARNING SIGN: Client rejects advice, mandates solution, but not asked to sign a hold harmless agreement
- WARNING SIGN: A finished product is specified in the contract (even though you need to develop it first), yet the contract doesn't say it's a developmental effort!
- WARNING SIGN: Senior managers mark up "reds" to "yellows" and "yellows" to "greens" on status briefing slides
- WARNING SIGN: The only information senior managers want to see is on a quad chart

Where's Your Project Plan?

While project plans are important, they are not the same as "project management".

When over-emphasis is put on one problem area like schedules or briefing charts, other overlooked problems are lurking elsewhere in the project, but it all boils down to a lack of following accepted global project management practices.

- WARNING SIGN: Overemphasis on producing or updating Gantt charts and other illustrations; but little emphasis on other PMBOK tools like risk assessments
- WARNING SIGN: No project documentation until the week before the Project Management Review (PMR)—as if any smart executive can't tell that these things were just put together in the last couple of days
- WARNING SIGN: Spreadsheets, quad charts and items of vogue that take priority over resolving project issues
- WARNING SIGN: Version after version after version of briefings are created to communicate project information rather than just presenting a straight-forward business problem and solution.

I'll Take a Booth without a Cell Phone!

How many times have you gone to supper or lunch and someone—even you—has to take a cell phone call about a project? Probably more than you want to admit. You know these clowns; they're in every organization, but executives think they're fabulous.

- WARNING SIGN: People keep cell phones, e-mail, PDAs, pagers on in meetings and leap up like Superman to respond when something comes in on one or the other
- WARNING SIGN: Someone's cell phone bill goes higher each month as the project progresses
- WARNING SIGN: Every little decision requires multiple cell or conference calls

Don't Bother Me with Details!

Projects, by their very nature, have a lot of details, most of which interlock with each other and very few can be ignored by managers when trying to understand project issues.

Every project is built of many small pieces, but how many times do you hear nothing is important except the big things? Think about this: Fasteners are small things, but awfully important to keeping your airplane or car working in one piece!

- WARNING SIGN: You're told, "Keep it short" which is shorthand for "Catch me up fast, I'm on my way to learn about the next fire that I don't know anything about"
- WARNING SIGN: You're told your communications are too long which is shorthand for "I only need to know enough to cover my [posterior]"
- WARNING SIGN: "Just do it" or "Just get it done" is heard on a frequent occasion
- WARNING SIGN: In reengineering projects, existing issues or core problems are not dealt with, but the reengineering staff is marginalized or denigrated
- WARNING SIGN: PMs operating in crisis are seen by managers as more engaged than those whose projects are quietly under control

What Layoffs?

You survive a layoff, your project is on track, but you're worried things are bad in the cash room. Virtually every organization's layoff has financial problems at its core.

- WARNING SIGN: Multiple, consecutive layoffs
- WARNING SIGN: Managers are in denial but you know the company is in financial or sales trouble
- WARNING SIGN: Invisible management
- WARNING SIGN: Reimbursements take longer and longer to come back to you
- WARNING SIGN: Clients take longer than usual to make purchase decisions
- WARNING SIGN: There are no new customers
- WARNING SIGN: The firm fires the project team as soon as the project is delivered.

The Out-of-Towner Speaks: Distance Means Credibility

You're the PM closest to the work at hand, but your manager takes the word of someone at a distant location as "more credible". You hear very faint strains of *"March of the Clowns"* in your mind as the "out of towner" speaks.

- WARNING SIGN: The out of towner has huge credibility with your boss, but hasn't looked at a single document related to the project's requirements or solution
- WARNING SIGN: The out of towner declines your offer to provide any and all project documentation by e-mail for his review and comment within the next few business days

- WARNING SIGN: The out of towner refuses your tactful and diplomatic invitation to attend a program management review or technical interchange meeting at your location so his ideas and comments can be vetted by the project team in front of your manager
- WARNING SIGN: Your manager is not concerned that the out of towner won't air his ideas and comments in an on-site program management review or technical interchange meeting
- WARNING SIGN: Your manager doesn't share his e-mail or phone calls with the out of towner, but claims that person is right

Disclaimer

The above lessons are not based on any one person or company, but rather reflect a mosaic built from my observations in over 30 years of project management. Of course, if you're guilty of one of these lessons, you're probably seeing yourself here and getting ticked off at me!

9.5 SUMMARY OF LESSONS LEARNED

Regardless of how well the project appears to be going, there always exists the need for project health checks. Health checks provide validation that work is progressing as planned and that critical issues are identified and addressed.

TABLE 9-2 *PMBOK® Guide* Alignment to Lessons Learned

LESSONS LEARNED	PMBOK® GUIDE SECTIONS
The person or people performing the health check must be impartial. Internally; using the PMO may be best.	1.4.4
Metrics that may not be part of the standard organizational process assets may be necessary.	2.1.4
Clearly understand the information that the governance committee wants to see as a result of the health check.	2.2.2
It is often a good practice to allow stakeholders to participate in the health checks.	2.2.1
Health checks should be included in the project's life-cycle phases.	2.4.2
Health checks are part of the monitoring and controlling processes.	3.6, 4.4
Health checks must include validation of the scope.	5.5
Health checks should be integrated into the risk management processes.	11.2, 11.3, 11.4, 11.6

A checklist of techniques with regard to health checks might include:

- ☐ Work with the stakeholders to establish a routine schedule for health checks.
- ☐ Establish a set of metrics for performing the health checks.
- ☐ Identify conditions where nonroutine health checks may be necessary.
- ☐ Identify whether internal or external personnel will be used for the health checks.
- ☐ Be honest in reporting the results of the health checks.
- ☐ If necessary, identify fix-it plans.

Table 9-2 provides a summary of the lessons learned and alignment to various sections of the *PMBOK® Guide* where additional or supporting information can be found. In some cases, these sections of the *PMBOK® Guide* simply provide supporting information related to the lesson learned. There are numerous sections of the *PMBOK® Guide* that could be aligned for each lesson learned. For simplicity sake, only a few are listed.

10

TECHNIQUES FOR RECOVERING FAILING PROJECTS

10.0 UNDERSTANDING TROUBLED PROJECTS

Professional sports teams treat each new season as a project. For some teams, the only definition of success is winning the championship, while for others success is viewed as just a winning season. Not all teams can win the championship, but having a winning season is certainly within reach.

At the end of the season, perhaps half of the teams will have won more games than they lost. But for the other half of the teams who had losing records, the season (i.e., project) was a failure. When a project failure occurs in professional sports, managers and coaches are fired, there is a shakeup in executive leadership, some players are traded or sold to other teams and new players are brought on board. These same tactics are used to recover failing projects in industry.

There are some general facts about troubled projects:

- Some projects are doomed to fail regardless of recovery attempts.
- It takes a great deal of political savvy and political courage to admit that a project is in serious trouble.
- The chances of failure on any given project may be greater than the chances of success.
- Failure can occur in any life-cycle phase; success occurs at the end of the project.
- Troubled projects do not go from "green" to "red" overnight.
- There are early warning signs, but they are often overlooked or misunderstood.
- Most companies have a poor understanding of how to manage troubled projects.
- Not all project managers possess the skills to manage a troubled project.
- Stakeholders with limited knowledge of project management can make the situation worse.

Not all projects will be successful. Companies that have a very high degree of project success probably are not working on enough projects and certainly are not taking on very much risk. These types of companies eventually become followers rather than leaders. For companies that desire to be leaders, knowledge on how to turn around a failing or troubled project is essential.

Projects do not get into trouble overnight. There are early warning signs, but most companies seem to overlook them or misunderstand them. Some companies simply ignore the tell-tale signs and continue on hoping for a miracle. Failure to recognize these signs early can make the cost of downstream corrections a very costly endeavor. Also, the longer you wait to make the corrections, the more costly the changes become.

Some companies perform periodic project health checks. These health checks, even when applied to healthy-looking projects, can lead to the discovery that the project may be in trouble even though on the surface the project looks healthy. Outside consultants are often hired for the health checks in order to get an impartial assessment. The consultant rarely takes over the project once the health check is completed but may have made recommendations for recovery.

When a project gets way off track, the cost of recovery is huge and vast or even new resources may be required for corrections. The ultimate goal for recovery is no longer to finish on time, but to finish with reasonable benefits and value for the customer and the stakeholders. The project's requirements may change during recovery to meet the new goals if they have changed. Some projects may be corrected with just a bandage to stop the bleeding, but the project continues on. Other projects may require a plaster cast where part of the project is immobilized so that further changes cannot be made. There may also be projects that must be anesthetized and all work stops to allow for a major operation to take place. But regardless of what you do, not all troubled projects can be recovered.

10.1 ROOT CAUSES OF FAILURE

As discussed previously, there are numerous causes of project failure. Some causes are quite common in specific industries, such as information technology, whereas others can appear across all industries. Below is a list of common causes of failure that can apply to just about any industry:

- End-user stakeholders not involved throughout the project
- Minimal or no stakeholder backing; lack of ownership
- Weak business case
- Corporate goals not understood at the lower organizational levels
- Plan asks for too much in too little time
- Poor estimates, especially financial
- Unclear stakeholder requirements
- Passive user stakeholder involvement after handoff
- Unclear expectations
- Assumptions, if they exist at all, are unrealistic
- Plans are based upon insufficient data
- No systemization of the planning process

- Planning is performed by a planning group
- Inadequate or incomplete requirements
- Lack of resources
- Assigned resources lack experience
- Staffing requirements are not fully known
- Constantly changing resources
- Poor overall project planning
- Enterprise environmental factors have changes causing outdated scope
- Missed deadlines and no recovery plan
- Budgets are exceeded and out of control
- Lack of replanning on a regular basis
- Lack of attention provided to the human and organizational aspects of the project
- Project estimates are best guesses and not based upon history or standards
- Not enough time provided for proper estimating
- No one knows the exact major milestone dates or due dates for reporting
- Team members working with conflicting requirements
- People are shuffled in and out of the project with little regard for the schedule
- Poor or fragmented cost control
- Each stakeholder uses different organizational process assets, which may be incompatible with the assets of project partners
- Weak project and stakeholder communications
- Poor assessment of risks if done at all
- Wrong type of contract
- Poor project management; team members possess a poor understanding of project management, especially virtual team members
- Technical objectives are more important than business objectives

These causes of project failure can be sorted into three broad categories:

Management mistakes: These are due to a failure in stakeholder management perhaps by allowing too many unnecessary scope changes, failing to provide proper governance, refusing to make decisions in a timely manner and ignoring the project manager's quest for help. This can also be the result of wanting to gold-plate the project. This is also the result of not performing project health checks.

Planning mistakes: These are the result of poor project management, perhaps not following the principles stated in the *PMBOK® Guide*, not having a timely "kill switch" in the plan, not planning for project audits or health checks and not selecting the proper tracking metrics.

External influences: These are normally the failures in assessing the environmental input factors correctly. This includes the timing for getting approvals and authorization from third parties and a poor understanding of the host country's culture and politics.

10.2 DEFINITION PHASE

Historically, the definition of success on a project was viewed as accomplishing the work within the triple constraints and obtaining customer acceptance. Today, the triple constraints are still important but it has taken a "back seat" to the business and value components of success. In today's definition, success is when the planned business value is achieved within the imposed constraints and assumptions, and the customer receives the desired value.

While we seem to have a reasonably good understanding of project success, we have a poor understanding of project failure. The project manager and the stakeholders can have different definitions of project failure. The project manager's definition might just be not meeting the triple or competing constraints criteria. Stakeholders, on the other hand, seem more interested in business value than the triple or competing constraints once the project actually begins. Stakeholders' perception of failure might be:

- The project has become too costly for the expected benefits or value.
- The project will be completed too late.
- The project will not achieve its targeted benefits or value.
- The project no longer satisfies the stakeholders' needs.

10.3 EARLY WARNING SIGNS OF TROUBLE

Projects do not become distressed overnight. They normally go from "green" to "yellow" to "red" and along the way are early warning signs that failure may be imminent or that immediate changes may be necessary.

Typical early warning signs include:

- Business case deterioration
- Different opinions on project's purpose and objectives
- Unhappy/disinterested stakeholders and steering committee members
- Continuous criticism by stakeholders
- Changes in stakeholders without any warning
- No longer a demand for the deliverables or the product
- Invisible sponsorship
- Delayed decisions resulting in missed deadlines
- High tension meetings with team and stakeholders
- Finger pointing and poor acceptance of responsibility
- Lack of organizational process assets
- Failing to close life-cycle phases properly
- High turnover of personnel, especially critical workers
- Unrealistic expectations
- Failure in progress reporting

- Technical failure
- Having to work excessive hours and with heavy work loads
- Unclear milestones and other requirements
- Poor morale
- Everything is a crisis
- Poor attendance at team meetings
- Surprises, slow identification of problems and constant rework
- Poor change control process

The earlier the warning signs are discovered, the more opportunities exist for recovery. However, it takes a great deal of political courage to tell senior management that they had false expectations about the project. You must relate this information to them as quickly as possible to stop the bleeding. All too often, project managers wait until the project is way off track and then the recovery process becomes more difficult. In any case, this is the time when a project health check should be conducted. In general, there is tremendous political and cultural resistance to kill a project. Health checks combined with successful identification and evaluation of the early warning signs can tell us that the distressed project:

- Can succeed according to the original requirements but some minor changes are needed
- Can be repaired but major changes may be necessary
- Cannot succeed and should be killed

There are three possible outcomes when managing a troubled project:

- The project must be completed, i.e., required by law.
- The project can be completed but with major costly changes to the requirements.
- The project should be canceled:
  - Costs and benefits or value are no longer aligned.
  - What was once a good idea no longer has any merit.

Some projects cannot be cancelled because they are required by law. These include compliance to government laws on environmental issues, health, safety and pollution. For these projects, failure is not an option. Denver International Airport and terminal 5 at London Heathrow are examples of projects that simply could not fail. The hardest decision to make is obviously to hit the "kill switch" and cancel the project. Companies that have a good grasp of project management establish processes to make it easy to kill a project that cannot be saved. There is often a great deal of political and cultural resistance to kill a project. Stakeholder management and project governance play a serious role in the ease by which a project can be terminated.

10.4 SELECTING RECOVERY PROJECT MANAGER (RPM)

Companies often hire outside consultants to perform a health check on a project. If the health check report indicates that an attempt should be made to recover the troubled project, then perhaps a new project manager should be brought on board with skills in project recovery. Outside consultants normally do not take over the troubled project because they may not have a good grasp of the company's culture, business and project management processes, politics and employee working relationships. Not all project managers possess the skills to be an effective RPM. In addition to possessing project management knowledge, typical skills needed include:

- Strong political courage and political savvy
- A willingness to be totally honest when attacking and reporting the critical issues
- Tenacity to succeed even if it requires a change in resources
- Understanding that effective recovery is based upon information, not emotions
- Ability to deal with stress, personally and with the team

Recovering a failing project is like winning the "World Series of Poker." In addition to having the right skills, some degree of luck is also required.

Taking over a troubled project is not the same as starting up a new project. Recovery project managers must have a good understand of what they are about to inherit, including high levels of stress. This includes:

- A burned-out team
- An emotionally drained team
- Poor morale
- An exodus of the talented team members that are always in high demand elsewhere
- A team that may have a lack of faith in the recovery process
- Furious customers
- Nervous management
- Invisible sponsorship and governance
- Either invisible or highly active stakeholders

Project managers that do not understand what is involved in the recovery of a troubled project can make matters worse by hoping for a miracle and allowing the "death spiral" to continue to a point where recovery is no longer possible. The death spiral continues if we:

- Force employees to work excessive hours unnecessarily
- Create unnecessary additional work
- Replace team members at an inappropriate time.

- Increase team stress and pressure without understanding the ramifications
- Search for new "miracle" tools to solve some of the issues
- Hire consultants that cannot help or make matters worse by taking too long to understand the issues

10.5 RECOVERY LIFE-CYCLE PHASES

A company's existing enterprise project management (EPM) methodology may not be able to help recover a failing project. After all, the company's standard EPM methodology, which may not have been appropriate for this project, may have been a contributing factor to the project's decline. It is a mistake to believe that any methodology is the miracle cure. Projects are management by people, not tools or methodologies. A different approach may be necessary for the recovery project to succeed.

Figure 10-1 shows the typical life-cycle phases for a recovery project. These phases can significantly differ from the company's standard methodology life-cycle phases. The first four phases in Figure 10-1 are used for problem assessment and to evaluate and hopefully verify that the project may be able to be saved. The last two phases are where the actual recovery takes place.

10.6 UNDERSTANDING PHASE

The purpose of the understanding phase is for the newly assigned RPM to review the project and its history. To do this, the RPM will need some form of mandate or a project charter that may be different than that of his or her predecessor. This must be done as quickly as possible because time is a constraint rather than a luxury. Typical questions that may be addressed in the mandate include:

- What authority will you have to access proprietary or confidential information? This includes information that may not have been available to your predecessor, such as contractual agreements and actual salaries.

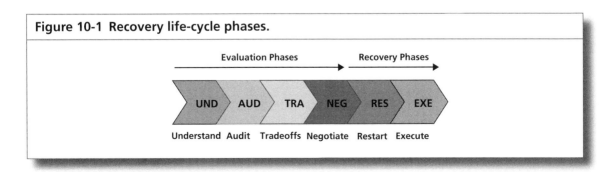

Figure 10-1 Recovery life-cycle phases.

- What support will you be given from the sponsor and the stakeholders? Are there any indications that they will accept less than optimal performance and a descoping of the original requirements?
- Will you be allowed to interview the team members in confidence?
- Will the stakeholders overreact to brutally honest findings even if the problems were caused by the stakeholders and governance groups?

Included in this phase are the following:

- Understanding of the project's history
- Reviewing the business case, expected benefits and targeted value
- Reviewing the project's objectives
- Reviewing the project's assumptions
- Familiarizing yourself with the stakeholders, their needs and sensitivities
- Seeing if the enterprise environmental factors and organizational process assets are still valid

10.7 AUDIT PHASE

Now that we have an understanding of the project's history, we enter the audit phase, which is a critical assessment of the project's existing status. Do not focus on the wrong issues during the audit phase. Look at what went wrong and what can be corrected rather than looking for someone to blame. The following is part of the audit phase:

- Assessing the actual performance to date
- Identifying the flaws
- Performing a root cause analysis
- Looking for surface (or easy-to-identify) failure points
- Looking for hidden failure points
- Determining what are the "must have," "nice to have," "can wait" and "not needed" activities or deliverables
- Looking at the issues log and seeing if the issues are people issues. If there are people issues, can people be removed or replaced?
- Prioritizing the problems and being prepared to address the most serious problems first
- Identifying what mistakes were made in the past so that lessons learned and best practices can be discovered to prevent a recurrence of the mistakes

The audit phase also includes the validation that the objectives are still correct, the benefits and value can be met but perhaps to a lesser degree, the assigned resources possess the proper skills, the roles and responsibilities are assigned to the correct team members, the project's priority is correct and will support the recovery efforts and executive support is in place. The recovery of a failing project cannot be done in isolation. It requires a recovery team and strong support/sponsorship.

The timing and quality of the executive support needed for recovery are most often based upon the perception of the value of the project. Five important questions that need to be considered as part of value determination are:

- Is the project still of value to the client?
- Is the project still aligned to your company's corporate objectives and strategy?
- Is your company still committed to the project?
- Are the stakeholders still committed?
- Is there overall motivation for rescue?

Since recovery cannot be accomplished in isolation, it is important to interview the team members as part of the audit phase. This may very well be accomplished at the beginning of the audit phase to answer the previous questions. The team members may have strong opinions on what went wrong as well as good ideas for a quick and successful recovery. You must obtain support from the team if recovery is to be successful. This includes:

- Analyzing the culture
- Data gathering and assessment involving the full team
- Making it easy for the team to discuss problems without finger-pointing or the laying of blame
- Interviewing the team members perhaps on a one-on-one basis
- Reestablishing work-life balance
- Reestablishing incentives, if possible

It can be difficult to interview people and get their opinion on where we are, what went wrong and how to correct it. This is especially true if the people have hidden agendas. If you have a close friend associated with the project, how will you react if they are found guilty of being part of the problem? This is referred to as an emotional cost.

Another problem is that people may want to hide critical information if something went wrong and they could be identified with it. They might view the truth as impacting their chances for career advancement. You may need a comprehensive list of questions to ask to extract the right information.

When a project gets into trouble, people tend to play the "Blame Game" trying to make it appear that someone else is at fault. This may be an attempt to muddy the water and detract the interviewer from the real issues. It is done as part of one's sense of self-preservation. It may be difficult to decide who is telling the truth and who is fabricating information.

You may conclude that certain people must be removed from the project if it is to have a chance for recovery. Regardless of what the people did, you should allow them to leave the project with dignity. You might say, "Annie is being reassigned to another project that needs her skills. We thank her for the valuable contribution she has made to this project."

Perhaps the worst situation is when you discover that the real problems were with the project's governance. Telling stakeholders and governance groups that they were part of the problem may not be received well. The author's preference is always to be honest in defining the problems even if it hurts. This response must be handled with tact and diplomacy.

You must also assess the team's morale. This includes:

- Looking at the good things first to build morale
- Determining if the original plan was overly ambitious
- Determining if there were political problems that led to active or passive resistance by the team
- Determining if the work hours and workloads were demoralizing

10.8 TRADEOFF PHASE

Hopefully by this point you have the necessary information for decision making as well as the team's support for the recovery. It may be highly unlikely that the original requirements can still be met without some serious tradeoffs. You must now work with the team and determine the tradeoff options that you will present to the stakeholders.

When the project first began, the constraints were most likely the traditional triple constraints. Time, cost and scope were the primary constraints and tradeoffs would have been made on the secondary constraints of quality, risk, value and image/reputation. When a project becomes distressed, stakeholders know that the original budget and schedule may no longer be valid. The project may take longer and may cost significantly more money than originally thought. As such, the primary concerns for the stakeholders as to whether or not to support the project further may change to value, quality and image/reputation. The tradeoffs that the team will present to the customer and stakeholders will then be tradeoffs on time, cost, scope and possibly risk.

One way of looking at tradeoffs is to review the detailed WBS and identify all activities remaining to be accomplished. The activities are then placed on the grid in Figure 10-2. The "must have" and "nice to have" work packages or deliverables are often the most costly and the hardest to use for tradeoffs. If vendors are required to provide work package support, then we must perform vendor tradeoffs as well, which include:

- Assessing vendor contractual agreements
- Determining if the vendor can fix the problems
- Determining if vendor concessions and tradeoffs are possible
- Establishing new vendor schedules and pricing

Figure 10-2 Tradeoff options.

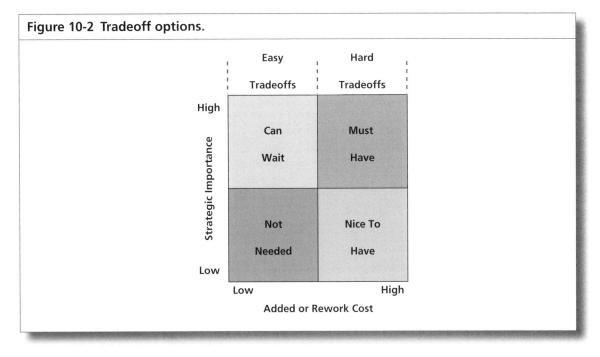

Once all of the elements are placed on the grid in Figure 10-2, the team will assist the RPM with tradeoffs by answering the following questions:

- Where are the tradeoffs?
- What are the expected casualties?
- What can and cannot be done?
- What must be fixed first?
- Can we stop the bleeding?
- Have the priorities of the constraints changed?
- Have the features changed?
- What are the risks?

It is important that the team prepare a checklist of early warning signs that indicate whether recovery is taking place or if the situation is deteriorating further.

Once the tradeoffs have been discovered, the RPM and the team must prepare a presentation for the stakeholders. There are two primary questions that the RPM will need to discuss with the stakeholders:

- Is the project worth saving? If the project is not worth saving, then you must have the courage to say so. Unless a valid business reason exists for continuation, you must recommend cancellation.
- If the project is worth saving, can we expect a full or partial recovery, and by when?

There are also other factors that most likely are concerns of the stakeholders and must be addressed. These factors include:

- Changes in the political environment
- Existing or potential lawsuits
- Changes in the enterprise environmental factors
- Changes in the organizational process assets
- Changes in the business case
- Changes in the assumptions
- Changes in the expected benefits and final value

10.9 NEGOTIATION PHASE

At this point, the RPM is ready for stakeholder negotiations provided that there still exists a valid business case. If the audit phase indicates that the bleeding cannot stop and a valid business case does not exist, then there may be no point to negotiate with the stakeholders unless there are issues with which the project manager is not familiar. Items that must be addressed as part of stakeholder negotiations include:

- Identifying items important to the stakeholders (e.g., time, cost, value)
- Identifying ways to maximize remaining value while minimizing additional investment
- Identification of the casualties that exist
- Identification of which constraints have changed
- Prioritization of the tradeoffs
- Honesty in your beliefs for recovery
- Not giving them unrealistic expectations
- Getting their buy-in
- Negotiating for the needed sponsorship and stakeholder support

Additional support from the stakeholders may be necessary to cut through bureaucracy that could impact rapid decision making. Stakeholders must be willing to insulate the team from any pressures that can impede the recovery process. It may be necessary to establish new channels of communications.

Be aware that the stakeholders may pressure you into committing to an unrealistic recovery plan. You should maintain your position on what is realistically achievable.

10.10 RESTART PHASE

Assuming the stakeholders have agreed to a recovery plan, you are now ready to restart the project. This includes:

- Briefing the team on stakeholder negotiations
- Making sure the team learns from past mistakes
- Introducing the team to the stakeholders' agreed-upon recovery plan including the agreed-upon milestones
- Identifying any changes to the way the project will be managed
- Fully engaging the project sponsor as well as the key stakeholders for their support
- Identifying any changes to the roles and responsibilities of the team members
- Restore team confidence
- Get buy-in for the new action plan for rapid recovery

There are three restarting options:

- **Full anesthetic:** Bring all work to a standstill until the recovery plan is finalized.
- **Partial anesthetic:** Bring some work to a standstill until the scope is stabilized.
- **Scope modification:** Continue work but with modifications as necessary.

Albert Einstein once said: "We cannot solve our problems with the same thinking we used when we created them." It may be necessary to bring on board new people with new ideas and different skills. However, there are risks. You may want these people full time on your project, but retaining highly qualified workers that may be in high demand elsewhere could be difficult. Since your project most likely will slip, some of your team members may be committed to others projects about to begin. However, you may be lucky enough to have strong executive-level sponsorship and retain these people. This could allow you to use a colocated team organization.

During the recovery process, time is usually a critical constraint. The RPM may find himself or herself in a position where they may have to completely change the culture of the project team. This may be difficult to do given the new constraints. The team may have been under severe pressure previously. It may be necessary to reestablish the work-life balance so people understand what is meant by the quality of life. This could allow the team to take advantage of new vacation schedules.

10.11 EXECUTION PHASE

During the execution phase, the project manager must focus upon certain back-to-work implementation factors. These include:

- Learning from past mistakes
- Stabilizing scope
- Rigidly enforcing the scope change control process

- Performing periodic critical health checks and using earned value measurement reporting
- Providing effective and essential communications
- Maintaining positive morale
- Adopting proactive stakeholder management
- Not relying upon or expecting the company's EPM system to save you
- Not allowing unwanted stakeholder intervention, which increases pressure
- Carefully managing stakeholder expectations
- Insulating the team from politics

Recovery project management is not easy, and there is no guarantee you can or will be successful. You will be under close supervision and scrutinized by superiors and stakeholders. You may even be required to explain all of your actions. But saving a potentially troubled project from disaster is certainly worth the added effort.

10.12 PROJECT RECOVERY VERSUS PROJECT RESCUE

Projects do not die without first attempting to be resuscitated through a recovery or rescue process. When someone is stranded at sea, we normally say that we have recovered or rescued the stranded passenger. We use the words rescue and recovery as being the same and most people cannot differentiate between the two. But in a project environment, when a project becomes distressed, these two words can have significantly different meanings, as illustrated in Table 10-1.

Once again, it is important to understand that in Table 10-1 we have taken an extreme view of the differences between recovery and rescue. Most people prefer to use the words interchangeably.

10.13 RECOVERY DECISION

When projects get into trouble, project managers usually react quickly looking for recovery plans. Project managers pride themselves on finding creative ways to resolve problems. Unfortunately, it may take a significant amount of money just to create a recovery plan and, without a clear understanding of the needs of the company, project managers can jump to a quick solution, which may decrease the chances of finding the best solution.

Recovering a failing project for the wrong reasons may be counterproductive. Understanding the needs of the company is critical. The needs may have changed over the course of the project.

Deciding whether to recover, rescue or euthanize a failing project is not easy. Project teams can spend enormous sums of money attempting to develop painful alternatives, but the final decision rests upon the shoulders

TABLE 10-1   Differences between Recovery and Rescue

PROJECT RECOVERY	PROJECT RESCUE
The project can be saved.	The project may not be able to be saved, but we must pretend it can be to protect people that cannot or are unwilling to accept failure in any form.
The recovery will contain some business value but perhaps not all of the value that was initially planned for.	The project may not contain any value at all, and we will cook the books to hide the truth.
Additional funding and scope reductions may be necessary to fulfill the recovery process.	Perhaps no additional funding will be provided, just lip service support.
End dates may be allowed to slip to get whatever value can be salvaged.	Schedule slippage may not be allowed.
An action plan will be developed.	Perhaps no funding is available for a new action plan.
Recovery projects are allowed to fail downstream if the business value cannot be attained.	The rescued project is not allowed to fail; it may be required by law.
Regardless of the outcome of an attempt at recovery, projects similar to this one will be attempted in the future.	Projects similar to this one will be avoided in the future.
Lessons learned and best practices are captured.	Documentation is at a minimum, and there is no attempt to discover lessons learned, best practices or who caused the problem.
Deliverables that are created are, in fact, used.	Deliverables that are created may simply become archived.
Sponsorship may not be at the executive levels.	Sponsorship may reach the CEO level perhaps due to media coverage.

of the governance committee. Typical questions that the governance committee might consider include:

- Is the project still aligned to strategic goals and objectives?
- Will the new targeted benefits or value be worth the recovery effort?
- Is the completion of the project still strategically important?
- Is senior management still committed to the success of the project?
- Will senior management continue showing support for the project?

Sometimes, the true degree of importance of the project is not conveyed to the project manager at project initiation and the project manager may not see "the big picture." There may be political reasons why management withheld critical information. On long-term projects, the needs of the business can change over the full life cycle of the project and, unless this information is known by the project manager, valuable recovery time can be wasted looking at the wrong recovery options.

10.14 SUMMARY OF LESSONS LEARNED

Not all projects will be completed successfully. Sometimes, health checks and early warning indicators provide project managers with sufficient time to recover a failing projects. Even then, there is no guarantee that the recovery process will be successful. Not all project managers possess the skills needed to recover a failing project. Significant tradeoffs may be necessary and the business case may need to change.

A checklist of some major techniques with regard to project recovery might include:

☐ Recognize as early as possible that the project may be in trouble.
☐ Make sure you clearly understand the project's business case.
☐ Perform health checks to get a clear picture of the project.
☐ You may have to rebuild the morale of the project team; understand what you are inheriting.
☐ Work with the team and decide what tradeoffs are possible and what can and cannot be salvaged.
☐ Present your findings to the stakeholders and get their position on whether they want you to continue.
☐ If necessary, be prepared for the project to be cancelled.

Table 10-2 illustrates a more detailed worksheet that can be used for recovery project management. The worksheet is based upon the recovery life-cycle phases shown in Figure 10-1.

TABLE 10-2 Project Recovery Worksheet

Understanding Phase

Have you reviewed the business case?	Yes	No
Is the business case still valid?	Yes	No
If not, do you understand the new business case?	Yes	No
Have the enterprise environmental factors changed?	Yes	No
Are the expected benefits still realistic?	Yes	No
If not, do you know the new benefits that are expected?	Yes	No
Can the targeted value still be achieved?	Yes	No
If not, do you know the new targeted value?	Yes	No
Have you reviewed the project's assumptions?	Yes	No
If the assumptions are no longer valid, do you know the new assumptions?	Yes	No
Are there any organizational process assets that you can use to help recover the project?	Yes	No

Audit Phase

Have you evaluated the actual performance to date?	Yes	No
Have you identified the surface failure points and their causes?	Yes	No
Have you identified what mistakes were made?	Yes	No
Have you identified any hidden failure points and their causes?	Yes	No
Have you determined which of the remaining activities and deliverables are an absolute necessity and which are not?	Yes	No
Have you interviewed the key team players?	Yes	No
Have you identified the people issues?	Yes	No
Can the people issues be resolved?	Yes	No
If the people issues cannot be resolved, can you find qualified replacement personnel?	Yes	No
Have you identified and prioritized the problems?	Yes	No
Does your company still consider the project of value?	Yes	No
Do the stakeholders, including the client, still consider the project of value?	Yes	No
Is everyone motivated for rescue?	Yes	No

Tradeoff Phase

Did you evaluate the vendor contractual agreements?	Yes	No
Did you determine if the vendors can fix their problems?	Yes	No
Are vendor tradeoffs and concessions possible?	Yes	No
Do any of the vendor contracts need to be repriced and renegotiated?	Yes	No
Have you determined what tradeoffs are possible?	Yes	No
Have you determined the risks and expect casualties from the tradeoffs?	Yes	No
Have the tradeoffs been prioritized?	Yes	No
Have you determined what can and cannot be accomplished?	Yes	No
Have you determined what must be done first?	Yes	No
Have the priorities of the constraints changed?	Yes	No
Have any of the features or deliverables changed as a result of the tradeoffs?	Yes	No
Can you stop the bleeding?	Yes	No
Is the project worth saving?	Yes	No
Will the changes impact the political environment?	Yes	No

(*Continued*)

TABLE 10-2 Project Recovery Worksheet (*Continued*)

Will the changes result in potential lawsuits?	Yes	No
Will the changes result in a new business case?	Yes	No
Negotiation Phase		
Have you determined what items are important to the stakeholders?	Yes	No
Have you identified funding requirements?	Yes	No
Have you identified potential casualties?	Yes	No
Have you prioritized the tradeoffs?	Yes	No
Have you been honest in your beliefs for recovery?	Yes	No
Have you given them realistic expectations?	Yes	No
Did you get their buy-in?	Yes	No
Did you negotiate for new levels of sponsorship and governance?	Yes	No
Restart Phase		
Did you brief the team on the results of stakeholder negotiations?	Yes	No
Does the team fully understand the past mistakes?	Yes	No
Does the team understand that the project's leadership may be different than before?	Yes	No
Does the team understand their new roles and responsibilities?	Yes	No
Did the team buy into the new action plan?	Yes	No
Execution Phase		
Did you reemphasize what was learned from past mistakes?	Yes	No
Does everyone fully understand the new scope requirements?	Yes	No
Have you implemented a rigid change control process?	Yes	No
Have you scheduled periodic health checks?	Yes	No
Is the morale of the team acceptable?	Yes	No
Have you attempted to limit stakeholder intervention?	Yes	No
Is the project team reasonably well insulated from politics?	Yes	No

TABLE 10-3 *PMBOK® Guide* Alignment to Lessons Learned

LESSONS LEARNED	PMBOK® GUIDE SECTIONS
All recovery processes should be aligned to the strategic business objectives.	1.4.3
Recovery cannot be done in isolation. Involvement by the operational stakeholders is necessary.	1.5.1.2, 2.2.1
Decisions made during the recovery process must still focus on the creation of business value.	1.6
Enterprise environmental factors may have changes.	2.1.5, 4.1.1.4
The definition of success may change during the recovery process.	2.2.3
A well-structured scope change control process should be in place.	4.5, 5.5
A new statement of work and possibly a new business case may need to be developed.	4.1.1.1, 4.1.1.2
Risk management techniques are essential during recovery	11.2, 11.3, 11.4, 11.6

Table 10-3 is a summary of the lessons learned and alignment to various sections of the *PMBOK® Guide* where additional or supporting information can be found. In some cases, these sections of the *PMBOK® Guide* simply provide supporting information related to the lesson learned. There are numerous sections of the *PMBOK® Guide* that could be aligned for each lesson learned. For simplicity sake, only a few are listed.

INDEX